CAMBRIDGE STUDIES IN INTERNATIONAL AND COMPARATIVE LAW

Books in the series

The Threat of Force in International Law
NIKOLAS STÜRCHLER

Indigenous Rights in the United Nations Context
ALEXANDRA XANTHAKI

International Refugee Law and Socio-Economic Rights
MICHELLE FOSTER

The Protection of Cultural Property in Armed Conflict
ROGER O'KEEFE

Interpretation and Revision of International Boundary Decisions
KAIYAN KAIKOBAD

Multinationals and Corporate Social Responsibility
Limitations and Opportunities in International Law
JENNIFER A. ZERK

Judiciaries within Europe
A Comparative Review
JOHN BELL

Law in Times of Crisis
Emergency Powers in Theory and Practice
OREN GROSS AND FIONNUALA NÍ AOLÁIN

Vessel-Source Marine Pollution
The Law and Politics of International Regulation
ALAN TAN

Enforcing Obligations *Erga Omnes* in International Law
CHRISTIAN J. TAMS

Non-Governmental Organisations in International Law
ANNA-KARIN LINDBLOM

Democracy, Minorities and International Law
STEVEN WHEATLEY

Prosecuting International Crimes
Selectivity and the International Law Regime
ROBERT CRYER

Compensation for Personal Injury in English, German and Italian Law
A Comparative Outline
BASIL MARKESINIS, MICHAEL COESTER, GUIDO ALPA AND AUGUSTUS ULLSTEIN

Dispute Settlement in the UN Convention on the Law of the Sea
NATALIE KLEIN

The International Protection of Internally Displaced Persons
CATHERINE PHUONG

Imperialism, Sovereignty and the Making of International Law
ANTONY ANGHIE

Necessity, Proportionality and the Use of Force by States
JUDITH GARDAM

International Legal Argument in the Permanent Court of International Justice
The Rise of the International Judiciary
OLE SPIERMANN

Great Powers and Outlaw States
Unequal Sovereigns in the International Legal Order
GERRY SIMPSON

Local Remedies in International Law
C. F. AMERASINGHE

Reading Humanitarian Intervention
Human Rights and the Use of Force in International Law
ANNE ORFORD

Conflict of Norms in Public International Law
How WTO Law Relates to Other Rules of Law
JOOST PAUWELYN

Transboundary Damage in International Law
HANQIN XUE

European Criminal Procedures
EDITED BY MIREILLE DELMAS-MARTY AND JOHN SPENCER

The Accountability of Armed Opposition Groups in International Law
LIESBETH ZEGVELD

Sharing Transboundary Resources
International Law and Optimal Resource Use
EYAL BENVENISTI

International Human Rights and Humanitarian Law
RENÉ PROVOST

Remedies Against International Organisations
KAREL WELLENS

Diversity and Self-Determination in International Law
KAREN KNOP

The Law of Internal Armed Conflict
LINDSAY MOIR

International Commercial Arbitration and African States
Practice, Participation and Institutional Development
AMAZU A. ASOUZU

The Enforceability of Promises in European Contract Law
JAMES GORDLEY

International Law in Antiquity
DAVID J. BEDERMAN

Money Laundering
A New International Law Enforcement Model
GUY STESSENS

Good Faith in European Contract Law
REINHARD ZIMMERMANN AND SIMON WHITTAKER

On Civil Procedure
J. A. JOLOWICZ

Trusts
A Comparative Study
MAURIZIO LUPOI

The Right to Property in Commonwealth Constitutions
TOM ALLEN

International Organizations Before National Courts
AUGUST REINISCH

The Changing International Law of High Seas Fisheries
FRANCISCO ORREGO VICUÑA

Trade and the Environment
A Comparative Study of EC and US Law
DAMIEN GERADIN

Unjust Enrichment
A Study of Private Law and Public Values
HANOCH DAGAN

Religious Liberty and International Law in Europe
MALCOLM D. EVANS

Ethics and Authority in International Law
ALFRED P. RUBIN

Sovereignty Over Natural Resources
Balancing Rights and Duties
NICO SCHRIJVER

The Polar Regions and the Development of International Law
DONALD R. ROTHWELL

Fragmentation and the International Relations of Micro-States
Self-determination and Statehood
JORRI DUURSMA

Principles of the Institutional Law of International Organizations
C. F. AMERASINGHE

THE THREAT OF FORCE IN INTERNATIONAL LAW

Threats of force are a common feature of international politics, advocated by some as an economical guarantee against the outbreak of war and condemned by others as a recipe for war. Article 2(4) of the United Nations Charter forbids states to use threats of force, yet the meaning of the prohibition is unclear. This book provides the first comprehensive appraisal of the no-threat principle: its origin, underlying rationale, theoretical implications, relevant jurisprudence, and how it has withstood the test of time from 1945 to the present. Based on a systematic evaluation of state and United Nations practices, the book identifies what constitutes a threat of force and when its use is justified under the United Nations Charter. In so doing, it relates the no-threat principle to important concepts of the twentieth century, such as deterrence, escalation, crisis management, and what has been aptly described as the 'diplomacy of violence'.

Nikolas Stürchler is a senior research fellow at the World Trade Institute, and a visiting lecturer in international and constitutional law at the University of Basel.

CAMBRIDGE STUDIES IN INTERNATIONAL AND COMPARATIVE LAW

Established in 1946, this series produces high quality scholarship in the fields of public and private international law and comparative law. Although these are distinct legal sub-disciplines, developments since 1946 confirm their interrelation.

Comparative law is increasingly used as a tool in the making of law at national, regional and international levels. Private international law is now often affected by international conventions, and the issues faced by classical conflicts rules are frequently dealt with by substantive harmonisation of law under international auspices. Mixed international arbitrations, especially those involving state economic activity, raise mixed questions of public and private international law, while in many fields (such as the protection of human rights and democratic standards, investment guarantees and international criminal law) international and national systems interact. National constitutional arrangements relating to 'foreign affairs', and to the implementation of international norms, are a focus of attention.

The Board welcomes works of a theoretical or interdisciplinary character, and those focusing on the new approaches to international or comparative law or conflicts of law. Studies of particular institutions or problems are equally welcome, as are translations of the best work published in other languages.

A list of books in the series can be found at the end of this volume.

The Threat of Force in International Law

Nikolas Stürchler

CAMBRIDGE
UNIVERSITY PRESS

CAMBRIDGE
UNIVERSITY PRESS

University Printing House, Cambridge CB2 8BS, United Kingdom

One Liberty Plaza, 20th Floor, New York, NY 10006, USA

477 Williamstown Road, Port Melbourne, VIC 3207, Australia

314-321, 3rd Floor, Plot 3, Splendor Forum, Jasola District Centre, New Delhi - 110025, India

79 Anson Road, #06-04/06, Singapore 079906

Cambridge University Press is part of the University of Cambridge.

It furthers the University's mission by disseminating knowledge in the pursuit of education, learning and research at the highest international levels of excellence.

www.cambridge.org
Information on this title: www.cambridge.org/9780521133616

First published 2007
First paperback edition published 2009

A catalogue record for this publication is available from the British Library

ISBN 978-0-521-87388-8 Hardback
ISBN 978-0-521-13361-6 Paperback

For as the nature of Foule weather, lyeth not in a showre or two of rain; but in an inclination thereto of many dayes together: So the nature of War, consisteth not in actual fighting; but in the known disposition thereto, during all the time there is no assurance to the contrary.

Thomas Hobbes, *Leviathan* part I, chapter 13, para. 62 (1651)

Neither side wanted war over Cuba, we agreed, but it was possible that either side could take a step that – for reasons of 'security' or 'pride' or 'face' – would require a response by the other side, which, in turn, for the same reasons of security, pride, or face, would bring about a counterresponse and eventually an escalation into armed conflict. That was what he wanted to avoid.

Robert F. Kennedy, *Thirteen Days* 49 (1968) (referring to his brother John F. Kennedy)

I think the whole thing is good neighbors. If you don't have good neighbors, you can forget the whole thing.

Chuck Searle, Shasta County cattleman; from Robert C. Ellickson, *Order Without Law* 1 (1991)

Contents

Foreword

For a long time the subject of threats of force between states as a distinct field of study was surprisingly neglected both by international lawyers and, even, by international relations scholars. From the legal side Romana Sadurska's 1988 article, 'Threats of Force', is one of the few items devoted to the issue, and its argument that there is a significant legal difference between a use and a threat of force under article 2(4) of the United Nations Charter was not widely accepted. In the *Nuclear Weapons Opinion* (1996) the International Court of Justice glossed over any possible distinctions between use and threat – despite their importance for the theory and practice of deterrence.

In one sense this is not surprising. Article 2(4) itself appears to equate the two: all United Nations members 'shall refrain in their international relations from the use or threat of force against the territorial integrity or political independence of a State'. On first impression a threat, sufficiently clear, imminent and credible, of a use of force which if carried out would be unlawful is itself unlawful. So international lawyers have tended to rest on the linkage between the two, without much further analysis – and to discount the point that responses to threats of force in state practice tend to be both rarer than and different in character to responses to the actual use of force.

More recently there have been detailed studies of international crises and comprehensive compilations of cases where threats of various kinds have been made, so that international lawyers can no longer complain of a lack of accessible material. Yet it is only with Nikolas Stürchler's book that this material has been carefully used. For the first time we have a historically informed and comprehensive account of the issue, bringing to bear international relations insights and historical research while retaining an international lawyer's perspective on the material.

It would have been easy in the welter of detail and the rough and divisive arena of military threats to lose touch, and faith, in any form of normativity. Yet Stürchler does not do so. After meticulous examination he concludes that '[t]he common wisdom that threats are met with indifference is false', and further that 'at least in threat-related cases, the assumption that silence equates approval is empirically false'; 'the surprising characteristic of state practice is that nations pay tribute to the no-threat principle without directly invoking it'. He provides other explanations of silence, which are realistic and do not involve the abdication of constraint. In particular 'governments seem to recognise that the UN best serves its objectives if it wears the hat of mediator whose impartiality is appropriate in situations where room for negotiation remains and recourse to force has not yet been decided upon. Interference by third parties would only render the task of the UN (or another honest broker) more difficult'. Outright military conflict is the worse evil, short of Munich-style appeasement: 'Governments recognise the special function of threats as markedly distinct from the use of force, to achieve results without resort to military conflict.' He suggests that 'state practice reveals a pattern whereby the unilateral threat of force finds limited accommodation under the umbrella of collective action designed to manage a crisis'.

He also underlines the continuity between international experience before and since September 2001: our world may not be brave, but neither is it especially new. Thus, in his view: 'Iraq in 2002–3 does not fall out of line with previous state practice, and this may be taken to indicate that the perception of UN members has not gone through a radical transformation.' And he ends with a clear call for international legal standards to be articulated and acted on, notwithstanding the widespread and even healthy tendency to focus on diplomatic efforts in crisis situations which, at all costs, prevent matters getting worse. As he says, 'a universal standard, applicable to all, that permits mutually exclusive claims of pre-emption can be neither a healthy nor an equitable prescription for order'.

This study fills a gap in the literature and does so with assurance, combining fine attention to detail and context with a broad vision. It will be widely read and appreciated.

James Crawford
Lauterpacht Centre for International Law
University of Cambridge
8 November 2006

Preface

I first came across the subject of this study through Roger Donaldson's documentary motion picture *Thirteen Days* about the Cuban missile crisis of 1962. Reading later about the crisis, I was intrigued by the fact that President Kennedy had read Barbara Tuchman's Pulitzer Prize winning *Guns of August*, a book that described the paradoxical circumstances through which, in 1914, Europe stumbled into a 'war which nobody wanted'. There are good reasons to believe that Kennedy took the lessons of the book seriously. He understood that the confrontation with the Soviet Union over the deployment of nuclear missiles on Cuba could lead to nuclear war even though both he and Khrushchev knew that such a war would be suicidal, and that neither of them could fully control what Thomas Schelling described as the 'dynamics of mutual alarm'. This understanding weighed heavily on Kennedy and probably on Khrushchev, too.

Not only was it inspiring to learn that an academically oriented book like the *Guns of August* could make a difference in world policy, it also struck me that a central element in the course of the Cuban missile crisis, the threat of force, was paid virtually no attention in the international law literature. Article 2(4) of the UN Charter expressly forbids states to take recourse to the threat of force. Yet what is to be understood by that prohibition, and how it has performed against the backdrop of sixty years of state and UN practice, has been left entirely unexplored. Perhaps this was out of the belief that the prohibition had long been subordinated to overriding political and military concerns: if the prohibition of the use of force was already fighting an uphill battle due to frequent violations, it would appear sensible to many international lawyers quietly to bury the issue of threats, which, if investigated, would only lend support to the undesirable conclusion that international law was only a pebble in the shoe of great powers.

Be that as it may, it seemed that the threat of force merited a deeper legal enquiry, even if this meant running the risk that the intuition of the law's insignificance would turn out to be correct. What has resulted from the effort to establish the facts objectively is the following study, an earlier version of which I submitted as a doctoral thesis at the University of Basel in summer 2005. Its main goal is to provide a legal appraisal of the regulation of military threats according to article 2(4) of the UN Charter, exposing the historical origin, underlying rationale, theoretical implications, relevant case law and state and UN practice involved. The study's secondary goal is to contribute a flash of insight on the operation of law in international crises. Throughout the text, the Cuban missile crisis is used as an illustration for the regulatory issues that arise in this context.

Is the threat of force topic, as originally conceived in 1945, still relevant today? It is commonplace after the events of September 2001 to debate the merits of the UN Charter principles in the light of new and emerging security threats that require, it is sometimes argued, a reconfiguration of the legal regime governing the threat and use of force. While it is true that law has evolved over time, the manner in which conflicts are conducted has not changed so radically that experience accumulated before September 2001 is no longer relevant. Rather, another goal pursued in this study was to highlight precisely what changes have taken place, and how this has affected the regulation of threats under the UN Charter. A limited set of trends and ideas have informed much thinking about the threat of force during the second half of the twentieth century, and it is their identification that allows for some extrapolations for the future.

In exploring these trends and ideas, the approach taken is an interdisciplinary one. Much research has been done on military threats in other disciplines. Scholars of international relations in particular have long preoccupied themselves with the phenomenon of war. Failure to understand how threats relate to war, and what their political and strategic dimensions are, is a recipe for ending up in a *dialogue de sourds* between scholars of international law and of international relations. I tried to place a foot in each camp so as to avoid that result.

I am aware of the argument that, however commendable a published thesis may be, it will not be read if it is too elaborate. Chapter 8 therefore packs together a general stock-taking with the main conclusions.

Otherwise, the plan of the book is to bring discussion of the no-threat principle, so to speak, up to speed with the one on the non-use of force. The first chapter starts with a historical account, leading up to what the drafters of the UN Charter had in mind when outlawing the threat of force. It provides the overall framework that is essential for understanding not only the original ideas and assumptions underlying article 2(4) of the UN Charter but also subsequent developments. In chapter 2 the focus is on potential interpretations. There are many possible interpretations which, even within the framework set out by the UN founders, are essentially incompatible with each other. Chapter 3 examines the contribution of the International Court of Justice to the no-threat principle; when the Court has applied it and what meaning it has been given. Chapters 4 to 7 are then devoted to the description of state practice. This part is the backbone of the book as it provides the empirical evidence to answer the most important questions regarding the content of the UN Charter. It also offers an understanding of the circumstances under which states issue threats in practice and, consequently, in which context law is supposed to give guidance. Finally, chapter 9 should be interesting to those inclined to wonder about what lies beyond the strict question of legality. It is an attempt, not intended to be comprehensive, to understand the substructure of the no-threat principle, and thereby bring to light some of the ways in which it may be said to facilitate dispute settlement and crisis defusing. This is a return to the theme of crisis management.

Perhaps it is also important to point out what cannot be found in the book. It does not delve into the theme of threats within the law of armed conflict, international criminal law or Chapter VII of the UN Charter (under the rubric of 'threats to peace'). The focus is on the legality of the military threats which states issue unilaterally. Specifically, it addresses the questions of what constitutes a threat of force according to article 2(4) of the UN Charter and on what grounds a recourse to a threat of force is justified. To keep the study within reasonable bounds, the emphasis is on the justification of self-defence. What I hope is that the book invites a reconsideration and revival of a topic that has been thoroughly neglected.

In the course of researching threats of force, I have accumulated various debts. I owe it to a host of sponsoring institutions that these debts are not financial. The Swiss National Science Foundation, the Janggen-Pöhn foundation, the Max Geldner foundation, the Freiwillige Akademische Gesellschaft and the Kalmann & Maria Lauer-Stein foundation all provided me with generous support for my two years of research at the Universities of Cambridge and Stanford. I thank them sincerely. My study would have turned out very differently if not for the opportunity to tap the wealth of inspiration and resources available at these places. Moreover, I am indebted to numerous people for inspiration and encouragement. They include Professor Anne Peters (Basel), Dr Christine Gray and Professor James Crawford (Cambridge), Professor James Fearon (Stanford), Professor Stephan Breitenmoser (Basel), Professor Robert Kolb (Bern), Professor Paul Richli (Lucerne), Lt Cr Scott Tait (US Navy) and Professor John Mayo (Georgetown). Thanks are also due to Susan Kaplan, Caroline Petherick, Richard Woodham and Rachel Liechti for making my English look better than it is, to Finola O'Sullivan from Cambridge University Press and to innumerable librarians who patiently helped me to find seemingly intractable documents. Many thanks also to Yasuko, Matius, Marjam, Jochen, Stephan, Henry, Geert, Owain, Neta, Delphine, François, Brooks and Shantanu for their companionship. And finally, I am indebted most of all to my parents, Tjoek and Dieter, whose unquestioning support has been the greatest gift. It is to them that I dedicate this book.

Basel, 25 November 2006
Nikolas Stürchler
njs@cantab.net

This book reflects the personal views of the author. It does not in any manner implicate the views of the Swiss Federal Department of Foreign Affairs.

Abbreviations

Act. Droit Int.	Actualité de Droit International
Afr. Aff.	African Affairs
Afr. Cont. Rec.	Africa Contemporary Record
Am. JIL	American Journal of International Law
Am. PSQ	American Political Science Quarterly
Am. PSR	American Political Science Review
Am. UILR	American University International Law Review
Ann. Am. Acad. P&SS	Annals of the American Academy of Political and Social Science
ASEAN	Association of Southeast Asian Nations
Asian Surv.	Asian Survey
ASIL Insights	American Society of International Law Insights
BGBl	Bundesgesetzblatt
Brit. Cmd	British Command Papers
Brit. JPS	British Journal of Political Science
Brit. YBIL	British Yearbook of International Law
Cal. WILJ	California Western International Law Journal
Cath. ULR	Catholic University Law Review
CENTO	Central Treaty Organization
Chris. S. Mon.	Christian Science Monitor
Conf. Mgmt. & PS	Conflict Management and Peace Science
COW	Correlates of War Project
Dept. St. Bull.	Department of State Bulletin
DMZ	Demilitarised zone
DPRK	Democratic People's Republic of Korea (North Korea)

EEZ	Exclusive Economic Zone
Enc. Pub. IL	Encyclopaedia of Public International Law
EU	European Union
Eur. JIL	European Journal of International Law
F. Aff.	Foreign Affairs
F. Press Cyp.	Foreign Press on Cyprus
FBIS	Foreign Broadcast Information Service
FRUS	Foreign Relations of the United States
GAOR	General Assembly Official Records
Geo. LJ	Georgetown Law Journal
Hague YBIL	Hague Yearbook of International Law
Harv. ILJ	Harvard International Law Journal
HIIK	Heidelberg Institute on International Conflict Research
IAEA	International Atomic Energy Agency
ICB	International Crisis Behaviour Project
ICC	International Criminal Court
ICJ	International Court of Justice
ICJ Plead.	ICJ Pleadings, Oral Arguments, Documents
ICJ Rep.	International Court of Justice Reports
ILC	International Law Commission
ILM	International Legal Materials
Ind. JIL	Indian Journal of International Law
Int. & Comp. LQ	International and Comparative Law Quarterly
Int. Aff.	International Affairs
Int. Org.	International Organization
Int. Sec.	International Security
Int. Stud. Q.	International Studies Quarterly
J. Conf. Resol.	Journal of Conflict Resolution
J. Cont. Hist.	Journal of Contemporary History
J. Mod. Afr. Stud.	Journal of Modern African Studies
J. Pal. Stud.	Journal of Palestine Studies
J. Peace Res.	Journal of Peace Research
J. Theo. P.	Journal of Theoretical Politics
JL & Econ.	Journal of Law and Economics
KEDO	Korean Peninsula Energy Development Organization
KFOR	Kosovo Force
KLA	Kosovo Liberation Army

L. & Cont. Prob.	Law and Contemporary Problems
Latin Am. Wkly Rep.	Latin America Weekly Report
Leid. JIL	Leiden Journal of International Law
LNOJ	League of Nations Official Journal
LNTS	League of Nations Treaty Series
MAD	Mutual Assured Destruction
Mich. LR	Michigan Law Review
Mil. LR	Military Law Review
Mn.	Marginal note
MOAB	Massive Ordnance Air Blast
NAM	Non-Alignment Movement
NATO	North Atlantic Treaty Organization
Nav. War. CIL Stud.	US Naval War College International Law Studies
Neth. YBIL	Netherlands Yearbook of International Law
New Eng. J Pub. Pol.	New England Journal of Public Policy
New. Eng. LR	New England Law Review
NPT	Nuclear Non-Proliferation Treaty
Nw. ULR	Northwestern University Law Review
NYT	New York Times Historical Archive
OAS	Organization of American States
OAU	Organization of African Unity
Ocean Dev. & IL	Ocean Development and International Law
ODS	United Nations Official Document System
OIC	Organization of Islamic Conference
Oil & Gas J.	Oil and Gas Journal
OPEC	Organization of Petroleom Exporting Countries
OR	Official Records
OSCE	Organization for Security and Co-operation in Europe
PCIJ	Permanent Court of International Justice
PLA	People's Liberation Army
PLO	Palestine Liberation Organization
Pol. Analysis	Political Analysis
PRC	People's Republic of China
Proc. Acad. PS	Proceedings of the Academy of Political Science
PSQ	Political Science Quarterly
Pub L.	Public Law

Rec. des Cours	Recueil des Cours
Resum.	Resumption
ROK	Republic of Korea (South Korea)
San Diego ILJ	San Diego International Law Journal
SC	Security Council
Schw. Jb. IR	Schweizerisches Jahrbuch für Internationales Recht
SCOR	Security Council Official Records
Stan. JIL	Stanford Journal of International Law
Stan. LR	Stanford Law Review
Stat.	Statute
Supp.	Supplement
Taiwan CNA	Taiwan Central News Agency
The Nat. Interest	The National Interest
UCK	Ushtria Clirimtare E Kosoves (Kosovo Liberation Army)
UK	United Kingdom
UNC	United Nations Charter
UNCIO	United Nations Conference on International Organization
UNCLOS	United Nations Convention on the Law of the Sea
UNEF	United Nations Emergency Force
UNMOVIC	United Nations Monitoring, Verification and Inspection Commission
UNTS	United Nations Treaty Series
UNYB	United Nations Yearbook
UPI	United Press International
USA	United States of America
USN & World Rep.	US News and World Report
USSR	Union of Soviet Socialist Republics
Va JIL	Virginia Journal of International Law
VCLT	Vienna Convention on the Law of Treaties
Verf. & R. Übersee	Verfassung und Recht in Übersee
Wash. Post	Washington Post
WHO	World Health Organization
Wkly Comp. Pres. Doc.	Weekly Compilation of Presidential Documents
World P.	World Politics

WVa LR	West Virginia Law Review
Yale JIL	Yale Journal of International Law
Yale LJ	Yale Law Journal
YBILC	Yearbook of the International Law Commission
ZaöRV	Zeitschrift für ausländisches öffentliches Recht und Verfassungsrecht

1 Birth and infancy of a Charter rule: the open framework

My dear Briand, I have been reading this wonderful book . . . *Vom Kriege* [by] Karl von Clausewitz . . . I came upon an extraordinary chapter . . . entitled 'War as an Instrument of Policy.' Why has not the time come for the civilized governments of the world formally to renounce war as an instrument of policy?

Nicholas Murray Butler to Aristide Briand (June 1926), describing the origins of the Kellog-Briand Pact[1]

Article 2(4)'s blind spot

After sixty years of United Nations (UN) activity, there seems little of a peg on which to hang yet another investigation into the regime of force. The UN Charter law regulating the initiation of interstate military action has been examined innumerable times. Its main pillars, article 2(4), article 51 and chapter VII, are well known. The outlawing of force as the first pillar is one of the key dictates of international law:

All Members shall refrain in their international relations from the threat or use of force against the territorial integrity or political independence of any state, or in any other manner inconsistent with the Purposes of the United Nations.[2]

Surprisingly, however, even the most comprehensive discussions of the force regime have turned a blind eye to one of its components: the

[1] Nicholas Murray Butler, *Across the Busy Years: Recollections and Reflections* vol. II, 202–3 (1940) (footnotes omitted).

[2] Article 2(4) *Charter of the United Nations and the Statute of the International Court of Justice*, 39 Am. JIL Supp. 190–229 (1945) (26 Jun. 1945).

prohibition of *military threats.*[3] Article 2(4) expressly forbids 'the threat or use of force'. Yet what is to be understood by the first part of that phrase, and how the UN and individual states have treated it, has until now remained entirely unexplored.[4] To chart this hitherto blank territory on the map of international practice, and to discover what it means for the international law discipline, is the subject of this study.

Properly speaking it is a rediscovery of previously charted territory. In June 1945 the UN Charter signatories agreed to the wording of article 2(4) as it was prepared by the US State Department prior to the Dumbarton Oaks conversations. By informal consensus of the drafters, as will become clear, the objective was to recast the language of the League of Nations Covenant, whose ban of 'war' by then carried the stigma of failure; it had failed to contain international violence between 1919 and 1945. The new wording in the UN Charter was created to overcome the deficiency that governments could deny the existence of a state of war by simply omitting to attribute that word to their military actions. The terms 'threat' and 'force' were designed to describe a single wrong and put an end to self-declaratory formalism.

Curiously, the idiomatic unity of 'threat or use of force' quickly dissolved. The two terms all too soon met entirely different fates. Since 1945, it was 'force' that was most evidently spotlighted, debated, politicised, reinterpreted, tested against practice and sometimes dismissed altogether. The 'threat' of force neither shared any of that celebrity nor did it undergo similar attempts to adapt it to changed circumstances. There have been no claims that threats ought to be lawful for humanitarian, ideological or overriding security concerns. Nor, for example, have proposals emerged to link them with the right to self-defence. Paradoxically, old and new resolutions of the UN and nearly all

[3] For the purposes of this study, I treat 'military threat' and 'threat of force' as synonyms. I take article 2(4) United Nations Charter (UNC) as being limited to military force and threats to impose economic or political sanctions as being beyond its scope. See Leland M. Goodrich, Edvard Hambro and Anne Patricia Simmons, *Charter of the United Nations: Commentary and Documents* 49 (3rd edn, 1969); Albrecht Randelzhofer, 'Art. 2(4)', in Bruno Simma (ed.), *The Charter of the United Nations: A Commentary* vol. I, 112–36 (2nd edn, 2002), at Mn. 15–19; Rolf M. Derpa, *Das Gewaltverbot der Satzung der Vereinten Nationen und die Anwendung Nichtmilitärischer Gewalt* (1969).

[4] The notable exceptions are J. Craig Barker, *International Law and International Relations* 122–36 (2000); Nigel D. White and Robert Cryer, 'Unilateral Enforcement of Resolution 687: A Threat Too Far?', 29 Cal. WILJ 243–83 (1999); Romana Sadurska, 'Threats of Force', 82 Am. JIL 239–68 (1988); Hilaire McCoubrey and Nigel D. White, *International Law and Armed Conflict* 55–62 (1992); Ian Brownlie, *International Law and the Use of Force by States* 88–9, 364–5 (1963).

important security agreements of the post-war period still echo the 'threat or use of force' formula, but none has ever attempted to lay the groundwork for elaboration on the threat issue.[5] Not only has there been a lack of discussion that might lead to reinterpretation, but also of simple primary understanding. The no-threat rule is established on paper – there is no shortage of treaty evidence for this – yet in the complex back and forth of scholarly enquiry and evolutionary identification of the law, article 2(4) 'part two' has been completely left out of the loop.

The completeness of this omission is surprising and its consequences are obscure. Omission means, for one thing, that at present there can be little agreement on the content of the law. What makes a threat of force unlawful? When is its use justified? Under what circumstances is a treaty invalid according to article 52 of the Vienna Convention of the Law of Treaties?[6] Without records of the case law of courts, the practice of UN organs, state behaviour and scholarly opinion, the existing literature, like a hall of mirrors, reflects seemingly empty space. As a result, short of embarking on an in-depth study of the subject, the legal advisor who is asked to comment on the lawfulness of suspicious action is left with nothing to hold on to other than the text of the UN Charter itself. That text is highly indeterminate. One can derive little certainty from the word 'threat' alone or the context of its placement. Numerous interpretations are plausible. Even if one could trump all others, few

5 Brownlie, *Use of Force by States*, at pp. 120–9. See the General Assembly resolutions A/RES/380 *Peace Through Deeds* (17 Nov. 1950); A/RES/2131(XX) *Declaration on the Inadmissibility of Intervention in the Domestic Affairs of States and the Protection of Their Independence and Sovereignty* (21 Dec. 1965); A/RES/2625 (XXV) *Declaration on the Principles of International Law concerning Friendly Relations and Co-operation Among States In Accordance With the Charter of the United Nations* (24 Oct. 1970); A/RES/42/22 *Declaration on the Enhancement of the Effectiveness of the Principle of Refraining from the Threat or Use of Force in International Relations* (18 Nov. 1987). For important multilateral treaties see article 1 *American Treaty on Pacific Settlement (Pact of Bogotá)*, 30 UNTS 55 (30 Apr. 1948); article 19 *Charter of the Organization of American States*, 119 UNTS 3 (30 Apr. 1948); article 1 *Inter-American Treaty of Reciprocal Assistance (Rio Treaty)*, 21 UNTS 324 (9 Feb. 1947); article 1 *The North Atlantic Treaty*, 34 UNTS 243 (4 Apr. 1949); article 1 *Southeast Asia Collective Defence Treaty (Manila Pact)*, 209 UNTS 28 (8 Sep. 1954); article 1 *Treaty of Friendship, Co-operation and Mutual Assistance (Warsaw Pact)*, 219 UNTS 3 (1 May 1955); articles 52 and 53 *Vienna Convention on the Law of Treaties*, 1155 UNTS 331 (23 May 1969); articles 19(2)(a), 39(1)(b) and 301 *United Nations Convention of the Law of the Sea*, 1833 UNTS 3 (10 Dec. 1982); article 4(f) *Constitutive Act of the African Union*, 479 UNTS 39 (11 Jul. 2002).

6 Article 52 Vienna Convention on the Law of Treaties (VCLT) reads: 'A treaty is void if its conclusion has been procured by the threat or use of force in violation of the principles of international law embodied in the Charter of the United Nations.' For a discussion see below, chapter 9, at pp. 285–9.

decisions on the UN Charter, as the long history of the use of force debate exemplifies, have been arrived at purely by reliance on a text-based analysis. The Charter is a treaty and its text the primary source of law, but there is much more to it than that: today the law is extracted by consulting a complex interplay of documented history, which includes the UN Security Council, the General Assembly, the International Court of Justice, UN member practice and the academic literature.[7] None of these can be left out of a proper investigation if the goal is to instil such accuracy into article 2(4) that is capable of guiding interstate conduct. It is this same accuracy that the legal advisor will need to respond firmly to a government's enquiries.

Omission also has consequences on a deeper, systemic level. If the law is unknown and if no trip-wires of unlawfulness have been defined, there can be no convincing condemnation of wrongful behaviour. At the same time, public international law is highly dependent on diplomatic protest for the very sake of identifying the law. It is said that when states acquiesce to violations, the pertinent rule itself will undergo erosion.[8] Resorting to the aging Lotus principle, states accord to themselves the freedom to act when they ought not. The systemic result is that omission is self-confirming. It feeds presumptions of indeterminacy, which in turn affect the patterns of behaviour on which lawyers depend to extract the law.[9]

Arguably, neglect in the literature would not be of any real consequence if the no-threat principle were inherently indeterminate, to the effect that any research on the content of the law beyond the Charter text would be bound to fail. The notion of threat is difficult to grasp. Nonetheless, I argue that this is a groundless assumption. Indeterminacy stems less from an inbuilt fuzziness of the Charter language (or ordinary language) than from the absence of solid enquiry. 'Force' too, is hard to define, yet there has been no shortage of scholarly and governmental attempts to root out uncertainties.[10] As in any system of law, rules simply need to be spelt out for specific cases, the accumulation of authoritative cases sharpening the meaning of the original norm. It follows that indeterminacy can be at least partially overcome by the introduction of evidence. The 'case history' on interstate threats,

[7] Michael Byers, book review, 'Recourse to Force: State Action Against Threats and Armed Attacks', 97 Am. JIL 721–5 (2003).
[8] Knut Ipsen, *Völkerrecht* §15 Mn. 112 (5th edn, 2004).
[9] Thomas M. Franck, *The Power of Legitimacy Among Nations* 50–66 (1990).
[10] Especially A/RES/3314 (XXIX) *Definition of Aggression* (14 Dec. 1974).

as we will see in detail, is rich enough to eliminate some of the ambiguities in which article 2(4) is presently shrouded. To recover this hidden treasure is desirable not only from an academic viewpoint, but also for the very sake of rendering the UN Charter rules and principles operational and able to discharge their proper function.

If states evidently thought it wise to have the rule against threats instituted in 1945, why has it been so manifestly omitted? A confluence of factors suggest themselves. To begin with, the advent of the Cold War shortly after the signing of the UN Charter sent strong signals to state leaders from both ideological camps that they could not afford to tempt each other with weakness. From Washington's perspective (the perspective of the major sponsor of the UN Charter), there could not be another Munich failure. The lesson of Hitler's coerced surrender of the Czechoslovakian Sudeten territory in 1938 was that appeasement and the 'peace in our time' formula did not work.[11] Unopposed aggression would simply breed further aggression. Wrongdoers had to be opposed from the very beginning with the language of action and the word of force.[12] States could not rely on the UN Security Council, which was caught in paralysis, for their own safety. If force turned out to be a sporadic necessity, even more did the deterrent threat establish itself as a continuous shield against expansionist plans of adversaries. For this reason, while the first use of force remained politically sensitive on a case-by-case basis, the threat of swift military action became an integral part of US grand strategy.[13] The overriding objective of winning the Cold War could only mean that the Charter's shining commitment to renouncing international violence, which relied on replacing confrontation with cooperation, would fall prey to the dictate of *Realpolitik*. Among the first victims in the Charter's retreat to pragmatism ranked its signatories' promise to forgo the threat of force.

This retreat was pushed further with the advance of military technology.[14] With the development of the atomic bomb and its

[11] G. F. Hudson, 'Threats of Force in International Relations', in Martin Wight (ed.), *Diplomatic Investigations: Essays in the Theory of International Politics* 201–5 (1966).

[12] Robert J. Beck, 'Munich's Lessons Reconsidered', 14 Int. Sec. 161–91 (1989).

[13] David Mayers, 'Containment and the Primacy of Diplomacy: George Kennan's Views, 1947–1948', 11 Int. Sec. 124–62 (1986).

[14] Thomas M. Franck, 'Who Killed Article 2(4)? or: Changing Norms Governing the Use of Force by States', 64 Am. JIL 809–37 (1970), at 820–2; and the follow-up article, Thomas M. Franck, 'What Happens Now? The United Nations After Iraq', 97 Am. JIL 607–20 (2003).

proliferation into the hands of the Soviet Union, Britain, China and France, the reliance on threats turned from a strategy of preference into one of survival. Between the USA and the Soviet Union, deterrence and the maintenance of military balance grew into the best remedy to avoid all-out war.[15] Force would now be promised in the hope that the promise would never have to be fulfilled.[16] While the case for deterrence was strongest for nuclear weapons, it was never confined to them. The delivery of advanced conventional arms, too, could increase the military prowess of countries without nuclear weapons to the sudden disadvantage of adversaries, making the threat of force a more pervasive foreign policy tool than before. This was in itself not a new situation. The American Civil War (1861–5) was the first conflict in which the devastating effects of mass production and mechanised weaponry, enabled through the industrial revolution, were experienced. What distinguished the second half of the twentieth century from previous periods was the multiplication of destructive power well beyond earlier capacities. In the face of military build-ups, states would find themselves ever more compelled to rely on the politics of confrontation and their own acquisition of cutting-edge arms to safeguard their national security. The logic of the Latin adage *si vis pacem para bellum* (if you wish for peace, prepare for war)[17] and the resulting arms race reverberated with particular strength in the technology-empowered post-World War II order. Examples abound to this day, as in the current conflicts between the two Koreas, Turkey and Greece, India and Pakistan, and mainland China and Taiwan, where both sides seek to gain security by expanding their ability to impose unacceptable costs on the other. The embittered ideological divisions in the world, together with the multiplication of destructive power, pushed the call to forsake all forms of military threats into the realm of the merely desirable.

After 1989, the influence of the Cold War rationale lessened while the gulf between the technology haves and have-nots widened. In the First Gulf War, the casualty ratio between US and Iraqi soldiers amounted to an unprecedented 1:1,000.[18] In the following years, primarily the USA began to argue that the credible threat of force

[15] Richard Ned Lebow and Janice Gross Stein, 'Deterrence and the Cold War', 110 PSQ 157–81 (1995).

[16] Thomas C. Schelling, *Arms and Influence* 18–26 (1966).

[17] Attributed to Flavius Vegetius Renatus, *Epitoma Rei Militari* book 3, prologue (2004) [390], in the form '*Qui desiderat pacem, praeparet bellum*'.

[18] William J. Perry, 'Desert Storm and Deterrence', 70 F. Aff. 66–82 (1991), at 67.

was a necessary ingredient of diplomacy in dealing with notorious norm-breakers.[19] Bosnia, Kosovo, Macedonia, Somalia, Haiti, North Korea, Taiwan, East Timor, Iran and Iraq loomed large as cases where coercive diplomacy could make a difference.[20] Although seriously flawed, the humanitarian dimension of efforts such as in the former Yugoslavia had the effect of making it difficult to defend a completely pacifist stance. Moreover, the threat of force had qualities that no military battle could deliver. Applied successfully, it could persuade wrongdoers to comply without a single death occurring. If it failed, it demonstrated that diplomatic means had been exhausted to no avail and that force was truly the last resort. While the dictate of 1945 had been 'peace over justice' under all circumstances, the notion of 'justice over peace' had now clearly gained momentum and weakened claims that the eventual use of force was unlawful.[21] The crucial difference from the threat of force debate is that it was never started.

Traced attempts to regulate threats before 1919

Two related strands of thought may be said to run through historic attempts to regulate the recourse to force. On the one hand, there has been the social attempt to create a communal system that would diminish incentives to go to war. States could be persuaded not to wage war once doing so offered no advantages. On the other hand, there has been the legal attempt to establish the wrongfulness of coercive military action. States could be persuaded directly through the weight of moral judgment. A decisive turning point arrived when the two strands of thought came together: first, with the advent of the League of Nations, and later and more thoroughly, with the UN. An international system that offered an effective remedy for an injured state could also legitimately demand that recourse to forcible self-help be banned as a matter of law.[22] For much of its history, however, the international system offered no such remedies, and legal concepts to regulate threats of force were embryonic at best.

[19] For a proponent of the continued utility of threats see James A. Nathan, *Soldiers, Statecraft, and History: Coercive Diplomacy and the International Order* 167–71 (2002).

[20] Barry M. Blechman and Tamara Cofman Wittes, 'Defining Moment: The Threat of Force in American Foreign Policy Since 1989', in Paul C. Stern (ed.), *International Conflict Resolution After the Cold War* 90–122 (2000).

[21] Susan J. Atwood, 'From Just War to Just Intervention', 19 New Eng. J. Pub. Pol. 55–75 (2003–4).

[22] Thomas M. Franck, *Fairness in International Law and Institutions* 253 (1995).

In the middle ages, ideas for regulating force between nations have run side by side with larger plans for a comprehensive system of peaceful coexistence. Such plans regularly provided for the establishment of a confederation of sovereign states, whose task was to persuade nations to settle their disputes without resort to violence.[23] But ultimately, such ideas were predominantly visionary. They were not held to be a dictate of the law. Natural law theorists such as Alberico Gentili, Hugo Grotius, Thomas Hobbes and Samuel Pufendorf did not think of war as illegitimate in itself.[24] Disagreement concentrated on rightful reasons to wage one, and within that context, threats were only of ancillary concern in the question of whether the fear of a neighbouring nation could justify a pre-emptive war.[25] Kant later proposed that standing armies be abolished because 'they incessantly menace other states by their readiness to appear at all times prepared for war'.[26] This was well conceived, but again visionary and not an official statement of policy of any government.

While the early writers of international law had still lived in an age when threats were not particularly useful for foreign endeavours, the situation had changed dramatically by the nineteenth century with the advance of technology and the industrial revolution. The invention of the steamboat, the railway and the telegraph not only led to the shrinking of the world and the first wave of globalisation but also to the ability to extend increased military power over greater distances.[27] European states regularly threatened and used force to advance their imperial goals in Asia, South America and Africa. British 'gunboat diplomacy', made famous in the first Opium War of 1840–2 against China, was acknowledged practice. The USA, too, asserted with the Monroe doctrine the right to exercise hegemonic influence over the Americas. In Asia, the 'black ships' of Commodore Matthew C. Perry forced Japan to sign the treaty of Kanagawa in a successful mission to gain trade concessions in 1854. Coercion was a foreign policy tool of great convenience, while the ordering idea of balance of power was

[23] Sylvester John Hemleben, *Plans for World Peace through Six Centuries* (1943).

[24] Grotius himself championed the right to self-preservation and the right to punishment for violations of the law of nature: see Hugo Grotius, *The Law of War and Peace* book I, chap. 2, paras. 1–6 (1925) [1625]; Richard Tuck, *The Rights of War and Peace: Political Thought and the International Order from Grotius to Kant* 86, 102, 108 (1999).

[25] Tuck, *The Rights of War and Peace*, at pp. 18–31, 52, 130, 161, 167, 183 and 227.

[26] Immanuel Kant, *Zum Ewigen Frieden: Ein Philosophischer Entwurf* preliminary article 3 (1984) [1795].

[27] William R. Keylor, *The Twentieth-Century World: An International History* 27–8 (4th edn, 2001).

preoccupying the minds of continental statesmen as a means of maintaining systemic order.[28] Intervention in the affairs of smaller nations was widely accepted practice among large Western powers, while headlong confrontation between equals risking pan-European war – the fruit of the balance of power concept – was not.[29] If Western leaders worried about the threat of war, it was because they worried about its potential to bring about war among themselves. After the defeat of Napoleon Bonaparte, the informal Concert of Europe attempted to settle contentious issues that threatened the stability between the great sovereign powers (Great Britain, Prussia, Austria, Russia and France) by a division into territorial blocks, a system of alliances and periodic international conferences. Above all, it was designed to counter another French-incited battle over the mastery of Europe. Since revision of the status quo was dangerous to the established order, it was opposed. States accorded to themselves the occasional right to reinstate the balance by force and showed no signs of surrendering portions of their sovereignty that would reduce their capacity to do so.[30]

Nineteenth-century international law did not object to this basic scheme. Scholars were now much more confident in their reliance on positive, consent-indicating acts of states to shape legal obligations, and under these terms, threats as part of war (or as the trumpets heralding its commencement) were permitted.[31] Nations retained the right to wage war on a scale, at a time and for a reason of their own choosing.[32] When Lassa Oppenheim, a strong adherent to positivist thinking about international law, summarised the *lex lata*, he reasoned along the categorical lines of Vattelian sovereignty: 'States are Sovereign, and as consequently no central authority can exist above them able to enforce compliance with its demands, war cannot, under the existing conditions and circumstances of the Family of Nations, always be avoided … International Law … at present cannot and does not object to States

[28] Alan J. P. Taylor, *The Struggle for Mastery in Europe* xix-xx (2nd edn, 1974); Alfred Vagts and Detlev Vagts, 'The Balance of Power in International Law: A History of an Idea', 73 Am. JIL 555–80 (1979), at 564–76.

[29] Thomas G. Otte, 'Of Congress and Gunboats: Military Intervention in the Nineteenth Century', in Andrew M. Dorman and Thomas G. Otte (eds.), *Military Intervention: From Gunboat Diplomacy to Humanitarian Intervention* 19–52 (1995).

[30] Brownlie, *Use of Force by States*, at pp. 46–9.

[31] Maurice Bourquin, 'Le Problème de la Sécurité Internationale', 49 Rec des Cours, vol. III, 473–542 (1934), at 477.

[32] Robert Kolb, *Ius Contra Bellum: Le Droit International Relatif au Maintien de la Paix* Mn. 27–40 (2003).

which are in conflict waging war upon each other instead of peaceably settling their differences.'[33] Paradoxically, however, and also as a derivative from the concept of sovereignty, international law did forbid intervention in the affairs of other sovereign states under the law of peace. In the absence of war, the threat of force was seen as a form of intervention which had to obey the rules governing armed reprisals.[34] Under these rules, a government's armed reprisal was lawful if used as a proportional response to prior injury by another state. Hence it was formally possible that a state issuing a military threat violated international law. But obviously, this fell far short of establishing a solid prohibition, and its modest ethos was very little in evidence in practice. Not only were prior injury and proportionality rather woolly restraints; at heart stood an axiomatic contradiction: governments remained free to remove these restraints by simply declaring, instantly and at the stroke of a pen, a state of war and with it the breakdown of the law of peace. The residual freedom to go to war had such sanction under the law that the delicate fences built around the use of 'armed reprisals' were too easily shattered.[35]

Towards the turn of the century the European mindset gradually began to change. Governments increasingly became democratically accountable. Wars took a heavier toll on the general population and a nation's economic resources. Information was spread widely through newspapers.[36] The principle of non-intervention was beginning to be taken more seriously, particularly outside Europe.[37] The first international attempt to regulate the threat of military force came from the American continent. In 1890, in the midst of the European 'scramble for Africa', Argentina and Brazil, at an inter-American conference, found wide approval for their proposal which condemned territorial conquest and that submitted that 'all cessations of territory made subsequent to

[33] Lassa Oppenheim, *International Law: A Treatise* vol. II, 52–3 (1906). On the 'Vattelian' basis see Emer de Vattel, *Le Droit des Gens ou Principes de la Loi Naturelle, Appliquée à la Conduite et aux Affaires des Nations et des Souverains* book I, chapter 2 (1958) [1758].

[34] In the nineteenth century the principle of non-intervention was predominantly understood to interdict armed force as a compulsive means, including the threat of force. See Axel Gerlach, *Begriff und Methoden der Intervention im Völkerrecht* 24–8 (1967). But the law was anything but settled on the matter, see Brownlie, *Use of Force by States*, at pp. 44–5; P. H. Winfield, 'The History of Intervention in International Law', 3 Brit. YBIL 130–49 (1922–3).

[35] Kolb, *Ius Contra Bellum*, at Mn. 39.

[36] Brownlie, *Use of Force by States*, at p. 26.

[37] Gerlach, *Intervention im Völkerrecht*, at pp. 18–19.

the present declarations shall be absolutely void if made under threats of war or the presence of an armed force'.[38] Although the resolution had been passed with the consent of all sixteen governments attending the conference, it did not attain the status of treaty law as originally intended.[39] On a more global basis, the 1899 and 1907 Hague Convention for the Pacific Settlement of International Disputes simply read: 'With a view of obviating, as far as possible, recourse to force in relations between the States, the Signatory Powers agree to use their best efforts to insure the pacific settlement of international differences.'[40] In 1907 the Drago-Porter Convention outlawed the collection of contract debts between governments by military force. However, force remained lawful when the debtor state essentially refused or neglected to comply during any of the stages of the designated arbitration process.[41] At the same Hague Peace Conference, Tsar Nicholas II's expressed desire to make Europe disarm was unsuccessful. It took the Concert of Europe's spectacular failure to prevent the outbreak of World War I in 1914 to convince states that its central edifice – consultation – was inadequate to rein in the machinery of war once it was put into motion.[42]

The League and interwar system

Significant but insufficient changes took place after World War I.[43] The League of Nations Covenant of 1919 marked a new systemic approach to the regulation of force on a universal footing. The Covenant declared any war or threat of war to fall within the competence of the League,

[38] Quoted from 'Rights and Duties of States in Case of Aggression, Part II: Aggressors', 33 Am. JIL Supp. 886–98 (1939), at 890–1 (15 Jan. 1890). See also John B. Moore, *A Digest of International Law as Embodied in Diplomatic Discussions, Treaties and Other International Agreements* vol. I, 292 (1906).

[39] Brownlie, *Use of Force by States*, at p. 25.

[40] Article 1 *Convention for the Pacific Settlement of International Disputes* (29 Jul. 1899 and 18 Oct. 1907 respectively), reprinted in Permanent Court of Arbitration, *Basic Documents* 1–39 (1998).

[41] Article 1 *Convention Respecting the Limitation of the Employment of Force for Recovery of Contract Debts* 2 Am. JIL Supp. 81–5 (1908) (18 Oct. 1907).

[42] Barbara W. Tuchman, *The Guns of August* (1962); David Stevenson, 'Militarization and Diplomacy in Europe Before 1914', 22 Int. Sec. 125–61 (1997); Stephen Van Evera, 'The Cult of the Offensive and the Origins of the First World War', 9 Int. Sec. 58–107 (1984).

[43] John Mueller, 'Changing Attitudes Towards War: The Impact of the First World War', 21 Brit. JPS 1–28 (1991). On general post-war sentiments and politicising leading to the establishment of the League see Margaret MacMillan, *Peacemakers: The Paris Peace Conference and Its Attempt to End War* (2003).

which would take appropriate action for the preservation of peace.[44] Signatories agreed to submit serious disputes either to the League's Council or to arbitration, pending whose decisions they were obliged not to 'resort to war'.[45] During the waiting period, any resort to war was *ipso facto* an act of war against all members of the League and thus unlawful.[46] However, in the absence of a settlement or even three months after one had been achieved the right of the parties to go to war bounced back.[47] The unwieldy design of the League and above all the unwillingness of states to commit to its purposes soon led to the organisation's inactivity and, eventually, to its quiet death in the harsh setting of the 1930s.[48] Japan's invasion of Manchuria in 1931, the Spanish Civil War of 1936–9 and the Italian conquest of Ethiopia in 1936 all went a long way towards chipping away what little was left of the League's credibility. When Germany threatened Austria, Czechoslovakia and Lithuania with invasion, the League was already distanced, abandoned by important members, and had lost most of its prestige.

On the face of it the League Covenant had nothing to say about military threats apart from the organisation's entitlement to act upon such threats. In case of external aggression or 'any threat or danger of such aggression' the Council was mandated to advise upon the means by which the obligation of non-aggression ought to be fulfilled.[49] Article 11 added that: 'Any war or threat of war, whether immediately affecting any of the Members of the League or not, is hereby declared a matter of concern for the whole League, and the League shall take action that may be deemed wise and effectual to safeguard the peace of nations.'[50] Military threats between member states fell squarely within the responsibilities of the Council. But by giving the Council authorities in such matters, the Covenant obviously still fell short of obliging directly member states to refrain from threats themselves. Such was only the

[44] Articles 11, 15(6, 7) *Covenant of the League of Nations*, 13 Am. JIL Supp. 128–40 (1919) (28 Jun. 1919).

[45] Article 12(1) *League Covenant.* [46] Article 16(1) *League Covenant.*

[47] Article 15(7) *League Covenant.* In this respect the Covenant followed the 'cooling off' concept of the pre-war Bryan treaties. See Brownlie, *Use of Force by States*, at p. 23; Kolb, *Ius Contra Bellum*, at Mn. 44–5.

[48] F.P. Walters, *A History of the League of Nations* (1952). Defending the League's setup Victor-Yves Ghebali '*Avaritia et ambitio* dans les relations internationales de l'entre-guerres: la gestion des conflits internationaux par la Société des Nations', in Michel Porret (ed.) *Guerres et paix: Mélanges offerts à Jena-Claude Favez* 715–39 (2000).

[49] Article 10 *League Covenant.* [50] Article 11(1) *League Covenant.*

case if 'resort to war' also encapsulated military pressure other than blunt physical imposition or *vis absoluta*.

Two opposing schools of thought existed. According to the first, which adhered to the 'state of war' doctrine, war was a technical term of the 1907 Hague Convention.[51] It preconditioned governments formally to declare war or alternatively to issue an ultimatum conditioning a state of war on non-compliance with clear and unambiguous demands.[52] States that did not formally announce their intention to enter a state of war were not in conflict with article 12 of the League Covenant.[53] The threat of force was unlawful only in the form of an ultimatum, whose definition was not precisely agreed upon but, in general, was narrowly construed.[54] Writing in 1906, Lassa Oppenheim defined an ultimatum as 'the technical term for a written communication by one state to another which ends amicable negotiations respecting a difference, and formulates for the last time, and categorically, the demands to be fulfilled if other measures are to be averted'.[55] Ondolf Rojahn, in one of the rare recent discussions of the term, described the ultimatum as follows:

> [The ultimatum is] a unilateral declaration which consists of a peremptory and unequivocal warning by one State to another that unless certain stated conditions are complied with within a fixed period of time, a particular legal relationship between the parties will be created, changed or dissolved ... usually

[51] Brownlie, *Use of Force by States*, at pp. 26–44, 384–401; Yoram Dinstein, *War, Aggression and Self-Defence* 29, 136 (3rd edn, 2001).

[52] Article 1 *Convention Relative to the Opening of Hostilities*, 2 Am. JIL Supp. 85–90 (1908) (18 Oct. 1907), which reads: 'The contracting Powers recognize that hostilities between themselves must not commence without previous and explicit warning, in the form either of a declaration of war, giving reasons, or of an ultimatum with conditional declaration of war.'

[53] Brownlie, *Use of Force by States*, at pp. 38–41. On the classic ultimatum in international law see Heribert Johann, *Begriff und Bedeutung des Ultimatums im Völkerrecht* (1967); Norman Hill, 'Was There an Ultimatum Before Pearl Harbour?', 42 Am. JIL 355–67 (1948). For an examination from the political science see Paul Gordon Lauren, 'Coercive Diplomacy and Ultimata: Theory in Practice and History', in Alexander L. George and William E. Simons, *The Limits of Coercive Diplomacy*, 23–40 (2nd edn, 1994). For an account of its historic development see Stephen C. Neff, *War and the Law of Nations: A General History* 105, 185 (2005).

[54] Ondolf Rojahn, 'Ultimatum', 4 Enc. Pub. IL 1006–18 (2000), at 1006.

[55] Lassa Oppenheim, *International Law: A Treatise* vol. II, 30–1 (1906). Oppenheim distinguishes between an ultimatum that is simple: 'if it does not include an indication of the measures contemplated by the Power sending it'. And one that is qualified 'if it does indicate the measures contemplated' (emphasis in original).

but not necessarily transmitted in writing [and demanding] a clear and categorical reply.[56]

Non-military ultimata did not fall into this category: for the 1907 Hague Convention, the 'legal relationship' at stake needed to be the state of war versus the state of peace. War in the formal sense triggered a host of legal consequences; the laws of war, neutrality, treaty, commerce, and national constitutional procedures hinged on the determination of whether war existed or not.[57]

The second school understood war in a non-technical sense. War was an observable condition that did not depend on how states labelled it.[58] Hostile 'measures short of war' (or *mesures coercitives*), the bone of contention at the time,[59] were argued to be in breach of the League Covenant. These could take the form of reprisals, pacific blockades, naval demonstrations or interventions with limited objectives.[60] Demonstrations of force thus fell under this category, expanding the circle of unlawful conduct beyond the traditional ultimatum. Arguably, the same authors would have supported a wider definition of the ultimatum that would have put an end to the strict state of war conditionality.

However, in light of the larger theme of 'war' narrowly or broadly conceived, the threat issue was a minor point and scholars rarely debated it. The design of the Covenant was invented to make cool heads prevail by, reduced to its core, installing a mechanism to delay the outbreak of war. The compromise in 1919 was that the peaceful settlement of disputes could be achieved by committing states to

[56] Rojahn, 'Ultimatum', at 1006. *Black's Law Dictionary* 1558 (8th edn, 2004) defines the ultimatum as: 'The final and categorical proposal made in negotiating a treaty, contract, or the like. An ultimatum implies that a rejection might lead to to a break-off in negotiations, or, in international law, to a cessation of diplomatic relations or even to war.' Ekkehard Bauer, 'Ultimatum', in Hans-Jürgen Schlochauer (ed.), *Wörterbuch des Völkerrechts* 467–8 (2nd edn, 1962) defines it as an '*eindeutige letzte Mitteilung eines Standpunktes oder einer Forderung, verbunden mit der Angabe einer Frist, binnen deren der Standpunkt anerkannt oder die Forderung erfüllt werden muss, und eine Drohung für den Fall der Nichterfüllung* [a final, unambiguous notification of a point of view or demand combined with the statement of a grace period within which the point of view needs to be recognised or the demand met, and a threat in case of non-compliance]'. See further Johann, *Begriff und Bedeutung des Ultimatums im Völkerrecht*, at pp. 10–71.

[57] Brownlie, *Use of Force by States*, at p. 27.

[58] Hersch Lauterpacht, '"Resort to War" and the Interpretation of the Covenant during the Manchurian Dispute', 28 Am. JIL 43–60 (1934), at 47.

[59] Kolb, *Ius Contra Bellum*, at chapter II.

[60] Brownlie, *Use of Force by States*, at p. 26; Neff, *War and the Law of Nations*, at p. 293.

negotiations and mediation at least for a short time, but they ultimately retained the right to use force.[61] Taking that concept to its logical conclusion, the League system could only demand that a threat of force had to be suspended during the designated waiting period and that the promise of force not be immediately implemented. It could hardly have required that a threat be entirely retracted. But this was nowhere clearly stated, and the League, being primarily devised as a political institution, did not resolve the deep ambiguity of its statute. When Italy under Mussolini issued an ultimatum against Greece and eventually bombarded and occupied Corfu in the autumn of 1923, the conclusions reached by the special commission of jurists of the League read as a capitulation to indeterminacy:

> Coercive measures which are not intended to constitute acts of war, may or may not be consistent with the provisions of Articles 12 to 15 of the Covenant, and it is for the Council, when the dispute has been submitted to it, to decide immediately, having due regard to all the circumstances of the case and to the nature of the measures adopted, whether it should recommend the maintenance or the withdrawal of such measures.[62]

The interwar period brought forth over 200 instruments that often took the League Covenant as their model and thus did not overcome its semantic ambiguity.[63] Only gradually and sporadically did awareness grow that the notion of war was a conceptual failure and, by that token, states also started to pay some consideration to the threat of force, beyond the ultimatum, in their law-making schemes. A first abortive attempt by the League Assembly, the 1924 Geneva Protocol, made specific reference to the threat of aggression. Its article 8, which never came into force, stated that the signatories would:

> ... undertake to abstain from any act which might constitute a threat of aggression against another State. If one of the signatory States is of the opinion

[61] Brownlie, *Use of Force by States*, at p. 56.

[62] *Interpretation of Certain Articles of the Covenant and Other Questions of International Law: Report of the Special Commission of Jurists*, 5 LNOJ 523–9 (April 1924), at p. 524. For details see Quincy Wright, 'Opinion of Commission of Jurists on Janina-Corfu Affair', 18 Am. JIL 536–44 (1924); Neff, *War and the Law of Nations*, at pp. 298–300; International Crisis Behaviour Project, version 6.0 (ICB), 'Corfu Incident', crisis 28.

[63] According to an early UN survey, a total of 234 treaties for the pacific settlement of international disputes were signed between 1928 and 1948. See *United Nations Systematic Survey of Treaties for the Pacific Settlement of Disputes, 1928–1948* 1179 (1949). Quoted from Brownlie, *Use of Force by States*, at p. 67.

that another State is making preparations for war, it shall have the right to bring the matter to the notice of the Council.[64]

Thrusts into the same direction were more successful on the American continent, which sought to strengthen the principle of non-intervention. The 1925 Central America Inquiry Convention forbade military preparations and mobilisations pending the work of a commission investigation.[65] In 1933 sixteen American states ratified the Montevideo Convention on Rights and Duties of States, which stipulated in article 11:

> The contracting states definitely establish as the rule of their conduct the precise obligation not to recognize territorial acquisitions or special advantages which have been obtained by force whether this consists in the employment of arms, in threatening diplomatic representations, or in any other effective coercive measure. The territory of a state is inviolable and may not be the object of military occupation nor of other measures of force imposed by another state directly or indirectly or for any motive whatever even temporarily.[66]

Schemes including European states were more traditional. The Locarno Treaties of 1925, occupied with remnant tensions between France and Germany over the post-war order established at Versailles, tellingly lacked any reference to the threat of force.[67] The important Kellog-Briand Pact of 1928, too, made no specific mention.[68] France had initiated the pact in the hope of gaining the bilateral commitment of the USA against the feared resurgence of German aggression. Shying away from any entanglement with the European alliance system, the

[64] Article 8 *Protocol for the Pacific Settlement of International Disputes*, 19 Am. JIL Supp. 9–17 (1925) (2 Oct. 1924). A 1923 League draft for a *Treaty of Mutual Assistance*, 16 LNOJ Spec. Supp. 203–6 (1923) recognised preparations for military mobilisation as indicative of aggression that should trigger League action, but did not provide for a prohibition of the threat of aggression itself. See *Commentary on the Definition of a Case of Aggression*, 12 LNOJ Spec. Supp. 183–5 (1923), at para. 6; Benjamin B. Ferencz, *Defining International Aggression: The Search for World Peace; A Documentary History and Analysis* vol. I, 10–13 (1975).

[65] Quincy Wright, 'The Outlawry of War', 19 Am. JIL 76–103 (1925), at 81.

[66] Article 11 *Convention on Rights and Duties of States*, 165 LNTS 19 (26 Dec. 1933). The ratifying states were: Brazil, Chile, Colombia, Costa Rica, Cuba, Dominican Republic, Ecuador, El Salvador, Guatemala, Haiti, Honduras, Mexico, Nicaragua, Panama, the USA and Venezuela.

[67] *Treaty of Guarantee between Germany, Belgium, France, Great Britain and Italy*, 154 LNTS 290 (16 Oct. 1925).

[68] *General Treaty for the Renunciation of War*, 94 LNTS 57 (27 Aug. 1928).

US State Department under Franck Kellog countered with a proposal for a multilateral pact.[69] This proposal proved highly successful in reaching virtually universal acceptance among the international community of states at the time.[70] It condemned the recourse to war 'for the solution of international controversies', renouncing it as 'an instrument of national policy in their relations with one another'.[71] It added in article 2 that 'the settlement or solution of all disputes or conflicts of whatever nature or of whatever origin they may be, which may arise among them, shall never be sought except by pacific means'.[72] The Saavedra-Lamas Treaty, concluded in 1933, equally condemned wars of aggression, and its signatories pledged 'that the settlement of disputes or controversies of any kind that may arise among them shall be effected only by the pacific means which have the sanction of international law'.[73] There is no evidence from the *travaux préparatoires* that states considered the inclusion of military threats in any of these pacts.[74]

It is unsurprising that in view of the abundance of at best loosely consistent treaties, the content of law was in the eye of the beholder and nowhere near an exact science. For example, article 2 of the Kellog-Briand Pact, taken literally, merely binds states to seek a peaceful solution to their disputes but not to find one.[75] Scholarly debate continued to revolve around the question of whether hostile measures short of war fell under the purview of the treaties.[76] For example, the International Law Association, in the summer of 1934, concluded in the clearest terms that: 'A signatory state which threatens to resort to armed force for the solution of an international dispute or conflict is guilty of a violation of the Pact.'[77] A number of states subsequently

69 Keylor, *Twentieth-Century World*, at p. 120.

70 Sixty-three states ratified the Kellog-Briand Pact. A remainder of four states (Bolivia, El Salvador, Uruguay and Argentina) did not, but ratified the Saavedra-Lamas Pact (see n. 73). See Brownlie, *Use of Force by States*, at p. 75; Ipsen, *Völkerrecht*, at §59 Mn. 8.

71 Article 1 *General Treaty*. 72 Article 2 *General Treaty*.

73 Article 1 *Anti-war Treaty of Non-aggression and Conciliation*, 163 LNTS 393 (10 Oct. 1933).

74 Brownlie, *Use of Force by States*, at p. 89; M. André Mandelstam, *L'interprétation du Pacte Briand-Kellog par les Gouvernements et les Parlaments des Etats Signataires* 2–22 (1934); Robert H. Ferrell, *Peace in Their Time: The Origins of the Kellog-Briand Pact* (1952).

75 Brownlie, *Use of Force by States*, at pp. 84, 90.

76 Quincy Wright, 'The Meaning of the Pact of Paris', 27 Am. JIL 39–61 (1933), at 39; John Fischer Williams, 'Recent Interpretations of the Briand-Kellog Pact', 14 Int. Aff. 346–68 (1935); Quincy Wright, 'The Munich Settlement and International Law', 33 Am. JIL 12–32 (1939), at 23; Brownlie, *Use of Force by States*, at pp. 84–92.

77 Article 2 *Budapest Resolutions of 1934 on the Briand-Kellog Pact of Paris*, 29 Am. JIL 92–4 (1935) (10 Sep. 1934).

denounced any such interpretation.[78] However, available evidence suggests that states took a less formal view of their obligations after 1919 than at the turn of the century; in judging the actions of others or by concluding treaties that no longer made reference to war in a technical sense. The notion of ultimatum as a term of art, too, had gone out of fashion. The Kellog-Briand Pact stands testimony to a step away from formalism, a step that statesmen had not been ready to make with the Geneva Protocol of 1924.[79] In the most comprehensive study on the subject, Ian Brownlie reports in his survey that states invoked the Kellog-Briand Pact whether or not any party conceded a state of war in the formal sense.[80] For example, they practiced non-recognition of territorial acquisitions in instances where military threats (beyond the classic ultimatum) had laid the ground for non-violent occupation,[81] a practice put into motion by US Secretary of State Henry Stimson's famous response to the Japanese occupation of Manchuria in 1932.[82]

Attempts to regulate military threats before 1945 were the result of transition from the notion of 'war' towards the non-technical 'threat or use of force'.[83] On the one hand was the fading state of war doctrine; on the other, the emergent idea that interstate violence was unlawful irrespective of how the belligerents characterised it. The blatant ultimatum to procure concessions carried the stigma of aggression and

[78] Miroslas Gonsiorowski, 'The Legal Meaning of the Pact for the Renunciation of War', 30 Am. PSR 653–80 (1936).

[79] Kolb, *Ius Contra Bellum*, at Mn. 70–6.

[80] Brownlie, *Use of Force by States*, at p. 395; Kolb, *Ius Contra Bellum*, at Mn. 66, 84.

[81] Brownlie, *Use of Force by States*, at pp. 88, 410–23. Rojahn, 'Ultimatum', at 1007 further reports that state practice and the prevailing legal doctrine in the meantime had concluded that the ultimatum also 'covers other forms of warning such as the termination or suspension of treaties . . . , the severence of diplomatic relations . . . , or the establishment of a blockade, provided the entry into force of the legal consequences announced in the warning is clearly made dependent on non-compliance with the stated demands'.

[82] Known as the 'Stimson Doctrine'. See *The Far Eastern Crisis: Occupation of Manchuria by Japan and Statement of Policy by the United States*, 1932 FRUS vol. III, 1–754; Kolb, *Ius Contra Bellum*, at Mn. 91–101; Neff, *War and the Law of Nations*, at pp. 296, 321. In two identical communications to the Japanese and Chinese governments, Stimson wrote that 'the American Government . . . does not intend to recognize any situation, treaty, or agreement which may be brought about by means contrary to the covenants and obligations of the Pact of Paris of August 27, 1928, to which treaty both China and Japan, as well as the United States, are parties'. Quoted from Quincy Wright, 'The Stimson Note of January 7, 1932', 26 Am. JIL 342–8 (1932), at 342. The UN General Assembly *Friendly Relations Declaration* confirms that: 'No territorial acquisition resulting from the threat or use of force shall be recognized as legal.'

[83] Edward Gordon, 'Article 2(4) in Historical Context', 10 Yale JIL 271–8 (1985).

illegality. Other forms of coercion short of war, such as naval demonstrations, pacific blockades or preparations for war, were of at least doubtful legality. Agreements and case-by-case diplomatic practice in the aftermath of the League Covenant indicated states' willingness to apply its provisions progressively. Since the law demanded that states settle their disputes by peaceful means, it was only consistent to insist that nations conduct their foreign policy without any reference to force, and that the fruits of such reference, for example, in the form of coerced treaties, would find no legal sanction. Accordingly, in the interwar period, scholars and states had begun to argue in line with the Stimson doctrine, that a treaty imposed by military force was void.[84] It seems that only the side by side of old and new treaties - thus the lack of a clear break with the past - kept arguments about the use and threat of force to retain their aura of extreme ambiguity. It is for this reason that the Gordian knot of claims and counter-claims remained uncut until 1945.

The Charter's original conception of restraint

With the outbreak of World War II the shortcomings of the interwar force regime had become glaringly obvious. States no longer declared war on one another. Germany had rearmed itself in brazen violation of its obligations under the Treaty of Versailles. In the course of the 1930s, illusions over the League of Nations' political influence to rein in military adventures of the major states of the time were entirely dispelled.

The increasing certainty of an Allied victory after the summer of 1943 brought the long-pending question of Europe's post-war order to the fore. The US State Department under President Roosevelt took the lead in planning a new world organisation that should avoid the League's shortcomings. Roosevelt and Churchill had already broadly committed themselves in the 1941 Atlantic Charter to the future United Nations Organization. Inspired by Wilsonian internationalism, point eight of the Atlantic Charter stated that:

> . . . all of the nations of the world, for realistic as well as spiritual reasons must come to the abandonment of the use of force. Since no future peace can be

[84] Stuart S. Malawer, 'Imposed Treaties and International Law', Cal. WILJ 1-178 (1977), at 19-25 (writers), 25-41 (states). See also his interesting discussion of article 19 *League Covenant* and subsequent practice, at 42-74.

maintained if land, sea or air armaments continue to be employed by nations which threaten, or may threaten, aggression outside of their frontiers, they believe, pending the establishment of a wider and permanent system of general security, that the disarmament of such nations is essential.[85]

Later Stalin and Chiang Kai-shek joined ranks with Roosevelt and Churchill with the 1943 Moscow Declaration, which endorsed a legal ban of military force and disarmament of the Axis powers after the War.[86]

Neither the idea of non-use of force nor of disarmament was new. Both elements had been alive in the minds of the peacemakers in Versailles after World War I. But within the US State Department towards the end of World War II, the novel idea of proposing a legal linkage between the two was suggested. Following intense internal debate, the Department's 29 April 1944 version of the future Charter read:

The organization should be empowered to make effective the principle that no nation shall be permitted to *maintain or use armed force* in international relations in any manner inconsistent with the purposes envisaged in the basic instrument of the international organization or to give assistance to any state contrary to preventive or enforcement action undertaken by the international organization.[87]

The official US Charter proposal submitted to the Allied powers on 18 July 1944 preserved the same wording.[88] On an identical basis, Roosevelt explained to the US public on 15 June 1944 that his administration was seeking 'effective agreement and arrangements through which nations would maintain, according to their capabilities, adequate forces to meet the needs of preventing war and of *making impossible deliberate preparations for war* and to have such forces available for joint action when

[85] *Joint Declaration by the President of the United States of America and Mr Winston Churchill representing His Majesty's Government in the United Kingdom, known as the Atlantic Charter*, 1946–7 UNYB 2 (14 Aug. 1941). On the negotiation process leading to the Atlantic Charter see Ruth B. Russell and Jeannette E. Muther, *A History of The United Nations Charter: The Role of the United States 1940–1945*, at pp. 34–43 (1958).

[86] *Moscow Declaration on General Security*, 1946–7 UNYB 3 (14 Oct. 1943).

[87] *Possible Plan for a General International Organization* (29 Apr. 1944), reprinted in Harley A. Notter (ed.), *Postwar Foreign Policy Preparations 1939–1945* (1949), at p. 583 (emphasis added). The most intensive drafting period with the State Department took place between December 1943 and August 1944.

[88] Chapter I, letter A, article 3 *United States Tentative Proposals for a General International Organization* (18 Jul. 1944), 1944 FRUS vol. I, 653.

necessary'.[89] The available documents thus suggest that blueprints for the future UN Charter envisioned a legal order whereby the breach of disarmament obligations, which the victorious Allied powers could confidently expect to impose on the Axis powers, would constitute *ipso facto* a violation of the Charter. The mere maintenance of an armed force inconsistent with designated limits was to be in direct violation of the Charter and would trigger early and determined Security Council action.

Properly speaking the idea was one of arms control. While the failure to remain disarmed was conceived of as a direct violation of the future UN Charter, the dictate of disarmament was not meant to be absolute. Clearly, states were entitled to retain the arms necessary to meet the collective security goals of the new organisation. The UN would rely on the contributions of member states to counter aggression with communal force.[90] States were also not expected to give up the military forces necessary to guarantee domestic order and to secure a minimum of individual self-defence.[91] However, excesses such as those of Germany after World War I were not to be tolerated again. The concern for a proper functioning of the collective security system mandated that the Security Council deter and if need be take action when faced with militarisation and military build-up, and this should be reflected in the principles of the Charter restraining members not only from the recourse to armed force, but also from the threat thereof.[92]

The 'maintenance or use [of] armed force' Charter version, however, did not survive the internal editing process within the State Department. It was never signed into law. In the midst of the Four Powers exchanges (which started on 21 August), the run up to the Dumbarton

89 Quoted from Notter, *Postwar Foreign Policy Preparations*, at p. 269 (emphasis added).

90 Robert C. Hilderbrand, *Dumbarton Oaks: The Origins of the United Nations and the Search for Postwar Security* 22, 26 (1990). US Secretary of State Cordell Hull opened the Dumbarton Oaks conversations with the assurance that 'any peace and security organization would surely fail unless backed by force to be used ultimately in case of failure of all other means for the maintenance of peace. That force must be available promptly, in adequate measure, and with certainty. The nations of the world should maintain, according to their capacities, sufficient forces available for joint action when necessary to prevent breaches of the peace'. Quoted from Cordell Hull, *The Memoirs of Cordell Hull* vol. II, 1676 (1948). See also the provisional estimates for the military forces that were planned to become available to the Security Council (article 43 UNC), 1946–7 UNYB 403. See further Michael Howard, 'The United Nations and International Security', in Adam Roberts and Benedict Kingsbury (eds.), *United Nations, Divided World: The UN's Roles in International Relations* (1988), at p. 39.

91 Russell and Muther, *A History*, at p. 239. 92 *Ibid.*, at pp. 234, 456.

Oaks Conference and last-ditch amendments to the Tentative Proposals in late August 1944, the disarmament linkage was dropped.[93] Using the latest proposals as a basis for discussion, the conversations in one of Washington DC's Georgetown mansions between the USA, the UK, the Soviet Union and China left the issue of disarmament untouched.[94] When the discussions came to an end, the official Dumbarton Oaks Proposals of 7 October to provide the basis for the San Francisco Conference contained the formula 'threat or use of force' as it now stands: 'All members of the Organization shall refrain in their international relations from the threat or use of force in any manner inconsistent with the purposes of the Organization.'[95]

The reasons for the text changes are nowhere explicitly stated. It is possible that the term 'threat' was intended as a simple synonym for 'maintenance'. It is equally possible that State Department officials sought to revise the substance of the text, concluding perhaps that extending the outlawry of force to mere maintenance of armed force was too far-reaching, or too narrow to unduly exclude other forms of coercion. Some drafts exchanged in the State Department show that both versions were used side by side for some time, but do not indicate whether distinct meanings were associated with them. However, there were two good reasons why keeping the 'maintenance formula' would have been a mistake. First, this formula depended entirely on the acceptance of a system of general disarmament, including agreement on numerical limits for the military equipment and troop power of individual states, which had yet had to be established. Anticipating complicated and potentially fruitless negotiations, the decision was to postpone the question of disarmament.[96] Imposing disarmament duties on Germany and Japan was one thing; to procure the consent of all states to a universal disarmament scheme quite another. Second, no matter how easily an agreement could have been procured, whether it was wise to do so within the context of the future UN organisation was

[93] As far as is possible to judge from the available documents, the Subcommittee on General Organization had agreed to do so by 29 August 1944. See *Memorandum by the Under Secretary of State (Stetttinius) to the Secretary of State*, 1944 FRUS vol. I, 747. For final editing in the State Department see Notter, *Postwar Foreign Policy Preparations*, at p. 299.

[94] Edwin Borchard, 'The Dumbarton Oaks Conference', 39 Am. JIL 97–100 (1945), at 100.

[95] Chapter II, Principle 7 of the *Proposals for the Establishment of a General International Organization*, 1946–7 UNYB 4 (7 Oct. 1944).

[96] *Memorandum by the Under Secretary of State (Stetttinius)*, 1944 FRUS vol. I, 824, 894; *Record of Informal Meeting With Diplomatic Representatives of Certain American Republics, Held, at Washington, January 31, 1945, 3 p.m.*, 1945 FRUS vol. I, 44.

another question. One of the conceptual failures of the Treaty of Versailles had been the troublesome interweaving of the League Covenant with the peace arrangements governing Germany's post-war duties. When the latter came under increasing criticism in the interwar period, the League of Nations took part of the brunt. It was therefore better to approach the disarmament issue as a separate package. The UN Charter could make reference to disarmament but should not be conditioned by it.[97] Years later, it turned out that this was the correct decision. The comprehensive disarmament scheme that the original draft preconditioned could not possibly materialise within the context of rapidly deteriorating East-West relations. Perhaps in wise foresight, the technical translation of 'war' to 'threat or use of force' prevailed in 1944 as being the better, more well-rounded formula.

The story from then on is a short one. When it came to negotiating the principle of non-use of force at San Francisco, no objections were raised to this part of article 2(4).[98] If the transcripts of the San Francisco Conference are any guide, the threat of force clause passed through the rush of negotiations with scant consideration. States were much more preoccupied with possible exceptions to the non-use of force rule and the powers of the Security Council. They paid virtually no attention to the inclusion of threats into the prohibition. The only statement of any substance regarding threats was the proposal of Brazil to expand article 2(4) to include the threat or use of economic measures.[99] This was rejected by 26 votes to 2.[100] The only change to article 2(4) as a whole was an amendment proposed by Australia, adding the famous 'against the territorial integrity or political independence of any member state' clause.[101] The participants' unanimous adoption of that proposal resulted in the phrasing of the present Charter:

> All Members shall refrain in their international relations from the threat or use of force against the territorial integrity or political independence of any state, or in any other manner inconsistent with the Purposes of the United Nations.[102]

[97] Article 26 UNC. Compare with the more far-reaching article 8 *League Covenant*.

[98] See the comments of governments on the Dumbarton Oaks Proposal, 3 UNCIO 100–10 (1946).

[99] 3 UNCIO 253 Doc. G/7 (6 May 1945), 334 Doc. 784 I/1/27 (5 Jun. 1945).

[100] 3 UNCIO 335 Doc. 784 I/1/27 (5 Jun. 1945).

[101] Brownlie, *Use of Force by States*, at pp. 265–8; Thomas M. Franck, *Recourse to Force: State Action Against Threats and Armed Attacks*, at p.12 (2002).

[102] Article 2(4) UNC.

As with many new rules, the limits of clarity were harder for their legislators to see, who had modelled the UN Charter on the bold German and Japanese actions heralding the outbreak of the war. No one in San Francisco would have doubted the threatening nature of their deeds, and to that extent the outlawry of threats must have appeared sufficiently transparent. Moreover, the major achievement of San Francisco was seen in the agreement on the basic pillars of collective security, whose success depended not so much on the precise definition of international wrong as on the commitment of the permanent Security Council members.[103]

That commitment soon cracked under the strain of superseding imperatives. The rift between Moscow and Washington cut through the UN Security Council, making it impossible for that body to discharge its proper function.[104] The first debates in its corridors in Lake Success focused on the presence of remnant troops in former combat zones and their timely withdrawal to home bases – in Iran, Greece, Indonesia, Syria and Lebanon.[105] The UN, off to a bad start, could not operate and therefore could not address early cases involving potentially unlawful threats that carried the seed of military confrontation – in Berlin, Turkey, Finland and Yugoslavia.[106] Only in a single incident, never to be repeated in Cold War history and due to a blatant mistake by the Soviet Union, did the Security Council authorise military force to protect South Korea and repel invasion from North Korea in the summer of 1950. Yet by then no one doubted that, despite formal efforts by the General Assembly, the well-intentioned idea of global disarmament and cooperation had been outpaced by a renewed race to arms.[107]

This is not to suggest that article 2(4) suffered irreparable harm. Its wording, strictly speaking, neither confirmed nor denied that military build-ups amounted to a 'threat of force' and should have compelled UN members to act. The *travaux préparatoires* to the contrary suggested that military build-ups were a central concern at least of the USA. Moreover, the trend of the pre-Charter period – unlawfulness of ultimata and of measures short of war – had gained currency at the expense of strict

[103] Franck, *Recourse to Force*, at p. 19.
[104] Stanley Meisler, *United Nations: The First Fifty Years* 21–36 (1995).
[105] 1946–7 UNYB 327–92.
[106] ICB, 'Turkish Straits', crisis 111; ICB, 'Soviet Note to Finland I', crisis 122; ICB, 'Berlin Blockade', crisis 123; ICB, 'Soviet Block Yugoslavia', crisis 131.
[107] Keylor, *Twentieth-Century World*, at pp. 275–83.

formalism.[108] The 'threat or use of force' formula stood for a rejection of the state of war doctrine. But in the light of the uncertainty, UN political organs would have been well advised to map out impermissible state behaviour in greater detail. With the Cold War, the international climate had grown utterly non-conducive for this almost as soon as the Charter came into force. For better or for worse, and perhaps to a greater extent than they had expected, the San Francisco signatories had left the refinement of the no-threat rule to further practice.

The Nuremberg and Tokyo trials

Two months after Germany's unconditional surrender of 7 May 1945, the occupational powers France, Great Britain, the USA and the Soviet Union declared in the London Four Powers Agreement their intention to indict and prosecute the major war criminals of the European Axis.[109] In the Pacific, Japan surrendered to the terms of the Potsdam Declaration of 26 July 1945, where the USA, China, Great Britain and the Soviet Union had pledged to mete out 'stern justice' against Japanese war criminals.[110] The Nuremberg and Tokyo trials were devised as a measure to root out high-ranking militarism and secure the establishment of an orderly society in post-war Germany and Japan. Yet the precedent of criminal responsibility, and the closely connected theme of aggression first raised in the League of Nations in 1923, came to preoccupy the UN at length. For the purposes of this study, the organisation's attempt to define aggression is of some import.[111] The two trials represent the first step in this attempt.

Among the divisive issues in Nuremberg and Tokyo was that of individual responsibility for attacks against, *inter alia*, Poland, Yugoslavia, Greece, the Soviet Union, China and the USA, acts constituting what was commonly described as the 'supreme crime' of waging a war of aggression. Clearly the new UN Charter could not apply to the

108 See on measures short of war Neff, *War and the Law of Nations*, at p. 318.

109 *Agreement for the Prosecution and Punishment of the Major War Criminals of the European Axis*, 39 Am. JIL Supp. 257–64 (1945) (8 Aug. 1945). Annexed to the London Agreement was the statute of the Nuremberg tribunal. Nineteen states joined the London Agreement before the Nuremberg trials came to an end.

110 *Unconditional Surrender of Japan*, 39 Am. JIL 264–5 (1945) (1 Sep. 1945).

111 For historical accounts see Brownlie, *Use of Force by States*, at pp. 159–64; Benjamin B. Ferencz, 'Defining Aggression: Where it Stands and Where it's Going', 66 Am. JIL 491–508 (1972); Ferencz, *Defining International Aggression*; Ahmed M. Rifaat, *International Aggression: A Study of the Legal Concept: Its Development and Definition in International Law* (1979).

circumstances before the war. Consequently, the pre-war uncertainties about the meaning of the League Covenant (to which Japan had remained a party) and the Kellog-Briand Pact should have been put to the test. In identical provisions however, the statutes of both tribunals declared:

> The following acts, or any of them, are crimes coming within the jurisdiction of the Tribunal for which there shall be individual responsibility: (a) Crimes Against Peace: namely, planning, preparation, initiation or waging of a war of aggression, or a war in violation of international treaties, agreements or assurances, or participation in a common plan or conspiracy for the accomplishment of any of the foregoing.[112]

This, of course, was a formulation with no pedigree in the law of the pre-war era and unprecedented in its sweeping scope: judges were authorised to sentence defendants for the planning, preparation, initiation and waging of wars of aggression no matter whether, through such acts, they had violated international treaties.[113]

On that basis, the Nuremberg tribunal was unambiguous in its condemnation of German leaders.[114] It asserted that both the *Anschluss* of Austria in 1938 and the seizure of Czechoslovakia in 1939, procured by the direct intimidation of government officials and the threat of invasion, amounted to acts of aggression.[115] With regard to Austria, the tribunal stated in no uncertain terms that 'the facts plainly prove that the methods employed to achieve the object were those of an aggressor. The ultimate factor was the armed might of Germany ready to be used if any resistance was encountered'.[116] At Nuremberg no one hesitated to declare that the German threat of force amounted to aggression. In fact,

[112] Article 6 *Charter of the International Military Tribunal*, 39 Am. JIL Supp. 258–64 (1945) (8 Aug. 1945); Article 5 *Charter of the International Military for the Far East*, http://www.yale.edu/lawweb/avalon/ (19 Jan. 1946).

[113] See e.g. Knut Ipsen, 'Das "Tokyo Trial" im Lichte des Seinerzeit Geltenden Völkerrechts', in Rolf Dietrich Herzberg (ed.), *Festschrift für Dietrich Oehler zum 70. Geburtstag* 505–15 (1985).

[114] *Judgment of the International Military Tribunal for the Trial of German Major War Criminals*, 41 Am. JIL 172–333 (1 Oct. 1946), at 214. The tribunal declared that 'certain of the defendants planned and waged aggressive wars against twelve nations, and were therefore guilty of this series of crimes. This makes it unnecessary to discuss the subject in further detail, or even to consider, at any length the extent to which these aggressive wars were also "wars in violation of international treaties, agreements or assurances"'.

[115] *Nuremberg Judgment*, at 192–7.

[116] *Nuremberg Judgment*, at 194.

drafts of the Nuremberg Charter circulated among the London 'big four' (the UK, the USA, the Soviet Union and France) indicated that this was precisely their understanding of the rules. According to an Anglo-American draft, amended on 28 June 1945, criminal responsibility was stated to exist, *inter alia*, for the 'invasion or threat of invasion of, or initiation of war against, other countries in breach of treaties, assurances between nations or otherwise in violation of international law'.[117]

The Tokyo tribunal followed the lead of Nuremberg in a 1,218-page final judgment, arduously documenting the plans and progress of the Japanese élite for the creation of a greater Asia under their rule. It concluded that Japan had prepared and acted in aggression against France in Indochina:

> The Tribunal is of the opinion that the leaders of Japan in the years 1940 and 1941 planned to wage wars of aggression against France in French Indo-China. They had determined to demand that France cede to Japan the right to station troops and the right to air bases and naval bases in French Indo-China, and they had prepared to use force against France if their demands were not granted. They did make such demands upon France under threat that they would use force to obtain them, if that should prove necessary. In her then situation France was compelled to yield to the threat of force and granted the demands ... The occupation by Japanese troops of portions of French Indo-China, which Japan had forced France to accept, did not remain peaceful. As the war situation, in particular in the Philippines, turned against Japan the Japanese Supreme War Council in February 1945 decided to submit the following demands to the Governor of French Indo-China: (1) that all French troops and armed police be placed under Japanese command, and (2) that all means of communication and transportation necessary for military action be placed under Japanese control. These demands were presented to the Governor of French Indo-China on 9th March 1945 in the form of an ultimatum backed by the threat of military action. He was given two hours to refuse or accept. He refused, and the Japanese proceeded to enforce their demands by military action ... The Tribunal finds that Japanese actions at the time constituted the waging of a war of aggression against the Republic of France.[118]

[117] Robert H. Jackson, *Report of Robert H. Jackson, United States Representative to the International Conference on Military Trials, London, 1945* 86 (Dept State Pub 3080, 1949). Quoted from Brownlie, *Use of Force by States*, at p. 163. A definition of aggression was dropped on the grounds that it would complicate issues unnecessarily and might reflect unfavourably on Allied military operations (at p. 163).

[118] *Judgment of the International Military Tribunal for the Far East* (12 Nov. 1948), reprinted in John R. Pritchard and Sonia M. Zaide (eds.), *The Tokyo War Crimes Trial: The Complete Transcripts of the Proceedings of the International Military Tribunal for the Far East* vol. XX, 49582–4 (1981).

The tribunal condemned the indicted Japanese leadership on the same grounds for its coercive policy towards the Dutch East Indies.[119] On 11 December 1946, the General Assembly unanimously endorsed the Nuremberg principles.[120]

Since the judgments did not formally rely on the breach of international treaties to sentence the leaders of the Axis, clarification of the no-threat rule is not straightforward. Aggression was a popular term of art in both treaties and diplomatic exchanges of the interwar period.[121] To some extent article 2(4) of the UN Charter was an extension of this practice. The Charter text, however, only referred to aggression in Chapter VII, which deals solely with the responsibilities of the Security Council.[122] It is therefore difficult to see how the military trials, apart from the precedent of individual responsibility, could have fed into the revised regime of force after 1945.[123]

Post-Charter efforts dealing with the threat of force: defining aggression

In recognition of the legal deficiencies surrounding the Nuremberg and Tokyo trials, the General Assembly at the initiative of the Soviet Union mandated the newly established International Law Commission (ILC) with two tasks: first, to draft a comprehensive international criminal code[124] and, second, to work out a more precise definition of aggression.[125] Special Rapporteur Spiropoulos of the ILC all too soon reported back that a legal definition of aggression would be fruitless and the ILC had stopped working on the second project by 1951.[126] Instead, the study of aggression was to be continued as part of the project on an

119 *Tokyo Judgment*, at 49584–5.

120 A/RES/95 (I) *Principles of International Law Recognized in the Charter of the Nürnberg Tribunal and in the Judgment of the Tribunal* (11 Dec. 1946).

121 Brownlie, *Use of Force by States*, at pp. 351, 356.

122 Aggression appears in articles 1(1), 39 and 53 UNC within the same context. The French version of the Charter in addition refers to 'armed, attack' in article 51 as '*agression armée*'.

123 Christine Gray, *International Law and the Use of Force* 150 (2nd edn, 2004).

124 A/RES/177 (II) *Formulation of the Principle Recognized in the Charter of the Nürnberg Tribunal and the Judgment of the Tribunal* (21 Nov. 1947).

125 A/RES/378B (V) *Duties of States in the Event of the Outbreak of Hostilities* (17 Nov. 1950).

126 Jean Spiropoulos, 'Second Report of the Special Rapporteur on the Draft Code of Offences Against the Peace and Security of Mankind', 1951 YBILC vol. II, at 43–69. The report concluded that: 'Bearing in mind the preceding remarks, ou[r] conclusion is that the notion of aggression is a notion *per se*, a primary notion, which, by its very essence, is not susceptible of definition … even if the definition of aggression were

international criminal code. Among the offences to be defined should be the crime of aggression. That too, however, led to a near stop to the drafting activities in December 1954. The ILC submitted a draft code that leaned heavily on the Nuremberg Charter but incorporated article 2(4) of the UN Charter, distinguishing between preparing and actively threatening aggression. Criminal was to be, *inter alia*, the following:

(2) Any threat by the authorities of a State to resort to an act of aggression against another State. (3) The preparation by the authorities of a State of the employment of armed force against another State for any purpose other than national or collective self-defence or in pursuance of a decision or recommendation of a competent organ of the United Nations.[127]

This draft did not fall on fertile ground in the General Assembly, and other proposals by Assembly committees proved equally abortive. Not until 1974, after US President Nixon had proclaimed an end to the 'era of confrontation' with the Soviet Union and *détente* was well under way, was the Assembly able to agree on a text.[128] Resolution 3314 now explained at the very beginning:

Aggression is the use of armed force by a State against the sovereignty, territorial integrity or political independence of another State, or in any other manner inconsistent with the Charter of the United Nations, as set out in this Definition.[129]

The preamble further declared that 'aggression is the most serious and dangerous form of the illegal use of force'. According to resolution 3314, the use of force was the only component of aggression and nowhere was reference made to the threat of force. In putting the concept of aggression into the Charter framework, the members agreed to define aggression as a sub-case of article 2(4)'s prohibition of the use of force.[130] Only severe forms of force should entail the penal liability that article 5 vaguely asserted.[131]

theoretically possible, it would not be desirable, for practical reasons, to draw up such a definition' (at paras. 165, 168).

127 *Draft Code of Offences Against the Peace and Security of Mankind*, 1954 YBILC vol. II, at 149.

128 Benjamin B. Ferencz, 'Aggression', 1 Enc. Pub. IL 58–65 (1992), at 60.

129 Article 1 A/RES/3314 *Definition of Aggression* (14 Dec. 1974).

130 Ferencz, *Defining International Aggression*, vol. II, at p. 29; Rifaat, *International Aggression*, at p. 267.

131 Article 5(2) reads: 'A war of aggression is a crime against peace. Aggression gives rise to international responsibility.' See Ferencz, *Defining International Aggression*, vol. II, at pp. 43–5.

Yet ultimately, the task of narrowing down the specific circumstances of criminal liability was bestowed a second time upon the ILC, which was requested to reattempt drafting an acceptable code of criminal offences by the Assembly in 1981.[132] Leafing through the reports and meeting records of the ILC between 1981 and 1996, one cannot help but regret the repetitiveness of proposals revolving around slightly modified texts. Picking up the 1954 draft, the Commission at first upheld the distinction between threat and preparation for aggression.[133] A threat in the context of the draft, the Special Rapporteur noted:

> … does not result from a dispute or a situation which, in itself, constitutes a danger to peace [in the sense of article 33 and 34 of the UN Charter]. Rather it is the intention expressed or manifested by a State to commit an act of aggression. The concrete evidence of this intention is blackmail or intimidation, either oral or written. The threat may also consist of material deeds: the concentration of troops near a State's borders, a mobilization effort widely publicized by the media, etc. It is in this second sense that the term is used in Article 2, paragraph 4, of the Charter …[134]

The majority of the ILC agreed that the draft should uphold the threat of aggression as a separate crime.

The proposed crime of preparing aggression, however, soon fell into disrepute as ILC members felt that it was impossible to distinguish between unlawful and lawful conduct. When did it begin? How was it different from legitimate preparations for defence? To some it amounted to an 'excessive extension of the scope of the concept of offences against peace'.[135] Other members of the ILC saw a fundamental flaw in the notion itself. According to them there were only two possible outcomes: 'either the aggression did not take place, in which case no wrong would seem to occur, or else it did, in which case the preparation merged in the aggression itself'.[136] While several members remained in favour of a crime of preparation,[137] the Commission eventually decided to drop the notion from the draft in 1988. The prevailing view was that in purely legislative terms, making preparation

[132] A/RES/36/106 *Draft Code of Offences Against the Peace and Security of Mankind* (10 Dec. 1981).

[133] 1985 YBILC vol. II, part one, at 73–5. [134] *Ibid.*, at 73. [135] *Ibid.*, at 74.

[136] *Report of the Commission to the General Assembly on the Work of its Thirty-seventh Session*, 1985 YBILC vol. II, part two, at 17.

[137] Doudou Thiam, *Sixth Report on the Draft Code of Crimes against the Peace and Security of Mankind*, 1988 YBILC vol. II, part one, at 58–9.

for war a crime was undesirable and the Nuremberg Charter should be overturned in this regard.

By 1989 the ILC had arrived at a different definition of the threat of aggression, based on an enumerative approach and the attempt to provide more objective means for its detection. As a crime against peace, article 13 of the draft now listed the following:

> Threat of aggression consisting of declarations, communications, demonstrations of force or any other measures which would give good reason to the Government of a State to believe that aggression is being seriously contemplated against that State.[138]

The accompanying commentary now declared that here the word threat denoted:

> ... acts undertaken in view to making a State believe that force will be used against it if certain demands are not met by that State. Under the terms of the article, the threat of aggression may consist in *declarations*, that is to say expressions made public in writing or orally; *communications*, that is to say messages sent by the authorities of another Government by no matter what means of transmission; and, finally, *demonstrations of force* such as concentrations of troops near the frontier. This enumeration is indicative, as shown by the words 'or any other means'.[139]

Some members thought that the constituent elements should be strengthened to include seriousness, imminence, planning, an element of intent, or reference to determination by the Security Council.[140] Although the wording remained highly contentious among the thirty-four Commission members, the consensus remained to retain the threat of aggression as a crime, recognising its preventive value.[141] With slight modifications article 13 was submitted to the plenary of states in 1993.[142]

Most governments that commented on article 13 expressed dissatisfaction with it. Australia, the Netherlands, the UK, and the USA contended that the threat of aggression as a crime was a novelty with no basis in customary law. Paraguay, Turkey, the UK and Switzerland concluded that the rule was too imprecise for the purposes of a criminal

[138] 1989 YBILC vol. II, part two, at 68.
[139] 1989 YBILC vol. II, part two, at 68 (emphasis in original).
[140] 1989 YBILC vol. II, part two, at 69. See also 1989 YBILC vol. I, at 292 *et seq.*
[141] 1989 YBILC vol. I, at 279. [142] 1991 YBILC vol. I, at 203.

code or, as the USA explained, unfit for a court of law because it could be misused for political purposes.[143] Ultimately, states disagreed with the ILC that the threat of aggression should have a place in a future criminal code. The Commission soon decided to follow suit 'because of the nebulous character of the underlying concept and the lack of rigour required by criminal law'.[144] It churned out a final draft in 1996 in the run-up to the establishment of the International Criminal Court. Article 16 of the draft read:

> An individual who, as leader or organizer, actively participates in or orders the planning, preparation, initiation or waging of aggression committed by a State shall be responsible for a crime of aggression.[145]

Evidently, after half a century in the making the ILC had come full circle to produce a slightly modified replica of the Nuremberg Charter that relied on different 'phases' of aggression.[146] States that commented on the threat of force in the ILC draft did not want it to entail criminal responsibility. As for the impact of the draft on the regulation of threats under the UN Charter, the ILC gave assurance that it did not 'not relate to the rule of international law which prohibits aggression by a State'.[147] Negotiations in Rome in 1998 establishing the International Criminal Court (ICC) revealed that states were no more able to arrive at a binding consensus on a crime of aggression than they had been after World War II.[148] The 1996 ILC draft did not find its way into

143 1993 YBILC vol. II, part one, at 60–106. 144 1995 YBILC vol. II, part two, at 22.

145 Article 16 *Draft Code of Crimes Against the Peace and Security of Mankind*, A/51/10 (1996), at para. 50.

146 On the 1996 draft see Jean Allain and John R. W. D. Jones, 'A Patchwork of Norms: A Commentary on the 1996 Draft Code of Crimes Against Peace and Security of Mankind', 8 Eur. JIL 100–17 (1997).

147 See the commentary to the draft code, *Report of the International Law Commission on the Work of its Forty-eighth Session*, GAOR Supp. 10, A/51/10 (1996), at 85. And further: 'The action of a State entails individual responsibility for a crime of aggression only if the conduct of the State is a sufficiently serious violation of the prohibition contained in Article 2, paragraph 4, of the Charter of the United Nations. In this regard, the competent court may have to consider two closely related issues, namely, whether the conduct of the State constitutes a violation of Article 2, paragraph 4, of the Charter and whether such conduct constitutes a sufficiently serious violation of an international obligation to qualify as aggression entailing individual criminal responsibility. The Charter and Judgment of the Nürnberg Tribunal are the main sources of authority with regard to individual criminal responsibility for acts of aggression.'

148 Silva A. Fernández de Gurmendi, 'An Insider's View', in Mauro Politi and Giuseppe Nesi (eds.), *The International Criminal Court and the Crime of Aggression* 175–88 (2004), at p. 176.

the Rome Statute. Rather, article 5(2) of the Statute flatly postpones jurisdiction of the court over the crime of aggression until a definition 'consistent with the relevant provisions of the Charter of the United Nations' is found and adopted by the state parties.[149]

Among the sparse post-Charter efforts dealing with the no-threat rule, the ILC project on aggression is the only instance where the UN has given some systematic thought on the meaning of the term 'threat of force'. Since 1945 there has been no comparable effort to define the threat of force by any other UN organ. The General Assembly widely supported the prohibition of threats in its resolutions, but this at best expressed the continued adherence of an increasing number of UN members to that Charter principle, and not an attempt to define threats any further. The Assembly came closest to refining the law by stating in its 1970 Friendly Relations Declaration that the threat of force to acquire territory was unlawful.[150] One is left to guess just what this could add to the Charter formulation.

It is therefore tempting, in examining article 2(4), to refer to the ILC drafts to fortify claims that military threats ought to be defined in a particular fashion.[151] ILC drafts are often cited as authoritative restatements of customary international law.[152] However, the preceding exposition of the Commission's work shows that one would be

149 Article 5(2) *Rome Statute of the International Criminal Court*, 2187 UNTS 90 (20 Nov. 1998). The Preparatory Commission brought to life at the end of the Rome conference is mandated to carry on the task of finding a consensus. See *Final Act of the United Nations Diplomatic Conference of Plenipotentiaries on the Establishment of an International Criminal Court*, res. F, para. 7, A/Conf.183/10 (17 Jul. 1998). The Commission's working group, at the time of writing, has not come up with a consensus. See http://www.icc-cpi.int/asp/aspaggression.html.

150 A/RES/2625 (XXV) *Declaration on the Principles of International Law concerning Friendly Relations and Co-operation Among States In Accordance With the Charter of the United Nations* (24 Oct. 1970). See also A/RES/2131(XX) *Declaration on the Inadmissibility of Intervention in the Domestic Affairs of States and the Protection of Their Independence and Sovereignty* (21 Dec. 1965). It postulates that 'armed intervention and all other forms of interference or, attempted threats . . . are condemned'. The term 'attempted threats', however, does not seem to be a statement of substance.

151 Cases in point are: Brownlie, *Use of Force by States*, at p. 365; Nigel D. White and Robert Cryer, 'Unilateral Enforcement of Resolution 687: A Threat Too Far?', 29 Cal. WILJ 243–83 (1999), at 252. See also the oral presentation of Indonesia in the *Nuclear Weapons* proceedings before the International Court of Justice: Indonesia, *Verbatim Record*, CR 95/25 (3 Nov. 1995), at para. 35 *et seq.*

152 See e.g. the ILC's work on state responsibility, cited by the International Court of Justice in *Gabčíkovo-Nagymaros (Hungary* v. *Slovakia)*, 1997 ICJ Rep. 7 (25 Sep. 1997), at paras. 51–2, dealing with necessity precluding wrongfulness.

ill-advised to yield to such a temptation. There was little agreement among the thirty-four members of the Commission, perhaps with the exception that preparations for aggression should play no part in the context of criminal responsibility. More strikingly, there was an unfortunate lack of any effort by the ILC to check the traditional sources of international law. It relied, virtually exclusively, on the Nuremberg principles, the UN Charter and the 1974 Definition of Aggression.[153] It did not consult the drafting history of the Charter, the practice of UN principle organs or, even more surprisingly, the case law of the International Court of Justice (ICJ). There never was any clarification within the Commission and thus none can be derived from it. Post-Charter drafting and theorising in the corridors of the UN headquarters has contributed little to the development of certainty about the meaning of threats in article 2(4).

The drafter's broad intent

The historical context of the UN Charter suggests that not every conceivable hazard emanating from a country was considered an unlawful threat in the meaning of article 2(4). Such a view would have been contradictory to the real-life circumstances that the Charter reflected and acknowledged: the Allied powers asserted the right to maintain military capabilities, and disparities of power were acknowledged to exist; to help enforce measures of the Security Council under Chapter VII, weapons and military force were indispensable; the right to self-defence in article 51 implied that the maintenance of some level of arms was lawful.

At the same time, the history of article 2(4) provides evidence that at the moment the UN Charter came into being, the general understanding was to reject the state of war doctrine, which had failed the League of Nations, and replace it with strictly objective standards. The formula 'threat or use of force' was to include the ultimatum and so-called measures short of war. The experiences of World War II still fresh in their memories, the victors of the war sought ways to outlaw the belligerent policies of a Hitler or Tojo. Early signs of those policies were military build-ups betraying aggressive intent, especially if they stemmed from the former Axis powers. The Charter itself provided in

[153] *Second Report on the Draft Code of Offences against the Peace and Security of Mankind*, 1984 YBILC vol. II, part one, at 14.

article 107 that World War II enemy states still needed to fear submission by force.[154] The post-war constitutions of Germany and Japan reflect the preoccupation with preparation for aggression. Article 9 of the Japanese constitution reads:

> [Chapter II: Renunciation of War] (1) Aspiring sincerely to an international peace based on justice and order, the Japanese people forever renounce war as a sovereign right of the nation and the threat or use of force as means of settling international disputes. (2) In order to accomplish the aim of the preceding paragraph, land, sea, and air forces, as well as other war potential, will never be maintained. The right of belligerency of the state will not be recognized.[155]

And article 26 of the German Grundgesetz postulates:

> [Ban on War] (1) Acts with the potential to and undertaken with intent to disturb the peaceful relations between nations, especially to prepare war or aggression, are unconstitutional ... (2) Weapons designed for warfare may not be manufactured, transported, or marketed except with the permission of the Government ...[156]

If such policies should appear again from any state, they should face timely and determined resistance. No state with aggressive intent should be allowed to reap the fruits of its policy. It could not make any difference to the law that force was not used merely because military intimidation had produced the desired result. Only dimly did the Charter drafters consider another rationale for the no-threat rule: that states, once caught in a spiral of threats and counter-threats, should be called to not make true their threat in order to preserve their credibility. This lesson, impressed on statesmen in 1914, fell into disrespect with the experiences of Munich in 1938.[157]

In short, it is between the two poles – lawful deterrence of aggression and unlawful threat of aggression – that the Charter sought to secure

[154] Article 107 UNC, now obsolete, reads: 'Nothing in the present Charter shall invalidate or preclude action, in relation to any state which during the Second World War has been an enemy of any signatory to the present Charter, taken or authorized as a result of that war by the Governments having responsibility for such action.' Read in conjunction with article 53(2).

[155] Article 9 *Constitution of Japan* (3 Nov. 1946), translation from http://www.oefre.unibe.ch/law/icl/.

[156] Article 26 *Grundgesetz der Bundesrepublik Deutschland*, I BGBl 1 (23 May 1949), translation from Axel Tschentscher, *The Basic Law (Grundgesetz): The Constitution of the Federal Republic of Germany (May 23rd, 1949)* 31 (2002).

[157] This disrespect, however, was not absolute. See below, chapter 2, p. 50.

international peace. This main thrust of intent, although formulated in the broadest terms, is clear.[158]

However, the delegates at San Francisco did not contemplate in depth the legal meaning of the term 'threat of force', and neither did their successors devote much attention to a clear definition. In their minds, the UN was above all conceived not to make law but to implement it.[159] The no-threat rule was devised as a principle, an axiom for correct interstate conduct. It did not specify the exact parameters of cross-border behaviour. Clarity was desired but not achieved.

In the early exchange of drafts and opinions between the Soviet Union, the USA and the UK, the UK government emphasised in response to the first tentative proposal by the US State Department:

> The Organisation should be as simple and flexible as possible. Thus the statement of its principles and objects becomes specially important, since they lay down the conditions in which action is taken by the members of the Organisation.[160]

Yet article 2(4) is without doubt open to interpretation as governments advocate claims made in response to changed circumstances. These changes were, for example, that the advent of long-range missile systems and the possibility of their instant delivery rendered the criterion of preparing for aggression anachronistic. The doctrine of deterrence, too, developed and took on another meaning in the nuclear age.[161]

There has been no enquiry into ways in which the no-threat rule could be consistently applied or even understood today. No coherent opinion prevails in the literature as to the legal limits for states to threaten with force. To provide plausible interpretations of article 2(4) within the drafter's framework of intent is the object of the next chapter. The subsequent chapters investigate how far individual state, communal and court practice corresponds to the range of plausible interpretations identified.

[158] On the legal relevance of intent see articles 31(1) and 32 *Vienna Convention of the Law of the Treaties* (VCLT).

[159] Oscar Schachter, 'United Nations Law', 88 Am. JIL 1–23 (1994), at 1.

[160] *Tentative Proposals by the United Kingdom for a General International Organisation, Memorandum A: Scope and Nature of the Permanent Organisation, Copy Transmitted by the British Embassy to the Department of State on 22 July 1944*, 1944 FRUS vol. I, 670.

[161] Paul Bracken, 'Mobilization in the Nuclear Age', 3 Int. Sec. 74–93 (1978–9); John Lewis Gaddis, *The Long Peace: Inquiries Into the History of the Cold War* 104–46 (1987).

2 The menu of choice: a guide to interpretation

> Doubtless India would hold . . . that its action is aimed at a just end. But, if our Charter means anything, it means that States are obligated to seek a solution of their differences by peaceful means, are obligated to utilize the procedures of the United Nations when other peaceful means have failed.
>
> US Ambassador Adlai Stevenson in the UN Security Council, 18 December 1961, referring to the Indian seizure of Goa[1]

From intent to content

According to the *Oxford English Dictionary*, the noun 'threat' is related to 'throng' (a crowd) and appears to go back to the sense 'to press'. This eventually came to mean a 'declaration of hostile determination or of loss, pain, punishment, or damage to be inflicted in retribution for or conditionally upon some course; a menace. Also *fig.* an indication of impending evil'. The French Charter uses the word *menace*, which, according to the dictionary, denotes: 'A declaration or indication of hostile intention, or of a probable evil or catastrophe; a threat.'[2] Thus it seems that the ordinary meaning of the expression 'threat of force' is not very helpful to identify the real-life implications of article 2(4) of the UN Charter. It merely suggests that a hostile intent must be communicated in some form, and that this communication must contain a reference to the use of force.

The preceding chapter described how the historical origins of article 2(4), too, have left wide margins of interpretation as to the exact parameters of illicit action. No injustice is therefore done to the Charter

[1] SCOR S/PV.987 (18 Dec. 1961), at para. 76.
[2] *Oxford English Dictionary*, http://dictionary.oed.com.

signatories if one explores the various competing interpretations of the no-threat rule as they could be spelled out for specific circumstances. This chapter introduces and discusses five major ways how the threat of force ban may be meaningfully understood.[3] In doing so, its aim is also to flesh out the set of ordering ideas that inform the thinking about military threats and their prohibition.

Formulated as propositions, the five interpretations on offer are that the legal appraisal of a threat relies on (1) the (un)lawfulness of the *use of force* envisaged, (2) the (in)ability of a threat to meet the UN Charter's *peace objective*, (3) the obligation of *peaceful settlement of disputes*, (4) the *imminence* of a threat and (5) the *coerciveness* of a threat. The following sections examine each proposition in turn.

Proposition that threat and force are coupled

One issue left open in San Francisco is the following: is the threat of force subject to exactly the same parameters as the use of force itself? Or do different standards apply? The Charter could be read as supporting both theories: as a first proposition, an illicit threat could be a conditional promise to use force in circumstances in which that use of force would itself be illegal. If state A is not allowed to use force against state B in a given situation, the promise to use it would be equally unlawful. If it is entitled to use force, it may also threaten to use it. As a result, the hotly debated question of whether and under what circumstances resort to force is justifiable (for example, in self-defence, for humanitarian purposes, for the protection of nationals abroad) would apply equally to military threats. The second proposition, which forms the basis for the following section, is that threats of force could be uncoupled from the use of force doctrine and defined according to an independent, *sui generis* legal standard. A threat could be illegal even if the projected use would not be, and conversely a state could be allowed to threaten with force that it ultimately was not entitled to use.

[3] The intention here is not to give preference to a particular 'school' of interpretation, but rather to explore the practical possibilities as they present themselves. On the 'schools' of treaty interpretation see Sir Gerald Fitzmaurice, 'The Law and Procedure of the International Court of Justice: Treaty Interpretation and Certain Other Treaty Points', 28 Brit. YBIL 1–28 (1951). On UNC interpretation specifically see Georg Ress, 'Interpretation', in Bruno Simma (ed.), *The Charter of the United Nations: A Commentary* vol. I, 13–32 (2nd edn, 2002).

It is on this choice between the two interpretations that scholars have pioneered discussion where governments have not. Ian Brownlie first touched the subject in 1963, when he proposed that threat and use are directly coupled:

A threat of force consists in an express or implied promise by a government of a resort to force conditional on non-acceptance of certain demands of that government. If the promise to resort to force in conditions for which no justification for the use of force exists, the threat itself is illegal.[4]

Brownlie apparently derived his view from pre-Charter practice regarding threats that paved the way for occupation without armed resistance.[5] His view has been repeated and endorsed in the sparse literature as an authoritative reading of the Charter text.[6] The International Court, too, has embraced it. When the Court rendered its advisory opinion on the legality of nuclear weapons in 1996, it took the cue offered to it by the British government, whose written statement had made direct reference to Brownlie's passage quoted above.[7] The Court stated in para. 47:

In order to lessen or eliminate the risk of unlawful attack, States sometimes signal that they possess certain weapons to use in self-defence against any State violating their territorial integrity or political independence. Whether a signalled intention to use force if certain events occur is or is not a 'threat' within Article 2, paragraph 4, of the Charter depends upon various factors. The notions of 'threat' and 'use' of force under Article 2, paragraph 4, of the Charter stand together in the sense that if the use of force itself in a given case is illegal – for whatever reason – the threat to use such force will likewise be illegal. In short, if

4 Ian Brownlie, *International Law and the Use of Force by States* 364 (1963).

5 Brownlie, *Use of Force by States*, at pp. 88–9. He also cites Lassa Oppenheim, *International Law: A Treatise* vol. II, 133, 295–8 (7th edn, 1952). Oppenheim, however, does not address the issue.

6 Nigel D. White and Robert Cryer, 'Unilateral Enforcement of Resolution 687: A Threat Too Far?', 29 Cal. WJIL 243–83 (1999), at 251, 254; Matthew A. Myers, 'Deterrence and the Threat of Force Ban: Does the UN Charter Prohibit Some Military Exercises?', 162 Mil. LR 132–79 (1999), at 171; Anne Hsiu-An Hsiao, 'Is China's Policy to Use Force Against Taiwan a Violation of the Principle of Non-Use of Force Under International Law?', 32 New Eng. LR 715–42 (1998), at 723; Hilaire McCoubrey and Nigel D. White, *International Law and Armed Conflict* 55, 56 (1992); Belatchew Asrat, *Prohibition of Force under the UN Charter: A Study of Art. 2(4)* 138–44 (1991); Yoram Dinstein, *War, Aggression and Self-Defence* 81 (2001).

7 *Written Statement of the Government of the United Kingdom* 72 (16 Jun. 1995), http://www.icj-cij.org/.

it is to be lawful, the declared readiness of a State to use force must be a use of force that is in conformity with the Charter. For the rest, no State – whether or not it defended the policy of deterrence – suggested to the Court that it would be lawful to threaten to use force if the use of force contemplated would be illegal.[8]

The Court did not explain how it arrived at its conclusion, nor do the separate or dissenting opinions provide insight. None do comment on this aspect of the majority opinion.

What are the merits of an interpretation that welds threat and force together? What may be assumed to be the reasoning of Brownlie and the ICJ appears at first hand easy and convincing. Could it possibly make sense in international law to allow a threat of invasion if the invasion itself was patently unlawful? If threat and use were not to stand together, would this not open wide the floodgates to abusive claims? If disconnected from the illegality-justification-architecture of the use of force, states could claim any threats to be in conformity with unknown criteria not contained in the UN Charter. Adopting such an interpretation would be to ridicule the purpose of article 2(4). It would amount to a *reductio ad absurdum* that would negate the absolute character of article 2(4) and introduce an undesirable loophole. This bears out the attitude of a Court diligently attempting to preserve the UN Charter principles and to protect them against erosive claims of exceptions and justifications, a trend that prompted Thomas Franck in the 1970s to conclude that article 2(4) was dead altogether.[9]

One problem with the Brownlie formula is that it may be difficult to apply it in reality. For one thing, states often use ambiguity as a deliberate strategy when threatening the use of force.[10] The measure 'contemplated' is intentionally ill-defined to leave the target state uncertain

[8] *Legality of the Threat or Use of Nuclear Weapons (Advisory Opinion)*, 1996 ICJ Rep. 226 (8 Jul. 1996), at para. 47. It may be worth pointing out that according to the ICJ, the threat is illegal if the use of force is illegal for whatever reason *within* the UNC, as becomes clear from the second last sentence of the paragraph. Compare further para. 78, in which the Court states that: 'If an envisaged use of weapons would not meet the requirements of humanitarian law, a threat to engage in such use would also be contrary to *that* law' (emphasis added). A conditionality on the legality of force according to humanitarian law or international law at large was not intended. But see John Burroughs, *The (Il)legality of Threat or Use of Nuclear Weapons: A Guide to the Historic Opinion of the International Court of Justice* 41 (1997).

[9] Thomas M. Franck, 'Who Killed Article 2(4) or: Changing Norms Governing the Use of Force by States', 64 Am. JIL 809–37 (1970). See the rebuttal by Louis Henkin, 'The Reports of the Death of Article 2(4) Are Greatly Exaggerated', 65 Am. JIL 544–8 (1971).

[10] The term of art among foreign policy practitioners is 'strategic ambiguity'.

about the real consequences of defiance. Clear-cut ultimata are rare. As a result, any judgment on the threat of force would have to struggle with the problem that legality hinged on the evaluation of a vague reference to force. Depending on what the reference is, legality would depend much on yet-to-materialise circumstances. For example, it may be unclear whether the use of force alluded to will occur on foreign soil (a practical problem in disputes over territory), whether it will be of a sufficient scale, whether it will be proportional, whether it will occur in self-defence, or whether the UN Security Council will eventually approve the use of force under Chapter VII of the UN Charter. Although the International Court demands judgment according to the circumstances at the time of the threat (and not those that would prevail when the force was used), the question remains of just how the readiness to use force should be assessed if the circumstances are ill-defined. In practice, it is often hard to tell if the situation referred to by the threatening state is one the law approves of or not.

This is exacerbated by the problem of cross-referencing. A difficulty with the Brownlie formula lies in a reverse scenario which runs counter to the author's intention. Not only is every threat illegal where force is illegal, but, obviously, any justification put forward for the use of force will work equally well for the threat of such force. As noted, the threat of one state is difficult enough to judge, but it becomes a near-impossible task when two or more states are threatening each other. The Cuban missile crisis serves to illustrate this point. When, in October 1962, the US government under John F. Kennedy discovered that the Soviet Union was building secret nuclear missile bases in Cuba, it made it clear that if Russian ships bound for the island broke through its naval blockade it would feel compelled to engage them by force. Khrushchev, upon learning of Kennedy's demands, contended that Washington was not entitled to intervene in what was Cuba's right to make deterrent preparations against a possible US invasion. Could it be said that the Soviet Union threatened force in collective self-defence, or was it rather the US threat which was justified in exerting its right to self-protection? Much may be and has been said to add to the details of Cuban missile crisis. It may be argued, for example, that the Soviet Union pursued geopolitical interests as opposed to collective security interests. The Organization of American States had unanimously agreed to the naval blockade. The attempted invasion of the Bay of Pigs in April 1961, on the other hand, had delivered ample indication that toppling Fidel

Castro had indeed been on the agenda of the USA. And so forth.[11] But for present purposes, the practical result of the Brownlie formula is that if two states on a collision course simultaneously threaten each other, the cross-references to self-defence would cancel each other out and both sides could proceed with the conviction of perfect legal authority. Whether references to self-defence are genuine could then be formally determined only by asking whether the governments had reported the counter-threats to the Security Council, as article 51 requires.[12] If article 2(4) is supposed to develop a preventive role, the Brownlie formula would be of little use since it implies that the law should remain silent until arms speak for themselves. The justification of self-defence would lend itself even more easily to abuse for the threat of force than for the actual use of force. In pursuit of the broader goals of the UN Charter, this is hard to accept.

In the setting of the 1996 advisory opinion of the ICJ the considerations above were perhaps implausible. It would have been difficult to argue that the threat to use nuclear weapons was unlawful whereas a nuclear strike was not. To take an example in this context: during the Suez crisis in 1956, the Soviet Union threatened both the UK and France with nuclear force if they did not roll back their military offensive against Egypt, whose Gamal Abdel Nasser had nationalised the Suez Canal. It also demanded that Israel, which had colluded in the Anglo-French attack, withdraw its troops from the Sinai peninsula.[13] Here, too, it is plausible along the lines of the ICJ (that a threat is illegal if the use of force is illegal) that the Soviet promise – targeting the civilian population centres of London, Paris and Tel Aviv – was in conflict with the requirements of necessity and proportionality of the use of force, and thus already unjustified under the *jus ad bellum*. But the argument here is that there may be other ways of reading article 2(4) that would avoid, in settings which the ICJ did not ponder, the disadvantages of complete dependence of threats on the use of force.

[11] For example, Abram Chayes, *The Cuban Missile Crisis: International Law and the Rule of Law* (1974).

[12] Christine Gray, *International Law and the Use of Force* 101–4 (2nd edn, 2004). States, however, have never reported counter-threats to the Security Council. This may be indicative for an informal consensus that no reporting is required, or alternatively, that article 51 does not apply since it is predicated on the existence of an armed attack. See below, chapter 7 for a discussion of the right to self-defence.

[13] ICB, 'Suez Nationalization War', crisis 152. For a legal evaluation see Louis Henkin, *How Nations Behave: Law and Foreign Policy* 250–68 (2nd edn, 1979).

As to the ICJ's argument that of the thirty-five states participating in the proceedings 'no State – whether or not it defended the policy of deterrence – suggested to the Court that it would be lawful to threaten to use force if the use of force contemplated would be illegal',[14] that argument does not go very far in its support. The written statements and oral pleadings before the Court divided states according to whether they were against or in favour of nuclear weapons.[15] Pro-nuclear states would defend the legality of both the use and threat of nuclear weapons to the same extent as their opponents would advocate the illegality of the two. There was no reason for either side to claim otherwise, and thus their statements do not appear as evidence of *opinio juris* as the Court infers.

Proposition that threat and force are uncoupled

The central contention of the second proposition is that military threats ought to be judged on their own merits and that no reference to the use of force is needed. Threats are *sui generis*. Advocating this proposition is a double-edged sword, as it can be wielded both to weaken the no-threat rule (threats are always lawful) or to strengthen it (threats are always unlawful). Once the reference to the illegality-justification-architecture of the use of force is gone, the door is open for both more restrictive and more permissive legal criteria.

In 1988 Romana Sadurska pioneered the argument in the direction of the permissive end:

> The Charter prohibits the use of force in violation of the political independence and territorial integrity of a state *because* it may lead to international instability, breach of the peace and/or massive abuses of human rights. But if that is the rationale of Article 2(4), then there is no justification for the claim that the use of force and the threat of force should be treated equally. Typically, an effective threat of force will not have the same destructive consequences as the use of force. (As a matter of fact, in specific cases, an effective threat may be an economical guarantee against open violence.) Therefore, there is no reason

[14] *Legality of the Use by a State of Nuclear Weapons in Armed Conflict (Advisory Opinion)*, 1996 ICJ Rep. 66 (8 Jul. 1996), at para. 47.

[15] See the remarks in the written statements of the governments of the USA at 45, the UK at 72–3, France at 24–7, Solomon Islands at 23–6, Mexico at 7–9, Nauru at 24–30 and Malaysia at 9–11 and 16–19. See http://www.icj-cij.org/.

to assume that the threat will *always* be unlawful if in the same circumstances the resort to force would be illicit.[16]

Sadurska further submits that threats are potentially lawful if states can credibly invoke overriding security concerns, genuine self-help, or apply threats with prudence and economy.[17] The ultimate touchstone is whether a state is threatened with force to the effect that 'the benefits for the overall security and welfare of the community balanced the harm resulting from the conduct of the threatener'.[18] One may contend that Sadurska's view, associated with the New Haven school, is dangerously permissive to powerful states in precisely the ways that the ICJ in 1996 tried to prevent.[19] But her most important argument, that threat of force and use of force should be treated differently because they are different in kind, certainly merits consideration.

There are two arguments why threats should be treated differently from the actual use of force. Sadurska mentions the first, namely, that threats in fact sometimes help to uphold international security and in this way indirectly serve the central purpose of the UN Charter, conveniently stated in its preamble, 'to save succeeding generations from the scourge of war'. The closely related second argument is that the threat of force is not of the same gravity as the use of force. In his widely acclaimed book 'How Nations Behave', first published in 1979, Louis Henkin explains why, in his view, threat and use are two different things in the context of the Cuban missile crisis. In domestic law he says, one is always allowed to threaten with more force than one is allowed to employ. The actual use of force is the more serious offence. By analogy, President Kennedy did not act unlawfully by threatening military action should the Soviet Union refuse to withdraw its missiles from Cuba.[20] Within the Charter scheme, the threat of force is more likely to pass the test of proportionality, and its employment is therefore justifiable in circumstances where the use of force no longer would be.[21] This argument is subtle because it does not imply, as Sadurska's

[16] Romana Sadurska, 'Threats of Force', 83 Am. JIL 239–68 (1988), at 250 (footnotes omitted; emphasis in original).

[17] Sadurska, 'Threats of Force', at 260–6. [18] *Ibid.*, at 266.

[19] Compare Myers S. McDougal and Florentino P. Feliciano, *Law and Minimum World Order: The Legal Regulation of International Coercion* (1961); Rosalyn Higgins, *The Development of International Law Through the Political Organs of the United Nations* (1963); W. Michael Reisman and Andrew R. Willard (eds.), *International Incidents: The Law That Counts in World Politics* (1988).

[20] Henkin, *How Nations Behave*, at p. 298. [21] Sadurska, 'Threats of Force', at 250.

argument does, that threats of force sometimes do have benign effects on international security.[22] The claim is merely that they are less harmful than uses of force and thus more readily justifiable. Both arguments have in common, however, that the threat of force does not, or not as much, compromise the UN Charter's peace objective as the use of force does, and that this should be given due consideration in interpretation.

Much of this, then, is predicated on the assumption that the threat of force is indeed less conducive than the actual use of force to instability and breaches of the peace as Sadurska asserts, that threats more often help to prevent wars than they invite them. That is an empirical question, one which scholars of international relations have been unable to resolve. There seems to be evidence for both sides of the argument.[23] For example, researchers often attribute the outbreak of the Korean War in 1950 to the US mistake in defining its defence perimeter short of the Korean peninsula. Had the USA clearly included it, North Korea would have been effectively deterred from crossing the 38th parallel.[24] On the other hand, several ultimata issued by the People's Republic of China (PRC) and the US military command during the course of the Korean War resulted in a costly engagement of both armies.[25] According to scholars of international relations, competing with each other are two models of reality: the deterrence model and the spiral model.

22 Sadurska, 'Threats of Force', at 246–51 argues that the threat of force is an adequate self-help substitute for the failed collective security arrangement of the UNC, that it may help to solve disputes peacefully, and that occasionally it is a ritual substitute for the use of force itself. These reasons are taken by her to relax the no-threat rule such that behaviour to these ends is permissible. She does not, however, cite evidence for her assertions.

23 For example, scholars have attributed the fortunate fact that there has been no major war between industrialised countries since 1945 to a variety of incompatible reasons. Compare Kenneth Waltz, 'The Spread of Nuclear Weapons: More May Be Better', 117 *Adelphi Papers* (1981); John Mueller, *Retreat from Doomsday: The Obsolescence of Major Wars* 81–187 (1989); John Lewis Gaddis, *The Long Peace: Inquiries Into the History of the Cold War* 215–45 (1987); Richard Ned Lebow and Janice Gross Stein, *We All Lost the Cold War* (1994); Colin S. Gray, *Military Strategy* 298–302 (1999). On tit-for-tat on the micro level see, *inter alia*, Russell J. Leng and Hugh G. Wheeler, 'Influence Strategies, Success, and War', 23 J. Conf. Resol. 655–84 (1979); Paul Huth and Bruce Russett, 'Deterrence Failure and Crisis Escalation', 32 Int. Stud. Q. 29–45 (1988); Susan G. Sample, 'Military Buildups, War, and Realpolitik: A Multivariate Model', 42 J. Conf. Resol. 156–75 (1998); B. Lai, 'The Effects of Different Types of Military Mobilization on the Outcome of International Crises', 48 J. Conf. Resol. 211–29 (2004).

24 Alexander L. George and Richard Smoke, *Deterrence in American Foreign Policy: Theory and Practice* 141–2 (1974).

25 See below, chapter 5, at pp. 131–135.

The *deterrence model* holds that military threats may prevent war by convincing the adversary that going to war would be too costly or even self-destructive. Deterrence keeps rivals in check if they share similar military capabilities. Nuclear weapons are a famous 'equaliser', but the logic of deterrence extends to all weapon categories. Here is the place for the Latin adage *si vis pacem para bellum*. In contrast, the *spiral model* asserts that military threats and brinkmanship tend to escalate into war.[26] States engage in arms races; in crisis, they raise the ante through threats only to discover later that these threats, having failed, need to be implemented for the sake of credibility, personal pride or political necessity. Conflict then resembles a 'game of chicken', in which two motorists drive towards each other to see who is the first to swerve aside. If both fail to give in at the last moment, the disaster, like their commitment, is complete.[27] The spiral model is dynamic while the deterrence model is static. Thomas Schelling in 1966 described the logic involved like this:

> If all threats were fully believable ... Countries would hasten to set up their threats; and if the violence that would accompany infraction were confidently expected, and sufficiently dreadful to outweigh the fruits of transgression, the world might get frozen into a set of laws enforced by what we could figuratively call the Wrath of God ... And if all threats depended on some kind of physical positioning of territorial claims, trip-wires, troop barriers, automatic alarm systems, and other such arrangements, and all were completely infallible and fully credible, we might have something like an old fashioned western land rush, at the end of which – as long as nobody tripped on his neighbor's electric fence and set the whole thing off – the world would be carved up in a tightly bound status quo ... But uncertainty exists ... Violence, especially war, is a confused and uncertain activity, highly unpredictable, depending on decisions made by fallible human beings organized into imperfect governments,

[26] For a survey see Robert Jervis, *Perception and Misperception in International Politics* 58–116 (1976); Franck C. Zagare and D. Marc Kilgour, 'Deterrence Theory and the Spiral Model Revisited', 10 J. Theo. P. 59–87 (1998). For an early attempt to marry the concept of escalation with international law see Hanspeter Neuhold, *Internationale Konflikte: Verbotene und erlaubte Mittel ihrer Austragung* 264–7 (1977). The escalation argument was considered by the ICJ in its *Nuclear Weapons Advisory Opinion*, at para. 43.

[27] Seminal Bertrand Russell, *Common Sense and Nuclear Warfare* (1959); Hermann Kahn, *On Escalation: Metaphors and Scenarios* (1965); Thomas C. Schelling, *Arms and Influence* 116–25 (1966). Interestingly, the words 'bellum' and 'duellum' share the same origin. See Quincy Wright, *A Study of War* 175 (updated and abridged edn, 1964). See further Oran R. Young, *The Politics of Force: Bargaining During International Crises* (1968); Zagare and Kilgour, 'Deterrence Theory and the Spiral Model Revisited'; William Poundstone, *Prisoner's Dilemma: John von Neumann, Game Theory, and the Puzzle of the Bomb* (1992).

depending on fallible communications and warning systems and on the untested performance of people and equipment. It is furthermore a hotheaded activity, in which commitments and reputations can develop a momentum of their own.[28]

The spiral and deterrence models remain contested descriptions of real-life militarised conflicts. But it appears that anyone who advocates that the UN Charter generously permits threats implicitly relies on the deterrence model.[29] Narrowly construed, the deterrence model lends itself to the less sweeping assertion that unilateral deterrence indirectly serves the Charter's peace objective and therefore should be beyond the scope of article 2(4). Broadly construed, even more active threats would fall outside of the purview of the UN Charter. The latter is what Romana Sadurska suggests when she invokes overriding security concerns or genuine self-help as criteria for the lawfulness of a military threat.

However, the historical context suggests that either permissive interpretation should be met with caution. It is true that the UN Charter partially relies on deterrence to dissuade states from resorting to force. It endorses the threat of military action to induce compliance. But there is little doubt that deterrence was intended to flow from the Security Council, whose initiation of collective action as a whole was meant to discourage defection. Only as a fail-safe deterrent should states retain the right to act in self-defence.[30] The drafter's intent thus suggests that Sadurska construes article 2(4) in ways that *prima facie* run, notwithstanding her assertions, counter to the design of the UN Charter. In order to defend either permissive interpretation, it would be necessary to show that states in their practice subsequent to the adoption of the UN Charter supported the deterrence model over the spiral model, at least in some yet to specified circumstances. This hypothesis is dealt with further below.[31] Suffice it to note here that testing the hypothesis provides an inroad into clarifying the UN Charter, and that it is the two models that provide the theoretical basis for it.

[28] Schelling, *Arms and Influence*, at pp. 92–3.

[29] A supporter of the deterrence model is Judge Schwebel in the *Nuclear Weapons Advisory Opinion*, where he argues that the USA effectively dissuaded Saddam Hussein from using chemical and bacteriological weapons against US troops during the first Gulf War (his dissenting opinion starts at p. 311).

[30] Thomas M. Franck, *Recourse to Force: State Action Against Threats and Armed Attacks* 45 (2002).

[31] See below, chapters 7–8.

The two models also prove useful in the analysis of the proportionality argument. The idea of proportionality originates from an ethical principle seeking 'moderation' and 'the avoidance of any excess behaviour'.[32] If the spiral model is correct, moderation means that the standard for proportionality cannot be only whether force is more excessive than the threat of force, but also whether the risks of future violence are excessive, whether, in a self-fulfilling prophecy, the signal of violence is imprudently brought to its tragic conclusion.[33] One could then argue that the static view fails to consider that the UN Charter is as much concerned with the process of conflict prevention as it is with dealing with the results. Louis Henkin's reference to domestic law does not take into account that conflict escalation is not a concern between individuals in municipal law. That physical injury is the more serious offence than the threat of such injury is true, but this difference is above all relevant in the context of criminal responsibility. The rationale is different in the context of preventing war between states.

It is not difficult to see that the second variation to the uncoupling of threat and force, which leans towards a comprehensive threat ban, builds on the spiral model. In some circumstances such an interpretation of article 2(4) of the UN Charter would condemn threats when the use of force contemplated was, according to the Brownlie formula, technically lawful, for example, in self-defence. It could deny states the right to threaten back.[34] It would have disapproved of the Soviet nuclear threat in 1956 because it deliberately risked all-out war with Britain, France, Israel, and the US. Kennedy's threat during the Cuban missile crisis would have been at variance with the UN Charter for the same reasons, quite independently of whether the 'hemispheric'

[32] Jost Delbrück, 'Proportionality', 3 Enc. Pub. IL 1140–4 (1997), at 1140; On the function of minimising the disruption of international peace and security see Judith Gardam, *Necessity, Proportionality and the Use of Force by States* 16 (2004).

[33] See the consideration of the ICJ in its *Nuclear Weapons Advisory Opinion*, at para. 43: 'Certain States have ... suggested that in the case of nuclear weapons, the condition of proportionality must be evaluated in the light of still further factors. They contend that the very nature of nuclear weapons, and the high probability of an escalation of nuclear exchanges, mean that there is an extremely strong risk of devastation. The risk factor is said to negate the possibility of the condition of proportionality being complied with.' The Court, however, merely observed that such risks were 'to be borne in mind by States believing they can exercise a nuclear response in self-defence in accordance with the requirements of proportionality' (*ibid.*).

[34] In a sense, this is compatible with Sadurska's finding that states appreciate prudence and economy in judging the lawfulness of a threat of force. See Sadurska, 'Threats of Force', at 265–6.

menace of a foreign missile deployment on Cuba itself already amounted to a threat of force.

Roughly thirty protracted conflicts account for close to 60 per cent of all international crises in the twentieth century.[35] An interpretation inspired by the spiral model relies on the observation that amid many conflicts, and especially protracted conflicts, it is difficult if not impossible to tell which side 'provoked' the outbreak of hostilities. Information is often imperfect; initial hostile acts are regularly small in scale and difficult to attribute to a government. Blame is often a shared commodity. If the spiral model applies, the prohibition of the threat of force independent of justificatory rhetoric could, through the political organs of the UN, bring pressures to bear on crisis actors that would serve preventive diplomacy in ways superior to those of the Brownlie formula. An advantage of a legal call for restraint, prudence and forbearance (that is not based on a *quid pro quo*) provides statesmen with a face-saving 'way out' or 'tie' when for the sake of bargaining reputation, personal fervour or out of a fatal error they would have proceeded with headlong confrontation.[36]

Three objections may be raised against an interpretation leaning towards a comprehensive threat ban. First, if the deterrence model is more accurate, to forbid the threat of force would be to deny states the very means to fortify their safety and forestall armed conflict. Second, applying the spiral model runs counter to a pervasive theme in international law: reciprocity. Only in rare cases, such as when there are humanitarian concerns, does international law deny states to respond to non-compliance with non-compliance.[37] Third, many scholars would argue that a strict prohibition would be patently incompatible with the right to self-defence, which states guard jealously.[38] While the first and

35 Michael Brecher and Jonathan Wilkenfeld, *A Study of Crisis* 820–1 (1997). See the annex for an overview table.

36 Schelling, Arms and Influence, at pp. 116–20; Neuhold, *Internationale Konflikte*, at pp. 262–3. See further below, chapter 9, at pp. 283–4. A famous example for misjudgment is the eve of World War I, when statesmen across Europe felt certain that the war would last for a matter of months at the most.

37 For a brief overview of the regulation according to the Geneva Conventions see Knut Ipsen, *Völkerrecht* §16 Mn. 12–13 (5th edn, 2004).

38 For example, Bosnia Herzegovina argued that the UN-imposed arms embargo (S/RES/713) violated its right to self-defence against Serbia and Montenegro. See Christine Gray, 'Bosnia and Herzegovina: Civil War or Inter-State Conflict? Characterization and Consequences', 67 Brit. YBIL 155–97 (1996), at 190–5.

second objections are rather a matter of principle, the third can be relativised on legal grounds. The text of article 51 of the UN Charter provides space for a contrary assertion. There is room for the uncontemplated – and perhaps revolutionary – interpretation that a threat of force can be justified only when, and not before, an armed attack is underway.[39] Following the deterrence model, such a view is patently untenable. Following the spiral model, the restriction makes sense. One could argue that the view that unilateral threats are conditional upon a prior armed attack is incompatible with the rationale of the Charter. As mentioned above, the Charter does not object to defiance against aggression. In general it confers legitimacy to such efforts, and there is an implied rejection of appeasement and the 'peace in our time' formula applied in Munich in 1938. The UN Charter distinguishes between aggressor and victim, with the latter enjoying the right to self-defence. But to conclude from this that only the deterrence model informed the thinking of representatives at San Francisco in 1945 would be simplistic. Elements of the spiral model can also be traced in the UN Charter. It postulates the obligation to settle disputes peacefully (implying a duty to exercise forbearance), and seeks to do away with secret military alliances in favour of an arrangement of collective security (recognising the tendency of 'deterrence blocs' to fail in containing wars). And as shown in chapter 1, the drafter's preoccupation with arms build-ups and preparations for aggression means that no licence for unlimited 'deterrence' was intended.

As Thomas Franck reports, at the San Francisco conference, a US delegate inquired about the case where 'a fleet had started from abroad against an American republic but had not yet attacked'. Commander Strassen replied that 'we could not under this provision attack the fleet but we could send a fleet of our own and be ready in case an attack came'.[40] The original sense of exercising maximum restraint in order to give time for diplomacy is evident. Such a solution might not always

[39] Article 51 UNC reads: 'Nothing in the present Charter shall impair the inherent right of individual or collective self-defence if an armed attack occurs against a Member of the United Nations, until the Security Council has taken measures necessary to maintain international peace and security. Measures taken by Members in the exercise of this right of self-defence shall be immediately reported to the Security Council and shall not in any way affect the authority and responsibility of the Security Council under the present Charter to take at any time such action as it deems necessary in order to maintain or restore international peace and security.'

[40] *Minutes of the Thirty-Eighth Meeting of the United States Delegation, Held at San Francisco, Monday, May 14, 1945, 9:05 a.m.*, 1945 FRUS vol. I, 707–12, at 709. See Franck, *Recourse to Force*, at p. 50.

produce workable results. Norman Bentwich recalls that 'the overwhelming majority by which the San Francisco Conference added a self-defence clause to the Dumbarton Oaks Proposals was a measure of its lack of confidence in the perfection of the system of collective security based upon the Charter' and designed as an 'emergency measure'.[41] If lack of perfection must be part of an interpretation of the UN Charter today, as is often argued, it means having to navigate between a law-deleting, all-encompassing defence clause and the genuine reliance on deterrence, however prudent, to secure freedom from force.

Again an empirical enquiry into state practice recommends itself. The hypothesis to be tested then would be whether the spiral model began to inform the thinking of governments more often since 1945.[42] Taking the spiral model as a guide, it is plausible that under circumstances where threats only breed further threats and bold signals hasten even bolder responses, the continuation of brinkmanship is today understood by states to be incompatible with article 2(4). Inflammatory rhetoric and commitments to respond with force to the slightest provocation would be unlawful. This is in the belief that genuine reference to self-defence in fact reduces danger since it points to a non-hostile attitude conducive to peaceful settlement.[43]

The views states have taken in practice since 1945 in this regard, of the tension between the deterrence and the spiral model, is the subject of chapter 7. For present purposes, it is helpful to understand that what the theories of this section have in common is that they take the objectives of the UN Charter as point of reference and seek to bestow an *effet utile* on to its component parts.[44]

41 Norman Bentwich and Andrew Martin, *A Commentary on the Charter of the United Nations* 106, 108 (2nd edn, 1951). A proper functioning of the Security Council would have made article 51 redundant. For a summary of the San Francisco deliberations see *The Acting Secretary of State to Diplomatic Representatives in the American Republics*, 1945 FRUS vol. I, 831–7.

42 See below, chapters 7–8.

43 Before the World Wars, the non-aggression pact was a pervasive method to provide mutual assurances at a time when the belief in offensive military strategies was equally pervasive. Recently North Korea demanded that the USA pledge non-aggression despite identical obligations imposed by the UN Charter. So, too, did the Soviet Union demand the pledge of non-invasion of Cuba in 1962. The specific promise not to act in the offensive, not to strike first, not to act unless attacked, is a valued assurance even in the modern era.

44 This is what Sir Hersch Lauterpacht generously called 'Filling of Gaps by Reference to the Needs of the International Community and the Effectiveness of Treaty Obligations' in Hersch Lauterpacht, *The Function of Law in the International Community* 123 (1933).

Proposition that article 2(4) joins in with article 2(3)

It is evident to scholars today that the UN Charter recognises different forms of threats in the material sense: at the sharp end, threats of armed force; at the broad end, threats to international peace.[45] Neither a threat to peace nor a breach of the peace according to article 39 in Chapter VII is necessarily constituted by a violation of the UN Charter.[46]

This difference became very plain right at the start of the UN's history. When in 1950 the Security Council authorised US-led UN troops to repel the North Korean attack against South Korea, US lawyers in defence of resolution 83 were keen to point out that it did not matter that neither of the two Koreas were members of the UN nor, as a matter of international law, two independent countries entitled to the protection of article 2(4). The Security Council's competences were formulated without reference to any such conditions.[47] Ever since, the Security Council, on a case-by-case basis, has widened the circle of its competences in response to different emergency situations: in the Congo over civil war; in South Africa and the former Rhodesia over racism; in Somalia over mass starvation; or in Haiti over the overthrow of an elected regime.[48] In short, Chapter VII waved an early farewell to article 2(4), whose prohibition of military threats was of no concern to the Security Council.

However, it has simply been assumed that article 2(4)-type threats are of an entirely different nature to those of Chapter VII. A systematic reading of the UN Charter does not necessarily support such a conclusion. Article 2(3) of the Charter declares as a principle that:

> All Members shall settle their international disputes by peaceful means in such a manner that international peace and security, and justice, are not endangered.

[45] The UNC uses the notion of 'threat' in articles 1(1), 2(4), 39 and 99. Chapter VII authorises the Security Council to act upon 'threats to the peace, breaches of the peace, and acts of aggression'. This is the unifying theme of all references to threats other than article 2(4). See also Quincy Wright, *The Role of International Law in the Elimination of War* 61 (1961); 1985 YBILC vol. II, part one, at 73.

[46] Hans Kelson, 'Collective Security and Collective Self-Defense Under the Charter of the United Nations', 42 Am. JIL 783–96 (1948), at 788.

[47] Josef L. Kunz, 'Legality of the Security Council Resolutions of June 25 and 27, 1950', 45 Am. JIL 137–42 (1951), at 139.

[48] Franck, *Recourse to Force*, at pp. 40–4; Mirko Zambelli, *La Constatation des Situations de l'Article 39 de la Charte des Nations Unies par la Conseil de Sécurité: Le Champ d'Application des Pouvoirs Prévus au Chapitre VII de la Charte des Nations Unies* 194–264 (2002).

It is generally agreed that the obligation to obtain a peaceful settlement is an active duty and that states cannot remain idle in the face of brewing conflict.[49] They must set in motion the procedures for peaceful settlement that the Charter describes in Chapters VI and XIV.[50] If one reads article 2, para. 4 in conjunction with para. 3, it is plausible to argue that states have a positive duty to conduct negotiations free from any reference to military force. If the use of force cannot be an instrument of national policy, according to article 2(3) it is equally impermissible to hint at the possibility that it could.

This is no small suggestion. In fact, military threats are often just that: a bargaining chip that signals the willingness of a government to run the risk of military a clash. Adopting a joint interpretation of the two paragraphs would mean, for example, that parties to a dispute had an active obligation not to conduct military exercises, tests, movement of forces, military build-ups or engage in verbal militarism. Most importantly, the ambiguity in which such actions are cloaked in practice would not work to remove the presumption of unlawfulness. The ICJ ruled in the *Oil Platforms* case that the burden of proof for the existence of an 'armed attack' rests with the state claiming self-defence.[51] By analogy it would be conceivable to require that the active duty to refrain from militarised acts also entails that if such acts nonetheless occur, there is a presumption that they are illegal. As with members of a jury, the *appearance* of prejudice alone, and not the proof in actual fact, would be enough for the law to intervene.

It is not excessively unworldly to suggest in a further step that in conjunction with Chapter VI and VII of the UN Charter, states have a farther reaching general duty to actively *prevent* situations that would put international peace and security at undue risk.[52] Such a view seems to have guided Georg Dahm in 1960, who concluded that

[49] *North Sea Continental Shelf Cases (Germany* v. *Denmark and the Netherlands)*, Merits, 1969 ICJ Rep. 3 (20 Feb. 1969), at paras. 83–101.

[50] Norman Bentwich and Andrew Martin, *A Commentary on the Charter of the United Nations* 13 (2nd edn, 1951).

[51] *Oil Platforms Case (Islamic Republic of Iran* v *United States of America), Merits*, 2003 ILM 1334–485 (6 Nov. 2003), at paras. 57, 61.

[52] In this sense the distinction between 'dispute' and 'conflict' according to John Collier and Vaughan Lowe, *The Settlement of Disputes in International Law* 1 (1999) is not upheld here. In the context of article 2(3), a dispute is not only 'a specific disagreement relating to a question of rights or interests in which the parties proceed by way of claims, counter-claims, denials and so on', but also 'a general state of hostility between the parties'.

war-mongering could not be reconciled with the UN Charter's prohibition of the use and threat of force.[53] By the same token, the UN General Assembly has condemned inflammatory propaganda as a pattern of aggression.[54] Article 20(1) of the UN Covenant on Civil and Political Rights now demands that: 'Any propaganda for war shall be prohibited by law.'[55] Leaning on the Security Council's recent expansion of Chapter VII, article 2(4) could also be said to prohibit – *de lege ferenda?* – a government's deliberate deportation of refugees, the bringing about of conditions of mass starvation, the defiance of disarmament obligations, to name examples, if the use of force against another state is a likely consequence of the situation.[56] Article 2(4) would then closely correspond to Chapter VII threats to peace. Bringing about a threat to peace would constitute a violation of the UN Charter.

One may entertain serious doubts whether such a reading does not stretch the limits of good faith interpretation. Article 2(4) is international in character.[57] Some Chapter VII-type threats sit ill with the preoccupation of article 2(4) with military force. A country's failure to hold democratic elections or to uphold human rights cannot be in violation of the no-threat rule. Moreover, the margins of discretion could be so wide, abstract and over-generalised that the resulting rule retains hardly any specific meaning. Yet considering article 2(4) in its context, in the light of the Charter's object and purpose, is an adequate guide to interpretation.[58] It suggests that in reading article 2(4) together with article 2(3), the no-threat rule ought not necessarily to be construed narrowly, and that it is in principle receptive to dynamic

[53] Georg Dahm, Völkerrecht vol. II, 358 (1960): '*Mit dem Verbot der Anwendung und Androhung von Gewalt ergibt sich auch: Verbot der Anstiftung und der Hetze zum Krieg* [With the prohibition of the use and threat of force also follows prohibition of stirring up and inciting war].'

[54] A/RES/380 *Peace Through Deeds* (17 Nov. 1950). See Quincy Wright, 'The Crime of War Mongering', 42 Am. JIL 128–36 (1948); John B. Whitton, 'The United Nations Conference on Freedom of Information and the Movement Against International Propaganda', 43 Am. JIL 73–87 (1949); Arthur Larson, 'The Present Status of Propaganda in International Law', 31 L. & Cont. Prob. 439–51 (1966); John B. Whitton, 'Hostile International Propaganda and International Law', 398 Ann. Am. Acad. P&SS 14–25 (1971). But see further Krateros Ioannou, 'Propaganda', 3 Enc. Pub. IL 1135–8 (1997), arguing that UN practice has not yet hardened into law forbidding propaganda.

[55] *United Nations International Covenant on Civil and Political Rights* (UNCCPR) 78 UNTS 277 (16 Dec. 1966).

[56] For a recent example see *New York Times* (NYT), 'After Battle in Capital, Chad Threatens to Expel Sudanese' (15 Apr. 2006).

[57] Albrecht Randelzhofer, 'Art. 2(4)', in Simma, *Commentary* vol. I, 112–36, at Mn. 29.

[58] Article 31(1) *Vienna Convention on the Law of Treaties*, 1155 UNTS 331 (23 May 1969).

interpretation. This is so because, as we have seen, it is possible to expand the meaning of the no-threat rule *within* the UN Charter system to accommodate implications and connections that were not actively thought of in 1945. Neither the institutional history of the UN nor the Charter's text provide a categorical answer.

Proposition that article 2(4) requires imminence

Depending on the position taken, article 2(4) is either located far away from Chapter VII, or, as proposed in the previous section, they are loosely related. Quite independent of that question, to those who are primarily concerned with precision in what the UN Charter forbids, there is little doubt that the no-threat rule needs to be interpreted narrowly.

An evident possible criterion is that the threat of force, in order to be unlawful, must be imminent. A sense of urgency ought to prevail. Based on this criterion, Belatchew Asrat argued that the Iraqi construction of the Osirak (Tamuz-1) nuclear reactor in 1981 did not constitute a threat of force vis-à-vis Israel. He also contends that the Soviet preparations of nuclear missiles on Cuba in 1962 did not amount to a violation of article 2(4), since: 'The missiles had not yet reached the completed and credible stage that could have made them usable for, hence capable of, manifesting immediate hostility to one or more States of the Americas.'[59]

There is no particular novelty in this idea, despite the absence of any reference in the Charter text to the concept of imminence. Rather, it is a proposition that implies article 51 of the UN Charter, which many claim permits states to act in anticipatory self-defence if faced with an imminent attack and if exposure to a fatal strike has grown patently apparent.[60] This Asrat infers as he cites incidents where countermeasures taken in response to a perceived threat were the issue. If article 2(4) is said to be violated only in cases where a state is gearing up for assault, the no-threat rule would turn out as the exact counterpart to the authority of the victim state to take military action in early response, provided that the threat envisaged amounted to the intensity

59 Belatchew Asrat, *Prohibition of Force under the UN Charter: A Study of Art. 2(4)* 140 (1991).
60 Derek W. Bowett, *Self-Defence in International Law* 187–93 (1958); Franck, *Recourse to Force*, at pp. 97–108. Arguing against are Brownlie, *Use of Force by States*, at pp. 275–8; Gray, *Use of Force*, at pp. 129–33, 181–4. See further Albrecht Randelzhofer, 'Article 51', in *Simma, Commentary* vol. I, 788–806, at Mn. 39–40; *Stanimir* A. Alexandrov, *Self-Defense Against the Use of Force in International Law* 149–65, 295–6 (1996).

of an attack. This early response could include, if anticipatory defence is said to be right, not only the use of force but also a counter-threat designed to deter the feared attack.

One may question, however, whether such a proposal is not built on sand. There is no hint in the UN Charter in its support. The standard argument for a right of anticipatory self-defence is that custom in the pre-Charter era was largely permissive to pre-emptive action and that the Charter did not remove the entitlement to act as necessity dictates.[61] The *Caroline* precedent, requiring the necessity for self-defence to be 'instant, overwhelming, leaving no choice of means, and no moment for deliberation' is often cited without qualification as a codification of customary law permissive of anticipatory self-defence.[62] There is no need to engage in a debate on whether that claim is correct.[63] Article 2(4) does not have a comparable history. In fact, we have seen in chapter 1 that the threat of force formula was primarily intended to capture measures short of war. There is no evidence that such measures, as understood by nations at the time, had to constitute the prelude to actual fighting. Quite to the contrary, such measures, for example, a naval blockade, were often only deemed successful if this outcome was averted. In light of these considerations the proposition of imminence is unconvincing.

Even if that were not a concern, one may wonder what is to be gained by introducing imminence as a criterion of law. It is not clarity. For example, the contention that the Soviet missiles on Cuba, once deployed and ready for a strike, would pose an imminent threat is untenable. Deployment is not synonymous with imminent employment.[64] Modern military technology renders the concept of imminence deeply ambiguous. It fails to take into consideration that many military

[61] For example, Abraham D. Sofaer, 'International Law and the Use of Force', 4 *The Nat Interest* 53–64 (Fall 1988).

[62] Letter from Daniel Webster to Lord Ashburton (6 Aug. 1842), reprinted in John B. Moore, *A Digest of International Law as Embodied in Diplomatic Discussions, Treaties and Other International Agreements* vol. II, 412 (1906); Sir Robert Y. Jennings, 'The Caroline and McLeod Cases', 32 Am. JIL 82–99 (1938). For recent invocations of the *Caroline* incident see John Yoo, 'International Law and the War on Iraq', 97 Am. JIL 563–76 (2003); Miriam Sapiro, 'Iraq: The Shifting Sands of Preemptive Self-Defence', 97 Am. JIL 599–607 (2003); Abraham D. Sofaer, 'On the Necessity of Pre-emption', 14 Eur. JIL 209–26 (2003).

[63] For a rare (but also problematic) critique see Maria Benvenuta Occelli, '"Sinking" the Caroline: Why the Caroline Doctrine's Restrictions on Self-Defense should not be regarded as Customary International Law', 4 San Diego ILJ 467–90 (2003).

[64] Concurring Dinstein, *War, Aggression and Self-Defence*, p. 169; Quincy Wright, 'The Cuban Quarantine', 57 Am. JIL 546–65 (1963), at 549–53.

threats are not preparations to the use of force but, as mentioned, are intended to procure concessions from a target state without having to resort to force.[65] The better argument is that imminence may occasionally be a good indicator for, but not a precondition of, an unlawful threat of force.[66]

Proposition that article 2(4) requires coercion

The desire to define the threat of force along the lines of its foreign policy utility leads to coercion becoming the defining ingredient in the no-threat formula. This proposition requires that the threatening government engages in *coercive diplomacy* (or, to use a stronger term, blackmail), whereby it makes the use of force conditional on the non-compliance with specified demands.[67] Albrecht Randelzhofer expresses the belief in the UN Commentary that: 'It is not sufficient that another State reacts or believes it is reacting to a presumed threat of force. Only a threat directed towards a specific reaction on the part of the target State is unlawful under the terms of Art. 2(4).'[68] Such a reaction typically revolves around claims over territory, title over natural resources, suppression of cross-border infiltration, inducement of regime change, or dissuasion of a particular military move that would be considered of hostile intent. Historically, measures short of war were indeed often designed to extract concessions. Reprisals in the pre-Charter era were permissible as a form of self-help that aimed at redress for a previous wrong. Demonstrations of force, too, often were designed to deter the commission of an offence. As we have seen, the Charter did seek to remove these forms of forceful policy.

It is helpful briefly to analyse what the foreign policy utility of threats are. To begin with, coercive diplomacy is not a term of art in international law but a political concept that became popular during the Cold War. Alexander George defined coercive diplomacy as the idea to 'back one's demand on an adversary with a threat of punishment for

65 Alexander L. George, *Forceful Persuasion: Coercive Diplomacy as an Alternative to War* (1993).

66 Concurring White and Cryer, 'A Threat Too Far?', at 253.

67 The proposition is supported by Brownlie, *Use of Force by States*, at p. 364; Sadurska, 'Threats of Force', at 242; Robert Kolb, *Ius Contra Bellum: Le Droit International Relatif au Maintien de la Paix* Mn. 391 (2003). See also the written statement of France in the *Nuclear Weapons Proceedings, Exposé Ecrit du Gouvernment de la République Française* 25 (20 Jun. 1995), http://www.icj-cij.org/.

68 Randelzhofer, 'Art. 2(4)', at Mn. 38.

noncompliance that he will consider credible and potent enough to persuade him to comply with the demand'.[69] It involves four basic variables: a demand; the means used for creating a sense of urgency; the threatened punishment for non-compliance; and the possible use of incentives.[70] It is a proactive tool of statecraft for gaining leverage and procuring concrete results through the allusion to military action. Demands can take two forms: first, *compellence*, where the intent is to make the target state actively do something, or second, *deterrence*, where the intent is to make the target state refrain from doing something.[71] Deterrence tends to be infinite in its timing and indeterminate in regard to what constitutes compliant behaviour. Compellence has to be definite.[72] The 1962 US demand for the removal of Soviet missiles from Cuba was a case of compellence. The sixty-year-old US demand vis-à-vis mainland China not to attempt an invasion of Taiwan is a case of deterrence.

Following such a line of reasoning, article 2(4) could be said to include the ultimatum of the pre-Charter era (compellence) and, more broadly, the open-ended military pressure that does not require a prompt response and/or leaves doubt as to the precise terms of compliance (deterrence). Alternatively, it could be said to include only one of them. The UN Charter's recognition of the right to self-defence and to reasonable levels of armaments to that end lends plausibility to the view that deterrence is not strictly unlawful. Compellence is more 'offensive'; deterrence more 'defensive'. The Charter may be read to recognise this distinction similar to the view of Randelzhofer noted above.

In practice, however, there is often no clear line between the two forms of coercion. As lawyers know from criminal law, the distinction between omission and action is occasionally difficult to draw. For example, one could argue that during the Cuban missile crisis in 1962, the USA intended to *compel* the Soviet Union to stop the building of nuclear missile bases, but also to *deter* penetration of its naval blockade or future Soviet advances against Berlin. Demands are often multi-dimensional and ambiguous,[73] and therefore narrowing down the

[69] George, *Forceful Persuasion*, at p. 4. [70] *Ibid.*

[71] See Schelling, *Arms and Influence*, at pp. 69–78. One of the differences between compellence and deterrence is that compellence is more difficult to achieve since it requires actively undoing an action. Potential loss of face increases resistance (at p. 82).

[72] Schelling, *Arms and Influence*, at pp. 72–3.

[73] Schelling, *Arms and Influence*, at pp. 78–86; Walter J. Peterson, 'Deterrence and Compellence: A Critical Assessment of Conventional Wisdom', 30 Int. Stud. Q. 269–94 (1986).

no-threat rule to a prohibition of compellence would probably be too simple. By the same token, the term 'coercive diplomacy' used by political scientists is not as restrictive.

There are further lessons to be learnt. First, coercive diplomacy includes the use of force to coerce. The capacity to harm does not stop once the first shot has been fired, but continues as the level of violence – the threat of further violence – is augmented.[74] Coercion may work in armed conflict itself, and certainly when the level of hostility has not yet peaked into all-out war and thus the means to compel are not yet exhausted.[75] (Even the most destructive single use of force, the bombing of Hiroshima and Nagasaki, arguably served the purpose of hastening Japanese capitulation in World War II.) Second, the means to convey a credible threat, the 'art of commitment', are those that give a threat its physical face: military manoeuvres, demonstrative tests, mobilisations of troops, logistic build-ups, passage of warships, maritime blockades, border incidents, airspace violations, ostentatious reconnaissance operations and simple verbal assurances or hints that military action will not be in short supply.[76] The author signals that he or she is willing to run the risk of military confrontation, that his or her visible commitment will leave credibly little choice but to proceed to resort to force.[77] Thus coercion as a criterion for article 2(4) suggests that threats may be issued both verbally and through force demonstrations, and that there is no conceptual difference between the threat of an initial use of force and one of a further, intensified use of force.

[74] Stephen J. Cimbala, *Coercive Military Strategy* 16 (1998).

[75] Schelling, *Arms and Influence*, at pp. 105–9.

[76] Eduardo Jiménez de Aréchaga, 'International Law in the Past Third of a Century', 159 Rec. des Cours vol. I, 1–344 (1978), at 88 has written accordingly: 'A threat of force could also be implicitly conveyed by certain acts such as "a demonstration of force for the purpose of exercising political pressure", the sudden concentration of troops in a border area in a situation of existing border dispute, or a display of force by means of warships close to the coasts of another state. A general mobilization could, in the context of a serious dispute, constitute a threat of force.' (The reference in the text is from the *Corfu Channel Case (United Kingdom* v *Albania), Merits*, 1949 ICJ Rep. 4 (9 Apr. 1949), at 35.)

[77] Schelling, *Arms and Influence*, at pp. 99–109. The commitment typically takes either a physical form by putting military hardware into action and/or a verbal, immaterial form where a government commits itself in private or in public to a certain policy. Public commitment involves more prestige and thus conveys more credibility. See James Fearon, 'Domestic Audiences and the Escalation of International Disputes', 88 Am. PSR 577–92 (1994); James Fearon, *Threats to Use Force: Costly Signals and Bargaining in International Crises* (1992).

How does the notion of coercion fit into the Charter's regime of force? That the element of coercion also runs through the use of force was readily acknowledged in the days when reprisals were an accepted tool of every state to bring norm-breakers back in line with their duties under international law.[78] But, strictly speaking, coercion and coercive diplomacy are not terms of art in UN law. Under municipal law, the outlawry of coercion flows from the legislator's intent to guarantee a minimal freedom of choice to each citizen.[79] International law protects the same interests under the principle of non-intervention, which preserves the right of states to exercise sovereignty in matters which are rightfully theirs to decide without outside interference.[80] Traditionally, however, the concept of free choice was of no concern for the *jus ad bellum*. Before 1945, it was widely held that treaties concluded under the threat or use of force were lawful despite severe impairment of free will.[81] This has changed recently,[82] but the regulation of force is still not formally linked to the idea of free choice. That does not rule out, however, that the element of coercion is not transposable to the notion of threat of force. Applying the coercion criterion to article 2(4), the no-threat rule would be identical to the non-intervention rule but for the difference that coercion needs to involve a military dimension.[83]

That said, it is worth considering whether the UN Charter goals – enshrined in article 1 – are in line with the concept of according states a minimum freedom of choice. Article 2(7) does indeed guarantee states freedom of choice as a guard against dictatorial interference by the UN

[78] Hans Widmer, *Der Zwang im Völkerrecht* (1935).

[79] *Black's Law Dictionary* 275 (8th edn, 2004) defines coercion as 'compulsion by physical force or threat of physical force' and criminal coercion, *inter alia*, as: 'Coercion intended to restrict another's freedom of action by ... threatening to commit a criminal act against that person.' See also Sadurska, 'Threats of Force', at 241.

[80] *Military and Paramilitary Activities In and Against Nicaragua (Nicaragua* v *USA), Merits*, 1986 ICJ Rep. 14 (27 Jun. 1986), at para. 205. The concept of coercion is also incorporated in the ILC *Articles of State Responsibility*, GAOR Supp. 10, A/56/10 (annex to A/RES/56/83, 12 Dec. 2001). For a commentary on article 18 see James Crawford, *The International Law Commission's Articles on State Responsibility: Introduction, Text and Commentaries* 156–8 (2002).

[81] Stuart S. Malawer, 'Imposed Treaties and International Law', Cal. WILJ 1–178 (1977), at 156; H. G. de Jong, 'Coercion in the Conclusion of Treaties: A Consideration of Articles 51 and 52 of the Convention on the Law of Treaties', 15 Neth. YBIL 209–47 (1984), at 244; Dinstein, War, *Aggression and Self-Defence*, p. 37.

[82] Articles 52 and 53 *Vienna Convention on the Law of Treaties*, 1155 UNTS 331 (23 May 1969).

[83] This understanding seems to have guided the ICJ in the *Corfu Channel Case (United Kingdom* v *Albania), Merits*, 1949 ICJ Rep. 4 (9 Apr. 1949). See below, chapter 3, at pp. 68–74 for a discussion of the judgment.

organisation. However, since the Charter's primary objective is the prevention of war, freedom of choice is a welcome but far from exclusive ordering principle. As long as military coercion accurately captures the kind of state-to-state brinkmanship that by experience invites armed conflict, there is overlap. The one instance when there is none is when a state is girding for war and compliance (if any demands have been stated) no longer deflects the use of force. Coercion implies that the target state is given a choice.[84] It is here that the term coercive diplomacy is perhaps too restrictive, since the blatant preparation for the use of force can hardly become lawful once coercive strategy has failed and the promise of force is implemented. The Charter's primer on peace preservation and war preclusion in this case complements the concept of coercion.

Subject to further examination in this book will be how far modern state practice reflects the logic of coercive diplomacy. At this stage it is highly plausible that the presence of coercion, and particularly compellence, is a strong indicator of unlawfulness.[85] Coercion as a criterion is helpful to show that the threat of force is not, when properly understood, the mere preparation for the use of force. Quite the contrary. If threats succeed, states can procure concessions at much lower political and economic costs than any strategy of direct military force ever could. They need not be, and often are not, a mere precursor of war, but are an end in themselves. They are a foreign policy tool in their own right in situations where nations joust over influence in matters that affect their core interests. This a genuine reading of the UN Charter, intended to strengthen its assigned function, should not ignore.

Conclusions

In the words of Edmund Burke, laws, like houses, lean on one another.[86] This chapter introduced a series of interpretations that all lean on 'neighbouring' provisions of international law: the principle forbidding the actual use of force, the right to self-defence, the principle of proportionality, the obligation to settle disputes peacefully, the concept of threat to peace, and the principle of non-intervention. Consulting these six provisions fits well into the canon of interpretation of the Vienna

[84] Schelling, *Arms and Influence*, at 74–5.
[85] White and Cryer, 'A Threat Too Far?', at 253.
[86] Quoted from the *Oxford Dictionary of Quotations* 159 (4th edn, 1992).

Convention on the Law of Treaties, which in article 31(3)(c) recommends the consultation of 'any relevant rules of international law applicable in the relations between the parties',[87] thus to achieve a degree of coherence in regulation. All six provisions govern conflict situations. The first three specifically relate to military conflict, the last three relate to conflict between states in general.

The ordering ideas identified are equally important. They are few in number: preservation of peace, deterrence (including balance of power), escalation and coercion. The focus of the first three is on the effect of threats on a conflict, whereas coercion is more associated with the rationale that leads states to issue threats in the first place. Although not formally incorporated in the UN Charter as a right, these ordering ideas form the *Vorverständnis* for most theorising about threats and their prohibition.

That said, a question that briefly needs to be addressed is how the prohibition of threats relates to other obligations under international law in case of conflict. This is the question of *jus cogens*.[88] In view of the concepts discussed in this chapter, it may seem possible to provide different answers. For example, it is plausible to argue that if the practice of deterrence in fact enhances international security, a comprehensive ban on military threats ought not be part of the *ordre public* that is an attributed quality of *jus cogens* norms.[89] If not peremptory, threats are justifiable to safeguard rights that are peremptory, such as respect for core human rights. Conversely, if threats often invite wars, the *ordre public* quality of the no-threat rule is hardly contestable and it would certainly hold *jus cogens* status. But what is uncertain in theory is quite clear in practice: the evidence that the no-threat principle is peremptory is quite strong. The ICJ in 1986 squarely declared that the ban on threats was an integral part of the 'principle of non-use of force' encapsulating the whole of article 2(4). The inference was that its peremptory character should not be cast into doubt.[90] A positivist approach, following article 53 of the Vienna Convention, supports the same view: article 52 of the Vienna Convention (which postulates that treaties procured by the threat or use of force are invalid) would be hard to explain otherwise, and the reference to the prohibition on 'threat or use of force' is frequent in international instruments, evidencing the

[87] Article 31(3)(c) VCLT. [88] Articles 53 and 64 VCLT.
[89] Rosalyn Higgins, *Problems and Process: International Law and How We Use It* 20–1 (1994).
[90] *Military and Paramilitary Activities*, at paras. 190, 227.

highest level of universal consent.[91] The UN Charter also asserts its supremacy in its article 103. It is therefore safe to conclude that article 2(4) of the UN Charter is *jus cogens* as a whole, without distinction to be made between the threat of force and the actual use of force.[92]

However, certainty about the formal status of the no-threat principle does not remove the uncertainty as to its content. As this chapter demonstrated, the 'menu of choice' on offer is considerable, the inevitable result being that article 2(4) is weighed down by legal ambiguity that a good faith reading of the Charter, no matter how objectively attempted, cannot brush aside. One important reason seems to be that threats, by their very nature, are elusive. Language is clumsy and defining thresholds difficult. At the same time, there is persuasiveness in simple rules because violations are easy to detect. The all-or-nothing distinctions, such as 'all torture is unlawful' or 'all chemical weapons are unlawful' have a higher normative quality than interpretations that depend on a varyingly complex measure of degree.[93] In this regard the no-threat rule is at a peculiar disadvantage in comparison to the no-force rule: the firing of the first shot, the armed crossing of national boundaries, the laying of mines, the interception at sea, the aerial bombardment, are all natural thresholds that states readily acknowledge. Clarity fades in various sub-cases, but the use of force has a distinct quality whose first use begs for justification. Threats, on the other hand, transcend boundaries, are gradual and revolve around past behaviour and reputation, occasionally construed out of a mere series of hints and surreptitious activities. They are real only in the minds of people. It is for this reason that an interpretation that relies on the weighing up of various values, such as security, prudence, necessity or proportionality, are of limited use. 'Any kind of restrained conflict', Thomas Schelling reasoned, 'needs a distinctive restraint that can be recognized by both sides, conspicuous stopping places, conventions

91 See the comments of governments at the Vienna Conference on the Law of Treaties, A/Conf.39/11, meetings 52–67 (26 Mar. to 24 May 1968) on what came to be article 53 VCLT. The general consensus seems to have been that the whole of article 2(4) UNC, if not the whole of article 2, was *jus cogens*.

92 It may be mentioned for the sake of completeness that one could then assert, as has been proposed by Oscar Schachter for *jus cogens* norms in general, that article 2(4) as a whole is immune against derogation by non-compliant state practice. See Oscar Schachter, 'Entangled Treaty and Custom', in Yoram Dinstein (ed.), *International Law at a Time of Perplexity* 717–38 (1989), at p. 734.

93 Schelling, *Arms and Influence*, at pp. 131–41; Thomas M. Franck, 'Legitimacy in the International System', 82 Am. JIL 705–59 (1988), at 715–25.

and precedents to indicate what is within the bounds and what is out of bounds, ways of distinguishing new initiatives from just more of the same activity'.[94] Among the interpretations on offer, preference should be given to the one that brings to the fore that potential, however difficult it may be to achieve. Good interpretation will lead to clarity.

To that end, two things will be done in the following chapters. First, we will examine the practice of the ICJ and explore the interpretation that its judges have bestowed on the no-threat rule. Second, we will embark on the more demanding task of identifying, recording and analysing the practice of states, in order to arrive at an understanding of how governments themselves have interpreted article 2(4) in a host of international cases since 1945.

[94] Schelling, *Arms and Influence*, at p. 135.

3 Precedents of the International Court of Justice

Scarcity of case law

In its six decades of history, there are only three International Court of Justice (ICJ) cases relevant to the threat of force theme. The cases cover radically different facts and the threat of force was not a central part of the deliberations. In the first case, the *Corfu Channel* case,[1] threats of force were not explicitly mentioned but only implied; in the second case, the *Nicaragua* judgment,[2] their invocation was of marginal importance; and in the third case, the *Nuclear Weapons* advisory opinion,[3] they would push the Court to the limits of its judicial capacity.

In some other instances, states have claimed exposure to threats before the ICJ but that claim, or their cases as a whole, did not make it to the merits phase. Libya brought forward the illegality of threats in the *Lockerbie* proceedings,[4] yet the parties agreed to remove it from the Court's docket in September 2003.[5] In the *NATO* cases, Yugoslavia alleged that NATO member states had illegally used threats of force before and during the Kosovo intervention, but did not include this

1 *Corfu Channel Case (United Kingdom v Albania), Merits*, 1949 ICJ Rep. 4 (9 Apr. 1949).

2 *Military and Paramilitary Activities in and Against Nicaragua (Nicaragua v USA), Merits*, 1986 ICJ Rep. 14 (27 Jun. 1986).

3 *Legality of the Threat or Use of Nuclear Weapons (Advisory Opinion)*, 1996 ICJ Rep. 226 (8 Jul. 1996).

4 *Questions of Interpretation and Application of the 1971 Montreal Convention Arising from the Aerial Incident at Lockerbie (Libyan Arab Jamahiriya v United States of America, United Kingdom), Application*, 1992 ICJ Plead., http://www.icj-cij.org/ (3 Mar. 1992).

5 'Cases removed from the Court's List at the joint request of the Parties', 2003 ICJ Press Release 29 (10 Sep. 2003).

claim in its submissions.[6] The Spanish-Canadian *Fisheries Jurisdiction* case, in which Spain invoked article 2(4) of the UN Charter in regard to the coerced interception of its fishing boats by Canadian patrol vessels, was dismissed on procedural grounds.[7] The same fate befell the Greek-Turkish dispute over the Aegean continental shelf.[8] There were also three further near misses.

First, in the 1973 jurisdiction phase of the Anglo-Icelandic *Fisheries Jurisdiction* case over Iceland's extension of its fisheries zone to fifty miles (the 'Cod War'), the threat of force issue was indirectly addressed but no facts were submitted in its support. Iceland, which did not formally take part in the proceedings, indicated in a letter to the ICJ that the 1961 bilateral agreement establishing the jurisdiction of the Court had been formed under 'extremely difficult circumstances, when the British Navy had been using force to oppose the 12-mile fishery limit established by the Icelandic Government in 1958'.[9] This sole assertion stood against a wealth of British evidence showing that activities of the Royal Navy off the Icelandic coast had essentially ceased one year before the conclusion of the agreement, that it had been negotiated on a *quid pro quo* basis, was initiated by Iceland itself, and that subsequently the Prime Minister of Iceland had expressed his 'sincere thanks for ... a fortunate solution of the matter'.[10] Working on the basis of the facts presented, the judges found the assertion of duress was unsubstantiated. They concluded that the 1961 exchange of notes had been 'freely negotiated by the interested parties on the basis of perfect equality and freedom of decision on both sides' and that: 'No fact has

[6] *Legality of Use of Force (Yugoslavia* v. *Belgium et al.), Application*, 1999 ILM 950–962 (29 Apr. 1999), submissions; See further *Verbatim Records*, CR/99/14 (10 May 1999) and CR/99/25 (12 May 1999).

[7] *Fisheries Jurisdiction Case (Spain* v. *Canada), Application*, ICJ Plead. 3–9 (28 Mar. 1995); *Fisheries Jurisdiction Case (Spain* v. *Canada), Jurisdiction*, 1998 ICJ Rep. 3 (4 Dec. 1998), at para. 89.

[8] *Aegean Sea Continental Shelf Case (Greece* v. *Turkey), Request for the Indication of Interim Measures of Protection*, 1976 ICJ Rep. 6 (11 Sep. 1976), at para. 15(ii); *Aegean Sea Continental Shelf Case, Jurisdiction*, 1978 ICJ Rep. 3 (19 Dec. 1978).

[9] *Letter of 29 May 1972 addressed to the Registrar of the International Court of Justice by the Minister of Foreign Affairs of Iceland*, the relevant passage reprinted in the *Fisheries Jurisdiction Case (United Kingdom* v. *Iceland), Jurisdiction*, 1973 ICJ Rep. 3 (2 Feb. 1973), at para. 24.

[10] *Memorial on Jurisdiction submitted by the Government of the United Kingdom of Great Britain and Northern Ireland*, 1975 ICJ Plead. vol. I 123 (13 Oct. 1972), at paras. 48–53. The quotation is from para. 53. See further *Oral Arguments on Jurisdiction of the Court*, 1975 ICJ Plead. vol. I 242 (2 Feb. 1973), at para. 259.

been brought to the attention of the Court from any quarter suggesting the slightest doubt on this matter.'[11] A year later, the UK in its final submissions to the Court dropped its own allegation that Iceland had engaged in the threat of force against British fishing boats.[12] In short, no facts were presented that could support a claim of breach of article 2(4), and thus no precedent results from the *Fisheries Jurisdiction* judgment that were of value.[13]

Second, in the *Oil Platforms* case, Iran charged, in the context of the destruction of three offshore oil platforms by the US during the Iran-Iraq War, that the USA had adopted 'a patently hostile and threatening attitude towards the Islamic Republic that culminated in the attack and destruction of the Iranian oil platforms'.[14] It pointed out 'a threatening and provocative position vis-à-vis Iran with the deployment of substantial naval and air forces just off the shores of the Islamic Republic'.[15] Iran claimed violation of a Treaty of Amity of 1955, on which the jurisdiction of the case hinged, and relied on the UN Charter as a yardstick for determining whether that treaty had been violated. However, Iran revised its submissions such that the ICJ was not called to rule on the alleged threatening attitude of US military forces in the Persian Gulf.[16]

Finally, in the *Genocide* case, Bosnia and Herzegovina submitted that since its independence from Yugoslavia in March 1992, it had been-subject to the 'constant threat of extermination' by Serbia and

11 *Fisheries Jurisdiction Case, Jurisdiction*, at para. 24. It is worth noting, however, that in the same ruling, Judge Luis Padilla Nervo hinted in his dissenting opinion that the British Royal Navy presence off the Icelandic coast had unduly influenced the 1961 exchange of notes between the two countries. See Padilla Nervo, *Dissenting Opinion*, at paras. 46–7.

12 *Fisheries Jurisdiction Case (United Kingdom* v. *Iceland), Merits*, 1974 ICJ Rep. 3 (25 Jul. 1974), at paras. 11–12.

13 The 'Cod War' between Iceland and the UK took on more serious proportions after the judgment. See the crises in 1973 and 1975 documented in ICB, 'Cod War I', crisis 254; ICB, 'Cod War II', crisis 263; 1973 UNYB 264–5; 1975 UNYB 317–9.

14 *Oil Platforms Case (Islamic Republic of Iran* v. *United States of America), Merits*, 2003 ILM 1334–85 (6 Nov. 2003), at para. 18(c). That the USA had used armed force in destroying the oil platforms was never contested, and thus the question of establishing a breach of article 2(4) UNC did not stand in the forefront. Rather, the question was whether the USA rightfully invoked self-defence. See *Merits*, at paras. 45, 57.

15 *Oil Platforms, Application*, 1992 ICJ Plead., http://www.icj-cij.org/, Jurisdiction (2 Nov. 1992).

16 *Oil Platforms, Merits*, at para. 19.

Montenegro,[17] and the latter was in breach of article 2(4).[18] Yet again, in its revised submissions to the Court, there is no further pursuit of the claim.[19]

Under these circumstances it is perhaps not surprising that the extent of clarification available from the rulings of the ICJ on the threat of force is limited. The search for the golden nugget in the Court's judicial history brings to light precious little. Those few of its decisions which touch on the issue have never attempted to explain the rules pertaining to threats of force in a comprehensive manner. Nonetheless, the three principle precedents on the threat of force prohibition bear the signature of a court aware of at least some of the choices described in the last chapter. The manner in which the ICJ addressed – and for that matter, partially solved – these problems is instructive.

UK–Albania (Corfu Channel, 1949)

The UK, the power policing Greek cities after the withdrawal of the German occupation forces and supporter of the incumbent pro-British regime, crushed a communist insurgency in November 1944. During the Greek civil war many of the guerrillas escaped to Yugoslavia, Albania or Bulgaria, all of which provided sanctuary and military support.[20] The first case of the ICJ, and an early test for the infant UN Charter rules on force, concerned a series of incidents that took place in 1946 in the North Corfu Channel, reflecting tensions between Britain and the newly autonomous state of Albania at the onset of the Cold War. The channel, three miles wide and located between the Greek island of Corfu and the Albanian mainland, connected the Aegean and Adriatic Seas and provided strategically important access to harbours in Corfu. Resenting British involvement in Greece, Albania asserted exclusive territorial sovereignty over the strait. Britain, for its part, had previously conducted several unopposed naval operations in the strait to remove German mines under the authority of the Mediterranean Zone Mining Board, of which, however, Albania was not a member.

[17] *Application of the Convention on the Prevention and Punishment of the Crime of Genocide (Bosnia and Herzegovina* v. *Yugoslavia), Application*, 1993 ICJ Plead., http://www.icj-cij.org/ (20 Mar. 1993), at para. 21.

[18] *Crime of Genocide, Application*, at para. 135(f).

[19] *Memorial of the Government of the Republic of Bosnia and Herzegovina*, at paras. 293–5 (15 Apr. 1994).

[20] ICB, 'Greek Civil War I', crisis 98; ICB, 'Greek Civil War II', crisis 112.

On 15 May 1946, several warning shots were fired at two British cruisers, the *Orion* and the *Superb*, by Albanian batteries from ashore.[21] In a communication the Albanian government under Premier Hoxha maintained that 'foreign warships and merchant vessels had no right to pass through Albanian territorial waters without prior notification to, and the permission of, the Albanian authorities'.[22] The UK government, on the other hand, maintained the channel to be an international waterway and insisted on a right of innocent passage. It declared:

> ... the rule of international law regarding straits gives both to ships of war and to merchant vessels in time of peace as well as in time of war a right of innocent passage through straits which form routes for international maritime traffic between two parts of the high seas. His Majesty's Government recognise no right on part of the territorial Power concerned to demand fulfilment of conditions before entry into such waters is permitted. In these circumstances His Majesty's Government cannot accept the reply of the Albanian Government to their last communication as being satisfactory and they cannot agree that British shipping passing through the Straits of Corfu should give prior notification of their passage to the Albanian authorities. Furthermore the Albanian Government should take note that should Albanian coastal batteries in future open fire on any of His Majesty's vessels passing through the Corfu Channel fire will be returned by his Majesty's ships.[23]

Four months later on 22 October, the destroyers *Saumarez* and *Volage* (the first British ships to pass through the strait after the exchange), both struck a moored contact mine and suffered substantial damage. One of the ships was wrecked. Some forty-four sailors were killed and around fifty were wounded.[24]

Outraged, Britain announced its intention to sweep the channel of mines and that it held Albania responsible for the incident, to which Albania responded that it would regard such action as a 'premeditated

[21] *Corfu Channel Case (United Kingdom* v. *Albania), Merits*, 1949 ICJ Rep. 4 (9 Apr. 1949), at para. 27; On the judgment see William W. Bishop Jr, 'The Corfu Channel Case (Merits)', 43 Am. JIL 558–89 (1949); Il Yung Chung, *Legal Problems Involved In The Corfu Channel Incident* (1959); Leslie Gardiner, *The Eagle Spreads His Claws: A History of the Corfu Channel Dispute and of Albania's Relations with the West 1945–1965* (1966); J. Mervyn Jones, 'The Corfu Channel Case: Merits', 26 Brit. YBIL 447–53 (1949).

[22] *Corfu Channel (Merits)*, at para. 27.

[23] The text of the note communicated to the Albanian Minister in Belgrade on 2 August 1946, 1949 ICJ Plead. vol. I, at 72.

[24] NYT, 'Britain Overrides Albania on Strait' (13 Nov. 1946); NYT, Albania Assailed for Mined Channel' (20 Nov. 1946).

violation of Albanian sovereignty'.[25] On 13 November the British navy returned to the channel in *Operation Retail* with substantial naval covering forces, including an aircraft carrier and several war vessels kept at a distance. A squadron swept for mines and, after their successful removal, took two of them to Malta for inspection.[26] On 12, 13 and 27 November, the Albanian government sent telegrams to the UN Secretary-General filing protests against 'provocative incursions' of the British naval units in its territorial sea.[27] The UK, in turn, demanded a formal apology and reparations from Albania for a 'deliberately hostile act'. It said that its investigation had brought to light that Albania, if it had not laid them itself, at least must have known of the mines and that they had been put into place recently.[28] In the absence of an apology the UK would have 'no alternative but to bring the matter before the Security Council of the United Nations as a serious threat to and a breach of international peace and security'.[29] Tirana, however, did not apologise, and neither did London retract its demand for an apology.[30] A lengthy discussion within the Security Council ensued. Faced with the certainty of a Soviet veto blocking Albania's condemnation, the Council recommended referral of the Corfu Channel mine dispute to the ICJ. As a result of the Council's resolution, the two governments concluded a Special Agreement establishing its jurisdiction.[31]

The ICJ initially answered the question of whether Albania was responsible under international law for the explosions of 22 October, which it found it was.[32] The question was then whether the UK had violated Albania's sovereignty by reason of, first, its intrusion into Albanian waters on 22 October and, second, its minesweeping actions on 12 and 13 November.[33] Albania did not contend that the UK had illegally threatened with force; it asserted solely that its territorial sovereignty had been violated.[34] Albania did not become a member of

[25] *Corfu Channel (Merits)*, at para. 33; NYT, 'Britain Overrides Albania On Strait' (13 Nov. 1946).

[26] *Corfu Channel (Merits)*, at paras. 13–15.

[27] *Corfu Channel (Merits)*, at para. 19.

[28] NYT, 'Britain Overrides Albania On Strait' (13 Nov. 1946).

[29] NYT, 'British Demand Albania Apologize Or Mine Case Will Be Sent To U.N.' (11 Dec. 1946).

[30] NYT, 'Britain Irked by Albanian Reply' (28 Dec. 1946).

[31] NYT, 'Soviet Veto Blocks Rebuke of Albania' (26 Mar. 1947); NYT, 'World Court Gets Albanian Dispute' (10 Apr. 1947).

[32] *Corfu Channel (Merits)*, at para. 26.

[33] *Corfu Channel (Merits)*, at para. 26.

[34] In fact, neither did the UK ask the Court to decide whether the 12-minute long firing by Albania in the direction of the British warships on 15 May 1946 constituted an

the UN until 1955; at the time of the events described above, it was not in a position to invoke the UN Charter as a source of mutual treaty obligation.

Regarding the passage of British ships on 22 October that resulted in the mine accident, the ICJ decided that the UK had indeed been entitled to innocent passage.[35] That decided, the question then turned to whether the passage had been innocent.[36] Albania held that it had not been, on the grounds that the British vessels had been on a political mission, and were sailing in diamond combat formation with the crew on action stations. It further pointed out that the number of ships and their armaments exceeded that which was necessary in order to attain their objective and showed an intention to intimidate and not merely to pass.[37] The Court agreed that there had to be a test based on the manner in which the passage had been carried out. It found, however, that the British passage passed the test: it said that contrary to Albania's assertion, the ships had not been in combat formation, the guns were not loaded and no indications existed that the passage was not peaceful. The crew was commanded to be on action stations, but the Court believed this to be reasonable in light of the events of 15 May.[38] As the Court observed, the warships:

> ... passed one after another through this narrow channel, close to the Albanian coast, at a time of political tension in this region. The intention must have been, not only to test Albania's attitude, but at the same time to demonstrate such

unlawful threat of force. Such a claim would have been more difficult to make, however, because the Albanian fire occurred exclusively within its own sovereign territory – beyond the scope of article 2(4). Whether the right of innocent passage makes the firing 'international' for the purposes of the UN Charter is unclear.

35 *Corfu Channel (Merits)*, at para. 29. The Court held that Albania, because of exceptional circumstances (Greece considered itself at war with Albania), did have a right to issue regulations, but not to prohibit passage. Therefore, the UK did not violate Albania's sovereignty solely by not asking for authorisation.

36 Compare today's regulation in article 19 *United Nations Convention of the Law of the Sea*, 1833 UNTS 3 (10 Dec. 1982). '(1) Passage is innocent so long as it is not prejudicial to the peace, good order or security of the coastal State. Such passage shall take place in conformity with this Convention and with other rules of international law. (2) Passage of a foreign ship shall be considered to be prejudicial to the peace, good order or security of the coastal State if in the territorial sea it engages in any of the following activities: (a) any threat or use of force against the sovereignty, territorial integrity or political independence of the coastal State, or in any other manner in violation of the principles of international law embodied in the Charter of the United Nations; (b) any exercise or practice with weapons of any kind; ...'

37 *Corfu Channel (Merits)*, at para. 30. 38 *Corfu Channel (Merits)*, at para. 30.

force that she would abstain from firing again on passing ships. Having regard, however, to all the circumstances of the case, as described above, the Court is unable to characterize these measures taken by the United Kingdom authorities as a violation of Albania's sovereignty[39] ... Lastly, as the Court has to judge of the innocent nature of the passage, it cannot remain indifferent to the fact that, though two warships struck mines, there was no reaction, either on their part or on that of the cruisers that accompanied them.[40]

One can surmise from this extract that British passage was innocent for two main reasons. First, the special circumstances of previous Albanian warning shots on 15 May justified preparedness to respond to Albanian fire. The UK had been entitled to signal its readiness to return fire. Second, despite the two mine explosions that had inflicted considerable damage on vessels and crew, the British commander had refrained from a military response. This, the judges well understood, was evidence for a posture of restraint and not one of undue provocation.

In regard to *Operation Retail* of 12 and 13 November, the same factors were weighted differently. The UK did not argue that its operation was lawful under the heading of innocent passage. Rather, it sought to justify its actions by reference to the Mediterranean Zone Board authority and, secondarily, the necessity of securing *corpora delicti* before they could be removed from the scene of the crime.[41] The ICJ was not convinced by these arguments. Rejecting a right to self-help or to secure evidence under the circumstances, the Court concluded that the minesweeping had occurred in violation of Albanian territorial sovereignty.[42] In a first passage, in which it refuted a unilateral right to secure evidence, the Court remarked:

The Court can only regard the alleged right of intervention as the manifestation of a policy of force, such as has, in the past, given rise to most serious abuses and such as cannot, whatever be the present defects in international organization, find a place in international law. Intervention is perhaps still less admissible in the particular form it would take here; for, from the nature of things, it would be reserved for the most powerful States, and might easily lead to perverting the administration of international justice itself.[43]

[39] *Corfu Channel (Merits)*, at para. 30. [40] *Corfu Channel (Merits)*, at para. 32.

[41] Malgosia A. Fitzmaurice, 'The Corfu Channel Case and the Development of International Law', in Nisuke Ando et al. (eds.), *Liber Amicorum Judge Shigeru Oda* vol. I, 119–46 (2002), at p. 144.

[42] *Corfu Channel (Merits)*, at para. 35. [43] *Corfu Channel (Merits)*, at para. 35.

A few sentences later it added:

> The method of carrying out 'Operation Retail' has also been criticized by the Albanian Government, the main ground of complaint being that the United Kingdom, on that occasion, made use of an unnecessarily large display of force, out of proportion to the requirements of the sweep. The Court thinks that this criticism is not justified. It does not consider that the action of the British Navy was a demonstration of force for the purpose of exercising political pressure on Albania. The responsible naval commander, who kept his ships at a distance from the coast, cannot be reproached for having employed an important covering force in a region where twice within a few months his ships had been the object of serious outrages.[44]

The ICJ's reading of the facts is hardly straightforward, but the basic decision is still sufficiently clear. Alluding to the UN Charter, it held that a demonstration of naval force could violate it, but was unconvinced that *Operation Retail* amounted to such a violation.[45] To qualify as violation of article 2(4), the British mission would have needed to exert political pressure on Albania, for which the Court found insufficient evidence. It could not reprimand the UK for its limited objective of securing the removal of the mines, which relied on the signalled readiness to repel an attack and thus to deter any further transgression on the side of the Albanian authorities. The UK had never argued that intervention was justified on the grounds of self-defence.[46] Yet it seems that the Court relied on the notion of self-defence when it declared that the British commander's precautions against a potential attack could not be faulted. The UK was not condemned beyond the violation of the non-intervention principle.[47]

All in all, the ICJ seems to have captured the view that naval demonstrations aimed at extracting political concessions were incompatible with the new UN Charter. It was willing to weigh up several

44 *Corfu Channel (Merits)*, at para. 35.

45 For a different interpretation see Romana Sadurska, 'Threats of Force', 83 Am. JIL 239–68 (1988), at 263–4, where she argues against Oscar Schachter, 'International Law: The Right of States to Use Armed Force', 82 Mich LR 1620–46 (1984), at 1626.

46 Chung, *Legal Problems*, at p. 247.

47 Judge S. Krylov, *Dissenting Opinion*, at paras. 76–7 and Judge P. Azevdeo, *Dissenting Opinion*, at para. 109 condemned the British assembly of naval forces as considerably more serious and disproportionate. Judge B. Ecer, *Dissenting Opinion*, at paras. 129–30, on the other hand, concluded that the nature of the British mission was not proven to be offensive by intent. See also Judge A. Alvarez, *Individual Opinion*, at para. 47.

additional factors, among them the regional propensity for hostilities and the specific conduct of the governments involved in exercising either thoughtful moderation or deliberate provocation. The signal that force might be used in order to secure the safe passage of ships could neither be viewed as excessive nor provocative. The reluctance to apply direct physical force and the previous behaviour of the Albanians amounted to extenuating circumstances for the British vessels penetrating foreign territorial waters – not enough to justify the violation of the non-intervention principle, but enough to avoid a breach of the UN Charter.

USA–Nicaragua (paramilitary activities, 1986)

Thirty-seven years later, the ICJ had to judge US foreign policy towards Nicaragua.[48] Under Ronald Reagan, the USA demanded the establishment of a democratic government to replace the Sandinista regime which, by way of a socialist revolution against the dictatorial Samosa dynasty, had come to power in 1979. The USA underlined its demands by conducting operations against Nicaragua's ports, oil installations, merchant ships and naval bases, and by furnishing support to the contras group fighting against the Sandinistas, which in turn had received logistical help from the Soviet Union. Civil war raged, exacting a hefty toll of some 50,000 deaths.[49]

Nicaragua contended that joint US-Honduran military manoeuvres in 1982–5, supplemented by incursions of low-flying aircraft in November 1984, constituted an impermissible threat of force. It claimed that the manoeuvres formed part of a 'general and sustained policy of force intended to intimidate the Government of Nicaragua into accepting the political demands of the United States government'.[50] It further submitted that the USA had repeatedly violated Nicaragua's sovereignty by 'efforts of direct and indirect means to coerce and intimidate the Government of Nicaragua'.[51]

[48] *Military and Paramilitary Activities in and Against Nicaragua (Nicaragua* v. *USA), Merits*, 1986 ICJ Rep. 14 (27 Jun. 1986). For a case study of US policy towards Nicaragua and the debate within the UN Security Council in November 1984 see below, chapter 6, at pp. 196–201.

[49] Rüdiger Dingemann, *Krisenherde der Welt: Konflikte und Kriege seit 1945* 554–62 (1996).

[50] *Military and Paramilitary Activities*, at para. 92.

[51] *Application Instituting Proceedings Submitted by the Government of Nicaragua*, 1986 ICJ Plead. vol. I, at para. 26(b) and (c).

As Nicaragua chose to document, there was no shortage of military exercises in the period 1982–5. In late 1982 US troops staged exercises jointly with the Honduran military on Honduran soil.[52] An exercise called *Ahuas Taras II* in August 1983 involved a troop contingent of over 5,000 men in the proximity of the Honduran-Nicaraguan land border, with flotillas of US warships patrolling both Nicaraguan coasts. By that time the US Department of Defense openly acknowledged that these actions were part of 'perception management' designed to exert pressure on the Sandinistas.[53] In October 1983, the USA invaded Grenada. In late 1984 and early 1985, the Reagan administration ordered the renewal of its naval presence in Nicaragua.[54] Manoeuvres *Ahuas Tara III* and *Universal Trek '85* were staged, with 4,500 and 6,600 troops, respectively, the latter mobilisation including twenty-four warships and the aircraft carrier *USS John F. Kennedy*, culminating in the largest ground and air manoeuvre conducted by the USA in Central America.[55] Anticipation of a US invasion peaked when, as a result of the suspected delivery of Soviet MiG-21 jets for the Sandinistas, the USA conducted low-altitude surveillance flights over Nicaraguan territory between 7 and 11 November 1984, which produced 'loud sonic booms and shattering glass windows', reportedly intimidating the local population.[56] Nicaragua put its military forces on alert and rearranged its troops for a defence of Managua.[57]

Nicaragua contended that the sum of US efforts amounted to an unlawful threat of force. As evidence, Nicaragua had submitted reports from the *Washington Post* and the *New York Times*. US activities had received wide media coverage, and for this reason the ICJ took the matter 'as one of public knowledge, and as such, sufficiently established'.[58] But while the Court accepted the facts presented by

[52] *Memorial of Nicaragua (Merits)*, at paras. 51, 58.
[53] *Memorial of Nicaragua (Merits)*, at paras. 79, 80.
[54] *Memorial of Nicaragua (Merits)*, at para. 119.
[55] *Memorial of Nicaragua (Merits)*, at para. 140.
[56] *Memorial of Nicaragua (Merits)*, at para. 278; *Military and Paramilitary Activities*, at para. 87.
[57] NYT, 'Nicaragua Puts Forces on Alert for a U.S. Invasion' (13 Nov. 1984). See further *Memorial of Nicaragua (Merits)*, at para. 148, where Nicaragua refers to a 1985 radio address by President Reagan in which he would not rule out armed intervention. See *Radio Address of the President to the Nation* (6 Apr. 1985), reprinted in *Memorial of Nicaragua (Merits)*, at annex C, attachment I.20. See further SCOR Supp. S/17098 (12 Apr. 1985).
[58] *Military and Paramilitary Activities*, at para. 92.

Nicaragua, it refused to engage in a full appraisal of their legal significance. It concluded without further ado:

The Court has also found (paragraph 92) the existence of military manoeuvres held by the United States near the Nicaraguan borders; and Nicaragua has made some suggestion that this constituted a 'threat of force', which is equally forbidden by the principle of non-use of force. The Court is however not satisfied that the manoeuvres complained of, in the circumstances in which they were held, constituted on the part of the United States a breach, as against Nicaragua, of the principle forbidding recourse to the threat or use of force.[59]

The judgment, moreover, remained silent on the over-flights of November 1984.[60] It can only be inferred from the lack of reference in the judgment's *dispositif* that the Court was unconvinced of their legal relevance.

The threat of force had played a minimal role in Nicaragua's submissions. It appears that for this reason the judges felt little need to address it thoroughly, particularly because it had already generously condemned US behaviour as being in breach of the non-use of force principle. But obviously this does not erase the regrettable result that its finding on the threat issue is enigmatic. The ICJ held that military manoeuvres could indeed amount to a (customary) violation of article 2(4) of the UN Charter. In line with its stance in its ruling as a whole, it took a strict view of states' obligations not to use force in any shape or form unless justified under the narrow conditions of self-defence. But, if there was no military threat under the circumstances described, then the question begs answering under which circumstances there would be. What additional actions would have been necessary on the part of the USA to pass the threshold that the Court implied existed? On this obvious question the judges preferred to remain silent.

However, Judge Schwebel, who held that US action had been covered by its right to self-defence and thus saw legality upheld for other reasons,[61] felt less inhibited to note in his exposition of the facts that:

In November 1981, eight months after the United States had terminated aid to Nicaragua, and three months after Nicaragua had failed to respond positively to

[59] *Military and Paramilitary Activities*, at para. 227.

[60] *Military and Paramilitary Activities*, at para. 250. The judgment asserts that the over-flights had been dealt with in para. 227, and that accordingly, 'that aspect of Nicaragua's claim [would] not be pursued further'. However, there is no discussion of over-flights in the section cited by the ICJ.

[61] *Dissenting Opinion of Judge Schwebel*, at para. 9.

a clear, high-level, urgent United States demand (by the Enders mission) to put an end to its material support for the Salvadoran insurgency in return for the resumption of United States aid and other inducements, the United States decided to exert military pressure upon Nicaragua in order to force it to do what it would not agree to do. The exertion of that pressure was welcomed by the Government of El Salvador, to which the United States by then was rendering large-scale material assistance to fend off rebel attacks and sustain a wounded economy. El Salvador made it clear that it regarded, and continues to regard, United States pressure upon Nicaragua as action in legitimate defence against Nicaraguan aggression and intervention against it.[62]

It is not without irony that the judge most inclined to excuse US foreign policy towards Nicaragua was also the one to observe that military threats were patently apparent.

There is a second relevant paragraph of the judgment in which Nicaragua's own actions were reviewed by the ICJ. Subsequent to the delivery of its decision on jurisdiction and the admissibility of Nicaragua's application, the USA chose not to take part in the merits phase. Its presentation of fact and law is curtailed. However, this did not prevent the Court from examining the major counter-argument outlined by the USA, which was that its actions had been justified under the label of collective self-defence.[63] It held that it was within its right to help El Salvador to retaliate against Nicaragua's military infiltration and turn the tables by orchestrating military operations on the aggressor's own soil. The ICJ rejected these and like claims.[64] Within that context, the Court dismissed the US contention, merely indicated in the US statement of facts,[65] that the militarization of Nicaragua gave grounds for justification:

62 *Dissenting Opinion of Judge Schwebel*, at para. 34.

63 *Counter-Memorial of the United States of America*, 1986 ICJ Plead. vol. II, at paras. 189–202.

64 *Military and Paramilitary Activities*, at paras. 226–82.

65 Under the title 'The Sandinista Régime Has Violated Its Domestic and International Promises' all that the USA presented as evidence to the ICJ in its *Counter-Memorial of the United States of America*, at paras. 218–19 was the following: 'The Sandinista regime has also engaged in a massive military build up. Far from the minimal force envisioned in its 1979 pronouncements, since the earliest days of the regime there has been an unprecedented expansion of military forces ... As of mid-1984, the military and security forces of Nicaragua on active duty numbered some 57,000 with 48,000 well-trained reserves and militia available for mobilization on short notice – some eight times the size of Somoza's forces at their peak during the 1978–79 fighting ... Moreover, the equipment at the disposal of these forces is vastly beyond that required for self-defence or internal security purposes. It includes in excess of 100 medium tanks – although no other country of the region possesses even one – as well as over 100 armored vehicles ... The threat posed by the size and offensive

> The Court now turns to another factor which bears both upon domestic policy and foreign policy. This is the militarization of Nicaragua, which the United States deems excessive and such as to prove its aggressive intent, and in which it finds another argument to justify its activities with regard to Nicaragua. It is irrelevant and inappropriate, in the Court's opinion, to pass upon this allegation of the United States, since in international law there are no rules, other than such rules as may be accepted by the State concerned, by treaty or otherwise, whereby the level of armaments of a sovereign State can be limited, and this principle is valid for all States without exception.[66]

With remarkable brevity, the Court had determined that, as of principle, military build-ups could not, unless specifically agreed upon by the state concerned, amount to an infringement of international law, let alone lend themselves to justifying forceful countermeasures.[67] None of the ten judges submitting dissenting or separate opinions disagreed. The idea that the maintenance of arms could directly compromise the UN Charter's non-violence dictate, once a matter carefully deliberated by the officers in the US State Department when drafting the UN Charter thirty years earlier, had vanished.

At the end of its long judgment, the ICJ determined by a majority of twelve to three that the USA was in breach of its obligation to refrain from the use of force.[68] The USA was not, apparently, in breach of customary law forbidding military threats, nor, in regard to the manoeuvres and over-flights complained of, was it in breach of the non-intervention principle, which the Court had readily applied to the USA elsewhere in the judgment.[69] 'The element of coercion, which defines, and indeed forms the very essence of, prohibited intervention' did not apply.[70]

What, then, are the implications for the no-threat rule? The foregoing exposition shows that the ICJ majority upheld two points. First, military build-ups categorically fall into the realm of sovereignty. A state is free to decide on its level of armaments. There is no conflict with the UN Charter. Second, military exercises may amount to an unlawful threat

capabilities of these forces has greatly increased the level of military tension in the region' (references omitted).

66 *Military and Paramilitary Activities*, at para. 269.

67 This hinted reference to the *Lotus* presumption was taken up by the ICJ in the third relevant case, *Legality of the Threat or Use of Nuclear Weapons (Advisory Opinion)*, 1996 ICJ Rep. 226 (8 Jul. 1996), at para. 21.

68 *Military and Paramilitary Activities*, at subpara. 4 of the *dispositif*.

69 *Military and Paramilitary Activities*, at subpara. 3 of the *dispositif*.

70 *Military and Paramilitary Activities*, at para. 205.

of force, depending on the circumstances in which they are staged. For reasons the judges did not explain, those conducted by the USA and Honduras did not qualify.

Nuclear Weapons Advisory Opinion (1996)

On 15 December 1994, the UN General Assembly passed a resolution that called upon the ICJ to answer the question: 'Is the threat or use of nuclear weapons in any circumstance permitted under international law?'[71] The resolution had been the result of a lengthy civil society effort to have the Court declare the inherent unlawfulness of nuclear weapons and thus, it was hoped, to promote worldwide nuclear disarmament.[72] Another request of the World Health Organization (WHO) addressed the ICJ with a similar plea.[73] While the Court (for formal reasons) refused to respond to that request,[74] it agreed to deliver an advisory opinion for the UN General Assembly.[75]

In order to understand the advisory opinion, a few remarks on the historic context deserve merit. Attempts to bring about nuclear disarmament date back to the immediate post-World War II period. With the 1946 Baruch plan, the USA proposed to turn its stockpile of atomic bombs over to UN surveillance under the condition that all other countries would likewise commit to equal abstinence and international verification. The plan failed, and it took the near nuclear brink of the 1962 Cuban missile crisis to provide the impetus for agreed limits on nuclear weapons testing, deployment, delivery and proliferation.[76]

71 A/RES/49/75K *General And Complete Disarmament* (15 Dec. 1994).

72 Ved P. Nanda and David Krieger, *Nuclear Weapons and the World Court* 69–86 (1998). For an 'activist' example see NYT, 'World Court Outlaw Nuclear Threats' (28 Dec. 1994).

73 In contrast to the one posed by the UN General Assembly, the WHO's question did not contain any reference to the threat of force. It read: 'In view of the health and environmental effects, would the use of nuclear weapons by a State in war or other armed conflict be a breach of its obligations under international law including the WHO Constitution?' See *Request for Advisory Opinion*, 1993 ICJ Rep. 1–7 (27 Aug. 1993), at para. 2.

74 *Legality of the Use by a State of Nuclear Weapons in Armed Conflict (Advisory Opinion)*, 1996 ICJ Rep. 66 (8 July 1996), at para. 21. (The short reference form *Nuclear Weapons Advisory Opinion* in this text refers to the opinion in response to the General Assembly request, not that of the WHO.)

75 *Nuclear Weapons Advisory Opinion*, at paras. 10–19.

76 Haralambos Athanasopoulos, *Nuclear Disarmament in International Law* 11–13, 17–18 (2000); William R. Keylor, *The Twentieth-Century World: An International History* 318–26 (4th edn, 2001). For the ICJ's consideration see *Nuclear Weapons Advisory Opinion*, at paras. 53–63. For a survey of treaties in place see Jozef Goldblat, *Arms Control: The New*

Nuclear free zones, which came in two waves (during the 1960s and 1990s), were successfully set up for non-nuclear states with respect to the Antarctic, the South Pacific, South America, the Caribbean, Africa and Southeast Asia,[77] and also the ocean seabed, the moon and outer space.[78] On a universal footing, the 1968 Nuclear Non-Proliferation Treaty (NPT) made nuclear weapons unlawful for the nuclear have-nots.[79] The deal in 1968 had been as follows: the non-nuclear states would help prevent the spread of nuclear weapons and pledge not to acquire any themselves. In return they were promised assistance by the official nuclear states with research on, and the production and use of, nuclear energy for peaceful purposes. In 1968 there were officially five states with nuclear weapons: the USA, the Soviet Union, the UK, France and the PRC, thus simultaneously the five veto wielding powers of the Security Council.[80] They were official because their continued possession of nuclear weapons was sanctioned by the NPT, to which all states (exceptions at the time being Cuba, Israel, India and Pakistan) were party.[81] Beyond their assistance for peaceful nuclear energy, the nuclear states sought to strengthen the non-proliferation regime

Guide to Negotiations and Agreements (2nd edn, 2002); UN Department of Disarmament Affairs, *The United Nations Disarmament Yearbook 2004* (2005).

77 *Antarctic Treaty*, 402 UNTS 71 (1 Dec. 1959); *South Pacific Nuclear Zone Free Treaty (Treaty of Raratonga)*, 24 ILM 1440 (6 Aug. 1985); *Treaty for the Prohibition of Nuclear Weapons in Latin America and the Caribbean (Treaty of Tlatelolco)*, 634 UNTS 281 (14 Feb. 1967); *Southeast Asia Nuclear Weapon Free Zone Treaty (Treaty of Bangkok)*, 35 ILM 635 (15 Dec. 1995); *African Nuclear Weapons Free Zone Treaty (Treaty of Pelindaba)* 35 ILM 698 (11 Apr. 1996).

78 *Treaty on Principles Governing the Activities of States in the Exploration and Use of Outer Space, including the Moon and Other Celestial Bodies (Outer Space Treaty)*, 610 UNTS 205 (27 Jan. 1967); *Treaty on the Prohibition of the Emplacement of Nuclear Weapons and Other Weapons of Mass Destruction on the Sea-Bed and the Ocean Floor and in the Subsoil Thereof (Seabed Treaty)*, 955 UNTS 115 (11 Feb. 1971); *Agreement Governing the Activities of States on the Moon and other Celestial Bodies (Moon Treaty)*, 18 ILM 1434 (5 Dec. 1979).

79 *Treaty on the Non-Proliferation of Nuclear Weapons (NPT)*, 729 UNTS 161 (1 Jul. 1968). Today, all states but India, Pakistan, Israel and North Korea are parties to the agreement.

80 The 'unofficial' ones were India, which had successfully test-detonated a nuclear device in 1974, and Israel, whose nuclear status became an open secret following the disclosures of one of its technicians, Mordechai Vanunu, in 1986. Pakistan was to follow in 1998. North Korea claimed possession of nuclear weapons in February 2005 and test-detonated its first nuclear weapon in October 2006.

81 In the meantime, Cuba (as the only non-nuclear non-signatory state) announced its intention to join the NPT, while North Korea withdrew from it in January 2003. See 'Cuba Says it will Accede to the Nuclear Non-Proliferation Treaty', Press Release G/DIS/3225 (1 Nov. 2002); Frederic L. Kirgis, 'North Korea's Withdrawal from the Nuclear Nonproliferation Treaty', *ASIL Insights* (Jan. 2003), http://www.asil.org/insights/insigh96.htm.

through unilateral security assurances: they pledged, first, never to use nuclear weapons against nuclear-free NPT signatories and, second, to offer immediate assistance should these signatories nonetheless ever face a nuclear strike.[82] The only restriction the NPT imposed on the official nuclear club members was contained in article VI. It obliged them 'to pursue negotiations in good faith' to cease the nuclear arms race and to agree on nuclear disarmament. On 11 May 1995, in accordance with article X(2) of the NPT, the Review and Extension Conference of the parties decided that the NPT would continue in force indefinitely,[83] while the five official nuclear states reaffirmed and harmonised their security assurances vis-à-vis the non-nuclear signatories to the treaty.[84] From the viewpoint of international law and its reliance on *opinio juris*, it is worth emphasising the near-universal acceptance of a complex treaty regime designed to curtail nuclear arms proliferation but that has not (yet) achieved their eradication.[85]

The views within the General Assembly were markedly different. When it came to the vote on the advisory opinion request in December 1994, seventy-eight states voted in favour of the resolution, forty-three against and sixty-four chose not to take sides.[86] Given the well-publicised intent of the resolution, the voting in effect pitched the nuclear have-nots against the nuclear haves and, indicative for present purposes, provided an informal poll of governments' opinions. Opposed to an Assembly majority were states with nuclear weapons, joined by those nations which had relied on their nuclear shield during much of the Cold War era. The Assembly majority, largely constituted by developing countries, wanted to ban nuclear arms altogether; it had striven to bring this point home by innumerous resolutions since the 1960s that condemned nuclear weapons in every shape and form.[87] An

[82] Goldblat, *Arms Control*, at 109–12.

[83] *Extension of the Treaty on Non-Proliferation of Nuclear Weapons*, NPT/Conf.1995/32/Dec.2 (1 May 1995).

[84] SCOR S/1995/261 (6 Apr. 1995) (Russia), S/1995/262 (6 Apr. 1995) (UK), S/1995/263 (6 Apr. 1995) (USA), S/1995/264 (6 Apr. 1995) (France), and S/1995/265 (6 Apr. 1995) (China). A unanimous Security Council endorsed this gesture. See S/RES/984 (11 Apr. 1995); SCOR S/PV.3514 (11 Apr. 1995). Note also the ICJ's reference to the assurances, *Nuclear Weapons Advisory Opinion*, at para. 45.

[85] Athanasopoulos, *Nuclear Disarmament*, at p. 34.

[86] 1994 UNYB 158.

[87] The first resolution condemning nuclear weapons was A/Res/1653 (XVI) *Declaration on the Prohibition of the Use of Nuclear and Thermo-nuclear Weapons* (24 Nov. 1961). See also the ICJ's discussion of a perceived bias in the formulation of the General Assembly request, *Nuclear Weapons Advisory Opinion*, at paras. 21–2, 68–73.

element of contradiction was at play to the extent that, one year before the ICJ delivered its advisory opinion, the Assembly majority had done two things: first, it had renewed its adherence to the NPT regime and, second, it had asked for the ICJ to declare the unlawfulness of those weapons that that very regime entitled the five permanent Security Council members to possess. It is difficult to square the endorsement of the NPT regime with the *opinio* that nuclear weapons are unlawful under all circumstances, unless one accepts that *opinio* to be *de lege ferenda*. Be that as it may, the ICJ was put in the uncomfortable position of having to gauge the nuclear leeway of those states that were least inclined to hear or heed its call.

In the course of the hearings before the ICJ, the formulation of the General Assembly request raised the question as to whether nuclear deterrence was reviewable by the Court. The General Assembly had not restricted its question to the usage of nuclear weapons in armed conflict as the WHO had done, but had expanded it to use and threat 'in any circumstance'. Did this mean that the Court needed to judge the lawfulness of nuclear deterrence or not? A short exposition of the views that governments expressed before the Court is helpful. These were essentially divided into two camps. The first camp argued that it was not for the Court to comment on nuclear deterrence, let alone the deployment, manufacture or possession of nuclear weapons. The Solomon Islands argued, for example, that:

> The use of the term 'threat' by the General Assembly in its request for an Advisory Opinion must ... be considered to be limited to the situation where one or more States clearly express an intention to use nuclear weapons against one or more specifically designated States or populations in precise circumstances. It is the illegality of this type of 'threat' – real and specific rather than theoretical and general – which should be considered by the Court in addressing this request for an Advisory Opinion.[88]

France, in its written statement to the ICJ, also saw the scope of 'threats' as essentially non-deterrent:

> *La doctrine de dissuasion est la clef de voûte de la sécurité de la France ... la France s'élève avec force contre une tentative qui tend à mettre en cause, par une démarche dirigée contre les seules armes nucléaires et au risque d'ébranler un des éléments du système mondial actuel pour le maintien de la paix et de la sécurité internationales, la politique des Etats*

[88] Solomon Islands, *Written Statement* (19 Jun. 1995), at 24.

dotés d'armes nucléaires et, au-delà, leur droit d'assurer leur défense par les moyens que leur permet le droit international en vigueur.[89]

Translated into political science parlance, this meant that only the legality of compellence, and not of deterrence, was for the ICJ to decide.[90] There was a distinction to be made between passive capability and active threats, of which only the latter could be unlawful and even then, according to some, only in the context of demands to extract undue concessions.[91] A second camp, among them Malaysia, Mexico, Nauru, Egypt and India, argued on the other hand that since no nuclear usage could fulfil the standards of law applicable in armed conflict, the threat inherent in their deployment could only be unlawful. Deterrence, the deployment of nuclear arms to forestall an armed attack, was unlawful and it was for the Court so to declare.[92]

Against this background, the ICJ eventually delivered its advisory opinion on 8 July 1996. It drew four main conclusions relevant for the present study: we have examined the first in chapter 2, following the Brownlie formula, threat and use stand together in the sense that the unlawfulness of a threat is predicated on the unlawfulness of the use of force envisaged. A threat cannot be lawful unless enforcing it can also be achieved lawfully.[93] The second, third and fourth conclusions are more ambiguous and subject to the analysis as follows: possession of nuclear arms *may* amount to a threat in the sense of article 2(4) of the UN Charter. Such possession *may* be justified by the right to self-defence. And finally, nuclear threats for purely self-defensive reasons and to secure the very survival of a state is *potentially* lawful.

89 France, *Written Statement* (20 Jun. 1995), at 2–3 ['The doctrine of deterrence is the keystone of French security . . . France strongly objects to the attempt to call into question, by a step directed solely against nuclear arms and at the risk of undermining one of the elements of the present global system for maintaining peace and international security, the policy of states endowed with nuclear arms, and beyond that, their right to assure their defence by means permitted by current international law'].

90 On the distinction see above, chapter 2, at p. 58.

91 France, *Verbatim Record*, CR/95/23 (1 Nov. 1995), at 64; Solomon Islands, *Verbatim Record*, CR/95/33 (14 Nov. 1995), at 63; UK, *Written Statement* (16 Jun. 1995), at 72–3; USA, *Written Statement* (20 Jun. 1995), at 46–7.

92 Malaysia, *Written Statement* (19 Jun. 1995), at 20; Indonesia, *Verbatim Record*, CR/95/25 (3 Nov. 1995), at 18, 24 et seq.; Qatar, *Verbatim Records*, CR/95/29 (10 Nov. 1995), at 27 et seq.

93 *Nuclear Weapons Advisory Opinion*, at para. 47. See above, chapter 2, p. 39.

Having adopted the Brownlie formula in para. 47, the focus of the ICJ in the advisory opinion is clearly on the legality of the use, and not the threat, of nuclear weapons. Since the legality of a nuclear threat depended entirely on the legality of the nuclear force envisaged, there was little merit in theorising in isolation about the threat of force. This is one reason why the Court's conclusions on threats are ambiguous and open to interpretation. But obviously, the question remained what it meant to 'threaten' under the Charter law. Was it necessary for a threat to be 'active' as some states had submitted, or was it sufficient to be 'passive' and implied? In dealing with this question in a cursory fashion, the Court stated in para. 48:

> Some States put forward the argument that possession of nuclear weapons is itself an unlawful threat to use force. Possession of nuclear weapons may indeed justify an inference of preparedness to use them. In order to be effective, the policy of deterrence, by which those States possessing or under the umbrella of nuclear weapons seek to discourage military aggression by demonstrating that it will serve no purpose, necessitates that the intention to use nuclear weapons be credible. Whether this is a 'threat' contrary to Article 2, paragraph 4, depends upon whether the particular use of force envisaged would be directed against the territorial integrity or political independence of a State, or against the Purposes of the United Nations or whether, in the event that it were intended as a means of defence, it would necessarily violate the principles of necessity and proportionality. In any of these circumstances the use of force, and the threat to use it, would be unlawful under the law of the Charter.[94]

The first sentences of the paragraph are instructive. 'Possession of nuclear weapons', the ICJ explained, 'may indeed justify an inference of preparedness to use them'. Giving the sentence its proper meaning, the judges adopted the view that the possession of nuclear weapons will in itself constitute a threat at least under most circumstances. The essence of deterrence is the signalled readiness to use force if necessary. In the special case of nuclear weapons, it was held that the capability to implement the threat alone is perfectly sufficient to convey that message.

If possession of nuclear arms does indeed fall under the purview of article 2(4), then implicitly so must their acquisition, assembly, stockpiling, installation, deployment and testing. According to the judges, neither is it necessary that states undertake more active preparations for a nuclear strike nor that they communicate a specific set of conditions

[94] *Nuclear Weapons Advisory Opinion*, at para. 48.

under which the promise of force would be realised. Both deterrence and compellence fall (or at least may fall) under the purview of article 2(4). And because deterrence is by nature a long-term affair, there is no requirement for imminence of a threat. To sum up, the allusion to nuclear force is enough. The idea that maintenance of arms may be a *prima facie* infringement of the no-threat rule, dead in the *Nicaragua* judgment, is alive and well here in regard to nuclear weapons.

Taking such an inclusive view of the threshold of article 2(4) of the UN Charter, full attention needed then to be brought to bear on the question of justification. In order to be lawful, any threat in breach of article 2(4) must be justified either as a self-defensive measure under article 51 or as one that is authorised by the Security Council according to Chapter VII of the Charter. Further, the threat must be necessary and proportional.[95] While leaving aside the hypothetical case of a Security Council authorisation, the advisory opinion contains two relevant observations on the right to self-defence: first, on the practice of deterrence and, second, on a so-called right to state survival.

In its examination of the practice of deterrence, the ICJ stated clearly – but for reasons that remain obscure in light of the General Assembly's bright-lined objective – that it did not want to comment on the legality of nuclear deterrence as such.[96] Deterrence as a term does not appear in the *dispositif*. Rather, the Court took the practice of deterrence as an indicator for the existence of customary international law regarding the threat or use of nuclear weapons.[97] If states could be shown to have endorsed nuclear deterrence, then it seemed plausible that deterrence as a *prima facie* violation of article 2(4) was justified under the rubric of self-defence. However, the Court observed in para. 67 that:

> ... it is a fact that a number of States adhered to [the practice known as the 'policy of deterrence'] during the greater part of the Cold War and continue to adhere to it. Furthermore, the Members of the international community are profoundly divided on the matter of whether non-recourse to nuclear weapons over the past

95 *Nuclear Weapons Advisory Opinion*, at paras. 38–44.

96 *Ibid.*, at para. 67. For another view see the *Declaration of Judge Shi*, http://www.icj-cij.org/, who argues that deterrence is political practice and therefore not relevant in international law. At the opposite extreme, emphasising the importance of the five nuclear powers, see the *Dissenting Opinion of Vice-President Schwebel*. The most comprehensive analysis is Judge Weeramantry's: see *Dissenting Opinion of Judge Weeramantry*, http://www.icj-cij.org/.

97 *Nuclear Weapons Advisory Opinion*, at para. 64.

fifty years constitutes the expression of *opinio iuris*. Under these circumstances the Court does not consider itself able to find that there is such an *opinio iuris*.[98]

Concluding its examination of the General Assembly resolutions consistently asserting the legality of nuclear weapons, the Court observed in para. 73:

... the adoption each year by the General Assembly, by a large majority, of resolutions recalling the content of resolution 1653 (XVI), and requesting the member States to conclude a convention prohibiting the use of nuclear weapons in any circumstance, reveals the desire of a very large section of the international community to take, by a specific and express prohibition of the use of nuclear weapons, a significant step forward along the road to complete nuclear disarmament. The emergence, as *lex lata*, of a customary rule specifically prohibiting the use of nuclear weapons as such is hampered by the continuing tensions between the nascent *opinio juris* on the one hand, and the still strong adherence to the practice of deterrence on the other.[99]

In expressing such a cautious view, the ICJ held that the law was in flux. It deliberately chose to leave final judgment to the further development of the law and the particular facts of a future case.

It may be useful to recall that article 2(4) of the UN Charter was signed into law at a time when the existence of nuclear weapons was unknown to most signatories. The expressed opinion and practice of states since 1945 was relevant to the question of whether the Charter's prescriptions had undergone some form of customary evolution, such as to clarify the legal status of deterrence.[100] In light of the available evidence, the Court determined that there was for the time being no conclusion possible in this regard. It seems to have considered the practice of deterrence and the fortunate abstention from nuclear war since 1945 of equal significance. As for the General Assembly resolutions, had the nuclear five been alone in their view, it would have been plausible to speak of them as persistent objectors. But the division into substantial blocks within the General Assembly and the universal acceptance of the NPT regime rendered such a conception implausible. Even if 'instant' custom had been a possibility, the division within the

[98] *Ibid.*, at para. 67.
[99] *Nuclear Weapons Advisory Opinion*, at para. 73.
[100] Article 31(3)b *Vienna Convention on the Law of Treaties*, 1155 UNTS 331 (23 May 1969).

General Assembly excluded the development of a prohibition of nuclear weapons.[101] As a result, state practice since 1945 lent itself neither to reject nor to confirm the hypothesis that nuclear deterrence was justified as a self-defensive measure according to article 51 of the UN Charter.

An objection to this is the famous *Lotus* presumption. According to the 1927 *Lotus* dictum of the Permanent Court, 'Restrictions upon the independence of States cannot ... be presumed',[102] and therefore, it would have been for the ICJ to declare that as long as there was no conclusive custom, nations retained an entitlement to practice nuclear deterrence as they saw fit. The Court rightly rejected this argument.[103] Quite independently of whether the *Lotus* presumption holds true today, the question for the UN Charter is whether specific acts fall under its provisions, i.e., whether promising nuclear retaliation infringes articles 2(4) and 51 of the Charter. The context is treaty interpretation. In it, applying a bias in favour of legality would be a misconception of the problem.[104]

The other relevant finding of the ICJ in the justificatory context is on the notion of state survival. Whereas the unanimous finding in para. 2C of the *dispositif* is cast in the familiar mould of an attack-defence scheme ('A threat or use of force by means of nuclear weapons that is contrary to Article 2, para. 4, of the United Nations Charter and that fails to meet all the requirements of Article 51, is unlawful'),[105] paragraph 2E of the *dispositif*, which came into being only by the President casting his vote, is not. In it the Court declared:

> It follows from the above-mentioned requirements that the threat or use of nuclear weapons would generally be contrary to the rules of international law applicable in armed conflict, and in particular the principles and rules of humanitarian law;
>
> However, in view of the current state of international law, and of the elements of fact at its disposal, the Court cannot conclude definitively whether the threat or use of nuclear weapons would be lawful or unlawful in an extreme

[101] On the notion of 'instant' customary law see Bin Cheng, 'United Nations Resolutions on Outer Space: "Instant" Customary Law?', 5 Ind. JIL 23–112 (1965).

[102] *The Case of the S. S. Lotus (France* v. *Turkey), Merits*, 3 PCIJ Rep, Series A, No. 10 (7 Sep. 1927), at 18.

[103] *Nuclear Weapons Advisory Opinion*, at paras. 21–2, 52.

[104] See below, chapter 4, at p. 103.

[105] *Nuclear Weapons Advisory Opinion*, at para. 2C of the *dispositif*.

circumstance of self-defence, in which the very survival of a State would be at stake.[106]

It is unclear from where the Court derived a right to state survival, and what the notions of 'state' and 'survival' mean in this context. Survival features nowhere in the UN Charter, nor have scholars recently submitted that it were customary law.[107] But following through on the ICJ's dictum, the qualification of state survival means this: in order to secure one's survival, an active threat to use nuclear weapons could be justified even if its implementation would usually be prohibited, for example, because it would violate provisions of the Geneva Conventions. Since the possibility that the use of nuclear arms in a situation of extreme survival is lawful cannot be excluded, neither can the threat of such use *de lege lata* be strictly prohibited.

It follows, conversely, that at least any threat of nuclear force that is not issued for the purposes of essential state survival and not for a grave emergency is illicit. Broader justifications for nuclear threats are excluded. The ICJ itself elaborates in para. 47 that 'it would be illegal for a State to threaten force to secure territory from another State, or to cause it to follow or not follow certain political or economic paths'.[108] Equally important, a nuclear threat to hasten the end of a war – even if fought self-defensively – or to discourage the use of chemical or biological weapons as an end in itself would not pass the Court's justification test.[109] Practically speaking, a nuclear threat against a limited conventional attack would also usually fail to qualify, unless one considers the imaginary case that, say, the Principality of Monaco was invaded by

106 *Ibid.*, at para. 2E of the *dispositif.* See further paras. 96–7.

107 The right to self-preservation was considered a natural right according to Grotius and his contemporaries. See Richard Tuck, *The Rights of War and Peace: Political Thought and the International Order from Grotius to Kant* (1999). But this hardly makes it a customary right. See further on the notion of state survival see Marcelo G. Kohen, 'The Notion of "State Survival" in International Law', in Laurence Boisson de Chazournes and Philippe Sands (eds.), *International Law, the International Court of Justice and Nuclear Weapons* 293–314 (1999). The advisory opinion in para. 96 merely takes as a given that the ICJ 'cannot lose sight of the fundamental right of every State to survival, and thus its right to resort to self-defence, in accordance with Article 51 of the UN Charter, when its survival is at stake'.

108 *Nuclear Weapons Advisory Opinion*, at para. 47.

109 Compare Richard A. Falk, 'Nuclear Weapons, International Law and the World Court: A Historic Encounter', 91 Am. JIL 64–75 (1997), at 69.

France.[110] To threaten retaliation for terrorist attacks too would hardly be justifiable. In light of these considerations, today's equivalent of the threatened (and implemented) bombing of Hiroshima and Nagasaki become deeply problematic under international law. While carving out a *de facto* exception for threats to secure survival, the advisory opinion narrows the space for threats of any other kind. A state may not actively signal its readiness to use nuclear force unless it is in danger of total destruction.[111]

What does this mean for the policy of nuclear deterrence as practiced during most of the Cold War? It seems that it is saved from condemnation, since 'mutual assured destruction' (MAD), which is at the heart of nuclear deterrence, is by definition a threat to ensure self-preservation. As long as it is declared in strictly defensive terms and for the sole purpose of securing a state's ultimate survival in an emergency, the law is, according to the advisory opinion, indeterminate. It gives neither its blessing nor malediction.

This indeterminacy is presumably upheld for the policy of extended deterrence of the Cold War period, with which nuclear weapon states 'extended' their nuclear shield to allies; the *dispositif* of the advisory opinion speaks of the survival of *a* state. But paras. 96 and 97, which refer to situations where self-defence may be invoked by a state for *its* survival, suggest otherwise. Whether, according to the ICJ, the indeterminacy of the law extends to threats in collective self-defence is thus not entirely clear.

All in all, the advisory opinion of the ICJ is not all that it could have been: a clear-cut guide on threats of force under article 2(4) of the UN Charter. Its counsel to the General Assembly is rather sibylline, not a succinctly formulated dictum. Nonetheless, it did make important statements on the threat of force in four respects: (1) nuclear deterrence *prima facie* amounts to a violation of article 2(4) of the UN Charter; (2) justification according to the Brownlie formula depends on the legality of implementing a deterrent threat; (3) the law is indeterminate as to the extent of justification endorsed by custom; and (4) justification equally cannot be excluded for threats of self-defence for the purpose of securing the very 'survival' of a state. Securing 'survival' may even

110 This example raises the disquieting question of what is meant by the survival of the 'state', as opposed to, e.g., its government, people or territory. Smaller countries seem to be entitled to threaten and use nuclear force more quickly than the large ones. I owe this insight to James Crawford.

111 Compare *Nuclear Weapons Advisory Opinion*, at paras. 41–3.

justify threats (and uses) of nuclear force which under normal conditions would be prohibited under international law. It is quite evident that, taken together, these requirements set out a narrow path by which nuclear threats – particularly of the active, compellent type – could find approval by the UN Charter. At the same time, it is doubtful whether the four findings could be extended to the threat of force in a non-nuclear context. Possession and survival, it would appear, are of limited relevance for coercive action 'short of war' with conventional weapons that the San Francisco signatories sought to repeal.

Conclusions

The jurisprudence of the ICJ on the threat of force is sparse and scattered. None of the three decisions discussed in this chapter substantially refer to one another. There is disappointingly little explanation, and the traditional methods of identifying international law – treaty, custom, general principles or *travaux préparatoires* – are largely absent.

More importantly, the three ICJ precedents are hard to synchronise as inconsistencies abound. In *Nicaragua* the Court argued that states were free to decide on military build-ups. Pulling in the opposite direction, the same Court suggested in 1996 that possession of arms alone was quite sufficient to bring article 2(4) into play, and that the threat of nuclear annihilation was inherent in the capability to wage a nuclear war. In *Nicaragua*, the ICJ displayed a reluctance to assume that a threat of force was constituted by military exercises. It engaged in a delicate balancing of crisis circumstances in the *Corfu Channel* case that was – in the scope and scale of the military actions examined – incompatible with the assertion of 1986. In *Corfu Channel*, the test was whether the British ships were engaged in an open 'demonstration of force for the purpose of exercising political pressure on Albania', giving due consideration to the political tensions in the region and the immediately preceding behaviour of the parties. The Reagan administration in 1986 was bold enough to assert that its intention was to do just that: to exercise political pressure against a foreign government.

In support of the ICJ, it should be noted that the facts of each case varied greatly. In none of them was the threat theme of decisive importance. Nonetheless, the discrepancies are regrettable and they weaken the persuasiveness of the Court's overall interpretation of article 2(4). Some doubts are warranted on whether the Court's reasoning withstands closer scrutiny. But despite inconsistencies, there are also commonalities worth highlighting. In chapter 2 we set out to explore various interpretations of the threat of force ban. The ICJ chose to follow some of these while implicitly rejecting others. It demonstrated no interest in the view that threat and use of force might be two separate things, i.e., that the right to self-defence might not justify a threat of force in all circumstances. No backing is to be found for a connection between article 2(4) and an obligation to peaceful settlement or, conversely, that a violation of article 2(4) necessitates imminence or active coercion. Nor is there much support for the contention that deliberate disruption of international peace could amount to an illicit threat, although the *Corfu Channel* ruling can be read to have taken that proposal into consideration. All three cases, however, expressed no doubt that a threat of force could be achieved by an act of demonstration through military exercises or naval operations. Finally, there was likewise no doubt in the mind of the judges that the no-threat rule is a living ingredient of the non-use of force principle, accorded the same peremptory status that all of article 2(4) enjoys.

The track record of the ICJ, in summary, is a mixed bag. The small number of cases, the coverage of very different factual scenarios and the evident lack of a coherent interpretation approach to address the no-threat principle leave much room for doubt on a topic that is as much complex as it begs for clarification.

4 Deciphering post-Charter practice: means and limits

It is better to be approximately right than exactly wrong.
John Tukey[1]

Expanding the search

The previous chapters have examined historical pedigree, systemic context and case law only to arrive at the conclusion that the legal regime governing threats of force still eludes rigid legal taxonomy. The UN Charter does not define the phrase 'threat of force'. Within the broad parameters of the drafter's intent, it remains unclear what degree of intensity or what specific conduct would violate article 2(4) or would exceptionally appear lawful under article 51. To read the *travaux* is to become aware of the lack – not presence – of concrete consent. Subsequent agreements and resolutions affirm but, unhelpfully, merely repeat the Charter text. The ICJ provides very limited and at times contradictory guidance. So far, however, we have not explored the question of whether UN members, who now number four times as many as in 1945, have learned to read article 2(4) differently in their sixty years of practice.

In short, the need arises to employ state practice to narrow the margins of uncertainty; to ascertain whether mobilisations of the military are permissible; which hostile promises are unjustifiable; and which responses, if any, to counter military threats are acceptable. 'The UN Charter', the ICJ explained in 1986, 'by no means covers the whole

[1] Quoted from a presentation given by Edward Tufte, *Beautiful Evidence*, Stanford (8 Dec. 2004). See also Art B. Owen, *Empirical Likelihood* 5 (2001).

area of the regulation of force in international relations'.[2] For a consideration of the threat of force, recourse to sources beyond the text of the Charter is necessary if the international judge is not to decide purely on the basis of *ex aequo et bono*. The following three chapters therefore will examine post-Charter practice and opinion on the threat of force.

Any international legal argument that seeks support from state practice, however, requires some prior stipulations on methodology. How does one determine post-Charter practice? It is a paradox that the question of custom – one of the sources available to fill the gaps in the evolving international legal system – is among the most controversial and least certain fields of that system. Article 38 of the ICJ Statute describes custom as 'a general practice accepted as law'.[3] Custom, as it is commonly portrayed, is the combination of consistent governmental practice supported by a sense of legal obligation, referred to as *opinio juris*.[4] But beyond that, international scholars and their 'schools' have proposed highly contradictory views of custom; what it is made of, how it is formed and how we sample it once it has formed. It is not the aim here to discuss the controversy in detail or even to attempt its resolution. Suffice it to describe the basic choices forming the cornerstones of this study, as they relate to the particularities of the no-threat principle. This will be done by addressing three basic questions:

1. What state practice is legally relevant?
2. What is the relationship between state practice and treaty interpretation?
3. How does one collect empirical evidence on state practice?

These are no idle questions. On the contrary, scholarly investigations of state practice often suffer from the methodological deficiency of what might crudely be called the 'piling up approach': the proposition of custom is fortified with the accumulation of exclusively supporting cases; instances of diverging state practice receive no attention or are not systematically identified. In a milder form, scholars only examine cases that are well known and abundantly documented (so-called

2 *Military and Paramilitary Activities in and Against Nicaragua (Nicaragua* v. *USA), Merits*, 1986 ICJ Rep. 14 (27 Jun. 1986), at para. 176.

3 Article 38(1)(b) *Statute of the International Court of Justice*, 39 Am. JIL Supp. 215–29 (1945) (26 Jun. 1945). On the genesis of article 38(1)b see Karol Wolfke, *Custom in Present International Law* 1–5 (2nd edn, 1993).

4 *North Sea Continental Shelf Cases (Federal Republic of Germany* v. *Denmark and The Netherlands), Merits*, 1969 ICJ Rep. 3 (20 Feb. 1969), at para. 77.

convenience samples). As any social scientist will attest, this approach would be a cause for concern. By any standard of research-based, inductive social enquiry, it is appropriate to ask where practice comes from, what criteria were applied for its selection and along what lines it was evaluated.[5] International law is not immune to these concerns. In fact, methodological approaches in the discipline at times vary so greatly that, in the words of Sir Robert Jennings, it is not uncommon for parties to submit the same record of practice to a tribunal, and 'not surprisingly each Party is always able to give the identical body of practice the stamp of its own particular thesis'.[6] The practical difficulties of relying on state practice as a source of authority are considerable indeed.

For this reason the theories and methods applied in the present study are discussed here. In international law, uncertainty operates on two levels: the vagueness of the concept of custom, on the one hand, and the purely practical difficulties in subjecting the concept to empirical testing, on the other. Both aspects crucially affect the outcome of any analysis of state practice. Any reporting of the results of a study on state practice in international law must therefore involve some prior stipulations on the working hypotheses that have been brought to bear on its analysis. These working hypotheses should ideally represent the most plausible approach in the face of both imperfect theory and an imperfect historical record.

Legally relevant state practice

The dual requirement for customary law implies an underlying causal relationship between *opinio juris* and state practice. A state adopts a specific behaviour *because* it holds beliefs about its legal duties or rights. In theory, rule conforming behaviour is not sufficient for the formation of custom if it is not motivated by the belief that the rule applies to that behaviour. Only if law is the motivational cause for what states do or do not do is their behaviour legally relevant state practice.

Article 2(4) contains a prohibition on acting. Strictly speaking, compliant behaviour would be that of abstention, not action. The most appropriate research question would therefore be whether states have

[5] This is not to discount the notion of precedent. But even a national court, in determining the case law, will have to look at all relevant cases and not only those that support the claims of one party.

[6] Sir Robert Y. Jennings, 'What is International Law and How Do We Tell It When We See It?', 37 Schw. Jb. IR 59–88 (1981), at 68.

abstained from the use of military threats, not whether they have chosen to use them.[7] There are considerable practical difficulties associated with such an investigation.[8] A major problem is that the examination of abstentions requires us to rely on counterfactual theories of causation, in this case the speculation about the instances in which states would have resorted to threats in the absence of a legal requirement not to do so.[9] Counterfactual arguments necessitate informed estimates of the probability that if A had not occurred, then B would have.[10] Theories in international law have not developed adequately to address this problem, and indeed it is difficult to see how it could be efficiently overcome.[11] Quite independently of the hypothetical causality problems, further difficulties arise with the abstention approach. How does one weigh non-occurrence against action? How ought claims of justification be assessed if positive acts are excluded from the enquiry? And, most importantly, where does one find records on states practicing such forbearance? These difficulties render the usefulness of an investigation of 'abstention practice' highly uncertain to say the least.

Instead, a central premise of this study is that the response of bystander governments – on their own or through the UN – to potential violations of the no-threat principle is legally relevant state practice. Wide protest indicates unlawfulness; wide approval indicates lawfulness. There is no causal inference between action and motivation,

[7] This approach is documented, yet not strictly applied, by the ICJ in *Legality of the Threat or Use of Nuclear Weapons (Advisory Opinion)*, 1996 ICJ Rep. 226 (8 Jul. 1996), at para. 65. See further *The Case of the S.S. Lotus (France* v. *Turkey), Merits*, 3 PCIJ Rep., Series A, No. 10 (7 Sep. 1927), at 28.

[8] Anthony D'Amato, *The Concept of Custom in International Law* 61–3 (1971); Louis Henkin, *How Nations Behave: Law and Foreign Policy* 48 (2nd edn, 1979); Gionata Piero Buzzini, 'Les Comportements Passifs des États et leur Incidence sur la Réglementation de l'Emploi de la Force en Droit International Général', in Enzo Cannizzaro and Paolo Palchetti (eds.), *Customary International Law on the Use of Force: A Methodological Approach* 79–117 (2005), at pp. 81–4. Gérard Cahin, *La Coutume Internationale et les Organisations Internationales: L'incidence de la Dimension Institutionelle sur le Processus Coutumier* 139–46 (2001).

[9] The Permanent Court of International Justice (PCIJ) noted similarly that 'the rarity of ... judicial decisions ... merely show[s] that States had often, in practice, abstained from instituting criminal proceedings, and not that they recognized themselves as being obliged to do so, for only if such abstention were based on their being conscious of having a duty to abstain would it be possible to speak of an international custom'. See *S.S. Lotus*, at 28.

[10] James Fearon, 'Counterfactuals and Hypothesis Testing in Political Science', 43 World P. 169–95 (1991).

[11] For an attempt see D'Amato, *The Concept of Custom*, at pp. 81–7.

but a vote between different legal options.[12] In political science terms, a way of thinking about this phenomenon is that every case is a 'claim' that is either rejected or accepted, the accumulation of cases amounting to customary expectations about how the international community will react. Through their responses, states individually influence the expectations of the political costs that any violator will incur, notably the stigma of being labelled a law-breaker.[13] It should be emphasised that this is not the same as requiring that a 'norm-challenger' need incur political costs amounting to a crushing penalty. The notion of custom does not require the active resistance to violation; the prototype scenario is simply to hold a belief about the applicable law consistently practiced by the majority of states over time. Short of measuring abstention, the next best approach to investigation is to ascertain whether states indicate approval or disapproval in the face of the 'failings' of their peers. To require active, material resistance such as an economic boycott would be to condition the advent of law on a powerful system of enforcement not suggested anywhere in article 38 of the ICJ Statute. That article merely requires that a general practice be 'accepted as law'.[14] It is this acceptance or rejection that needs to be put to the test.[15] Consequently, it is sufficient that third parties express their opinion as to whether suspicious conduct is or is not in conformity with shared expectations of rightfulness and regard to the established order.

This concept is contrary to the view that only physical acts – the acts of the potential norm-breaker – could constitute state practice, that verbal assertions of the law by states short of signing a treaty are meaningless for custom.[16] That approach is too narrow. It is too

[12] There is a causal inference on another level, namely, that third party reaction (the dependent variable) is triggered by the potentially unlawful conduct of a state (one of many explanatory variables).

[13] This notion is best captured in international relations by cooperation and regime theory. See Robert O. Keohane, *After Hegemony: Cooperation and Discord in the World Political Economy* 49–110 (1989). On the application of regime theory to customary law see Michael Byers, *Custom, Power and the Power of Rules; International Relations and Customary International Law* 27–9, 149 (1999).

[14] Article 38(1)(b) *ICJ Statute*.

[15] This position is contrary to the New Haven school, whose advocates tend to regard the opinion of governments as unimportant. See the 'incident' genre advocated by the New Haven school by W. Michael Reisman and Andrew R. Willard (eds.), *International Incidents: The Law That Counts in World Politics* (1988).

[16] Wolfke, *Custom in Present International Law*, at pp. 41–4; D'Amato, *The Concept of Custom*, at p. 88; A. Mark Weisburd, *Use of Force: The Practice of States Since World War II* 10–13 (1997).

expedient for states that wish to bend rules in their favour; new law is established by breaking it; law is not recognised unless it is enforced. The better approach, in the words of Michael Akehurst, is that: 'State practice covers any act or statement by a State from which views can be inferred about international law.'[17] The judicial legacy of the ICJ offers considerable support for such greater inclusiveness, even though it has not been entirely consistent.[18] Be that as it may, for the examination of the no-threat principle there is not much of a choice: considering that verbal threats – diplomatic notes or public speeches – may themselves be unlawful, the international judge will inevitably have to rely not only on physical acts but also on less tangible forms of state behaviour. It follows from this characterisation of relevant state practice that it includes not only physical acts, but also governmental statements, official instructions, claims, assurances and silent acknowledgements. So too, therefore, should the official reactions of states to legal claims by others be taken into account as indicative of whether or not their customary expectations have been met. The test of communal reaction is receptive to systematic enquiry. Additional instruments indicating legal opinions are supplementary evidence. That is the approach of this study.

As scholars appear to have correctly identified, the inclusive approach to state practice leads to the regrettable outcome that the distinction between state practice and *opinio juris* becomes blurred, to the extent that it disappears altogether.[19] There is good reason to agree with this analysis. However, that deficiency is one that is inherent in the notion of customary law itself – and therefore irreparable if the traditional twofold canon of practice and opinion is to be upheld. Whenever the duty under international law is one of abstention, the only state practice that physically manifests itself is that of the potential violator. The opinion of all other states lacks a physical face. What they practice is omission, and for their part *opinio juris* as the subjective element necessarily takes the leading role whenever that omission, as noted above, eludes fruitful factual enquiry. There is, at least for empirical purposes, no silver bullet to overcome the methodological problems that are predetermined by the two-sided notion of custom

17 Michael Akehurst, 'Custom as a Source of International Law', 47 Brit. YBIL 1–53 (1976), at 10. Instructive Byers, *Power of Rules*, at pp. 133–6.
18 For references see Byers, *ibid.*, at pp. 134–5.
19 For example Byers, *ibid.*, at pp. 136–41.

itself.[20] The pragmatic approach has to be, as the ICJ itself ruled, that 'general practice of States should be recognised as *prima facie* evidence that it is accepted as law',[21] and that practice is taken here to include what bystander governments say as much as what they do. Accepting such evidence is especially justified for article 2(4) of the UN Charter, which arguably applies *erga omnes*. States may invoke injury even if they have not been the target of violation.[22]

That said, there is then the question whether the reactions of third parties are tantamount to legal views, or whether they are more accurately described as political expediencies which should be of no concern to international law.[23] The literature on this subject is sparse. Most scholarship concentrates on the question of whether the resolutions of international organisations purport to be declaratory of custom, or are merely recommendations devoid of any legal significance. The question raised in this context is generally one of the philosophy of the foundations of international law, but rarely one of factual enquiry.[24] In a detailed study in 1984 of the General Assembly's voting behaviour on aggression, Thomas Franck advanced the thesis that, by and large, states did not apply double standards when condemning acts of force such as those in Grenada, Cambodia, Afghanistan, Western Sahara, East Timor or the Falklands. Franck explains:

> Most states in the United Nations are small and weak. They are more likely to be victims, rather than perpetrators, of aggression; and therefore their perceived national interest usually coincides with any application of the principle that

[20] Patrick J. Kelly, 'The Twilight of Customary International Law', 40 Va JIL 449–543 (2000), at 500–7, who argues that a choice is necessary for the sake of consistency in empirical investigation; a choice, however, that general theory does not provide.

[21] *North Sea Continental Shelf Cases*, at para. 83.

[22] *Barcelona Traction, Light and Power Company, Limited (Belgium v. Spain), Second Phase*, 1970 ICJ Rep. 3 (5 Feb. 1970), at paras. 33–4, according to which the prohibition of 'acts of aggression' is an obligation *erga omnes*. See recently Christian J. Tams, *Enforcing Obligations* Erga Omnes *in International Law* 118, 144–5 (2006); Martti Koskenniemi, *Fragmentation of International Law: Difficulties Arising from the Diversification and Expansion of International Law*, A/CN.4/L.682 (4 Apr. 2006), at pp. 158–9. Note that before the General Assembly's resolution 3314 in 1974 (which excluded threats from the Definition of Aggression), the most important precedents on aggression were the Nuremberg and Tokyo trials. These had qualified the threat of force as an act of aggression. See above, chapter 1, at pp. 25–8

[23] Rosalyn Higgins, *The Development of International Law Through the Political Organs of the United Nations* 7–8 (1963).

[24] For an overview see Rosalyn Higgins, *Problems and Process: International Law and How We Use It* 25–7 (1994), with further references.

force must not be used to resolve conflicts between nations. The reason a majority of states can usually be found to support a condemnation of the unilateral use of force is that most of the Third World, being weak and vulnerable, believes it to be to their advantage to reinforce the law against aggressive behavior, no matter which state violates it.[25]

Christine Gray, on the other hand, writes that 'a slight doubt arises because occasionally both the General Assembly and the Security Council seemed willing to condemn a state for a particular episode because of its past record'.[26] Franck concedes irregularities in regard to votes on Israel, while Gray lists Portugal and South Africa as examples where a reputation as a colonial or apartheid power invited the scorn of other countries. Mark Weisburd's study in 1997 on the use of force by states since 1945 reveals a more patchy practice, where only the most flagrant violations, in particular invasions, prompt the General Assembly to vote in a principled manner but even then the General Assembly is not free from political horse-trading.[27]

The system of ostracism in international forums is certainly imperfect; bias in judgment comes as no surprise. However, all that communal condemnation (or, conversely, wide approval) means is that the majority of states have deemed an action impermissible, that state conduct, under the case-by-case circumstances, was not tolerable according to agreed standards. In this sense the back and forth between norm-challenger and responding states, imposing reputational costs on the challenger, is really about laying down what are figuratively called the 'rules of the game', and therefore, even though far from directly, about law.[28] Whatever philosophical riddle this may raise, one is likely to agree with the wisdom of statistician John Tukey that, 'It is better to be approximately right than exactly wrong':[29] in the absence of more

[25] Thomas M. Franck, 'Of Gnats and Camels: Is there a Double Standard at the United Nations?', 78 Am. JIL 811–33 (1984), at 831. Frank confirms his finding in his recent book *Recourse to Force: State Action Against Threats and Armed Attacks* (2002). See also Oscar Schachter, 'Self-Defense and the Rule of Law', 83 Am. JIL 259–77 (1989), at 263–5, 272.

[26] Christine Gray, *International Law and the Use of Force* 19 (2nd edn, 2004).

[27] Weisburd, *Use of Force*. Inconsistencies are also detected by Ramses Amer, 'The United Nations' Reactions to Foreign Military Interventions', 31 J. Peace Res. 425–44 (1994).

[28] Following the same intuition Oscar Schachter, 'The Twilight Existence of Nonbinding International Agreements', 71 Am. JIL 296–304 (1977).

[29] See above, n. 1.

conclusive evidence, third party reaction may well be the best available approximation of the settled legal opinions of states.[30]

Under the assumption that condemnation and approval correspond to judgments of law, it is still open what condemnation or approval are or how they ought to be defined. Again these are no idle questions. The *modus operandi* of general international law is to assume the persistence of a new or modified rule whenever affected states remain silent, faithful to the Latin adage *qui tacet consentire videtur* – who is silent appears to consent. Custom can only be defied by persistent objection.[31] The concepts of acquiescence and estoppel work, mostly in bilateral relations, on similar grounds to tilt the burden of proof against the state that does not agree with an emerging consensus.[32] The assumption in favour of new law might be a good device to advance the rule of law in a rudimentary legal system where there is still uncharted ground for regulation. It may also be highly plausible where there is no reason to energetically applaud compliance with an 'ordinary' obligation, for example, the respect for diplomatic immunity or the abstention from environmental pollution. However, by the same token, in order for a rule to be upheld, it has to be actively defended. If silence implies consent, then states need to be proactive in protesting challenges to avoid the result that changes in the law may be invoked as of right by states who resent the status quo.[33]

Quite independent of considerations of fairness, it is again essentially an empirical question of whether or not a majority of states actually do regularly comment on the failings of their peers, and if not, whether their silence is the equivalent of conscious approval. As Nigel White and Robert Cryer have pointed out, the inference of consent from reluctance to condemn may well be a great fallacy for threat-related cases.[34] In what may be regarded as the most systematic study on the use of

[30] This is not to say that in order to identify the rules, as others have proposed, opinion does not matter. See, however, Reisman and Willard, *International Incidents*, chapter 1. This approach is nothing more than the description of what political costs states incur when violating international law.

[31] Instead of many: Knut Ipsen, *Völkerrecht* §16 Mn. 25–7 (5th edn, 2004).

[32] Ipsen, *Völkerrecht*, at §16 Mn. 21, §18 Mn. 15.

[33] I. C. MacGibbon, 'Some Observations on the Part of Protest in International Law', 30 Brit. YBIL 293–319 (1954), at 310.

[34] Nigel D. White and Robert Cryer, 'Unilateral Enforcement of Resolution 687: A Threat Too Far?', 29 Cal. WILJ 243–83 (1999), at 246. See further Michael Byers, 'The Shifting Foundations of International Law: A Decade of Forceful Measures against Iraq', 13 Eur. JIL 21–41 (2002), at 36; Byers, *Power of Rules*, at pp. 142–6.

force practice since 1945, Mark Weisburd reports that the communal choir is often barely vocal in its protests against *prima facie* violations of the non-use of force principle.[35] Thomas Franck's 2002 study seems to contradict this finding, but is confined to cases that had already found their way into Security Council debate.[36] A study in 2001 by Richard Hermann and Vaughn Shannon indicates that state protest is sporadic and motives are mixed.[37] Louis Henkin too reports that: 'It is unusual for nations not directly involved to respond to a violation even of a widely accepted norm.'[38] One can only speculate about other, less obvious violations of the law. In the sparse literature, commentators consistently assume that third states mainly ignore threats of force when they occur.[39] Sometimes there seems little reason indeed to expect a response, simply because one cannot expect all states to be constantly on active guard against contraventions of the UN Charter, least of all those states that Franck identified as the most unbiased: namely, small states that have no specific interest in the outcome of a dispute and see no advantage in siding with one of its parties. Lack of information, solidarity with allies, fear of adverse consequences, susceptibility to vote bribery, impartiality in order to support mediation, recognition of the futility of protest or simple indifference may well override well-intentioned support for a principled and properly oiled UN machine.[40]

35 Weisburd, *Use of Force*.

36 Concurring Michael Byers, book review, 'Recourse To Force: State Action Against Threats and Armed Attacks', 97 Am. JIL 721–5 (2003).

37 Richard K. Herrmann and Vaughn P. Shannon, 'Defending International Norms: The Role of Obligation, Material Interest, and Perception in Decision Making', 55 Int. Org. 621–54 (2001).

38 Henkin, *How Nations Behave*, at p. 58. See further D'Amato, *The Concept of Custom*, at p. 99.

39 This is a very common perception, with authors referring to each other. Compare Romana Sadurska, 'Threats of Force', 82 Am. JIL 239–68 (1988); at 254; Albrecht Randelzhofer, 'Art. 2(4)', in Bruno Simma (ed.), *The Charter of the United Nations: A Commentary* vol. I, 112–36 (2nd edn, 2002), at Mn. 38; Hilaire McCoubrey and Nigel D. White, *International Law and Armed Conflict* 58 (1992); White and Cryer, 'A Threat Too Far?', at 246; Anne Hsiu-An Hsiao, 'Is China's Policy to Use Force Against Taiwan a Violation of the Principle of Non-Use of Force in International Law?', 32 New Eng. LR 715–42 (1998), at 724; Henkin, *How Nations Behave*, at 136; Oscar Schachter, 'International Law: The Right of States to Use Armed Force', 82 Mich. LR 1620–6 (1984), at 1625; Ipsen, *Völkerrecht*, at §59 Mn. 19; Michael Bothe, 'Friedenssicherung und Kriegsrecht', in Wolfgang Graf Vitzthum (ed.), *Völkerrecht* 589–667 (3rd edn, 2004), at p. 600.

40 D'Amato, *The Concept of Custom*, at p. 70; Kelly, *Customary International Law*, at pp. 469–75, 519–23; Derek W. Bowett, 'International Incidents: New Genre or New Delusion?', 12 Yale JIL 386–95 (1987); Buzzini, 'Les Comportements Passifs des États',

It may be argued that silence based on such non-legal interests is still legally relevant because other governments do attach legal significance to silence no matter what motivated that silence. But the concern that silence might be construed as a permissive precedent is simply one legal motive for governments to voice their opinion. Other motives to remain silent (or alternatively, to speak up) compete with it. The question, then, is which of a set of factors dominate the choices of decision-makers in threat-related cases. This has not been investigated before, and therefore the case studies in this book include a short enquiry into what motivated state reactions. It is then possible to say which inferences about state abstentions are accurate.[41]

A final issue requires consideration. According to article 24 of the UN Charter, UN members have conferred on the Security Council the primary responsibility for the maintenance of international peace and security, and the Council acts on their behalf. To act against violations of article 2(4) falls squarely within the responsibilities of the Council under Chapter VII. This delegation of responsibility could mean that for the purposes of legally relevant practice, the judgment of the Security Council and necessarily that of its permanent members would hold special significance.[42] One way of seeing this would be to declare the Council's practice as 'representative' in the sense of the ICJ's *North Sea Continental Shelf* cases.[43] Applying such a theory, its formal resolutions as well as the stance of its individual members could be said to hold the front-row position in refining UN Charter law.

There are several problems with this approach. For one thing, there is little indication that the ICJ has given independent status to the acts of international organisations when determining customary law in force-related cases. It has consistently conceptualised custom as something done by and traceable back to states.[44] Its decision in the *North Sea Continental Shelf* cases did not relate to the practice of an international organisation. Even if it had, the practice of the Security Council is probably not 'very widespread and representative' and inclusive of

at 84–117; Olivier Corton, 'Breach and Evolution of Customary International Law on the Use of Force', in Cannizzaro and Palchetti, *Use of Force*, pp. 119–44, at pp. 131–4; Olivier Corton, 'The Controversies Over the Customary Prohibition on the Use of Force', 16 Eur. JIL 803–22 (2005), at 817–18; Cahin, *La Coutume Internationale*, at p. 345.

[41] For a discussion of results see below, chapter 8, at p. 257.

[42] Byers, *Recourse to Force*, at pp. 722–3.

[43] *North Sea Continental Shelf Cases*, at para. 73.

[44] Jan Klabbers, 'International Organizations in the Formation of Customary Law', in Cannizzaro and Palchetti, *Use of Force*, pp. 179–95, at pp. 188–91.

what the judgment called 'those States whose interests [are] specially affected'.[45] What the Court meant is that the practice of states to which the Geneva Convention on the Continental Shelf of 1958 was not open for signature, namely landlocked states, would not be relevant to demonstrate that article 6 of the treaty had hardened into general customary law. While their lack of participation was not legally relevant, that of the coastal states certainly was. Against this background, it would be difficult to argue that the Security Council had a stake in the rules of force that the wider UN community did not share, even more so if one keeps in mind that these rules have an acknowledged *erga omnes* quality. Given that military force is endemic in many regions of the world, there is a corresponding vast legacy of states outside the Security Council sharing a continuing interest in the scope of articles 2(4) and 51 of the UN Charter. Furthermore, interests may well diverge. There is an abundance of instances in which the General Assembly and the Security Council judged cases very differently; in fact, from the 1960s onwards when former colonies swelled the ranks of the plenary organ this happened increasingly often. Since the Indian seizure of Goa in 1961, Assembly and Council voting patterns regularly differ.[46] To speak of a genuine representation in the sense of the *North Sea Continental Shelf* cases would be misleading.

If Security Council members are particularly affected, it is as keepers of international peace. Article 24 of the UN Charter gives them the authority to maintain it, and perhaps this may be taken as a source of legitimacy for its expansion of competences under Chapter VII. But article 24 says nothing about giving sweeping treaty interpretation capacities to the Council.[47] It would be just as plausible for that function to be conferred on the UN's principle judicial organ, the ICJ, while the members kept the right to formal amendment of the UN Charter to themselves.[48] Finally, it stands to reason that the San Francisco signatories did not intend, and would not have accepted, that the permanent five could, by virtue of their veto capacity, place their own military activities outside the scope of article 2(4).

If one accepts the view that UN law is able to grow organically through practice, then it is only consistent to ask whether states

45 *North Sea Continental Shelf Cases*, at para. 73.

46 Thomas M. Franck, *Nation Against Nation: What Happened to the UN Dream and What the US Can Do About It* 53–8 (1985).

47 Jost Delbrück, 'Article 24', in Simma, *Commentary*, vol. I, at pp. 442–52.

48 See Chapter XVIII (articles 108 and 109) on the rules of amendment.

perhaps conferred interpretation capacities on the Security Council at a later stage. The practice of ignoring abstentions in Security Council votes and the development of peacekeeping operations spring to mind as innovations that members have generally accepted. But treaty interpretation in the hands of the Security Council seems not to be one of them. The division of labour between the Security Council and UN members has never been clear-cut. Since 1950, the General Assembly has recommended action on security-related issues, starting with the 'Uniting for Peace' resolution introduced by the USA during the Korean War. According to that resolution, the General Assembly may step in to assume Security Council responsibilities if the Council is unable to act.[49] Since the 1960s governments have increasingly chosen to work through non-UN channels, such as by direct diplomatic *communiqués* or through other international organisations. Prominent in security matters are the Organization of the Islamic Conference, the League of Arab States and the Non-aligned Movement. They serve to consolidate and communicate their views inside and outside the UN headquarters. It therefore seems that the UN's own practice does not support the notion that states have ceded to the Security Council exclusive authority to elaborate the content of articles 2(4) or 51. The Council was designed to be a political organ, deliberating above all on the appropriate response to international crises. It was not designed to be a judge or even a legislator.[50] While the UN seems to be a valuable forum for the exchange of opinion and for coordinating communal reaction, it is not the only one.[51] Legally relevant state practice is such that it embraces the usage of all UN members; the Security Council plays a supportive but not exclusive role.

The relationship between state practice and treaty

Having determined legally relevant state practice, the question arises what impact it has on the force regime of the UN Charter. Reference has already been made to the concept of customary law. Strictly speaking, however, state practice in our context is not an element of general custom. Reference to practice should help interpret article 2(4) of the

[49] A/RES/377(V) *Uniting for Peace* (3 Nov. 1950).

[50] Paul C. Szasz, 'The Security Council Starts Legislating', 96 Am. JIL 901–5 (2002), at 901.

[51] Erik Voeten, 'Outside Options and the Logic of Security Council Action', 95 Am. PSR 845–58 (2001).

UN Charter following article 31 of the Vienna Convention of the Law of Treaties. According to that article, 'subsequent practice' in the application of a treaty that 'establishes the agreement of the parties regarding its interpretation' shall be taken into account.[52] It serves as an indicator of what parties really mean by a provision. The signing of the Non-Proliferation Treaty, for example, arguably shed light on whether or not states conceived nuclear deterrence as a violation of UN law. The ICJ has confirmed the suitability of a dynamic interpretation in its *Namibia* advisory opinion of 1971, reasoning that:

> ... an international instrument has to be interpreted and applied within the framework of the entire legal system, prevailing at the time of the interpretation. In the domain to which the present proceedings relate, ... the *corpus iuris gentium* has been considerably enriched, and this the Court, if it is faithfully to discharge its functions, may not ignore.[53]

For this reason the ICJ readily accepted the proposition that abstention within the Security Council did not amount to a veto.[54] Accepting a dynamic interpretation is particularly useful when considering open-ended terms such as 'threat of force' and where changed circumstances, such as innovations in military technology, call for clarification. The practice of UN members forms a rich resource for filling the widening textual gap that has surfaced.[55]

What are the practical consequences of making a distinction between 'subsequent practice' and custom? The difference has to be seen in relation to the original treaty norm, article 2(4). It should be emphasised that state practice and legal opinion are crucial to give meaning to article 2(4), not as a means to challenge the Charter by derogatory force.

52 Article 31(3)(b) *Vienna Convention on the Law of Treaties*, 1155 UNTS 331 (23 May 1969). For comment see Anthony Aust, *Modern Treaty Law in Practice* 194–5 (2000); Karl Wolfram, *Vertrag und spätere Praxis im Völkerrecht* (1983); Georg Ress, 'Interpretation', in Simma, *Commentary*, vol. I, pp. 13–32, at Mn. 8–9; Mark E. Villiger, *Customary International Law and Treaties: A Manual on the Theory and Practice of the Interrelation of Sources* (2nd edn, 1997); Nancy Kontou, *The Termination and Revision of Treaties in the Light of New Customary Law* (1994).

53 *Legal Consequences for States of the Continued Presence of South Africa in Namibia (South-West Africa) Notwithstanding Security Council Resolution 276 (1970) (Advisory Opinion)*, 1971 ICJ Rep. 16 (21 Jun. 1971), at para. 53. See also Franck, *Recourse to Force*, at p. 8, Gray, *Use of Force*, at p. 8. Ress, *Interpretation*, at Mn. 26–33; Ipsen, *Völkerrecht*, at §11 Mn. 21.

54 *Namibia Advisory Opinion*, at para. 22.

55 Exemplary for the accretion of 'UN law' under constitutive instruments of international organisations, see Higgins, *Development of International Law*.

Since the normative content of article 2(4) is open to interpretation, it would be misguided to polarise state practice, as some form of the *rebus sic stantibus* rule, in its opposition. Rather, in view of its vagueness, the correct approach is that article 2(4) has first to be assessed in the light of the behaviour and expressed beliefs of states since 1945.[56] This is particularly appropriate for article 2(4). Few rules in international law have been affirmed as unanimously and consistently around the globe as the principle not to use and threaten force – in treaties, declarations, resolutions, constitutions and public speeches.[57] No state has opted to leave the UN for good, and none has directly challenged the validity of article 2(4). Newly independent states have readily endorsed it. As mentioned earlier, the San Francisco delegates broke with the past; they established among themselves a regime that is intolerant of what used to be called measures short of war. Today that regime is universally accepted. It therefore appears to follow that the basic condition of *opinio juris*, which for the formation of custom is subject to proof, is already fulfilled.[58] For article 2(4), the relationship between practice and treaty is that the opinion of states continues to be enclosed in the latter. At the heart of the matter then lies the question of how far this general consensus carries on into specific types of threats that plausibly fall under its purview. For example, communal reactions to naval demonstrations shed light on whether they are meaningfully understood as threats of force. This is the focus of subsequent chapters.

One objection to this conceptualisation is that it downplays the possibility of supervening custom. Following the ICJ, customary law and treaty law may exist side by side with different content,[59] but the latter cannot be fortified against all denial.[60] If new custom is openly defiant of older treaty law, then the conclusion must be that the treaty

[56] Compare the different presumptions underlying the arguments of Sadurska, 'Threats of Force', at 240; and arguing against her, White and Cryer, 'A Threat Too Far?', at 245–6: the authors base their arguments on the dichotomy between the Charter law, on the one hand, and state practice, on the other.

[57] See for a similar line of argument *Military and Paramilitary Activities*, paras. 186–90; White and Cryer, 'A Threat Too Far?', at 246.

[58] It may be worth noting that the 'Baxter paradox' may not be relevant here, even though the UN Charter was not declaratory of customary law in 1945. Post-treaty practice and opinion do not suffer from the problem that states cannot act on either of them outside their treaty obligations. See R. R. Baxter, 'Multilateral Treaties as Evidence of Customary International Law', 41 Brit. YBIL 275–300 (1965–6).

[59] *Military and Paramilitary Activities*, para. 175.

[60] For a survey of decisions see Kontou, *Termination and Revision*, at pp. 109–34.

has been overtaken by new law forged by new practice. This is the question of *desuetude*. In the context here, the question is at which point one should concede that subsequent practice no longer supports the 1945 consensus but departs from it.[61] That it has long passed this point is the thesis of a number of authors such as Michael Glennon. Glennon argues that in recent years we have witnessed the death of article 2(4) by a thousand cuts; if not the intervention in Kosovo in 1999, then the war in Iraq in 2003 certainly did the job.[62] 'State officials', he writes, 'may [act] utterly without regard to any treaty obligation and solely to advance an independent interest',[63] and therefore it is doubtful that state behaviour really relates to the UN Charter. Actual behaviour is often non-compliant behaviour and thus more likely derogatory custom-in-the-making.[64]

There is no point in returning here to the question of legally relevant state practice that to a large extent is part of Glennon's objection.[65] Suffice it to concentrate on the relationship between treaty and practice. In my view, the principle *pacta sunt servanda*, the described openness of the no-threat rule to a wide range of interpretations, and its relative status as a peremptory norm in international law should put some restraint on any hasty assumptions that that the no-threat rule is ailing as a whole.[66] There are further reasons. As Nancy Kontou has shown, in order to argue successfully for the revision or termination of

61 Kontou, *Termination and Revision*, at pp. 25–31; Byers, *Power of Rules*, at pp. 172–80; Villiger, *Customary International Law*, at Mn. 321–56. For the view that *jus cogens* norms are immune against derogation by non-compliant state practice see Oscar Schachter, 'Entangled Treaty and Custom', in Yoram Dinstein (ed.), *International Law at a Time of Perplexity* 717–38 (1989) at p. 734.

62 Michael J. Glennon, 'How International Rules Die', 93 Geo. LJ 939–91 (2005); Michael J. Glennon, 'Why the Security Council Failed', 82 F. Aff. 12–35 (2003); Michael J. Glennon, *Limits of Law, Prerogatives of Power: Interventionalism after Kosovo* (2001).

63 Glennon, *Limits of Law*, at p. 49.

64 Glennon, *How International Rules Die*, at pp. 972–80.

65 See the previous section and, for the sake of completeness, the famous dictum of the ICJ that: 'In order to deduce the existence of customary rules, the Court deems it sufficient that the conduct of States should, in general, be consistent with such rules, and that instances of State conduct inconsistent with a given rule should generally have been treated as breaches of that rule, not as indications of the recognition of a new rule. If a State acts in a way *prima facie* incompatible with a recognized rule, but defends its conduct by appealing to exceptions or justifications contained within the rule itself, then whether or not the State's conduct is in fact justifiable on that basis, the significance of that attitude is to confirm rather than to weaken the rule.' From *Military and Paramilitary Activities*, at para. 186.

66 Dissenting Sadurska, 'Threats of Force', passim.

a treaty, a state needs to demonstrate that, among other things, the new custom is different from that at the time of the conclusion of the original treaty, and that the parties did not intend to exclude that possibility.[67] It is necessary to show that parties no longer wish to apply the original treaty rules, and in practice, derogation takes the form of one or more parties advancing such a claim which then is explicitly or implicitly accepted by the other parties.[68] The thesis of Charter supervening custom fails this test. While one may concede that article 103 of the UN Charter literally does not afford protection against new customary law, there is little doubt that the UN signatories intended to bestow upon the treaty a permanent character, suitable for its purpose to establish a new post-war international order. While it is possible that the original resistance to change itself may be overcome through new custom,[69] there is too much evidence of continued participation and commitment to the UN Charter goals and principles over the past sixty years, as noted above, to make the thesis of a separately developed *opinio juris* plausible.[70] This evidence takes a mostly verbal form, but then again, so does the conclusion of treaties. Valid consent as a source of obligation equally underlies the formation of customary law, and as such, to ignore the relevance of continued communal consensus would be to take issue with international law itself. It may well be true that governments often pay lip service to the UN Charter. Talk is cheap. Hypocrisy is widespread. Knowledge of intentions is seldom perfect.[71] But this does not negate state's obligations according to the *modus vivendi* of the international legal system, which, for better or worse, currently does not require forthrightness to give rights and duties positive effect. The more appropriate view is that general consensus still underpins article 2(4) empirically, and it is this consensus which informs the systematic enquiry into state practice.[72]

Within that enquiry, another facet of the relationship between treaty and custom needs mentioning. Since the business is not one of ascertaining custom but of working within the established parameters of 'subsequent practice', there is, to the extent that it is still relevant

[67] Kontou, *Termination and Revision*, at pp. 146–9.

[68] *Ibid.*, at p. 145; Michael Akehurst, 'The Hierarchy of the Sources of International Law', 47 Brit. YBIL 273–85 (1974–5), at 275–6.

[69] Villiger, *Customary International Law*, at Mn. 324.

[70] Compare article 31(2) VCLT; Aust, *Modern Treaty Law in Practice*, at pp. 187–91.

[71] Glennon, *Limits of Law*, at pp. 56–60.

[72] In this sense *Military and Paramilitary Activities*, at para. 184.

today, no *Lotus* presumption in favour of lawfulness if state responses to different types of threats are not consistent.[73] Traditionally, the kindred principle *in dubio pro mitius* (in doubt for leniency) was said to assist treaty interpretation in international law. This principle demands that preference should be given to the interpretation that least impairs the sovereign freedom of parties. If the principle ever was persuasive – haven't states already given consent, and isn't one state's freedom another's lack of freedom? – it has arguably outlived its usefulness. The Vienna Convention's articles on interpretation, in 1969 unanimously held to be declaratory of customary law,[74] do not list it even as a supplementary means of interpretation. International courts, too, seem to have lost sight of it.[75] Therefore, should subsequent practice fail to inform the meaning of a treaty provision, no assumption is in place to give governments legal benediction. Other tools of interpretation are still available. In the unlikely event that they, too, have an unsuccessful outcome, then the law may be indeterminate but is not absent.[76]

The collection of state practice

Having discussed legally relevant practice and how it relates to the UN Charter, it is now possible to formulate a hypothesis which can be tested against empirical evidence. According to Karl Popper, in order to

73 *The Case of the S.S. Lotus (France* v. *Turkey), Merits*, 3 PCIJ Rep., Series A, No. 10 (7 Sep. 1927), at para. 18; *Legality of the Threat or Use of Nuclear Weapons (Advisory Opinion)*, 1996 ICJ Rep. 226 (8 Jul. 1996), at paras. 52, 62, 64–7, 97, 105E.

74 Eduardo Jiménez de Aréchaga, 'International Law in the Past Third of a Century', 159 Rec. des Cours, vol. I, 1–344 (1978), at 42.

75 For example, three judges opined in the *Arrest Warrant* case that 'the [*Lotus*] dictum represents the high watermark of *laissez-faire* in international relations, and an era that has been significantly overtaken by other tendencies' (emphasis in original). See *Case Concerning the Arrest Warrant of 11 April 2000 (Democratic Republic of Congo* v. *Belgium), Merits, Joint Separate Opinion of Judges Higgins, Koojimans and Burgenthal*, 2002 ICJ Rep. 2, at para. 51 (14 Feb. 2002); Rudolf Bernhardt, 'Interpretation in International Law', 2 Enc. Pub. IL 1416–26 (1995), at 1419; Georg Dahm, Jost Delbrück and Rüdiger Wolfrum, *Völkerrecht* vol. I/1, 222–3 (2nd edn, 1988); Hersch Lauterpacht, 'Restrictive Interpretation and the Principle of Effectiveness in the Interpretation of Treaties', 26 Brit. YBIL 48–85 (1949).

76 On the controversial issue of *non liquet* that this raises see Daniel Bodansky, '*Non Liquet* and the Incompleteness of International Law', in Laurence Boisson de Chazournes and Philippe Sands (eds.), *International Law, the International Court of Justice and Nuclear Weapons* 153–70 (1999); Hersch Lauterpacht, *The Function of Law in the International Community* 76–9 (1933).

be scientific, any theory a researcher proposes has to be *falsifiable*.[77] That is, in the examination of evidence, there must be an empirical outcome that could convince the researcher that his or her theory is wrong.[78] If one were to apply the results of this chapter so far, the hypothesis would be as follows: *states have consistently protested against the use of military threats of type* X. The dependent variable is the extent of protest or approval of states, which in turn is a proxy for consent. The corresponding null hypothesis would be that: *states have consistently approved, or have protested inconsistently against, military threats of type* X. In such a case one could infer that threats of type X do not fall under the purview of article 2(4) of the UN Charter. As noted earlier, the wider proposition that threats of force are prohibited in general has already been established.

In order to test the hypothesis, it is necessary at the outset to address three preliminary questions

1. What amounts to approval or protest?
2. What does consistency mean in this context?
3. What type of threats X, Y, or Z, should be examined?

The first question is quickly answered. For the purposes of this study, *protest* is taken to mean a formal statement or action expressing dissent or disapproval.[79] On the other hand, to *approve* is to give formal sanction, to officially agree.[80] In both cases it will be deemed sufficient if the view of a state may be plausibly inferred through a prior conduct of the state in question and the particular circumstances. There is no strict requirement for an official communication. Out of line with the general view held in the literature, silence is treated neither as approval nor as protest. As discussed above, it is submitted that in the absence of proof, it would be premature to assume that silence of states is the same as approval. It may equally reflect indifference, neutrality or indecision.[81]

Legally relevant state practice must be reasonably *consistent* over time, or, in the words of the ICJ, the relevant acts must 'amount to a settled practice'.[82] For present purposes, the relevant timeframe begins on Wednesday, 24 October 1945, when the UN Charter entered into force.

[77] Karl R. Popper, *Logik der Forschung* chapter 4 (7th edn, 1982) [1934].
[78] Gary King, Robert O. Keohane and Sydney Verba, *Designing Social Inquiry: Scientific Inference in Qualitative Research* 19, 100 (1994).
[79] *Black's Law Dictionary* 1260 (8th edn, 2004). [80] *Black's Law Dictionary*, p. 111.
[81] For a discussion of results see below, chapter 8, at p. 257.
[82] *North Sea Continental Shelf Cases*, at para. 77.

It is post-Charter practice that sheds light on the then novel prescriptions of article 2(4). So much is clear. However, the time period necessary for custom to 'settle', the ICJ itself declared, varies from case to case and cannot be generalised.[83] While it may make sense to require different consistency over time for different types of rules, strictly speaking this means that there is no definition and that any time horizon is potentially sufficient. This leaves the researcher with a 'Catch-22' situation: it is consistency that custom requires, yet the lack of a relevant timeframe itself renders the determination of consistency in custom illusory. It follows that the requirement that state practice is consistent, according to the current standards of international law, is not falsifiable. There is no testable hypothesis which can be shown to be wrong.[84] A testable hypothesis requires commitment to a specific standard, yet international law does not provide one.[85] For any study on state practice for which no agreed relevant timeframe exists, therefore, researchers have no alternative but to define one themselves.

For this study, the relevant timeframe is from October 1945 to the present. There is no decisive turning point, not even the end of the Cold War, that would lead to an expectation of radical changes in the way states assess the permissibility of acts in potential breach of the UN Charter. That is not to say that governments' preferences have not changed, but rather that change, too, is subject to the same enquiry. Practice is consistent if in the period under consideration it follows a recurring pattern, such that firm expectations of behaviour have formed. It is not consistent if it changes over time, and may simply reflect a lack of consistency, rather than new practice, if it changed only a few months ago.[86]

83 *North Sea Continental Shelf Cases*, at para. 74. For an account see D'Amato, *The Concept of Custom*, at pp. 56–61, 91–8.

84 Concurring Kelly, *Customary International Law*, at p. 507. See the related comments on custom and time by Martti Koskenniemi, *From Apology to Utopia* 399–421 (1989); James Crawford and Thomas Viles, 'International Law on a Given Day', in K. Ginther *et al.* (eds.), *Völkerrecht zwischen normativem Anspruch und politisher Realität: Festschrift für Karl Zemanek zum 65. Geburtstag* 45–68 (1994). This could be called a time paradox. But note the 'chronological paradox' described by Byers, *Power of Rules*, at pp. 130–3, which has a different meaning.

85 The same type of paradox applies to other elements of custom. The common response of many lawyers is to remain uncommitted to a specific standard. For example, it is said that a 'considerable' majority of states are necessary to render a new rule universal. See Higgins, *Development of International Law*, at p. 6. However, no matter how well intended, this is a poorly concealed capitulation to conjecture.

86 It is very common, but under the rules of customary law problematic, to attribute to the latest developments of practice a special significance. Of course the most recent

The sampling of relevant state practice encounters an identical problem. We do not know in advance what *type of threats* (for example, X, Y, Z) amount to a threat of force in the sense of article 2(4). Should one include acts of propaganda, military build-ups, troop mobilisations or the testing of nuclear weapons? If so, under what circumstances? Arriving at a definition is precisely what the researcher hopes to derive from state practice, yet there is no objective standard indicating along what lines information on it should be collected and evaluated.[87] In theory, there are an infinite number of configurations in which state practice could have aligned itself, i.e., revolving around regional differences, the issues at stake, the historical circumstances, the type of government, the weapons involved and so on. The problem is compounded by the inherent elusiveness of the term 'threat' itself.[88] A selection is inevitable.

In the present study, a preliminary survey of historical case data suggested that the best approach is to examine state practice according to the following categories: first, open threats to extract concessions; second, demonstrations of force; and third, threats in self-defence. The axes of enquiry are thus, first, how a threat is conveyed (word versus action), and second, in what conflict setting a threat is issued (offensive versus defensive). The underlying theory is that states differentiate between types of threats, and that in identifying the law this should be given due consideration. Previous analyses appear wrongly to assume that there is only one way how threats may manifest themselves. This

developments may indeed indicate a change of heart and that the expectations of states have shifted. But there is an inherent tension with the requirement for consistency that is irresolvable as long as time requirements are not predefined.

87 In the international law literature, ignoring selection biases has generally led studies to focus on a few nations or cases that received abundant media coverage. See Gray, *Use of Force*, at p. 10.

88 In a recent study of US coercive diplomacy since 1989, Barry Blechman and Tamara Wittes outlined what could be called a threat continuum. 'U.S. armed forces', they write, 'have been used demonstratively in support of diplomatic objectives in literally more than a thousand incidents during this period, ranging from major humanitarian operations to joint exercises with the armed forces of friendly nations to minor logistical operations in support of the United Nations (UN) or other multinational or national organizations. Moreover, the deployment and operations of U.S. forces in Europe, and in Southwest and East Asia on a continuing basis throughout the period, are intended to support U.S. foreign policy by deterring foreign leaders from pursuing hostile aims and by reassuring friends and allies.' See Barry M. Blechman and Tamara Cofman Wittes, 'The Threat and Use of Force in American Foreign Policy Since 1989', in Paul C. Stern (ed.), *International Conflict Resolution after the Cold War* 90–122 (2000), at p. 93 (footnotes omitted).

leads to problems. For example, if states consistently protest against demonstrations of force but never against verbal threats, not to differentiate the two types of threats would result in erroneous generalisations.[89] A brief look at the available evidence strongly suggests a differentiated approach. Indeed there is no reason why, in a way that is undisputed for the use of force, variations of threat behaviour should not each be given their proper consideration.[90]

What does state practice support? The two axes of enquiry may be translated into the following four propositions:

1. The proposition that article 2(4) prohibits *open threats to extract concessions*, where state A promises the first use or a higher level use of armed force on a particular issue under dispute with state B. A subset case is the ultimatum, where state A offers state B a 'last clear chance' to give in on a specific demand.
2. The proposition that article 2(4) prohibits *demonstrations of force*, where state A, in the form of non-routine military deployments, build-ups, manoeuvres, tests or other militarised acts, signals preparedness and resolve to use armed force on a particular issue under dispute with state B. The initiation of militarised acts in a period of high tension is a firm indication that a demonstration of force is in play.
3. The proposition that the right to self-defence in article 51 justifies state A to threaten with force, as defined above, in response to a threat of force by state B. Threats resorted to in this context are referred to as *countervailing threats*.[91]
4. The proposition that the countervailing threat of state A against state B is unlawful in *protracted conflicts*, where parties have (i) a long-standing and recurring history of previous escalatory clashes and (ii) are predisposed to perceive any militarised act by their long-time adversary as provocation that necessitates a firm response.

The propositions simultaneously serve as case definitions, i.e., they allow the classification of historical incidents as practice or precedent. Each of the four propositions follows a rationale as explained below.

89 See e.g. Sadurska, 'Threats of Force'.

90 As to the corresponding variations governing the use of force, compare the notion of 'indirect aggression' and other forms of force addressed in A/RES/3314 (XXIX) *Definition of Aggression* (14 Dec. 1974).

91 It is taken for granted here that a state has the right to resort to a threat if an armed attack has already occurred or is under way. This is what even a narrow reading of article 51 of the UN Charter accords to individual states as long as the Security Council has not taken over responsibility.

Propositions 1 and 2 imply that threats are either communicated explicitly and clearly, or through some militarised action that signals readiness to resort to force to 'settle' an international dispute. Expressed as a single formula, the requirement is for either strong words or strong deeds, or both. That is a simplification, but one that is intended to convey the essence of what the no-threat principle is all about. As a result, the present study confines the empirical survey to cases where threats of force are clearly attributable to a foreign policy objective under dispute with another state. The threat forms part of a message that the target state risks exposure to force if it does not back down. An element of coercion is at play.[92] Correspondingly, the simple girding for war without a bargaining dimension does not qualify, nor do mere precautionary measures. The need for an international dispute dimension will usually also exclude 'micro threats' between, for example, individual soldiers in combat or jets involved in a dogfight, to the extent that they do not form part of a larger strategy.[93] However, the foreign policy objectives pursued need not be communicated clearly. Decisive is the existence of an international dispute over an issue, for example, over the construction of a missile base or over the delimitation of a common border. As will become apparent, the cases of clear-cut demands, deadlines and explicit military threat that are the characteristics of an ultimatum are the exception in modern practice. This fact cannot be ignored if the intent is to provide answers to the legal questions raised by the actual dealings of states with one another today.

Propositions 3 and 4 flow from another thesis. The central issue is whether states distinguish in practice between the deterrence model and the spiral model explained in chapter 2. The two models provide fairly intuitive but contending views on what is prudent and legitimate conduct in international crises. The idea here is that states differentiate between cases where the deterrence model is more appropriate and those in which it is not. If the deterrence model holds, they will accept the threat of force to deter an aggressor. A possible example is that of Kuwait in the 1990s being entitled to promise the use of force to preclude an Iraqi invasion. If the spiral model holds, bystander states will deny either side in a conflict the right any further provocation and will

[92] Both compellence and deterrence are included. Force does not have to be promised to change the status quo (revisionism), but it may also have the objective of preventing others from changing it (conservatism).

[93] A naval blockade, e.g., would usually be part of such a larger strategy.

condemn military threats and countervailing threats whether or not they are technically self-defensive. The dispute between Pakistan and India over Kashmir is an example. Testing propositions 3 and 4 will reveal whether the theory is accurate along the lines of protracted conflicts. Edward Azar, Paul Jureidini and Ronald McLaurin have described the properties of protracted conflicts in the context of the Middle East:

> Protracted conflicts are hostile interactions which extend over long periods of time with sporadic outbreaks of open warfare fluctuating in frequency and intensity. They are conflict situations in which the stakes are very high – the conflicts involve whole societies and act as agents for defining the scope of national identity and social solidarity. While they may exhibit some breakpoint during which there is a cessation of overt violence, they linger on in time and have no distinguishable point of termination.[94]

The definition is not applied here with the same stringency. What is important for present purposes is that the parties are particularly sensitive to any militarised acts of their rivals and that unilateral 'provocations', based on the record of conflict between the parties, are likely to set off a spiral of violence. A feature of protracted conflicts is that the aggressor-victim distinction is hard to apply, and that blame is often attributable to both sides. The self-defence reference, which is implicitly premised on the ability to distinguish between aggressor and victim, does not suit these situations, and states, aware of this difficulty, could be said to interpret article 2(4) accordingly.

A word about the scope of this study is in order. Since it is impossible to examine state practice along all possible axes, there are obvious limitations to the number of inferences that can be made. This study will not provide answers, for example, on the legality of threats to protect citizens abroad, or threats directed against non-state actors. Some limitations also follow from the case definitions. As previously noted, coercion is not part of the case definition, thus the legality of threats outside that context must remain in doubt. Insights into some questions may be gained as a by-product of enquiry (for example, whether compellence is more often condemned than deterrence), and some observations may be pervasive enough to exclude mere coincidence. But any such assertions will have to be treated with caution.

[94] Edward E. Azar, Paul Jureidini and Ronald McLaurin, 'Protracted Social Conflict: Theory and Practice in the Middle East', 8 J. Pal. Stud. 41–60 (1978), at 50.

The sources of analysis

To date no comprehensive dataset is available on the occurrence of military threats worldwide, although by any standard they have been a prominent feature of world affairs since the beginning of the nineteenth century. According to Daniel Jones, Stuart Bremer and David Singer, states have been engaged in over 1,550 militarised interstate disputes during the period 1945–2001, of which some 450 took the exclusive form of threats or displays of force. Their study also shows that the second half of the twentieth century witnessed the highest occurrence of militarised interstate disputes since 1812, running parallel to the increase of states from then roughly twenty-four to nearly two hundred at present.[95]

Although political scientists have become interested in phenomena short of war, they have seldom made military threats the exclusive focus in their studies of international conflicts. Jones *et al.*, coded threats, displays and small-scale uses of force as essentially an explanatory variable for conflicts where the danger of war became explicit and overt.[96] Their study takes into account military threats only if they were the stand-alone tool of hostility; threats that were overtaken by the use of force or full-scale war within the same conflict were omitted.[97] Other studies, particularly during the Cold War, focused much attention on the concept of rational deterrence, seeking to determine when so-called immediate deterrence strategy works and when it does not.[98] A perusal of studies also reveals that there is no operational gold

[95] Daniel M. Jones, Stuart A. Bremer and J. David Singer, 'Militarized Interstate Disputes, 1816–1992: Rationale, Coding Rules, and Empirical Patterns', 15 Conf. Mgmt & PS 163–213 (1996). For their definition of 'militarized interstate disputes' see *ibid.*, at 168. For the data from 1812–2001 (version 3.02) see the updated Correlates of War Project (COW) database at http://www.correlatesofwar.org. For an historical study see Peter Karsten, Peter D. Howell and Artes Frances Allen, *Military Threats: A Systematic Historical Analysis of the Determinants of Success* (1984).

[96] Charles S. Gochman and Zeev Maoz, 'Militarized Interstate Disputes 1812–1976: Procedures, Patterns and Insights', 28 J. Conf. Resol. 585–616 (1984).

[97] Jones *et al.*, 'Militarized Interstate Disputes', at 186.

[98] The pioneering study is Alexander L. George and Richard Smoke, *Deterrence in American Foreign Policy: Theory and Practice* (1974). Other examples are Paul Huth and Bruce Russett, 'What Makes Deterrence Work? Cases from 1900 to 1980', 36 World P. 496–526 (1984); Robert Mandel, 'The Effectiveness of Gunboat Diplomacy', 30 Int. Stud. Q. 59–76 (1986); Alexander L. George and William E. Simons (eds.), *The Limits of Coercive Diplomacy* 270–92 (2nd edn, 1994); Frank P. Harvey, 'Practicing Coercion: Revisiting Successes and Failures Using Boolean Logic and Comparative Methods', 43 J. Conf. Resol. 840–71 (1999).

standard among scholars of international relations as to what constitutes a military threat. Jones *et al.*, for example, identify verbal indications of hostile intent as threats of force, while the physical display of force and the actual use of force are treated as distinct features of conflict.[99] None of the studies records third-party reactions along the lines of approval or condemnation. Nor do available datasets properly reflect the specific issues at stake, which defy easy coding.

Overall, this means that the standards developed by political scientists are not readily applicable to the exigencies of the international law approach, which cannot take the definition of threats of force for granted and must take into account communal reaction. The most useful approach turns out to be to rely on the narrative description of interstate disputes themselves. The best source of such descriptions is provided by Michael Brecher and Jonathan Wilkenfeld, whose compilation of 443 interstate crisis narratives between 1918 and 2003 relies on the painstaking combing of historical documents and news archives.[100]

According to the International Crisis Behaviour (ICB) coding rules of the two authors, a foreign policy crisis is defined as an event that fulfils three conditions: (1) a threat to basic values; (2) a high probability of involvement in military hostilities; and (3) an awareness of finite time for response to the threat.[101] Taken at face value, none of these three conditions suggest that the ICB database excludes threats that would be relevant for present purposes. That is, there is little indication of a selection bias. One may assume with confidence that a credible threat of force will increase the probability of military conflict, that it will put the target state under considerable pressure to respond promptly and that states do not issue threats when their core national interests are not at stake. There may be a problem with propaganda or threats within the context of lengthy crises where the level of tension is already high and thus sporadic threats do not really increase the chances of armed conflict. Such rhetorical charges and ritualised threats, however, are

[99] Jones *et al.*, 'Militarized Interstate Disputes', at 170–2.

[100] Michael Brecher and Jonathan Wilkenfeld, *A Study of Crisis* 40–64 (1997). The latest version (at the time of writing 6.0, Jan. 2006) of the ICB database is available online at http://www.cidcm.umd.edu/icb/.

[101] Michael Brecher, 'State Behavior in International Crises: A Model', 23 J. Conf. Resol. 446–80 (1979), at 447; Brecher and Wilkenfeld, *A Study of Crisis*, at p. 3. On the difficulties of definition see Warren Phillips and Richard Rimkunas, 'The Concept of Crisis in International Politics', 15 J. Conf. Resol. 259–72 (1978).

arguably not of primary concern. If a bluff or minor incident carries enough symbolic gravity to trigger a crisis, then it is included. The ICB database focuses on the subset of militarised interstate disputes where the likelihood of war is real and palpable, where governments perceive the stakes as being high enough to risk hostile encounter.[102]

A problem often encountered in this context is the difficulty of breaking down long rivalries into chains of successive crises. Indeed, this problem is well known to scholars of militarised conflicts. The number of casualties per unit of time gives clues as to the use of force, but for military threats there is no tangible equivalent. The trigger for a crisis is usually easier to detect. For example, the USA plunged into a crisis on 16 October 1962 at the moment CIA photographic intelligence revealed ongoing Soviet construction of nuclear missile bases on Cuba. However, the end to a crisis is rarely as precipitous. In their codebook Brecher and Wilkenfield code the end of a crisis as when 'the last crisis actor ... perceive[s] a decline toward pre-crisis levels of threat and potential for military hostilities'.[103] While this hardly makes coding easy, it is the best option available in a world of imperfect information. This means for this study that, for example, the various episodes in Iraq regarding no-fly zones or in Kuwait in the 1990s are separate cases, in response to each of which states are assumed to have formed a separate opinion. This is necessarily to the disadvantage of a view which would favour assessment of legality in the light of a lengthy past record, for example, that Iraq was a notorious norm-breaker at the time of invasion in 2003. It is certainly true that crises are interlinked, but for practical purposes it is impossible to interpret communal reaction as a reflection of decades of near military encounter. The behaviour on trial, so to speak, in the court of world opinion must be construed narrowly to arrive at sensible conclusions.

Drawing from the ICB crisis narratives, it is possible to assemble a new dataset that lists all interstate threats from October 1945 to December 2003.[104] Of the 335 international crises in that period, 111

[102] Russell J. Leng and J. David Singer, 'Militarized Interstate Crises: The BCOW Typology and its Applications', 32 Int. Stud. Q. 155–73 (1987) at 159. This is why there is a gap between the COW data and the ICB data. The former operates with a lower threshold for militarised interstate disputes. Fishing boat incidents are a case in point. The ICB dataset tends to exclude such incidents because it requires the presence of an international crisis.

[103] Brecher and Wilkenfeld, *A Study of Crisis*, at p. 48.

[104] The case studies rely on an earlier ICB case pool up to December 2002. Three new entries (Iran Nuclear 2002, Haifa Suicide Bombing 2003 and Syria–Turkey 1998 as

or one-third fulfil the case definitions spelled out above (see the annex for capsule summaries). These form the pool of legally relevant cases for the present study. The final section of this chapter is devoted to the question of how these cases ought to be compared and appraised.

The appraisal of state practice

History, according to Thomas Carlyle, is a distillation of rumour.[105] Therefore, historical analogies may be misleading whenever the events being examined are more different than alike. Moreover, as anyone in the business of collecting historical data will attest, gathering, classifying and analysing incidents is a difficult undertaking. Many cases defy easy categorisation.[106] Threats of force are no exception. The purpose of this section is to discuss the necessary choices involved.

A first step concerns the *necessity of sampling*. Several practical hurdles hamper the apparently desirable statistical-correlative analysis of the cases. The reaction of third states, the dependent variable in the present study, may be determined by an array of factors that one may not be able to account for, at least not in the context of quantitative research. Explanatory variables such as the strategic environment, friend or foe, risks of involvement, room for leverage, domestic support, personal adversity between leaders or peer pressure are hard to quantify, and data over a time span of sixty years is sparse.[107] For practical purposes, only a small number of cases can be studied in depth paying proper attention to the full set of factors that determine protest and approval. In view of the large number of incidents in UN history involving the threat or use of force, some form of sampling is inevitable. From the case pool gathered, twenty-four incidents provide the material for a comparative case study approach.[108] Statistical logic demands that the sampling is

addendum) were included in the annex, but came too late to be incorporated in the random case selection (see below).

105 Quoted from the *Oxford Dictionary of Quotations* 159 (4th edn, 1992).

106 Vesna Danilovic, 'Conceptual and Selection Bias Issues in Deterrence', 45 J. Conf. Resol. 97–125 (2001).

107 George and Smoke, *Deterrence in American Foreign Policy*, at p. 91. For a discussion of the array of contextual aspects complicating quantitative analysis see George and Simons, *The Limits of Coercive Diplomacy*, at pp. 270–92.

108 On the case study approach of 'structured, focused comparison' see Alexander L. George and Andrew Bennett, *Case Studies and Theory Development in the Social Sciences* 67–72 (2005).

representative of the case pool. Accordingly, with two exceptions (Kosovo 1999 and Iraq 2002–3), cases were randomly selected.

One might well object that the approach of random selection is too narrow-minded. The 'value' of cases as precedents varies in real life, and therefore a focus on major cases is more meaningful. Indeed, governments may be said to rely on important historical analogies to form their expectations of what states are entitled to do and how challenges to the law might be resisted.[109] During the Cold War, the practice of the Soviet Union and the USA was arguably more relevant to a greater number of states than, say, the practice between Uganda and Kenya. It is therefore tempting to focus on 'leading instances' of state practice, as Thomas Franck has done.[110] But this leads inevitably to the question of what a leading instance is. It stands to reason that precedents are not equally important for all states. Certainly the practice of India is more relevant to Pakistan than to Peru. What criteria could be used to justify a selection? Being aware that 'reason is the servant of the passions',[111] researchers should be wary of inviting an unintended bias that sways results in their favour.[112] The consensual basis of the UN Charter in any event does not seem to justify a particular selection, either towards leading cases, leading nations or leading times or places. In order to be representative of UN members, post-Charter practice sampling should remain blinded as to the perceived watershed quality of some crises.[113]

That said, targeted selection can make sense for the very reason that it may be used to investigate the gap between high-profile and low-profile cases. As noted above, Kosovo and Iraq were deliberately

[109] Yaacov Y. I. Vertzberger, 'Foreign Policy Decisionmakers As Practical-Intuitive Historians: Applied History and Its Shortcomings', 30 Int. Stud. Q. 223–47 (1986).

[110] Franck, *Recourse to Force*, at p. 52.

[111] David Hume, *A Treatise upon Human Nature* book 2, part 3 (1992) [1739], quoted from the *Oxford Dictionary of Quotations* 355 (4th edn, 1992).

[112] On the problem of selection bias see Barbara Geddes, 'How the Cases You Choose Affect the Answers You Get: Selection Bias in Comparative Politics', 2 Pol. Analysis 131–50 (1990); David Collier and James Mahoney, 'Insights and Pitfalls: Selection Bias in Qualitative Work', 49 World P. 56–91 (1996); Christopher H. Achen and Duncan Snidal, 'Rational Deterrence Theory and Comparative Case Studies', 41 World P. 143–69 (1989), at 160–3; However, random sampling is sometimes the wrong choice when dealing with small-*n* studies. See e.g. King *et al.*, *Designing Social Inquiry*, at pp. 124–8.

[113] A more plausible reason to focus on high-profile cases would be that they alone prompt universal reactions from UN member states, thus yielding a better picture of communal opinion than low profile cases ever do. But this is an assumption, and ignoring cases with low reaction rates not only takes the irrelevance of silence for granted but also invites a selection bias of unknown direction.

selected for inclusion in the present study as both are illustrative of a host of attributes that are usually missing in unexceptional cases, such as Security Council involvement. As long as there are enough representative case studies left and the reason for their choice is made explicit, the reader should be presented with a balanced appraisal of state practice.

For each of the three basic threat conditions described above – open, demonstrated and countervailing – there are eight cases clustered in a group. Regarding the first two threat conditions, demonstrations of force and open threats were treated as two mutually exclusive types of threats. No case in one group is included in the other. Also, cases with countervailing behaviour were excluded from the first two case clusters and pooled in the third group for separate analysis. This makes it possible to study communal reactions to each type of threat in isolation.

A difficulty arises out of the fact that although the distinction between types of threats is real in practice, states sometimes use several types in conjunction. For example, in 2002–3 the USA communicated its resolve to use force against Iraq both through diplomatic channels and through concentrations of its troops in Kuwait. When states employed open and demonstrative threats together, it was therefore necessary to classify cases according to which type of threat was preponderant in determining the perception of third parties. It seems appropriate, for example, that troop deployments to Kuwait served a supportive rather than autonomous function. Open threats are geared towards achieving a specific result and usually precede demonstrations of force by some time, while demonstrations of force tend to be more vague. Their objective is often not openly stated but merely implied. Developing criteria to separate countervailing from non-countervailing cases was also necessary. Indicative factors were threat credibility, crisis initiation and the intensity of military threats compared with others. For example, in the Turkish-Cypriot missile crisis in 1997–8, Greece voiced a single warning in response to Turkey's repeated promise to conduct air strikes against Cyprus if it installed anti-aircraft missiles on the island. The Greek reaction was a counter-threat, but appeared negligible in view of Turkey's military preponderance and initiative. This was also the perception of third parties such as the EU, and accordingly the classification as an 'open threat case' seemed sensible.

It scarcely needs mentioning that classification is sometimes difficult and that, as so often in practice, there are no 'pure' cases. To filter out other 'confounding factors', such as involvement of the UN Security

Council or the existence of humanitarian motives for an intervention, would mean to reduce the cases available for examination to a small fraction of the overall case pool. In this sense the three groups created are good but by no means perfect bases for hypothesis testing. That said, the three groups may be summarised as follows: (a) Explicit threats, excluding counter-threat scenarios; (b) demonstrations of force, excluding counter-threat scenarios; and (c) explicit threats or demonstrations of force exclusively in counter-threat scenarios. About one-quarter of all cases fall under each of types (a) and (b), while threats of type (c) account for half of the total. The ratio between types (a) and (b) disregarding countervailing context is 50:61.

Having lined up the cases, the next step is to specify the *mode of analysis*. A comparative study approach requires that each case is examined along the same criteria. In this analysis, each case study is a stand-alone historical record of communal reaction. Three dimensions are investigated each time:

1. What constituted the threat?
2. What was the third party reaction to that threat?
3. What factors prompted that reaction?

The first and second dimensions are matter of hard fact.[114] They make it possible to say which threats states treat as UN Charter violations. In this regard, it should be clear that only those facts are relevant that formed the basis for communal reaction. The fact, for example, that there was no evidence for weapons of mass destruction in Iraq prior to the invasion in 2003 is certainly legally relevant: pre-emptive self-defence becomes implausible as a basis for justification. But, obviously, this information was not available to UN members at the time when intervention was at risk, and therefore it is not relevant in the case study description. Likewise, learning later that a threat was a bluff cannot matter.[115]

[114] Primarily the following sources were consulted: The International Crisis Behavior database (ICB), the UN Yearbook (UNYB), the UN Official Document System (ODS), the UN General Assembly Official Records (GAOR), the UN Security Council Official Records (SCOR), the Foreign Broadcast Information Service (FBIS), the Foreign Relations of the United States (FRUS), and the New York Times Historical Archive (NYT). The repeated reliance on these sources ensured a minimum of consistency in description across case studies.

[115] The reliance on newspaper articles and foreign ministry documents throughout the case studies follows the same rationale: to make sure that the account of events was a close approximation of what bystander states knew at the time of the crisis.

The first and second dimension also make it possible to test the hypothesis that silence, as discussed earlier, is tantamount to approval. If silence implied consent, one would expect bystander governments to change from silence to explicit condemnation when faced with behaviour that runs counter to that acquiesced to before. If the same majority remains silent on competing claims, the inference of approval is false. For example, states faced with the claims of a twelve-mile and a fifty-mile territorial sea cannot plausibly acquiesce to both.

Study of the third dimension gives answer to the question of whether the international response was, by any measurement undertaken, caused by legal concerns or by ulterior motives. The reasoning applied is one of *Realpolitik*: what material interests were at stake, and how could individual states or the UN be said to have acted on those grounds? If there were no overriding geopolitical reasons at work, then one can be confident that governments indeed expressed something close to their 'settled' legal views. Here the analysis becomes partly conjecture. Ultimately, the true legal views will almost always have to be inferred from the circumstances. At least in threat-related cases, governments rarely frame their communications in purely legal terms and remain vague in naming exactly the action they condemn or approve. For this reason, for example, it is usually difficult to differentiate between reactions to threats and actual uses of force, various forms of threats within the same crisis, or even other possible infringements of international law such as the right to self-determination, self-defence, non-intervention, proportionality, and so on. These can be viewed as limitations that are inherent in any investigation of customary law.

Three final comments are in order. First, it is worth emphasising that the case studies do not contain a legal appraisal of given threats. Rather they provide evidence of state reactions to threats, only the accumulation of which allows valid inferences about the content of articles 2(4) and 51 of the UN Charter. The temptation to assess the lawfulness of state actions 'on the spot' at the case study stage should be resisted because it would be methodologically inconsistent. The content of the law reveals itself from the aggregated set of individual cases. The paradox that custom can only be identified in retrospect, so to speak through the rear-view mirror, is again an inherent feature of the notion of customary law.[116]

[116] Crawford and Viles, *International Law on a Given Day*.

Second, many international crises involve actors whose status under international law is contentious: the divided sovereignty of the two Koreas; the two Vietnams; the two Chinas; and many colonies bound to achieve independence at some stage enjoyed only partial recognition. Taiwan today is not a state, principally because it officially declares that it is not one.[117] It is another question, however, whether Taiwan enjoys the protection of article 2(4) of the UN Charter. The article in principle applies only between UN members in their 'international relations' with one another. However, there is some debate on whether the non-use of force principle, and the no-threat rule it contains, also applies to *de facto* regimes and *de facto* international boundaries.[118] Rosalyn Higgins points out, in regard to the 1961 Indian takeover of the Portuguese colony of Goa, that:

> The Charter reference to Article 2(4) to 'territorial integrity' must be taken to refer to well established *de facto* possession, and not to *de jure* title. Were this not so, attacks would be permitted in every boundary dispute, in every dispute to territorial title. Consequently, even if the Portuguese title to Goa was in doubt, an attack against its *de facto* possession is not justifiable under the Charter.[119]

In a study of the subject in 1968, Jochen Frowein, too, concluded that article 2(4) must apply to 'pacified' *de facto* regimes and that state practice lends support to that view.[120] It is established that in order to retain statehood, exactly defined or undisputed boundaries are not necessary.[121] Not only would the UN Charter afford no protection to entities of near-state quality otherwise, it would also have the

[117] James Crawford, *The Creation of States in International Law* 219–21 (2nd edn, 2006).

[118] A/RES/2625 (XXV) *Declaration on the Principles of International Law concerning Friendly Relations and Co-operation Among States In Accordance With the Charter of the United Nations* (24 Oct. 1970) declares that: 'Every State has the duty to refrain from the threat or use of force to violate the existing international boundaries of another State or as a means of solving international disputes, including territorial disputes and problems concerning frontiers of States.'

[119] Higgins, *Development of International Law*, at p. 187. See for the problem (and its avoidance) before the ICJ *Case Concerning the Land and Maritime Boundary Between Cameroon and Nigeria (Cameroon* v. *Nigeria), Merits*, 2002 ICJ Rep. 3 (10 Oct. 2002), at paras. 308–24. See Christine Gray, 'The Use and Abuse of the International Court of Justice: Cases Concerning the Use of Force After Nicaragua', 14 Eur. JIL 867–905 (2003), at 882–4.

[120] Jochen A. Frowein, *Das de Facto-Regime im Völkerrecht: Eine Untersuchung zur Rechtstellung 'Nichtanerkannter Staaten' und Ähnlicher Gebilde* 66–9 (1968). See further Ian Brownlie, *International Law and the Use of Force by States* 379–83 (1963).

[121] D. J. Harris, *Cases and Material on International Law* 100 (6th edn, 2004).

unsettling effect that the resort to force of such entities would find approval under the law.[122] Many interstate conflicts are fought over disputed territory.[123] The conditionality of all legality of the use of force on the attribution of sovereign title, as Higgins points out, would in effect cancel out a substantial part of the call for non-violence in article 2(4) since it would be impossible to determine who was the attacker and who the defender. This, arguably, was not the intention of the UN Charter founders. In the light of these considerations, firmly established *de facto* entities are included in the case pool of the present study.

The third comment concerns threats combined with the use of force. In many real-life cases, military threats are not the sole feature of conflict. The use of force often has a parallel role, and indeed, as demonstrated in chapter 2, force itself is occasionally the vehicle used to threaten force on a wider scale. For this reason, the case studies do not exclude in principle instances in which nations have actively used force against one another.

Chapter summary

Extracting law from state practice is an arduous task with many pitfalls. According to James Crawford, 'international law is the art of creating normativity out of reality'.[124] If this is so, it is of paramount importance what reality we are examining and what methods we use to decipher it. The basis for the present study is a set of three comparative case studies each comprising eight historical incidents. Each study describes the type of threat involved, the individual and communal response of states to it and, as far as possible, the reasons why they responded the way they did. Taken together, the cases compared here are intended to yield answers as to the legality of four hypotheses on the law: the legality of explicit threats to extract concessions; demonstrations of force; threats in self-defence; and threats in the context of protracted conflict. Further, the case studies will also shed some light on how the concept of

122 Brownlie, *Use of Force by States*, at p. 379.

123 John A. Vasquez, *The War Puzzle* 151 (1993); Paul K. Huth, *Standing Your Ground: Territorial Disputes and International Conflict* 4–5 (1996); Paul F. Diehl, *A Road Map to War: Territorial Dimensions of International Conflict* (1999); Mark M. Zacher, 'The Territorial Integrity Norm: International Boundaries and the Use of Force', 55 Int. Org. 215–50 (2001).

124 James Crawford, 'Foundations of International Law', lecture given at the University of Cambridge (autumn 2003).

no-threat may apply to a particular situation. That is, we may gain some insight into the set of scenarios where the UN Charter ought to provide some meaningful answers regarding the limits of lawful behaviour. That is the reality we seek and which international law must attempt to manage.

The limits of empirical research in the realm of international law have also become apparent. Since the international law discipline does not agree on definite standards for the collection and appraisal of state and UN practice, the results of any study must be read in the context of its own parameters. There is no question that on this basis, interpretations deduced from state practice remain vulnerable to theoretical objections. In addition, it is also true that it still has yet to be seen just how far results from state practice ought to be weighed against other evidence of the law that may surface in international instruments or the already discussed court precedents or the Charter *travaux*. The Vienna Convention on the Law of Treaties offers limited guidance. Yet there need be no doubt that a systematic, transparent and theoretically consistent approach to the identification of post-Charter practice is necessary.

5 Open threats to extract concessions

A line drawn into the sand

Open threats to extract concessions, the archetype of nineteenth-century gunboat diplomacy practiced by colonial powers to subjugate new territory to foreign rule and trade, have always had their uses. An anecdote of the Greek historian Polybius illustrates both the antiquity and the essential nature of such threats.

In the summer of 168 BC Antiochus IV Epiphanes, King of Syria, conducted a military campaign against Egypt and Cyprus. The Roman senate, whose legions had just emerged victorious from the Macedonian war against Perseus, dispatched a three-man mission to Alexandria led by Gaius Popilius Laenas as their legate. The senate's decree was that Antiochus should vacate Egypt and Cyprus immediately. Upon meeting Antiochus at the outskirts of Alexandria, Popilius promptly handed him the senate's written demand and, according to Polybius, 'acted in a manner which was thought to be offensive and exceedingly arrogant':

> He was carrying a stick cut from a vine, and with this he drew a circle round Antiochus and told him he must remain inside this circle until he gave his decision about the contents of the letter. The king was astonished at this authoritative proceeding, but, after a few moments' hesitation, said he would do all that the Romans demanded. Upon this Popilius and his suite all grasped him by the hand and greeted him warmly.[1]

Although subtly conveyed, there could not have been much doubt in Epiphanes' mind that Popilius had afforded him a last opportunity to

[1] Polybius, *The Histories*, book 24, para. 27 (1927) [ca. 150 BC].

cooperate. Under the circumstances the drawing a line into the sand sufficed to signal Rome's willingness to eject his army by military force.

Similarly, this chapter is concerned with cases where states commit themselves to the use of force by, figuratively speaking, drawing a line in the sand, a mental trip-wire encircling a target state with the promise of military action. State A promises the first use or higher-level use of armed force in a dispute on a particular issue with state B.[2] The goal is to extract a concession, which makes it necessary for the threatening state to signal, usually in verbal form, what kind of concession is sought. As with any communication, the clearer the context of a message, the less clear the message itself need be in order to be understood. An allusion, as in Antiochus' case, will often be entirely sufficient. When, in the twentieth century, states acquired the means to strike almost instantly and decisively through the improvements in military technology, such allusions to the use of force became both more effective and more dangerous than probably at any previous point in history.

Two precedents above all guided the UN Charter drafters. There was still the sporadic habit of conditional war declarations. But much more than that, there were Germany and Japan. On the eve of World War II, the clearest case of coercion by forceful intimidation may well be Germany's seizure of Czechoslovakia. Playing with the plea of France and the UK to avoid military confrontation, Hitler successfully negotiated the German appropriation of Czechoslovakia's Sudeten territory during the Munich crisis in September 1938. Later, in March 1939, faced with the choice of a German invasion or a violence-free 'invitation' of its troops, Czechoslovakia's President Hacha signed a prepared note of surrender authorising the *de facto* annexation of his country.[3] That, together with Japan's coerced occupation of French Indochina, were the historical analogies that informed the thinking of UN Charter signatories in June 1945.

The first genuine post-Charter case of an explicit threat occurred as early as 1947, when the Soviet Union delivered an ultimatum calling upon Prague to rescind its acceptance to participate in the Marshall Plan talks in Paris.[4] This still fits the pre-war manner of issuing a threat. Since then, however, there has been a tendency to clothe verbal

[2] For details on the case definition see above, chapter 4, at p. 113.

[3] ICB, 'Munich', crisis 64; ICB, 'Czechoslovakia's Annexation', crisis 68; NYT, 'The German Ultimatum' (26 Sep. 1938); NYT, 'Reich Ultimatum' (14 Mar. 1939); James L. Richardson, *Crisis Diplomacy: The Great Powers Since the Mid-Nineteenth Century* 135–60 (1994).

[4] ICB, 'Marshall Plan', crisis 115.

threats in a mantle of ambiguity. The almost gentlemanly declaration to condition the use of force on compliance with demands, which still operated occasionally in the early twentieth century, does not feature prominently after World War II.[5] Of the 111 threat cases identified since then, only in twenty-one instances (18.9 per cent) have states resorted to the open promise to use force, and the ultimatum in preparation for invasion is virtually extinct in the modern era (Iraq and Kosovo notwithstanding). In short, 'pure' forms of threat delivery have become rare. Often there is a series of signals at work which then are as often mirrored by the rival state. Threats implied by demonstration or issued in the context of self-defence are more frequent. Accordingly, the question arises how UN practice has reacted to such changed circumstances.

And yet, the UN Charter's basic disposition appears clear: Munich-style threats were to be unlawful, categorised as the coercive 'measures short of war' that no longer were to be accepted . In the same vein, Oscar Schachter reasoned in 1991 that 'a blatant and direct threat of force to compel another State to yield territory or make substantial political concessions (not required by law) would have to be seen as illegal under Article 2(4), if the words "threat of force" are to have any meaning'.[6]

UK–Israel (Sinai incursion, 1948)

During the first Arab-Israeli war over Israeli independence and the partition of Palestine, Jewish Haganah units inflicted crushing defeats on Egypt, one of the participants in the multi-pronged Arab invasion against the nascent state of Israel. By the end of 1948, the Arab armies were badly beaten. Israeli forces controlled the Negev and Egyptian troops were trapped in Faluja. On 23 December 1948 Israeli forces advanced in a second southward offensive into the Sinai peninsula and penetrated Egyptian territory.[7] In defiance of a third Security Council

[5] For example, in 1921 alone, France and the UK threatened with the occupation of the Ruhr should Germany not pay its war reparations (ICB, 'German Reparations', crisis 20), the Yugoslav and Czechoslovak governments threatened force against Hungary should it restore the Habsburg throne of Karl IV (ICB, 'Karl's Return to Hungary', crisis 21) and Yugoslavia promised force against Salzburg in the Austrian separatist crisis (ICB, 'Austrian Separatists', crisis 22).

[6] Oscar Schachter, *International Law in Theory and Practice* 111 (1991).

[7] ICB, 'Sinai Incursion', crisis 128; 1948–9 UNYB 183; NYT, 'Israeli's Negeb Thrust Reached Point 80 Miles from Suez Canal' (12 Jan. 1949).

truce, the objective of 'Operation Horev' was to complete the round-up of enemy forces and to compel the Egyptian government to negotiate an armistice.[8]

After attempts to rally Arab aid proved unsuccessful, Cairo appealed to Britain to press for a Security Council resolution demanding Israeli withdrawal. Britain at the time was Egypt's formal ally by way of the 1936 treaty of bilateral alliance.[9] Via the US embassy, Britain telegraphed to the Israeli government on 30 December that 'it regards the situation with grave concern and that unless Israeli forces withdraw from Egyptian territory British Govt [*sic*] will be bound to take steps to fulfil their obligations under Treaty of 1936 with Egypt'.[10] These obligations provided for British intervention by force. Diplomatic pressure on Israel was mounted by the prospect of a one-sided lifting of the Arab arms embargo. Furthermore, the British government indicated that, together with the USA, it would review its sponsorship of Israel's application to the UN on the grounds that it jeopardised its reputation as a 'peace-loving state'.[11]

Under the weight of that pressure, Israel assured the recall of its raiding forces but at first retained some of its troops in Sinai.[12] Tensions rose when Israeli forces shot down five British planes that had been sent to observe the Israeli withdrawal from Sinai.[13] London reacted strongly by sending military reinforcements to its base in Aqaba, Trans-Jordan, on 7 January 1949, and by sending a note to Israel that it reserved its rights as to 'all possible future actions'.[14] Israel ordered its troops out of the area on the same day and, in response to a Security Council call for a ceasefire, completed its withdrawal on 10 January.[15]

[8] NYT, 'U.N. Says Israelis Launch Negeb War by Land, Sea, Air' (24 Dec. 1948).

[9] *Treaty of Alliance Between His Majesty, in Respect of the United Kingdom, and His Majesty the King of Egypt*, Brit. Cmd 5370 (27 Aug. 1937). According to the treaty, the UK agreed to withdraw its military forces from Egypt with the exception of a 10,000 man garrison to protect the Suez Canal Zone and the maintenance a naval base at Alexandria. In return, Egyptian troops would evacuate the Sudan and the Egyptian government accepted a twenty-year treaty of alliance with Britain.

[10] *Memorandum of Conversation, by the Acting Secretary of State*, 1948 FRUS vol. V, part 2, 1701–4, at 1704.

[11] *Draft Telegram by the Acting Secretary of State to the Special Representative of the United States in Israel*, 1948 FRUS vol. V, part 2, 1690.

[12] NYT, 'Israelis Reported Still Inside Egypt' (7 Jan. 1949).

[13] NYT, 'Israelis Down RAF Planes; Britain Protests Strongly, Reinforces in Trans-Jordan' (9 Jan. 1949).

[14] *Ibid.* [15] ICB, 'Sinai Incursion', crisis 128.

In this very early case in the UN's history, the coercion of Israel to withdraw troops from Sinai did not stir any response from the fifty-odd members of the organisation.[16] The Security Council had called for a ceasefire between the parties on 29 December but had not addressed the British interference either in its resolution or in its discussion.[17]

Technical and pragmatic reasons prevailed. Although represented in its meetings, Israel was not yet a member of the UN (joining in May 1949). The UN had put a premium on mediation, not confrontation. Two of the Security Council's permanent members, the UK and, most importantly, the USA, exercised strong pressure against it. Israel therefore sensibly did not raise Britain's ultimatum in public. It could have gained little, since the ultimatum was in line with the Security Council's demands and occurred in response to an Israeli offensive against an already defeated Egypt. In fact, information on the British warning was not leaked to the press until at least 9 January.[18] When the Israeli provisional government eventually did protest against the British troop deployment to Aqaba, it did not prompt a reaction.[19] In the turmoil between Israel and its Arabian neighbours, the extension of British aid to the faltering Egyptian front in Sinai did not – and could not be expected to – stir international comment. Rather, the UN saw its role in the management of the war crisis, to the extent that the UK-US effort to curb Israel's drive into Egypt did not appear out of proportion to its objectives.

USA–DPRK, PRC–USA (38th parallel, 1950)

Threats on the Korean peninsula in 1950 were similarly embedded in wider war context with strong UN involvement. During the first phase of the Korean War, the daring landing of a 269-ship US naval strike force in Inchon on 15 September 1950 marked a decisive turning point. It provided the basis to disable the North Korean army's supply lines and to force it out of South Korea. By the end of September, UN-mandated troops under US General MacArthur's command stood at the 38th parallel, the provisional ceasefire line agreed upon by the Soviet Union and the USA at the end of World War II.[20] Allied victory stood at hand.

[16] 1948–9 UNYB 183–6. [17] 1948–9 UNYB 183–4; S/RES/66 (29 Dec. 1948).

[18] On the level of newspaper coverage see NYT, 'London Calm on Alleged Foray' (30 Dec. 1948); NYT, 'U.S. Warning is Reported' (4 Jan. 1949); NYT, 'Israelis Down RAF Planes; Britain Protests Strongly, Reinforces in Trans-Jordan' (9 Jan. 1949).

[19] NYT, 'Israel's Protest on Aqaba' (10 Jan. 1949). [20] ICB, 'Korean War II', crisis 132.

The UN mandate to 'repel the armed attack' of the North Korean People's Army had been fulfilled.[21]

But, as the USA reasoned, if UN troops were to stop at the 38th parallel, the USA would have found itself back to patrolling the ceasefire line and assisting South Korea. Its forces would be pinned down at the expense of strategically more valuable tasks elsewhere. Hence the temptation lingered to charge north and bring about a unified peninsula.[22] Between 1 and 9 October, three threat attempts were made to prevent continuation of the war to the north – two by the USA and one by the PRC. All three failed.

On 1 October, MacArthur called by radio broadcastings for the unconditional surrender of North Korean troops. They should 'lay down their arms and cease hostilities' to avoid 'total defeat and destruction'.[23] On the same day South Korean troops started to cross the 38th parallel.[24] The simple message was that MacArthur would move UN troops north if the surrender demand was disregarded. On 7 October the UN General Assembly passed a resolution calling for a 'united, independent, and democratic Korea' and 'stability throughout Korea'.[25] This the Supreme Commander took as an authorisation to proceed beyond the 38th parallel and end the conflict by occupation of the north. On 9 October, MacArthur authorised that the Eighth Army join the South Korean troops already on the move. At the same time he issued a second ultimatum, this time in the name of the UN, warning the North Korean government 'for the last time' to cease fighting. Unless it answered immediately he would 'at once proceed to take such military action as necessary'.[26] In so doing he had taken liberties with the USA's late September plan of operation which inhibited him from using non-Korean troops in the northern-border provinces and that there be 'no announcement of intended entry, nor a threat to counter our operations militarily in North Korea'.[27] Whatever the communication

[21] S/RES/83 (27 Jun. 1950).

[22] Dean Acheson, *Present at the Creation: My Years in the State Department* 451 (1969).

[23] NYT, 'War's End Sought' (1 Oct. 1950).

[24] NYT, 'South Koreans Cross 38th Parallel On 8th Army's Order, Move 7 Miles; Reds Ignore M'Arthur On Surrender' (2 Oct. 1950).

[25] A/RES/376 (V) *The Problem of the Independence of Korea* (7 Oct. 1950); 1950 UNYB 264–6. This resolution paved the way for the 'Uniting for Peace' precedent in November.

[26] NYT, 'M'Arthur Gives Reds an Ultimatum; Warns Them "For Last Time" to Yield; Allies Open Offensive in North Korea' (9 Oct. 1950); Acheson, *Present at the Creation*, at p. 455.

[27] Acheson, *Present at the Creation*, at pp. 452–3.

malfunctions in the US chain of command, MacArthur's ultimatum against Pyongyang proved ineffective. Kim Il Sung ordered his troops to continue their fight.[28]

While Truman's commander sought to impose a swift capitulation in the north, the PRC in turn attempted to prevent any Allied crossing of the 38th parallel.[29] Chinese troops had amassed in Manchuria and thus had established a means for intervention. The PRC had voiced several warnings in the course of September. But its clearest warning came in immediate response to MacArthur's first call to surrender on 2 October.

The Chinese Premier Zhou Enlai declared publicly that its people would not stand aside if the north was invaded.[30] On the next day he transmitted a private warning to the USA via the Indian embassy: if US forces crossed the 38th parallel into North Korea the PRC would enter the war. Yet Washington took it as a bluff, or, in then Secretary of State Dean Acheson's words, 'a warning, not to be disregarded, but, on the other hand, not an authoritative statement of policy'.[31] On the 19th, some 200,000 Chinese troops began pouring across the Yalu river to overwhelm MacArthur's troops marching to the border.

Despite their evident gravity and far-reaching consequences, the threats issued did not solicit noticeable comment. Against the backdrop of the Korean War and the antagonism between a US-led General Assembly and Northeast Asian communist nations, the reciprocal threats of early October drowned in more important news. The General Assembly did not discuss the Chinese warning, and neither did it discuss MacArthur's.[32]

A series of circumstances complicated the situation. First, most states as UN members had officially taken side in the war. US-led action was endorsed by a General Assembly majority. Further, neither South Korea nor North Korea were members of the UN at the time. While the former

[28] NYT, 'Premier of North Tells Army to Fight to End Against U.N.' (11 Oct. 1950).

[29] Thomas C. Christensen, 'Threats, Assurances, and the Last Chance for Peace: The Lessons of Mao's Korean War Telegrams', 17 Int. Sec. 122–54 (1992).

[30] Christensen, 'Lessons of Mao's Korean War Telegrams', at 129; NYT, 'Chou Says Peiping Won't Stand Aside' (2 Oct. 1950); NYT, 'North Of The 38th' (2 Oct. 1950).

[31] Acheson, *Present at the Creation*, at p. 452. See also the communication problems within the US Department of State, 1950 FRUS vol. VII, 849–2. See in the same volume the CIA's erroneous estimate at 933–4, and MacArthur's own at 953. See further Anne Sartori, 'The Might of the Pen: A Reputational Theory of the of Communication in International Disputes', 56 Int. Org. 121–49 (2002), where she attributes the USA's dismissal of the Chinese warning to China's repeated empty promises over Taiwan.

[32] 1950 UNYB 220–301.

was probably a state, entitled to the protections of article 2(4), the status of the latter was far from clear.[33] Depending on the position taken, North Korea, at least in theory, was entitled to the right to self-defence, and MacArthur's ultimatum was not covered by the rightful repellence of the North's prior attack to the South. On the other hand, it could have easily been argued that there was no North Korea at the time, and therefore the ceasefire line and the ultimata in early October were meaningless for the purposes of the use of force regime, since they were confined to the borders of one and the same nation. The difficulties were compounded by the UN mandate, which not only stamped its seal of approval to repel the attack against the South but also 'to restore international peace and security in the area'.[34] It raised questions of implied authorisation that the USA would later invoke repeatedly in other situations.[35] In the eyes of communist states, however, that mandate was tainted by the non-representation of the PRC, and, to a lesser extent, the blunder of Soviet non-appearance in the Security Council.[36] What would come to haunt the UN in Iraq in the 1990s was the argument that this entitled the USA to effect the end of the Pyongyang regime by force, effectively erasing the 38th parallel as the border between two countries. MacArthur's call for surrender, which he moreover issued without prior approval, therefore stands in ambiguous light at best. Correspondingly, the Chinese *communiqué* of 2 October could be interpreted as a measure of self-defence or, on the other hand, in violation of UN resolutions that forbid assistance to North Korea.

Under these circumstances, the question who acted first, usually taken as decisive in determining the rights and duties of states in the context of military force, became practically inconsequential. Even if a UN majority had been inclined to shed off their support for South Korea for an impartial voting on legality, such assessment would have been deeply ambiguous due to the entirely different framings of the facts on offer. Given the context, however, it seems plausible that states more or less approved of the US measures as part of the war effort while, as the

[33] James Crawford, *The Creation of States in International Law* 466–72 (2nd edn, 2006).

[34] S/RES/83 (27 Jun. 1950).

[35] Jules Lobel and Michael Ratner, 'Bypassing the Security Council: Ambiguous Authorizations to Use Force, Cease-Fires and the Iraqi Inspection Regime', 93 Am. JIL 124–55 (1999), at 138–9.

[36] 1950 UNYB 225, 229. See the statements of the USSR, Czechoslovakia, Poland, Ukrainian SSR, Byelorussian SSR, the Democratic People's Republic of Korea (North Korea, DPRK) and the PRC.

Truman administration had done, underestimating the significance of the PRC's (primarily bilaterally communicated) warning of intervention.

PRC–India (Sino-Indian border, 1965)

The British McMahon line demarks the border between India and the PRC. It is not recognised by the latter, which reinvigorated territorial claims after seizing Tibet in 1959. Periodic clashes between the two states erupted into open war in 1962 and resulted in a humiliating defeat for India.[37]

In August 1965, Pakistani paramilitaries began to infiltrate the Kashmir valley to create a large-scale uprising against Indian-controlled territory, plunging the simmering conflict over the former princely state into another episode of crisis. The infiltration from the north prompted India to send several thousand troops across the 1949 UN-brokered ceasefire line, in return triggering Pakistani armoured divisions to mount a counterattack. An undeclared war took hold.[38] In September, in the middle of UN mediation efforts to bring hostilities to a halt, the PRC denounced India's measures as 'naked aggression' against Pakistan and claimed that India was engaged in hostile provocations against it at the Sino-Indian border. India denied this.[39] Nonetheless, on 17 September Beijing issued an ultimatum against Delhi. Its diplomatic *communiqué* read:

> The Chinese Government now demands that the Indian Government dismantle all its military works for aggression on the Chinese side of the China-Sikkim boundary or on the boundary itself within three days of the delivery of the present note and immediately stop all its incursions along the Sino-Indian boundary and the China-Sikkim boundary, return kidnapped Chinese border inhabitants and seized livestock . . . ; otherwise the Indian Government must bear full responsibility for all the grave consequences arising therefrom.[40]

The note, delivered to the Indian *chargé d'affaires* at 1.00 a.m., came in less than a day after reports had arrived of unusually heavy concentrations of Chinese troops along the border in the Himalayas.[41]

[37] William R. Keylor, *A World of Nations* 257 (2003). [38] ICB, 'Kashmir II', crisis 216.
[39] NYT, 'Peking Says India Perils Asian Peace' (8 Sep. 1965).
[40] *Note dated 16 September 1965 from the Ministry of Foreign Affairs of the People's Republic of China to the Indian Embassy in Peking*, SCOR Supp. S/6692 (18 Sep. 1965).
[41] NYT, 'China Gives India 3 Days to Abandon Border Posts' (17 Sep. 1965).

India refused to acknowledge any border infringements, saying that it was 'absolutely convinced that the allegations contained in the Chinese note under reply are completely groundless' and that the Chinese demands at this time were 'nothing but interference [in the conflict between India and Pakistan] to prolong and to enlarge the conflict'.[42] China extended its deadline on 19 September for another three days,[43] then declared on the 21st, one day before the expiration of the new deadline, that India had complied with its demands – an assertion that Delhi contested.[44] This, however, terminated the crisis between India and China in 1965.

In this instance, India protested that China was fabricating charges to find 'a pretext for further aggression' and informed the Security Council that the responsibility for any eventual carrying out of its threat would lie squarely with the Chinese government.[45] It did not, however, choose to occupy the Council with the incrimination that Beijing's ultimatum amounted to a violation of international law, and neither did the three other major powers involved in the crisis – the USA, the UK and the Soviet Union – file a protest along such lines. Closest to a condemnation came the US ambassador to the UN, Arthur Goldberg, who commented that Communist China was pursuing policies 'clearly designed' to aggravate the conflict between India and Pakistan.[46] The Soviet Union and the UK, which along with the USA had retained impartiality in the Kashmir dispute, signalled that they agreed.[47]

The Security Council, too, thought it wiser not to honour the Chinese ultimatum with a formal response.[48] On 20 September (one day before China's retreat) it followed a proposal by the Netherlands and unanimously called 'on all States to refrain from any action which might aggravate the situation in the area'.[49] This was a light reprimand for

[42] *Note by the Minister of External Affairs of India Delivered on 17 September 1965 to the Embassy of the People's Republic of China in New Delhi*, SCOR Supp. S/6692 (18 Sep. 1965).

[43] NYT, 'China Extends Deadline, Gives India 3 More Days' (20 Sep. 1965).

[44] NYT, 'India Consents to a Cease-Fire on U.N. Terms' (22 Sep. 1965); NYT, 'Peking Warns India Anew' (24 Sep. 1965).

[45] *Note by the Minister of External Affairs of India Delivered on 17 September 1965 to the Embassy of the People's Republic of China in New Delhi*, SCOR Supp. S/6692 (18 Sep. 1965); 1965 UNYB 167; NYT, 'Shastri Replies' (18 Sep. 1965).

[46] NYT, 'U.N. is Preparing to Demand Halt in Kashmir War' (20 Sep. 1965).

[47] NYT, 'U.N. Council Debates Chinese Threat Against India' (18 Sep. 1965).

[48] SCOR S/PV.1242 (20 Sep. 1965).

[49] S/RES/211 (20 Sep. 1965). The Security Council was composed as follows: Bolivia, (Nationalist) China, France, Ivory Coast, Jordan, Malaysia, the Netherlands, USSR, the UK, the USA and Uruguay. Jordan abstained in the voting.

China, since other resolutions on the Kashmir dispute exclusively addressed the two main contenders, Pakistan and India, in order to achieve a cease-fire.[50] The Council judged that it was imperative to continue efforts to bring about a truce between India and Pakistan and that, it may be inferred, Chinese interference was unwelcome. In fact, early commentators were quick to classify China's ultimatum as a psychological gambit, intended to score political points against India, but not an indicator for real preparedness to open a new military front in the Kashmir war.[51] The subsequent withdrawal of the ultimatum showed that this estimate had been right. There was no further comment forthcoming outside the Security Council chambers.

Morocco–Spain, Algeria (Moroccan march, 1975)

In 1974, Spain announced it would relinquish control over Spanish Sahara (later Western Sahara), the largest portion of African territory still under colonial rule at the time. The adjacent Morocco, along with Mauritania, entertained a special interest in succession to Spanish control based on historical and ethnic ties and, unofficially, the discovery of rich phosphate reserves in the otherwise barren desert land.[52] The General Assembly's approach was to hold a referendum in Western Sahara under the supervision of the UN, in order for the people of the colony (some 75,000) to determine themselves the future status of their territory.[53]

On 16 October 1975, the ICJ furnished an advisory opinion upon request of the UN General Assembly. It declared, in essence, that although legal ties of Morocco and Mauritania existed to Western Sahara, they were not of such nature that would stand in the way of applying the principle of self-determination to the Spanish colony.[54] The same day, King Hassan II of Morocco declared that he interpreted the opinion as supporting Moroccan claims to sovereignty over the area

50 Compare the other Security Council resolutions of the year 1965: S/RES209 (4 Sep. 1965); S/RES/210 (6 Sep. 1965); S/RES/214 (27 Sep. 1965); S/RES/215 (5 Nov. 1965).

51 NYT, 'U.S. Analyzes Threat' (18 Sep. 1965).

52 ICB, 'Moroccan March', crisis 261; Thomas M. Franck, *Recourse to Force: State Action Against Threats and Armed Attacks* 121–7 (2002); Thomas M. Franck, 'The Stealing of the Sahara', 70 Am. JIL 694–721 (1976).

53 Antonio Cassese, *Self-determination of Peoples: A Legal Reappraisal* 214–18 (1995). On the General Assembly's policy see A/RES/1514 (XV) *Declaration on the Granting of Independence to Colonial Countries and Peoples* (14 Dec. 1960).

54 *Western Sahara (Advisory Opinion)*, 1975 ICJ Rep. 68 (16 Oct. 1975), at para. 162.

and that he intended to lead a 'green march' of 350,000 unarmed civilians into Western Sahara to hasten its integration into his kingdom.[55] The king had already pledged in August that Moroccans would recover 'their Sahara' by peaceful or other means by the end of the year. The *New York Times*, referring to Hassan's 16 October speech, reported that while the king assured the peaceful nature of the march, at another point he appeared to be implying that he would use Moroccan troops if necessary and that they would take recourse to force in self-defence if 'other than Spanish forces' were encountered. This clearly referred to Algeria, which opposed any aggrandisement of its regional rival and sought an easy economic outlet to the Atlantic. Algeria supported the Sahara independence movement, Polisario, and had recently reinforced its military units stationed along the border.[56]

Spain protested, immediately calling for an urgent Security Council meeting to make Morocco reverse its announced 'invasion', which Spain said endangered the international security of the region and ignored the rights of the people of the Sahara to self-determination.[57] It proclaimed that Spanish forces would fight back if attacked by regular Moroccan forces.[58] Via personal message to US Secretary of State Henry Kissinger, Morocco signalled its resolve to go ahead with the march unless Spain recognised its right to the Sahara territory, and that it was determined to recover it by 'all possible means'.[59] Reports followed that military units, including airborne and armoured forces, would follow the marchers at least a day's stride behind.[60] Intervention by Polisario fighters would be deemed as Algerian interference into Moroccan affairs.[61]

On 22 October, in an obvious compromise and after some semantic squabbling, the Security Council ordered Secretary-General Kurt Waldheim immediately to consult with the countries concerned and appealed to the parties to 'exercise restraint and moderation'.[62] A second resolution on 2 November repeated that call, urging 'all parties

[55] NYT, 'Moroccans Plan March in Sahara' (17 Oct. 1975).

[56] *Ibid.* As for translation problems regarding 'self-defence' against Spanish forces see NYT, 'Moroccans Rally to Join Unarmed March into Spanish Sahara' (18 Oct. 1975).

[57] NYT, 'Madrid Bids U.N. Meet on Sahara' (19 Oct. 1975).

[58] NYT, 'Morocco, Unyielding, Gets Set for March' (20 Oct. 1975). [59] *Ibid.*

[60] NYT, 'Moroccans Will Begin Moving Toward Sahara Border Today' (21 Oct. 1975). 'Responsibility for any attack', the king said, could 'therefore be clearly assigned'.

[61] NYT, 'Moroccans Will Begin Moving Toward Sahara Border Today' (21 Oct. 1975).

[62] S/RES/377 (22 Oct. 1975); NYT, 'U.N. Council Asks "Moderation" by All in Sahara Dispute' (23 Oct. 1975).

concerned and interested to avoid any unilateral or other action which might further escalate the tension in the area'.[63] A Costa Rican proposal specifically to forbid the advance of the Moroccan march was rejected, yet revived on 6 November when the efforts of Secretary-General Waldheim had yielded no results. The new resolution now clearly called upon the King of Morocco 'immediately to withdraw from the Territory of Western Sahara all the participants in the march'.[64]

In the meantime, a diplomatic shuffle between Spain, Morocco, Mauritania and Algeria ensued. With Generalissimo Franco terminally ill, the faction of the Spanish government taking the upper hand began to favour a trilateral partition agreement with Morocco and Mauritania that would offer it valuable returns from the phosphate mines and fishing rights – quietly at the expense of Spain's prior plans to have the local Sahrawis decide their fate in exercise of the right to self-determination.[65]

Spain's new course of action was only briefly interrupted by Algeria, which warned of war if Morocco carried out the civilian march into the Sahara.[66] Because Spain depended on Algeria's natural gas exports, it briefly veered back to its former position. The Spanish representative in the Security Council now unambiguously contended that his country, in defending the administered territory and as *ultima ratio*, would repel the Moroccan march 'by every means available including use of armed force'.[67] A few days later it was reported that mines along the border were intended to dissuade the marchers from crossing the border, fortified with armoured vehicles and troops, yet withdrawing twelve kilometres inland to avoid a premature incident.[68]

63 S/RES/379 (2 Nov. 1975); NYT, 'U.N. Council Seeks To Have Sahara March Called Off' (3 Nov. 1975).

64 S/RES/380 (6 Nov. 1975); NYT, 'U.N. Council Calls on Morocco to Pull Out Saharan Marchers' (7 Nov. 1975).

65 NYT, 'In Moroccan March, Sand Stifles Fervor' (31 Oct. 1975).

66 NYT, 'Juan Carlos and Cabinet Confer on Sahara Crisis' (1 Nov. 1975); NYT, 'U.N. Council Seeks To Have Sahara March Called Off' (3 Nov. 1975), in reference to Algeria's statement in the Security Council; NYT, 'Action On Sahara Considered At U.N.' (2 Nov. 1975), in reference to Secretary Waldheim's report.

67 SCOR S/PV.1852 (2 Nov. 1975), at para. 24; 1975 UNYB 182; NYT, 'U.N. Council Seeks To Have Sahara March Called Off' (3 Nov. 1975); NYT, 'Action On Sahara Considered At U.139N.' (2 Nov. 1975); NYT, 'Moroccans Irate As Spain Revises Stand On Sahara' (2 Nov. 1975).

68 NYT, 'Spanish Troops Say They Planted Mines on Road From Morocco' (5 Nov. 1975). However, Spain officially claimed that the mines had been lain by Moroccans for the purpose of triggering an incident, see SCOR S/PV.1849 (20 Oct. 1975), at para. 34.

Yet eventually, the secret deal between Morocco, Spain and Mauritania was struck. On the 6 November, with some of its citizens already having crossed the border lining up at the Spanish line of defence, Morocco squarely confronted Spain with an ultimatum: to agree to bilateral negotiations lest the march would continue, and if resisted, would trigger engagement of the Royal Moroccan Armed Forces.[69] Spain gave in. On 9 November, King Hussan announced the ending of the march.[70] After the formal signing of the tripartite treaty on the 14th, which had bypassed the UN and outmanoeuvred Algeria, Mauritania began bombarding Polisario strongholds, while its forces started to pour in from the north to the capital of Aaiún.[71] The *fait* of annexation had been *accompli*, although at the price of a continuing and bloody civil unrest within the new territory.

The diplomatic reactions to the 'green march' and the tripartite treaty were mixed and at times contradictory. In the Security Council debates, the Spanish representative, de Piniés, left no doubt that his government considered the declared readiness of Morocco to push the green marchers over its southern border as 'intolerable threats', stating that the march was unlawful and constituted 'an act of force, prepared and carried out by Moroccan subjects and authorities in order to jeopardize the territorial integrity of the Sahara'.[72] Costa Rica and Algeria took sides with this interpretation,[73] but the remainder of the Council, to take the sarcastic words of the Swedish delegate, confined itself to 'earnestly hope that it will be possible to work out a settlement of the current crisis based on the principles of the Charter of the United Nations'.[74] It was not until the tensions rose in early November, with

[69] NYT, 'U.N. Council Calls on Morocco to Pull Out Saharan Marchers' (7 Nov. 1975).

[70] NYT, 'Hussan Calls Off March in Sahara' (10 Nov. 1975).

[71] NYT, 'Morocco and Mauritania in Sahara Pact with Spain' (15 Nov. 1975); NYT, 'Moroccan Troops In Sahara Capital' (12 Dec. 1975); NYT, 'Rebels Hold Out in Sahara Fighting' (19 Dec. 1975).

[72] SCOR S/PV.1849 (20 Oct. 1975), at paras. 6, 36; SCOR Supp. S/11851 (18 Oct. 1975). Spain had already complained in May 1975 about an intolerable intimidation of the Saharan people as a clear threat to use force to prevent their process of self-determination. See 1975 UNYB 176. In November 1975, the Security Council was composed as follows: Byelorussian Soviet Socialist Republic, Cameroon, China, Costa Rica, France, Guyana, Iraq, Italy, Japan, Mauritania, Sweden, Tanzania, the USSR, the UK and the USA. Spain, Morocco and later Algeria had been invited to explain their positions.

[73] See the statements by Costa Rica SCOR S/PV.1852 (2 Nov. 1975), at para. 38; Algeria SCOR S/PV.1853 (6 Nov. 1975), at para. 56.

[74] SCOR S/PV.1850 (22 Oct. 1975), at para. 75.

Spain in the most explicit terms assuring the recourse to force in self-defence, that the Council members became inquisitive of the exact nature of the Moroccan march.[75] While shying away from declaring unlawfulness, it was clearly uncomfortable with Morocco's course of action, which not only stood in potential violation of article 2(4) but also of the right to self-determination. As a result, it called Morocco to undo the border crossing on 6 November.

As for the tripartite agreement, which was conceivably the product of Moroccan pressure against Spain, the signals of the General Assembly on the events were more equivocal. That body gathered to discuss the matter of Western Sahara between 14 November and 4 December.[76] If the tripartite agreement had breached article 2(4) of the UN Charter, the agreement was void by virtue of the law of treaties.[77] The General Assembly passed two contradictory resolutions on the subject.[78] In the first, passed by eighty-eight votes to none, with forty-one abstentions, it requested Spain as the administering power of Western Sahara 'to take immediately all necessary measures, in consultation with all the parties concerned and interested, so that all Saharans originating in the Territory may exercise fully and freely, under United Nations supervision, their inalienable right to self-determination'.[79] In the second, adopted by fifty-six votes to forty-two votes, with thirty-four abstentions, the Assembly openly acknowledged the imposed tripartite agreement and simply requested its parties 'to ensure respect for the freely expressed aspirations of the Saharan populations', requesting the interim administration to take 'all necessary steps to ensure that all the Saharan populations originating in the Territory' would be able to exercise their 'inalienable' right to self-determination.[80] One resolution was intended to nullify the agreement of 14 November, the other was building on it. Only Algeria maintained that the agreement was in breach of Security Council resolutions and therefore null and void,[81] while Spain, now in reversal of its earlier stance in the Security Council, cited the agreement as in the spirit of article 33 of the UN Charter. A small number of states, Botswana, Ghana, Sri Lanka and Tanzania, facing an equally small

[75] SCOR S/PV.1853 (6 Nov. 1975). [76] 1975 UNYB 184–6.
[77] Article 52 *Vienna Convention on the Law of Treaties*, 1155 UNTS 331 (23 May 1969).
[78] Franck, 'The Stealing of the Sahara', at 717–18; NYT, '2 Rival Measures on Spanish Sahara Voted by U.N. Unit' (5 Dec. 1975).
[79] A/Res/3458(A)(XXX) *Question of Spanish Sahara* (10 Dec. 1975), at para. 7.
[80] A/Res/3458(B)(XXX) *Question of Spanish Sahara* (10 Dec. 1975). [81] 1975 UNYB 184.

crowd of explicit supporters, spoke out that the tripartite agreement did not conform with UN decolonisation decisions of the past.[82]

It is not easy to decipher the statements of states in a case where both the principles of non-use of threats and self-determination, for once prominently and outspokenly, stood on trial within the UN. Three states appeared to have threatened force: Morocco, Spain, and Algeria. Morocco, the initiator, tried to wrestle the Sahara from Spain in circumstances where a popular referendum of the local population would have led to independence. While the Security Council was hesitant to declare the unarmed march as a use of force, it was less ambiguous in its indication that it considered it an act of provocation that needed to be desisted. Spain and, more resolutely, Algeria responded with the promise that they would resist the Moroccan occupation by force. Here too, the Security Council at first tried to calm all parties, but in the end concentrated on Morocco as the main culprit of tension. The Spanish claim of self-defence, it is submitted, was thus indirectly vindicated. The two General Assembly resolutions, while seemingly giving partial legitimacy to the Madrid agreement (and hence the process of its agreement), have to be read as accommodating hardly reversible facts and the reluctance, perhaps of a majority, to condemn Morocco to the advantage of a colonial power.

Uganda–Kenya (Idi Amin, 1976)

In the 1970s, Uganda's Idi Amin combined repressive domestic rule with an activist but moody foreign policy. An unsuccessful 1972 attempt by his predecessor Milton Obote to retake control by force, launched from neighbouring Tanzania, amplified both tendencies.[83] In 1976, Idi Amin considered the idea of armed conflict with pro-USA Kenya and to a lesser extent with Tanzania.[84]

On 15 February 1976, Amin laid claims to the western part of Kenya and announced that, despite his preference for peace, he would consider engaging Kenya in war in order to recover it. The territory had belonged to British Uganda until 1909, when the old East Africa

[82] *Ibid.*

[83] Gilbert M. Khadiagala, 'Uganda's Domestic and Regional Security in the 1970s', 31 J. Mod. Afr. Stud. 231–55 (1993), at 237.

[84] 2004 ICB 'Uganda Claims', crisis 266; 1976–7 Afr. Cont. Rec. B237–8 (Kenya), 1976–7 Afr. Cont. Rec. B386–9 (Uganda).

Protectorate was transformed into the colony of Kenya.[85] Now Amin wanted it back. Should Kenya deny Uganda access to the sea, war would be the result.[86] To Uganda's precarious landlocked coffee economy and fuel-dependent army, lines of communication to the Indian Ocean were vital.[87] Around $54 million in trade debt was owed to Kenya,[88] and a new set of Soviet tanks and MiG-17 fighter aircraft (a gift for its recent hostile relations with Britain and the USA) provided further incentives for a forceful annexation of chunks of its neighbour's territory.[89] Uganda's army consisted of 20,000 soldiers. Kenya's economy-oriented Jomo Kenyatta ruled over a smaller force of 8,000.[90] Kenya's reaction nonetheless was swift and decisive. Kenyatta combined a statement of not yielding any territory with a stinging supply shortcut until March 1976.[91]

Tensions flared up when on the night of 3–4 July the same year, Israel conducted its famous Entebbe raid against Uganda to free hijacked hostages of an Air France passenger airbus headed from Israel to Paris.[92] A quarter of Uganda's air force ended up in flames as a result, accompanied by the death of the Ugandan soldiers who had guarded Entebbe airport.[93] In learning that the Israeli planes had refuelled in Nairobi after the attack, Amin in a radio speech on 5 July said that he wanted to 'impress on the international community the fact that Uganda has been aggressed by Israel with the close collaboration of some states, including Kenya and other neighboring states' and announced Uganda's right 'to retaliate in whatever way she can to redress the aggression against her'.[94] Before the UN Security Council, Uganda repeated its claim that Kenya had aided and abetted the Israeli clandestine operation.[95] Kenya, however, rejected any conspirator role in it. It retorted on 12 July that, since the Entebbe raid, systematic killings of Kenyan nationals living in

85 Aidan Southall, 'Social Disorganization in Uganda: Before, During, and After Amin', 18 J. Mod. Afr. Stud. 627–56 (1980), at 630.

86 2004 ICB 'Uganda Claims', crisis 266.

87 Southall, 'Social Disorganization in Uganda', at 631.

88 *Newsweek*, 'Uganda: Amin *v.* the World' (9 Aug. 1976).

89 Susan Aurelia Gitelson, 'Major Shifts in Recent Ugandan Foreign Policy', 76 Afr. Aff. 359–80 (1977), at 373.

90 1976–7 Afr. Cont. Rec. B389, B233.

91 1976–7 Afr. Cont. Rec. B386–7.

92 1976 UNYB 315–20; Franck, *Recourse to Force*, at pp. 82–6.

93 *Economist*, 'Uganda and Kenya; He Was Deflated' (10 Jul. 1976).

94 NYT, 'Amin Says Uganda Retains the Right to Reply to Raid' (6 Jul. 1976). See also the warning of bombing Kenya through Libyan aid reported in NYT, 'African Nations Bid U.N. Council Meet on Israeli Raid' (7 Jul. 1976).

95 1976 UNYB 315.

Uganda had started and that Ugandan troops had been massing along its border since 4 July.[96] Soviet-delivered tanks now underscored Amin's willingness to use force under the pretext of Kenya's alleged assistance to the humiliating Entebbe attack.

The main response of Kenya was to throttle its railway links to Kampala, in effect squeezing it off from vital goods (above all oil) that began to pile up at the port of Mombassa.[97] Uganda's army, it was speculated, apart from being underpaid and potentially disloyal, now also lacked the petrol to attack Kenya.[98] This time the Ford administration in the USA determined that it was necessary to take sides. Ostensibly on a routine mission, a US Navy P-3 Orion antisubmarine-warfare patrol plane landed in Nairobi on 10 July. The US frigate *USS Beary* arrived in Mombassa on 12 July, and a task group from the US Seventh Fleet – including the aircraft carrier *Ranger* – was ordered to steam toward Kenya as a third pointed signal of US support.[99] Although the US Defense Department described the arrival of the ships and planes as routine, officials privately said the visits were meant to display American support for Kenya in its dispute with Uganda.[100] A month earlier, Defense Secretary Donald Rumsfeld had arranged for a $70 million sale of twelve F-5 fighter jets to Kenya to bolster its ill-equipped military against Soviet-sponsored build-ups in neighbouring Somalia and Uganda.[101]

In rebuttal, Amin cut electricity supplies to Kenya and on 24 July warned that: 'If the economic blockade continues Uganda will have no alternative but to fight for her own survival.'[102] Although assertions of

[96] 1976 UNYB 316; SCOR Supp. S/12140 (12 Jul. 1976); *Facts on File*, 'Ugandan-Kenyan Ties Deteriorate' (17 Jul. 1976); NYT, 'Kenya Reports Killings' (11 Jul. 1976).

[97] NYT, 'Kenya Restricts Uganda's Key Rail Link to the Sea' (10 Jul. 1976).

[98] *Economist*, 'Getting Rid of Amin; Kenya's Attempt to Squeeze the Ugandan Tyranny to Death Deserves International Support' (31 Jul. 1976).

[99] NYT, 'U.S. Sends Frigate to Kenya in Show' (13 Jul. 1976); *Facts on File*, 'Ugandan-Kenyan Ties Deteriorate' (17 Jul. 1976); *Economist*, 'The Americans come to Kenya's Side' (17 Jul. 1976); *Newsweek*, 'The Fallout From Entebbe' (19 Jul. 1976) reports: 'The American moves last week appeared to be the first application of Henry Kissinger's new policy of strengthening America's ties with moderate Black African nations. At a Washington press conference, Kissinger said the Beary was on "a normal port visit," but the American moves were a bold warning to Amin not to let his post-Entebbe lust for revenge lead him into war.'

[100] NYT, 'U.S. Sends Frigate To Kenya In Show' (13 Jul. 1976).

[101] NYT, 'U.S. to Sell Kenya 12 F-5's In $70 Million Arms Deal' (17 Jul. 1976); *Facts on File*, 'U.S. Arms Pledged to Kenya, Zaire' (3 Jul. 1976).

[102] NYT, 'Amin Halts Supply of Power to Kenya, Threatens Attack' (25 Jul. 1976). See also NYT, 'Amin Says Gasoline Is Nearly Depleted And Hints "Action"' (26 Jul. 1976); *Facts*

harbouring no intentions to invade were announced intermittently, Amin, amid growing domestic protest against his rule,[103] informed the UN and the Organization of African Unity (OAU) that he was willing to take 'desperate action out of the need to survive'.[104] The OAU announced on 27 July that its Secretary-General, Eteki Mboumoua, would attempt to mediate the Uganda-Kenya dispute on 28 July.[105] However, there was little to negotiate since Kenya's economic blockade proved highly effective. On 27 July, Kenya conditioned normalisation of relations with Uganda on the removal of Ugandan troops from the Kenyan border, the cessation of threats to invade Kenya, full back payment for goods and services and an end to the killing of Kenyans in Uganda.[106] In form of a joint *communiqué* on 6 August, Uganda agreed to these conditions. Under its terms, all threats of the use of force between Kenya and Uganda were to cease immediately and troops were to withdraw from their common border. There was to be no more hostile propaganda broadcast or published. A six-nation commission of neighbouring countries was set up to help normalise relations.[107]

The crisis between Kenya and Uganda provoked no response from the UN. Apart from a feeble offer of mediation by the OAU and a subtle but firm demonstration of support by the USA, no third party became involved in the quarrel. Surprisingly perhaps, since Uganda's territorial claim, made while President Amin was chairman of the OAU, challenged one of that organisation's most cherished principles, namely the inviolability of African borders. Amin, too, certainly stood in no high regard among his African colleagues. In private, they applauded Amin's international humiliation resulting from the Entebbe incident.[108] Yet the OAU failed to raise even a whisper of protest.[109] Perhaps the factor most important in tempering UN opposition was the insight that Kenya

on File, 'Uganda Scores Kenya Over Oil Shortage' (31 Jul. 1976): An Ugandan military spokesman also hinted in a 17 July radio broadcast that Ugandan warplanes were capable of flying to Kenya's Indian Ocean port of Mombassa and back without refuelling.

103 1976–7 Afr. Cont. Rec. B377, B388.

104 NYT, 'Amin Hints Steps Against Kenyans' (27 Jul. 1976).

105 NYT, 'O.A.U. Mediation Attempt' (28 Jul. 1976).

106 NYT, 'Kenyans Set Conditions for Accord With Uganda' (28 Jul. 1976).

107 NYT, 'Kenya and Uganda in Accord on Ending Hostilities and Threats' (7 Aug. 1976); NYT, 'Kenyatta Signs Accord with Amin' (8 Aug. 1976); *Economist*, 'Kenya and Uganda; Idi Loses' (14 Aug. 1976); *Facts on File*, Kenya-Uganda Accord Signed' (14 Aug. 1976).

108 NYT, 'An African Reaction: Public Anger, Private Approval' (6 Jul. 1976).

109 *Economist*, 'Getting Rid of Amin; Kenya's Attempt to Squeeze the Ugandan Tyranny to Death Deserves International Support' (31 Jul. 1976).

could handle the crisis all by itself. Not Kenyatta, but Amin had appealed to the OAU, where his plea, perhaps indicative of disapproval, fell on deaf ears. Only Libya remained Amin's source of support by reportedly offering swift replacement for the planes lost in Entebbe. Kenya's formidable geographical position to trade oil supply for the normalisation of relations, backed by US support, provided all the necessary remedy to quench the fire endangering its territorial boundaries. All in all, this may well show that a silent majority of Amin's East African neighbours approved Kenya's economic countermeasures that were designed to silence Uganda's eagerness to blaze access to the Indian Ocean by the force of arms.

Cyprus–Turkey (missile crisis, 1997–1998)

In January 1997 the Greek Cypriot government made public an order for the purchase of Russian S-300 surface-to-air missiles. Cyprus did not have an air force. The missiles were designed to neutralise the air superiority that Turkey held since its 35,000-troop-strong invasion of 1974.[110] Concerned about its defence, Cyprus had concluded a military pact with Greece that provided for the construction of air and navy bases on the island. In the event of war, the new missile system was to shield off Turkish air strikes against these bases and provide an air corridor between Greece and Cyprus.[111] Furthermore, Turkey's jets would be unable to fly over Cyprus at will as it had done in the past. There were also hints that President Glafkos Clerides partly intended to renew international attention on the need for a solution to the island problem and simultaneously to use the missile plans as a bargaining chip for negotiations.[112]

Turkey promptly condemned the potential challenge to its air superiority and claimed that the missile purchase revealed hostile intent.[113] In a widely broadcast statement, Foreign Minister Tansu Ciller declared that 'if we have to strike to stop the Greek Cypriots then we will'.[114] Turkey would halt and board any ship bringing the missiles

[110] NYT, 'Cyprus Greeks in Missile Deal with Russia' (6 Jan. 1997).

[111] *The Scotsman*, 'Cyprus Raises Stakes with Missile Deal', 10 F. Press Cyp. 23–5 (6 Jan. 1997).

[112] *The World Today*, 'Squall Hits "Year of Cyprus"', 10 F. Press Cyp. 9–16 (Feb. 1997).

[113] 1997 UNYB 369; SCOR Supp. S/1997/111 (31 Jan. 1997); SCOR Supp. S/1997/732 (19 Sep. 1997).

[114] NYT, 'On Divided Isle of Cyprus, Missile Deal Widens Rift' (18 Jan. 1997).

to Cyprus – or attack them with air and commando forces if they were installed. Cyprus filed protests against the Turkish threat with the UN Security Council, asserting its right to self-defence and the need for effective deterrence.[115] While refusing to back down on the deal, the Greek Cypriot government pledged that it did not plan to deploy the missile system for the next sixteen months.[116]

A year later on 24 January 1998, Cyprus completed the construction of a military airbase alongside the civil airport of Paphos, one of the sites to be protected by the S-300 missile system. Again the Turkish government protested vigorously. Addressing the UN Secretary-General on 28 January, Turkey said that this had:

> ... added a highly destabilizing dimension to the military equation on the island and in the region, contravened Security Council resolutions calling on the parties to refrain from any action that could exacerbate the situation, and had brought the parties to the threshold of a crisis. The Turkish Government would not remain indifferent in the face of provocative and hostile actions and would act to protect the Turkish Cypriot people and preserve the balance between Turkey and Greece.[117]

Greece, standing shoulder to shoulder with Greek Cyprus, said that it would regard any attack as cause for war with Turkey.[118] Positions between Nicosia and Ankara did not change for much of 1998. Military build-up on both sides continued. In the course of the following months, both parties said they remained committed to reducing tensions while at the same time accusing each other of deliberate provocations.[119] Turkey protested against the landing of four Greek F-16 airplanes and a C-130 transport plane on 16 June, complaining that it posed a military threat.[120] Cyprus responded that the visit of Greek aircraft was covered by its right to self-defence.[121] On 19 July Cyprus protested against the dispatch of five Turkish warships, including two

[115] 1997 UNYB 369; SCOR Supp. S/1997/739 (26 Sep. 1997); SCOR Supp. S/1997/762 (29 Sep. 1997).

[116] NYT, 'U.S. Diplomat Visits Cyprus to Ease Strain' (13 Jan. 1997); NYT, 'Pledge on Missiles Eases Cyprus Crisis, Envoy Says' (14 Jan. 1997).

[117] 1998 UNYB 405; SCOR Supp. S/1998/81 (28 Jan. 1998).

[118] NYT, 'New Rumblings in Cyprus Raise Specter of War' (30 Apr. 1998).

[119] 1998 UNYB 406.

[120] SCOR Supp. S/1998/543 (18 Jun. 1998); NYT, 'Greece Sends Warplanes to New Base on Cyprus' (17 Jun. 1998); NYT, 'Greek and Turkish Jets Lead New Round of Cyprus Tensions' (20 Jun. 1998).

[121] SCOR Supp. S/1998/559 (23 Jun. 1998).

submarines, two frigates and a gunboat, to the port of Kyrenia, as well as the landing of seven military aircraft at the Lefkoniko airfield, to take part in ceremonies of the thirty-fourth anniversary of the Turkish invasion and occupation of the northern part of Cyprus.[122] Finally, yielding to international pressure, Cypriot President Glafkos Clerides announced in December 1998 that the government plans to deploy the missiles had been cancelled.[123]

In the course of 1997 and 1998, the UN Security Council[124] convened four times to discuss the Cyprus issue behind closed doors and on all occasions unanimously called on both sides to reduce tensions, cut their military spending and work towards disarmament.[125] The Council refrained from condemning any of the specific acts the parties had undertaken. It did not comment on the Turkish bombing threats, nor did it say that the S-300 missile plans were illegitimate. If it thought so, it chose not to point fingers at Ankara or Nicosia. Rather, it continued to mandate the Secretary-General to mediate in what has been his task ever since the island was divided in 1974. The General Assembly, too, did not take any positions. It merely passed the annual budget of the UN Peacekeeping force on Cyprus.[126]

Several European governments and the USA deplored the Cypriot plans to acquire the missiles but also strongly criticised the Turkish response deliberating military strikes. Washington sent Richard Holbrooke to mediate. London, for its part, declared that while it thought the missile plans were unwise, it recognised the Cypriot right to self-defence.[127] Concerned with the situation, the EU eventually threatened

[122] SCOR Supp. S/1998/671 (19 Jul. 1998).

[123] NYT, 'Cyprus Leader Cancels Plan to Deploy New Missiles' (30 Dec. 1998).

[124] The Security Council in 1997 was composed of the following states: Chile, China, Costa Rica, Egypt, France, Guinea-Bissau, Japan, Kenya, Poland, Portugal, Republic of Korea, Russian Federation, Sweden, the UK and the USA. In 1998: Bahrain, Brazil, China, Costa Rica, France, Gabon, Gambia, Japan, Kenya, Portugal, Russian Federation, Slovenia, Sweden, the UK and the USA.

[125] S/RES/1997/1117 (27 Jun. 1997), following meeting 3794; S/RES/1997/1146 (23 Dec. 1997) following meeting 3846; S/RES/1998/1178 (28 Jun. 1998) and S/RES/1998/1179 (29 Jun. 1998), following meeting 3898; S/RES/1998/1217 (22 Dec. 1998) and S/RES/1998/1218 (22 Dec. 1998), following meeting 3959. All meetings were held informally and the public records merely document the voting outcomes.

[126] 1997 UNYB 375; 1998 UNYB 416.

[127] NYT, 'U.S. Warns Turkey over Threat Aimed at Cyprus' (10 Jan. 1997); FBIS (Soviet Union), 'Daily Report: Moscow – Turkish Threats to Strike Cyprus "Destructive"' (15 Jan. 1997); FBIS (Western Europe), 'Daily Report: Britain Condemns Purchase of Russian Missiles' (15 Jan. 1997).

to suspend its accession talks with Cyprus if the weapons deployment were to occur. Following intense pressure from the EU, the USA and the UN, and detailed discussions with Greece, Cyprus announced on 29 December 1998 that it was cancelling its plans. The missiles would now be deployed on the Greek island of Crete, which meant that the Turkish airspace would no longer be threatened by the weapons.[128]

The dispute over the divided Cyprus was not novel. Ever since the occupation of 1974, Greece, Turkey and Cyprus had been repeatedly hostile to each other. Acquainted with the positions of the parties, the Security Council proceeded with its routine call for restraint but did not give the matter much further attention. Cyprus in fact knew that its missile acquisition was disapproved by the USA and European countries because it had previously attempted to buy an anti-aircraft system from them (leading to the Russian purchase), and in fact had even informed them in advance of its intentions when the Russian deal was in question.[129] The Cyprus question was of special concern to the EU, which had decided that Turkey's application for membership was 'premature', but found that it could start negotiations with Cyprus beginning in January 1998. Along with the pending North Atlantic Treaty Organization (NATO) enlargement, there was much reason for a big push to end the sweltering dispute. Under these circumstances it may be asked if Turkey really intended to use force against the missile bases, or whether other political calculations were not the primary reason for its aggressive stance. If so, the Europeans and the USA had little reason to pay the attention to Turkish threats that would have been necessary to pre-empt its premeditated benefits. In fact, the balance of power between Cyprus and Turkey was never substantially challenged. Turkey had 500,000 soldiers on the mainland as well as several hundred attack fighters, facing a Cypriot military force of some 11,000 soldiers and its ally, Greece, roughly 12,000 soldiers.[130]

In sum, it was felt that both sides were to blame – the Greek Cypriots for provocatively purchasing air-defence missiles, and the Turks for further increasing tensions by threatening military force. If the rules on threats were to flow from this case, it was that none of the parties had a

[128] ICB, 'Cyprus-Turkey Missile Crisis', crisis 423.

[129] NYT, 'Primakov in Cyprus' (2 Jul. 1998); US Department of State, Daily Press Briefing (6 Jan. 1997), http://www.fas.org/news/usa/1997/01/msg00005a.htm.

[130] *St Petersburg Times*, 'Cyprus Tension Crosses "Line"', 11 F. Press Cyp. 29–34 (26 Jun. 1998).

right to provoke the other even if just in response to the other's imprudent attempts to demonstrate military determination. At the same time, there can be little doubt that the Turkish promise to initiate air strikes against Cyprus posed the most dangerous course of action and that the criticism of the UN Security Council and of Western states must be read to have condemned that policy.

NATO–Yugoslavia (Rambouillet, 1999)

A full-scale insurrection led by the Kosovo Liberation Army (KLA) began in the former Yugoslavia in 1998. The Yugoslav government under President Slobodan Milosevic responded by increasing the Serb military presence in Kosovo. Ferocious assaults on Albanian villages and the killing of civilians caused a flow of some 200,000 to 300,000 refugees to improvised camps in the rural areas between April and September 1998.[131]

Worried that the Bosnian catastrophe would repeat itself, the UN Security Council issued sharp protests to Belgrade and demanded the end of hostilities. In a first resolution, it reinstalled the recently suspended arms embargo against Yugoslavia.[132] In September, it expressed grave concern over 'the excessive and indiscriminate use of force by Serbian security forces and the Yugoslav Army which have resulted in numerous civilian casualties and, according to the Secretary-General, the displacement of over 230,000 persons'.[133] It concluded that the situation in Kosovo amounted to a threat to peace and security in the region, and demanded that immediate steps be taken by both sides 'to avert the impending humanitarian catastrophe'.[134] It declared that it would 'consider further action and additional measures to maintain or restore peace and stability in the region'.[135] The situation in Kosovo nonetheless deteriorated further. It also became evident that despite the Security Council's reference to further measures, a resolution

[131] Organization for Security and Co-operation in Europe (OSCE), *Kosovo/Kosova, As Seen, as Told: An Analysis of the Human Rights Findings of the OSCE Kosovo Verification Mission* part 1, chapter 1 (Oct. 1998–Jun. 1999), http://www.osce.org/kosovo/. Further sources for the case study: ICB, 'Kosovo', crisis 429; Ivo H. Daadler and Michael E. O'Hanlon, *Winning Ugly: NATO's War to Save Kosovo* (2000); Franck, *Recourse to Force*, at pp. 163–70; Sean D. Murphy, 'Contemporary Practice of the United States Relating to International Law', 93 Am. JIL 628–67 (1999); Marc Weller, 'The Rambouillet Conference on Kosovo', 75 Int. Aff. 211–51 (1999); Urs Saxer, *Kosovo und das Völkerrecht: Ein Konfliktmanagement im Spannungsfeld von Menschenrechten, Kollektiver Sicherheit und Unilateralismus* (1999).

[132] S/RES/1160 (31 Mar. 1998). [133] S/RES/1199 (23 Sep. 1998). [134] *Ibid.* [135] *Ibid.*

authorising military force under Chapter VII of the Charter was out of reach. Russia and China had both indicated that they would cast their veto against such a resolution.[136] Russia in particular resented NATO's ongoing eastward expansion and wished to retain a free hand in Chechnya's secession rebellion.

Initiatives to handle the crisis in Kosovo henceforth took the form of concerted action outside the Security Council. In October 1998 US envoy Richard Holbrooke negotiated an agreement with Milosevic that demanded the removal of Serb forces and guaranteed eventual autonomy and free elections in Kosovo.[137] However, the stipulated deadline expired with no lessening of Serbian military presence in the province. The Serb marauding of the Kosovo village of Račak on 15 January 1999 eventually demonstrated that the Holbrooke-Milosevic agreement had failed, triggering a sea change in the US and NATO attitude towards the Kosovo crisis.[138]

After Račak, the UK and France, as members of the six-nation Contact Group, envisaged negotiations between Albanian and Yugoslav authorities in Rambouillet, close to Paris.[139] The Security Council endorsed the Contact Group's initiation of talks in a presidential statement that reiterated its 'full support for international efforts, including those of the Contact Group ... to reduce tensions in Kosovo and facilitate a political settlement on the basis of substantial autonomy and equality for ... Kosovo'.[140] In the same breath, it affirmed its commitment to the territorial integrity of Yugoslavia, reflecting the Russian and Chinese refusal to authorise the threat or use of force. Under the leadership of the Contact Group (excluding Russia), NATO now made clear that if the parties in Rambouillet would not come to a prearranged agreement it

136 NYT, 'Russia Vows to Block the U.N. from Backing Attack on Serbs' (7 Oct. 1998); Daadler and O' Hanlon, *Winning Ugly*, at p. 44.

137 1998 UNYB 381; Daadler and O' Hanlon, *Winning Ugly*, at pp. 45–62; Tarcisio Gazzini, 'NATO Coercive Military Activities in the Yugoslav Crisis (1992–1999)', 12 Eur. JIL 391–435 (2001), at 405–6; Patrice Despretz, 'Le Droit International et les Menaces d'Intervention de l'OTAN au Kosovo', Act. Droit. Int. (Nov. 1998), http://www.ridi.org/adi. The UN Security Council endorsed the agreement with S/RES/1203 (24 Oct. 1998); SCOR S/PV. 3937 (24 Oct. 1998). China and Russia abstained.

138 Daadler and O' Hanlon, *Winning Ugly*, at p. 64.

139 1999 UNYB 338; SCOR Supp. S/1999/77 (27 Jan. 1999); SCOR Supp. S/1999/96 (29 Jan. 1999). The Contact Group informally comprised the USA, the UK, France, Germany, Russia and Italy.

140 S/PRST/1999/5 *Statement of the Security Council President on behalf of the Council* (29 Jan. 1999).

was ready to employ military force.[141] On 30 January, the North Atlantic Council declared:

NATO's strategy is to halt the violence and support the completion of negotiations on an interim political settlement, thus averting a humanitarian catastrophe. Steps to this end must include acceptance by both parties of ... the completion of the negotiations on an interim political settlement within the specified timeframe; full and immediate observance by both parties of the cease-fire and by the FRY authorities of their commitments to NATO, including ... the ending of excessive and disproportionate force in accordance with these commitments.

If these steps are not taken, NATO is ready to take whatever measures are necessary in the light of both parties' compliance with international commitments and requirements, including in particular assessment by the Contact Group of the response to its demands, to avert a humanitarian catastrophe, by compelling compliance with the demands of the international community and the achievement of a political settlement. The Council has therefore agreed today that the NATO Secretary-General may authorize air strikes against targets on FRY territory.[142]

An official *communiqué* to Belgrade on the same day by Javier Solana, NATO's Secretary-General, read as follows:

Further to my letter of 28 January 1999, I am writing to underscore NATO's profound concern with the situation in Kosovo and our determination to ensure that the demands of the international community concerning this crisis are met. To this end, the North Atlantic Council has this evening authorized me to send you a final warning, a text of which is attached. I urge you to heed this warning and to take immediate steps to fulfil your obligations to the international community, including those established by the United Nations Security Council, the Organization for Security and Cooperation in Europe, the European Union, the North Atlantic Treaty Organization and the Contact Group. I have sent a similar message to Dr. Rugova. (Signed) Javier Solana.[143]

A major force demonstration made sure that NATO's promise to use force was credible. Preparations for air strikes had been continuously

[141] NYT, 'NATO Threatens Military Action to Stem the Violence in Kosovo' (29 Jan. 1999). The nineteen NATO members in 1999 were: Belgium, Canada, Czech Republic, Denmark, France, Germany, Greece, Hungary, Iceland, Italy, Luxembourg, the Netherlands, Norway, Poland, Portugal, Spain, Turkey, the UK and the USA.
[142] 'Statement by the North Atlantic Council on Kosovo', Press Release (99)12 (30 Jan. 1999).
[143] 1999 UNYB 339; SCOR Supp. S/1999/107 (2 Feb. 1999).

moving forward in the Balkan region and reached operational capability by the end of February. In the week of 20 February the USA, as the main military contributor, put a total of fifty-one US warplanes on alert, including twelve F-117A stealth fighters, twenty-five KC-135 refuelling planes and ten EA6B Prowler radar-jammers, to join more than 260 other US warplanes that were already in place in Europe. Five US warships and two US submarines of the Sixth Fleet were by then deployed in the Mediterranean and Adriatic Seas to fire cruise missiles in support of a potential air campaign.[144]

Yugoslavia immediately filed a complaint to the Security Council, citing Solana's *communiqué* as evidence for an open and clear threat of aggression that called for an emergency session of the Council.[145] The National Assembly of the Serbian Republic, while condemning NATO's threat, nonetheless accepted the invitation for talks in Rambouillet to start on 6 February.[146] The agreement presented by the Contact Group to Belgrade (the Rambouillet Accords) demanded the withdrawal of Yugoslav troops, a referendum in Kosovo to determine its future after three years of autonomy, and the deployment of 30,000 NATO troops to monitor compliance.[147]

While the Kosovo Albanians were persuaded to sign the Rambouillet Accords, Belgrade was not. It was not willing to allow NATO troops into Kosovo. Rather, it repeated its protest against the continued threat of pending NATO military action and the build-up by NATO countries of troops and arms.[148] On 23 March, Yugoslavia declared a state of imminent danger of war.[149] Recognising that Russia, as the leading opponent, could not be moved in the Security Council, the USA and the UK decided that NATO's crumbling credibility was on the line and that it was time to make good their promise to act. On 24 March 1999, NATO member states launched a 79-day air campaign against Yugoslavia, coming to an end on 10 June. On that day, Milosevic agreed to recall military forces from the embattled Kosovo and to have NATO ground forces secure the return of Kosovo Albanian refugees.[150] The Security

144 NYT, 'NATO Says it is Ready, but Awaits Key Aircraft' (20 Feb. 1999).
145 1999 UNYB 339. 146 1999 UNYB 339; SCOR Supp. S/1999/118 (4 Feb. 1999).
147 SCOR Supp. S/1999/648 *Interim Agreement for Peace and Self-Government in Kosovo* (7 Jun. 1999).
148 SCOR Supp. S/1999/177 (19 Feb. 1999) and S/1999/292 (17 Mar. 1999); NYT, 'No "Stonewalling" on Kosovo Peace, Milosevic is Told' (20 Feb. 1999).
149 SCOR Supp. S/1999/317 (24 Mar. 1999). 150 1999 UNYB 353.

Council thereupon established the multinational Kosovo Force (KFOR) in resolution 1244.[151]

Third-party responses to the Rambouillet ultimatum were at first hesitant. Before the NATO air strikes started, Belarus and Ukraine condemned the intention to use force to solve the Kosovo crisis.[152] Russia was openly critical of air strike plans.[153] Countries from south-east Europe, on the other hand, reiterated their full support for the efforts of the Contact Group.[154] Yet by and large, communal reaction during the Rambouillet talks was one of awaiting further events.

That changed when the bombings started. At Russia's bidding, the Security Council convened for two days to discuss the unfolding NATO bombing campaign in Kosovo.[155] During the debate, the exclusive focus of attention was the ongoing war and none of the countries represented lost much thought on the circumstances, however legally doubtful, that had led to its onset. Together with five NATO countries represented in the Council, Slovenia and Gambia defended the air campaign. Russia, China, Namibia and India (in the Council upon invitation), on the other hand, condemned the air strikes as a violation of international law. The rest would not clearly take sides.[156] On 26 March, the Security Council met to consider a draft resolution sponsored by Belarus, India and Russia by which the Council would have demanded an immediate cessation of the use of force against the former Yugoslavia and called for the urgent resumption of negotiations.[157] It was turned down by twelve votes to three.[158] Subsequently, Moscow said that it would suspend its diplomatic relations with NATO until the bombing of Yugoslavia had come to an end and demanded that the General Assembly hold a special meeting.[159] It also hinted that it would consider providing military support to Belgrade and reserved the right to take appropriate countermeasures.[160] Cuba, Belarus and China joined Russia in condemning

[151] S/RES/1244 (10 Jun. 1999).
[152] 1999 UNYB 241, 339; SCOR Supp. S/1999/208 (26 Feb. 1999); SCOR Supp. S/1999/194 (26 Feb. 1999); SCOR Supp. S/1999/309 (20 Mar. 1999).
[153] NYT, 'Doubts on NATO Air Raids as the Talks on Kosovo End' (18 Mar. 1999).
[154] 1999 UNYB 241; SCOR Supp. S/1999/319 (19 Mar. 1999).
[155] SCOR S/PV.3988 (24 Mar. 1999) and SCOR S/PV.3989 (25 Mar. 1999). The Security Council was composed as follows: Argentina, Bahrain, Brazil, Canada, China, France, Gabon, Gambia, Malaysia, Namibia, the Netherlands, Russia, Slovenia, the UK and the USA.
[156] Franck, *Recourse to Force*, at pp. 166–70.
[157] SCOR Supp. S/1999/328.
[158] 1999 UNYB 344; SCOR S/PV.3839 (12 Mar. 1999).
[159] 1999 UNYB 344; SCOR Supp. S/1999/358 (30 Mar. 1999).
[160] Daadler and O' Hanlon, *Winning Ugly*, at p. 127.

NATO attacks.[161] Outside of the Security Council chamber, the EU unsurprisingly lent strong support for NATO's actions,[162] and so did the countries of the South-Eastern Europe Cooperation after security assurances had been given by NATO.[163] The Movement of Non-Aligned Countries on 9 April expressed concern over the humanitarian situation in Kosovo, but rendered no conclusive opinion on the matter.[164] Yet in a press release in September the same year, Jordan declared on behalf of the movement that it rejected the right to humanitarian intervention, which it said had 'no legal basis in the United Nations Charter or in the general principles of international law'.[165]

Did the international system condemn NATO threats against Yugoslavia? The USA, referring to consensus among allies, had publicly declared that the strategy to resolve the crisis in Kosovo relied on 'combining diplomacy with a credible threat of force'.[166] Against this strategy there was, in view of Belgrade's stubborn defiance to adhere to humanitarian standards, comparatively little objection. Not until the war had begun did criticism over NATO's course of action become visceral and substantial, dividing the international community over the appropriateness of NATO's air campaign. The preceding threat itself solicited less attention.

An important problem complicates the reading of this case. To begin with, a number of issues were at stake: the legality of humanitarian intervention, the right to Kosovo-Albanian self-determination, implied Security Council authorisation, and so, too, the potential right to exercise military pressure to make Yugoslavia agree to the Rambouillet Accord. As Christine Gray reports, states were uncertain what formed the legal basis for NATO action.[167] In fact, NATO operated in full awareness that members disagreed in this regard.[168] As for the USA,

161 For an account of reactions see further Murphy, 'Contemporary Practice', at 633.
162 SCOR Supp. S/1999/429 (14 Apr. 1999); SCOR Supp. S/1999/490 (26 Apr. 1999).
163 SCOR Supp. S/1999/319 (24 Mar. 1999); Daadler and O' Hanlon, *Winning Ugly*, at p. 129.
164 1999 UNYB 345; SCOR Supp. S/1999/451 (21 Apr. 1999).
165 *Final Communiqué of the Meeting of Ministers for Foreign Affairs and Heads of Delegation of the Non-Aligned Movement* (23 Sep. 1999) at para. 171, http://www.nam.gov.za.
166 NYT, 'Allies Call Kosovo Rivals to Peace Talks in France' (30 Jan. 1999).
167 Christine Gray, *International Law and the Use of Force* 269 (2nd edn, 2004). See also Catherine Guicherd, 'International Law and the War in Kosovo', 41 *Survival* 19–34 (1999).
168 Daadler and O' Hanlon, *Winning Ugly*, at p. 45.

State Department spokesman James P. Rubin in a press conference on 16 March stated vaguely that:

> . . . there are principles of international law and specific provisions of international law that [the Serbs] have violated repeatedly. In addition, there is a danger to NATO allies in the region, which thereby brings in the NATO charter. In addition, there is the prospect of a further humanitarian catastrophe. These three reasons, in our view, are legitimate grounds, in our opinion, to threaten and, if necessary, use force. That is our view.[169]

In view of the fact that NATO did not offer a clear legal argument for its actions, the question arises whether it is not more accurate to describe state reactions as a single answer to a whole set of possible legal interpretations. For example, state reactions could have related to the use of force as such, or to its justification for humanitarian reasons. It could also have related to the threat of force preceding it, because in strategic terms, the Kosovo campaign was a single coercive undertaking: its aim was not to destroy Yugoslavia, but to bring Milosevic back to the negotiation table. In this sense use and threat of force could be said to have been judged as one and the same, the eventual start of the air campaign simply being the straw that broke the camel's back. The available evidence does not permit clear conclusions. The Security Council could neither condemn nor approve NATO's conduct, and the General Assembly did not cast votes as Russia had wanted.[170]

Nonetheless, the following seems evident enough: a majority of states could agree with the stance of the Contact Group that Yugoslavia's Kosovo campaign was unacceptable. Resolutions of the General Assembly focusing on human rights make this clear.[171] For humanitarian reasons, a majority of states was reluctant to criticise NATO's efforts to bring about a deal by the threat of force, and once Milosevic yielded to demands, to question the agreement's validity under the terms of the Vienna Convention on the Law of Treaties. Such a reading suggests that the threat of force prior to the start of bombing campaign was largely tolerated. Yet at the same time, the same majority entertained doubts over the advisability and permissibility of enforcing the demands through military action, particularly if this meant bypassing the UN Security Council. Many states

[169] James P. Rubin, *US Department of State Press Briefing* 8 (16 Mar. 1999), quoted from Murphy, 'Contemporary Practice', at 631.
[170] Saxer, *Kosovo und das Völkerrecht*, at pp. 37–9.
[171] A/RES/53/164 *Human Rights in Kosovo* (8 Dec. 1998).

therefore opposed the NATO bombings. Russia, for example, indicated that it could accept the threat of force in order to get a deal, but not its eventual implementation if the threat did not work.[172] In other words, it agreed to a bluff, but certainly not to the lifting of the Security Council's final say on the use of force. Hence a narrow common denominator may be said to have governed reactions to NATO's Yugoslavia policy: that the threat of force was exceptionally permissible as a means of crisis management and thus, paradoxically, as a means to avert the actual use of force, but that the aims pursued by the threat and its implementation be at the very least loosely determined by the UN Security Council. Clearly, controversy over the threat of force focused on its justification, and less over the threshold of article 2(4).

USA, UK–Iraq (regime change, 2002–2003)

After 11 September 2001, US foreign policy made a major shift towards the combat of global terrorism. Among the principle fears ranked the scenario of nuclear, biological or chemical weapons falling into the hands of 'rogue' regimes or terrorist networks inclined to launch an even more devastating attack on US soil.[173] The UN Security Council rapidly signalled its approval of self-defensive steps in the context of the attacks.[174]

On 7 October 2001 the newly elect Bush administration ordered the invasion of Afghanistan, whose Taliban regime had hosted parts of Al-Qaeda, a militant Islamic organisation that US intelligence suggested was responsible for the 9/11 attacks.[175] In 2002, the focus shifted to Iraq, with whom the USA had entertained acrimonious relations ever since that state's invasion of Kuwait. In the latest chapter of these relations, UN weapons inspections had come to an abrupt halt in 1998 after Baghdad had refused any further cooperation unless the UN seriously considered the lifting of economic sanctions.[176] A series of punitive air strikes conducted by the UK and the USA in operation *Desert Fox* had left Iraq

172 Daadler and O' Hanlon, *Winning Ugly*, at p. 74.

173 For a chronology of events leading the USA and the UK into Iraq see Todd S. Purdum, *A Time Of Our Choosing: America's War in Iraq* (2003); Ron Huisken, *The Road to War on Iraq* (2003); David Coates and Joel Krieger, *Blair's War* (2004); Bob Woodward, *Plan of Attack* (2004); 2002 UNYB 285–96.

174 S/RES/1368 (12 Sep. 2001). See also A/RES/56/1 *Condemnation of Terrorist Attacks in the United States* (12 Sep. 2001).

175 ICB, 'USA – Afghanistan', crisis 433.

176 Economic sanctions were in place since S/RES/687 (3 Apr. 1991).

unaltered and defiant vis-à-vis repeated demands of the Security Council to cooperate.[177] A US initiative in June 2001 to re-introduce inspectors into Iraq in exchange for 'smart sanctions' also left things unaltered.[178]

In the wake of 11 September 2001, the prospects of an unchecked Iraq acquiring advanced weapons capability became intolerable for US policy-makers.[179] Widening the scope of the 'war on terror', the Bush administration asserted that Baghdad entertained ties with Al-Qaeda and thus attempted to establish a link between the attacks of 9/11 and the necessity to take forceful action against Saddam Hussein. In his second State of the Union Address in January 2002, President Bush identified Iraq, Iran and North Korea as three 'axis of evil' states, whose aspirations to acquire weapons of mass destruction posed a 'grave and growing danger' where 'the price of indifference would be catastrophic'.[180] Following this speech, the UK government under Tony Blair took public position in Washington's support. Yet to make the reinforced alliance fly, Blair stressed the need for UN endorsement, so as to stem domestic tides of British opposition against any military engagement in cooperation with the USA.[181]

In August 2002, the Bush administration started to lay the groundwork for a possible invasion of Iraq. It announced that it would seek congressional approval for the use of force and started a campaign to convince foreign governments to follow the USA's lead.[182] It also published a new national security strategy, soon labelled the 'Bush doctrine' because of its break with previous policy, that carved out the right of the USA to go to war preventively and without signs of an impending attack.[183] On 12 September, President Bush explained to the UN General Assembly in New York that:

> If the Iraqi regime wishes peace, it will immediately and unconditionally forswear, disclose, and remove or destroy all weapons of mass destruction, long-range missiles, and all related material ... If Iraq's regime defies us again,

[177] ICB, 'UNSCOM II Operation Desert Fox', crisis 428; Sean D. Murphy, 'Contemporary Practice of the United States Relating to International Law', 93 Am. JIL 470–501 (1999), at 471–9.

[178] Huisken, *Road to War*, at p. 4. [179] *Ibid*, at p. 6.

[180] George W. Bush, 'Address Before a Joint Session of the Congress on the State of the Union', 38 Wkly Comp. Pres. Doc. 133–9 (29 Jan. 2002).

[181] Coates and Krieger, *Blair's War*, at pp. 48–52; Purdum, *A Time of Our Choosing*, at p. 75.

[182] Sean D. Murphy, 'Efforts to Address Iraqi Compliance', 96 Am. JIL 956–62 (1999), at 958.

[183] *The National Security Strategy of the United States of America* (19 Sep. 2002), http://www.whitehouse.gov/nsc/nss.html; Gray, *Use of Force*, at pp. 175–9.

the world must move deliberately, decisively to hold Iraq to account. We will work with the U.N. Security Council for the necessary resolutions. But the purposes of the United States should not be doubted. The Security Council resolutions will be enforced - the just demands of peace and security will be met - or action will be unavoidable.[184]

The Iraq problem, so the underlying tone, was now to be solved, not merely managed. To that end, the USA would no longer hesitate to remove Saddam Hussein by military force if necessary.[185] On 10 October 2002, the US Congress authorised President Bush to use US forces to 'defend the national security of the United States against the continuing threat posed by Iraq' and to 'enforce all relevant Security Council resolutions regarding Iraq'.[186] The members of Congress majority also endorsed the president's intention to 'obtain prompt and decisive action by the Security Council to ensure that Iraq abandons its strategy of delay, evasion and noncompliance and promptly and strictly complies with all relevant Security Council resolutions regarding Iraq'.[187]

Armed with Congressional authority, the Bush administration proceeded to round up approval by the UN Security Council to disarm Iraq by force if it continued to defy compliance with its obligations set out in resolution 687.[188] So far, Iraq's behaviour more often than not had stood at variance with the resolution's list of demands. During the negotiation process among the Security Council members, it became

184 George W. Bush, 'Address to the United Nations General Assembly in New York City', 38 Wkly Comp. Pres. Doc. 1529–33 (12 Sep. 2002). President Bush mentioned a series of further conditions that flowed from previous UN Security Council resolutions. Iraq was to: (1) immediately end all support for terrorism and act to suppress it; (2) cease persecution of its civilian population; (3) release, account for and assume liability for all missing Gulf War personnel resulting from the invasion of Kuwait in 1990; (4) immediately end all illicit trade outside the oil-for-food programme and accept UN administration of funds from that programme for the benefit of the Iraqi people. Finally, President Bush added that: 'If all these steps are taken, it will signal a new openness and accountability in Iraq. And it could open the prospect of the United Nations helping to build a government that represents all Iraqis - a government based on respect for human rights, economic liberty, and internationally supervised elections.'

185 NYT, 'Bush Has Received Pentagon Options on Attacking Iraq' (21 Sep. 2002).

186 *Authorization for Use of Military Force Against Iraq Resolution of 2002*, Pub. L. No. 107–243, 116 Stat. 1498–1502 (16 Oct. 2002), at section 3(a); NYT, 'Congress Authorizes Bush to Use Force Against Iraq, Creating a Broad Mandate' (11 Oct. 2002).

187 *Authorization for Use of Military Force*, at section 2(2).

188 S/RES/687 (3 Apr. 1991). In 2002, the Security Council was composed as follows: Bulgaria, Cameroon, China, Colombia, France, Guinea, Ireland, Mauritius, Mexico, Norway, Russia, Singapore, Syria, the UK and the USA.

clear that the USA sought to set a benchmark 'to do list' for Baghdad that, if not strictly complied with, would entitle the UK and the USA to proceed with an invasion of Iraq. Russia and France in particular opposed any self-triggering mechanism built into the proposed resolution and wished to retain final authority on the use of force within the Council chamber.[189] A painfully achieved compromise resulted in resolution 1441, passed unanimously on 8 November.[190] Acting under Chapter VII, the resolution in its operative part afforded Iraq 'a final opportunity to comply with its disarmament obligations under relevant resolutions of the Council'[191] and recalled the warning that Iraq would face 'serious consequences as a result of its continued violations of its obligations'[192] and finally, to remain seized of the matter.[193] Prime Minister Tony Blair now joined Bush's determination in no uncertain terms. After resolution 1441 had passed, he stated:

> To those who fear this resolution is just an automatic trigger point, without any further discussion point, paragraph 12 of the resolution makes it clear that it is not. But everyone now accepts that that if there is a default by Saddam, the international community must act to enforce its will. Saddam must now make his choice. My message to him is this: disarm or you face force. There must be no more games, no more deceit, no more prevarications, obstruction or defiance. Cooperate fully and, despite the terrible injustice you have often inflicted on others, we will be just to you. But defy the UN's will and we will disarm you by force. Be under no doubt whatever of that.[194]

Clearly now, the UK was standing shoulder to shoulder with the USA in assuring the use of force if full cooperation was not forthcoming.

Parallel to the unfolding of the Bush administration's diplomatic initiative, senior military officials travelled across Europe and Southwest Asia in late October and November to discuss basing agreements for US troops and aircraft.[195] Bearing fruit to these efforts, a continuous stream of US forces and war equipment began to shape a massive military presence in the Persian Gulf area. By mid-December, about 60,000 soldiers, sailors, marines and airmen had assembled within striking distance of Iraq, along with six aircraft carriers poised to

[189] 2002 UNYB 296. [190] S/RES/1441 (8 Nov. 2002).
[191] S/RES/1441 (8 Nov. 2002), at para. 3. [192] *Ibid.*, at para. 13. [193] *Ibid.*, at para. 14.
[194] *Statement of Prime Minister Tony Blair in response to the passing of UN Security Council resolution 1441* (8 Nov. 2002), quoted from Coates and Krieger, *Blair's War*, at p. 57 (emphasis omitted).
[195] NYT, 'U.S. Taking Steps to Lay Foundation for Action in Iraq' (18 Nov. 2002).

launch air attacks on short notice. Army forces conducted large-scale exercises in Kuwait that simulated Iraqi conditions for combat, and carrier-based jets patrolling the no-flight zone in southern Iraq carried out mock bombing runs against Iraqi airfields and military bases.[196] British troops began to arrive in January 2003.[197] By March, the Pentagon had stationed over 225,000 US soldiers ready for an invasion.[198] On 11 March, the US military also test-detonated the largest ever non-nuclear bomb (Massive Ordnance Air Blast, MOAB) at Eaglin Air Force Base in Florida. Defense Secretary Rumsfeld declared to the press that: 'The goal is to have the capabilities of the coalition so clear and so obvious that there is an enormous disincentive for the Iraqi military to fight . . . and there is an enormous incentive for Saddam Hussein to leave and spare the world a conflict.'[199]

Not only did the joint US-UK deployment provide formidable credibility to the two countries' commitment, but the mounting financial investment and prestige involved meant that a US withdrawal became more and more unlikely – if not politically unfeasible – since it would have been perceived as a political victory for Saddam Hussein.[200] Moreover, military experts had estimated that the optimal time window for waging war against Iraq was relatively narrow, given the strategic disadvantages of the desert heat and longer daylight times in the summer. A military strike against Iraq therefore had to take place no later than early April unless the credibility of a US attack should fade.[201] Once underway, the war machinery became increasingly difficult to stop.[202]

196 NYT, 'Buildup Leaves U.S. Nearly Set to Start Attack' (8 Dec. 2002); NYT, 'Top General Visit New War Room in Qatar' (21 Dec. 2002); NYT, 'U.S. Testing Missiles and Spy Planes in its Gulf Buildup' (23 Dec. 2002); NYT, 'Army Acts to Add Thousands of G.I.'s to its Gulf Force' (1 Jan. 2003); NYT, 'U.S. Force is Said to be Rising to 150,000 Troops' (12 Jan. 2003); NYT, '20,000 More Troops Sent to Persian Gulf' (15 Feb. 2003).

197 NYT, 'Britain Sending 26,000 More Troops to Gulf' (21 Jan. 2003).

198 NYT, 'U.S. Plan Sees G.I.'s Invading as More Arrive' (16 March 2003).

199 NYT, '"The Mother of All Bombs": 21,000-lb Monster Meant to Shock Iraq into Surrender' (12 Mar. 2003). The *New York Times* wrote that 'MOAB's devastating explosive power – which likely would make Iraqi troops think they are under a nuclear attack – also is in line with the Pentagon's overall strategic concept of trying to "shock and awe" the Iraqi regime into surrender'. See also NYT, 'Largest Conventional Bomb Dropped in a Test in Florida' (12 Mar. 2003);

200 NYT, 'Chicken a la Iraq' (5 March 2003).

201 NYT, 'Its Good to Go, But When?' (22 Sep. 2002); NYT, 'Questions of War and Timing' (10 Nov. 2002).

202 NYT, 'Bush Was Set on Path to War, British Memo Says' (27 Mar. 2006).

In the face of abundant evidence that the White House was preparing an invasion and that it had gone out of its way to win the Security Council to its cause, Iraq on 16 September declared its readiness to let UN weapons inspections resume – this time without any strings attached.[203] UNMOVIC and IAEA inspectors were allowed to enter the country on 27 November and, following the demands set out by resolution 1441, Iraq delivered a 12,200-page report on disarmament on 7 December 2002.[204] However, the report revealed little new. Most of all, it did not provide any proof that Iraq had really destroyed prohibited weapon systems that the inspectors knew about; and it did not indicate, as the resolution 1441 in essence had required, a fundamental change of heart on Saddam Hussein's part.[205] A continuous stream of discoveries by UN inspectors in Iraq's ammunition storage dumps and homes of nuclear scientists, too, fed Washington's case that Saddam Hussein was once again merely playing tricks. To others, however, these disclosures were a sign that the inspections were working; and that, given enough time, they would uncover illegal weapons programmes if any existed.[206]

In late January 2003, the Bush administration went one step further. While it had previously demanded that Iraq must prove that it had no weapons of mass destruction along the lines of the first Gulf War resolutions 678 and 687, it now (falsely) asserted to know that Iraq did possess them and that the weapons hunt was a farce.[207] In his next State of the Union Address, President Bush announced on 28 January 2003 that the USA would present intelligence to the Security Council concerning Iraq's 'illegal weapons programs, its attempts to hide those weapons from inspectors and its links to terrorist groups', reiterating at the same time that: 'We will consult, but let there be no misunderstanding: If Saddam Hussein does not fully disarm, for the safety of our people and for the peace of the world, we will lead a coalition to disarm him.'[208] Short of a spectacular surrender of weapons or the

[203] SCOR Supp. S/2002/1034 (16 Sep. 2002).
[204] NYT, 'Unhindered by Iraqi Officials, Arms Inspectors Visit 3 Sites' (28 Nov. 2002).
[205] Hans Blix, *Disarming Iraq* 111–13 (2004); NYT, 'In Blix's Words: Unresolved Issues' (20 Dec. 2002); NYT, 'U.N. Inspector Says Iraq Falls Short on Cooperation' (28 Jan. 2003).
[206] Purdum, *A Time of Our Choosing*, at p. 66.
[207] NYT, 'Why Bush Won't Wait' (25 Jan. 2003).
[208] George W. Bush, 'Address Before a Joint Session of the Congress on the State of the Union', 39 Wkly Comp. Pres. Doc. 109–16 (29 Jan. 2003).

breakdown of Saddam Hussein's reign altogether, it was difficult to see how an armed US intervention was to be avoided.[209]

The intelligence presented by US Secretary of State Collin Powell on 5 February in the Security Council failed to convince the majority of states that the weapons inspections was pointless. In mid-February and early March, the USA and UK therefore jointly embarked on a last-ditch campaign to win a second Security Council resolution that would have declared Iraq to have failed 'to take the final opportunity afforded to it by resolution 1441' and, living up to the 'serious consequences' promised, would now authorise the use of force.[210] Various officials from the administration now also felt that the objective was not only to disarm Iraq, but, as White House spokesman Ari Fleischer explained, to bring about regime change in Baghdad. This made a big difference, because the departure of Saddam Hussein could not be achieved by weapons inspections and was not mandated by UN resolutions.[211] On 24 February, London, Washington and newly found ally Madrid introduced a draft resolution to that effect. The objective was to gain at least nine votes in the Council even though Russia and France had indicated that they would cast their veto in disapproval.[212] But a majority in the Council felt that the UN inspectors should be given more time. The UK-US initiative bound to fail, the three sponsors withdrew their draft on 17 March.[213] That day, the leaders of Spain, Portugal, the UK and the US met on the Azores, declaring that 'If Saddam refuses even now to cooperate fully with the United Nations, he brings on himself the serious consequences foreseen in UNSCR [*sic*] 1441 and previous resolutions'.[214] The same evening at 8:01 p.m., President Bush addressed the US public on television:

> The United Nations Security Council has not lived up to its responsibilities, so we will rise to ours ... All the decades of deceit and cruelty have now reached an

209 Blix, *Disarming Iraq*, at p. 147. On the determination to go to war and the deliberation to provoke a confrontation see NYT, 'Bush Was Set on Path to War, Memo Says' (27 Mar. 2006).

210 NYT, 'U.S.-British Draft Resolution Stating Position on Iraq' (25 Feb. 2003).

211 NYT, 'Despite Obstacles to War, White House Forges Ahead' (2 Mar. 2003); Huiskin, *The Road to War on Iraq*, at p. 37.

212 NYT, 'U.S. Will Ask U.N. to State Saddam Hussein Has Not Disarmed' (14 Feb. 2003); NYT, 'Some on Security Council Want to Avoid Taking Sides on Iraq' (20 Feb. 2003); NYT, 'U.S. Seeks 9 Votes From U.N. Council to Confront Iraq' (21 Feb. 2003); NYT, 'U.S. Still Hopeful of 9 Votes at the U.N. for Iraq Measure' (13 Mar. 2003); *Washington Post* (Wash. Post), '6 "Undecideds" Face Tough Choice at U.N.' (14 Mar. 2003).

213 Wash. Post, 'U.S.-Backed Resolution Appears Doomed' (14 Mar. 2003).

214 'Statement of the Atlantic Summit: A Vision for Iraq and the Iraqi People', 39 Wkly Comp. Pres. Doc. 336–7 (16 Mar. 2003).

end. Saddam Hussein and his sons must leave Iraq within 48 hours. Their refusal to do so will result in military conflict, commenced at a time of our choosing. For their own safety, all foreign nationals – including journalists and inspectors – should leave Iraq immediately.[215]

After the ultimatum's deadline had expired for two hours, President Bush announced the commencement of operation *Iraqi Freedom.*[216] On 20 March, some 250,000 United States troops, with support from approximately 45,000 British, 2,000 Australian and 200 Polish combat forces, entered Iraq. On 14 April, the Pentagon declared major combat operations over.[217] Yet at the time of writing, hostilities continued between coalition forces and a mounting insurgency that has spiralled into civil war.[218]

In short, the USA was applying as much pressure against Baghdad as it could. In September, pressure derived largely from the assertion that the USA was growing impatient and that it would eventually act. Uncertainty about the Bush administration's resolve faded in the course of November and December, when more and more war material set the stage for combat sometime early in the next year – and probably no later than early spring. The White House assembled the largest troop deployment since 1991 and intensified its verbal war-drumming until 17 March, when it conditioned the non-use of force on the immediate departure of Saddam Hussein and his sons. Finally, by mid-February the global policy debate turned to efforts to rein in a White House that claimed that further UN inspections would yield no palpable results and that the only way to disarm Iraq permanently was physically to remove Saddam Hussein from power. Only radical changes by Iraq, everybody realised, could have taken the wind out of the US sails.

Throughout this period of preparation, states feeling compelled to voice their opinion on the appropriateness of the UK-US course of action faced an inescapable dilemma. Without exception, states agreed that Iraq had to comply with Security Council resolutions – it ought to disarm. Yet if past experience was any guide, that compliance would be forthcoming but under the fear of dire consequences.[219] Only the

[215] George W. Bush, 'Address to the Nation on Iraq', 39 Wkly Comp. Pres. Doc. 338–41 (17 Mar. 2003).
[216] George W. Bush, 'Address to the Nation on Iraq', 39 Wkly Comp. Pres. Doc. 342–3 (19 Mar. 2003).
[217] NYT, 'Pentagon Asserts the Main Fighting is Finished in Iraq' (15 April 2003).
[218] NYT, 'It's Official: There is Now a Civil War in Iraq' (23 Jul. 2006).
[219] Purdum, *A Time of Our Choosing*, at p. 80.

credible and sustained threat of force could compel Iraq into submission and avoid the terrible cost of war itself. On the other hand, anything short of full Iraqi compliance would, too, bolster the US call for intervention. Governments understood this unhappy logic and weighed into their diplomatic responses.[220]

When the Security Council passed resolution 1441 on 8 November, the result of a private word-for-word compromise over the previous weeks, its decision was unanimous.[221] The USA and the UK had traded control over an immediate war for a broader, UN-endorsed front against Saddam Hussein.[222] The USA and the UK assured explicitly in that process that the resolution contained no hidden trigger to jump-start an invasion without prior Council involvement. In return, the remaining Council members and the Arab nations equally explicitly sided with the position that Iraqi non-compliance was no longer acceptable and that enforcement action was at risk.[223] As a result, the Council had given at least partial blessing to the threat of force against Iraq, out of a simple hope that it would deflect, ironically, the necessity of foreign armed intervention. 'Serious consequences', as the resolution warned, in diplomatic euphemism meant military force. However, like resolution 1441 itself, that authorisation was based on a narrow consensus. Most of all, it could not give UN members such as the USA a *carte blanche* to proceed with threats beyond the parameters set out for Iraqi compliance or beyond the moment when the Council decided that threats were no longer appropriate. It certainly could not provide legal cover for any assurances that the USA and UK retained the right to determine non-compliance unilaterally. If the Security Council was bluffing, it was its own call to shoulder the consequences.

There is, of course, a fine line between such an interpretation and one that holds that states did view the USA's policy as lawful. Yet in prior meetings on the subject on 16 and 17 October, called into session by South Africa on behalf of the Non-Aligned Movement (NAM) and crowded by over fifty members of that organisation,[224] the Bush administration's push for an early US-led war against Iraq drew broad

220 William Shawcross, *Allies: The U.S., Britain, Europe and the War in Iraq* 117–18 (2003).

221 SCOR S/PV.4644 (8 Nov. 2002), at 2.

222 NYT, 'Security Council Votes, 15–0, for Tough Iraq Resolution' (8 Nov. 2002); NYT, 'Clock Ticks for Hussein' (9 Nov. 2002).

223 See the statements by the UK and US representatives to the UN Greenstock and Negroponte, SCOR S/PV.4644 (8 Nov. 2002), at 3–5.

224 SCOR Supp. S/2002/1132 (10 Oct. 2002). NAM members at the time totalled 115 states.

opposition. While backing the demand that Iraq ought to comply with previous resolutions and applauding the return of weapons inspections, non-aligned states had been unequivocally critical of what they felt was – correctly, as it turned out – the USA's foregone conclusion to use military force and its undue ruling out of viable diplomatic alternatives. Unanimously, they signalled their contempt for any US-led attack bypassing the Security Council.[225] As Pakistan commented, 'enforcement action involving the collective use of force has been and must remain an option of last resort, not the first policy choice'.[226] This, while short of condemning US and UK military pressure in UN Charter terms, mapped out early resistance of a majority, in particular Arab states, against the prospect of compelling Iraq into submission by force. A smaller group, including Denmark speaking on behalf of the EU, had anticipated the necessity of a unified approach and argued that it was essential that the international community 'remain resolute and put maximum pressure on the Iraqi Government in order to make it comply'.[227]

By early 2003, the USA had completed large portions of its military build-up in the Persian Gulf and had switched its rhetoric to regime change. The evident determination to carry out military action unilaterally despite ongoing UN inspections elicited mostly negative responses. The USA and UK now strongly advocated, in Secretary of State Colin Powell's words, that: 'The threat of force must remain.'[228] In the same vein, his British colleague Jack Straw reasoned that the UN Charter required 'to back a diplomatic process with a credible threat of force and also, if necessary, to be ready to use that threat of force'.[229] Yet a differently composed Council could not agree to proceed under these terms.[230] Among the staunchest dissenters, France's foreign minister

[225] NYT, 'Bush Garners Little Support at U.N. for an Attack on Iraq' (17 Oct. 2002).

[226] SCOR S/PV.4625 (16 Oct. 2002), at 18. See also the critical statements at 13 (Yemen), at 20 (UAE), at 24 (Tunisia); SCOR S/PV.4625 Resum I (16 Oct. 2002), at 7 (Arab League), at 9 (Thailand), at 13 (Indonesia); SCOR S/PV.4625 Resum II (17 Oct. 2002), at 2 (Switzerland), at 6 (Malaysia), at 8 (Lebanon), at 11 (India), at 12 (India), at 12 (Thailand), at 13 (Djibouti), at 14 (Liechtenstein), at 18 (Belarus), at 21 (Cambodia), at 22 (Jamaica), at 23 (Zimbabwe), at 25 (Qatar), at 27 (Nepal).

[227] SCOR S/PV.4625 (16 Oct. 2002), at 10 (Australia), at 11 (Kuwait), at 18 (New Zealand), at 19 (Argentina), 22 (Canada), at 22 (Japan), at 26 (Senegal); SCOR S/PV.4625 Resum II (17 Oct. 2002), at 19 (Albania); SCOR S/PV.4625 Resum III (17 Oct. 2002), at 15 (Norway).

[228] SCOR S/PV.4707 (14 Feb. 2003), at 21.

[229] SCOR S/PV.4707 (14 Feb. 2003), at 18.

[230] On 1 January, Colombia, Ireland, Mauritius, Norway and Singapore gave way to Angola, Chile, Germany, Pakistan, and Spain in the Security Council.

De Villepin countered that resolution 1441 was above all about inspections that should be continued,[231] while other Council members, such as Angola and Syria, categorically ruled out the use of force altogether. In a meeting on 18–19 February and again 11–12 March, the non-aligned states once again crowded the Council chamber. Speaking on behalf of the NAM, Malaysia declared that:

> The Non-Aligned Movement is gravely concerned over the precarious and rapidly deteriorating situation arising from the looming threat of war. We believe that war against Iraq will be a destabilizing factor for the region and for the whole world, as it will have far-reaching political, economic and humanitarian consequences for all. We, the Non-Aligned Movement, are committed to the fundamental principles of the non-use of force and of respect for the sovereignty, territorial integrity, political independence and security of all Member States of the United Nations.[232]

Of the over seventy additional countries attending the sessions, roughly a dozen voiced support for a move to use force. The EU retained a neutral position.[233] The message was that a majority of states wanted to give inspectors more time. The representative of Switzerland summarised: 'we understand the argument of those who consider that readiness to use force is essential in order to strengthen the position of the United Nations inspectors. We appreciate that view and the efforts of those who have expressed it. But the time to make such a decision has not yet come'.[234]

Did the international system condemn US and UK military pressure against Iraq as an unlawful threat of force? As demonstrated, considerations of the threat of force were of secondary concern. Diplomatic responses, similar to Kosovo in 1999, concentrated on the advisability of the use of force.[235] Yet on a closer look, there is evidence. Communal reaction to a tight timetable rigged towards military confrontation was overwhelmingly negative. A portion of the international community understood that maintaining pressure against Baghdad was essential to

231 SCOR S/PV.4701 (5 Feb. 2003), at 24. 232 SCOR S/PV.4717 (11 Mar. 2003), at 7.

233 NYT, 'European Union Says Iraq Must Disarm Fully and Quickly' (18 Feb. 2003).

234 SCOR S/PV.4709 (18 Feb. 2003), at 7.

235 On reactions after the invasion see SCOR S/PV.4726 (26 Mar. 2003) and SCOR S/PV.4726 Resum I (27 Mar. 2003); Gray, *Use of Force*, at pp. 181–4; Sean D. Murphy, 'Use of Military Force to Disarm Iraq', 97 Am. JIL 419–32 (2003), at 428; NYT, 'A Worried World Shows Discord' (19 Mar. 2003); NYT, 'Arab Ministers Urge U.S. Withdrawal' (25 Mar. 2003).

procure substantial results from Saddam Hussein. By that token, the Security Council approved early military pressure in November 2002 as a necessary evil to force Saddam Hussein to comply. However, the consensus achieved was pragmatic and narrow and, most of all, was to keep authority over the recourse to force in UN hands. The majority of states disagreed with the early 2003 shift to an open policy of regime change, which they held wrongfully bypassed and exceeded Security Council authorisation. This undid the slim consensus of 2002 that the no-threat rule had to be sacrificed in order to avoid an undesirable war. The threat of force lacked communal support in spring 2003, when states disapproved the US claim that a 'gathering threat', as President Bush had labelled it, entitled it to employ preventive force unilaterally. The same fate could be attributed to the claim that resolutions 678 and 687's revival provided legal cover for joint US-UK coercion.[236] Very few states gave any credence to that view.

Conclusions

There are other instances in which open threats to extract concessions played an important role in shaping the outcome of crises. During the Cuban missile crisis in 1962, Robert Kennedy made clear to Soviet Ambassador Anatoly Dobrynin on the night of 27 October that the USA needed a commitment by the following day that the missile bases on Cuba would be removed. Otherwise, he said, 'we would remove them'.[237] In 1965, Zambia issued an ultimatum against Rhodesia in order to prevent it from declaring independence from the UK.[238] During several largely underreported border clashes between the PRC and the USSR over the Ussuri river, the Soviet Union threatened to bomb China's nuclear facilities in Xinjiang province.[239] Since the end of the Cold War, Russia has threatened forceful action against Georgia in 1992 and 2002.[240] The USA, for its part, practiced coercive diplomacy based

[236] Thomas M. Franck, 'What Happens Now? The UN After Iraq', 97 Am. JIL 607–20 (2003).
[237] Robert F. Kennedy, *Thirteen Days: A Memoir of the Cuban Missile Crisis* 82 (1969).
[238] ICB, 'Rhodesia's UDI', crisis 218. [239] ICB, 'Ussuri River', crisis 231.
[240] ICB, 'Georgia – Abkhazia', crisis 407. In September 2002, Georgia protested against President Putin's broadcasted announcement which promised military action against Georgia if it did not suppress terrorist activities. Georgia referred to the statement as an undisguised threat of force. See SCOR Supp. S/2002/1033 (16 Sep. 2002). The announcement of President Putin took place on 11 September, exactly

on verbal promises and outside of a self-defence context against Haiti,[241] and repeatedly against Yugoslavia[242] and Iraq prior to the 2003 invasion.[243] Recently, the PRC issued a law that formally authorised its government to use of force in order to prevent Taiwan from declaring independence,[244] while in the Middle East the controversy over Iran's nuclear programme has occasioned a series of threats from Iran and the USA.[245]

The eight cases examined reveal a mixed picture. All belong to the same class of events. In all, open threats were the preferred tool to achieve a distinct foreign policy objective, yet they vary greatly in regard to the underlying facts and systemic responses. The British ultimatum against Israel in 1948, the Korean War threats of the USA and PRC in 1950, the PRC's ultimatum against India in 1965 and, finally, the threats of Uganda against Kenya in 1976 stirred reaction from only the closest military allies, not a widespread international reaction. On the other hand, Morocco's plans to annex Spanish Sahara met with resistance, and the Turkish threats against Cyprus also drew criticism. With regard to Yugoslavia in 1999 and Iraq in 2003, the system's reaction, too, was not one of indifference but compromise due to thorny circumstances. In the light of these particularities, the systematic comparison of the eight cases cannot support sweeping generalisations.[246]

If so, state practice in regard to open threats to extract concessions may appear at face value as inconsistent. It could be said that firm expectations on the reaction of third states have not formed and thus that the law that follows from the aggregate of cases is indeterminate.[247] It would be premature, however, to draw such a conclusion. Differentiation is called for.

one year after the 9/11 terrorist attacks. See NYT, 'Putin Warns Georgia to Root out Chechen Rebels Within its Borders or Face Attacks' (12 Sep. 2002); 2002 HIIK 11.

241 ICB, 'Haiti Military Regime', crisis 411. 242 ICB, 'Yugoslavia II: Bosnia', crisis 403.

243 ICB, 'Iraq No-Fly Zone', crisis 406; ICB, 'UNSCOM I', crisis 422; ICB, 'UNSCOM II Operation Desert Fox', crisis 428.

244 NYT, 'Beijing Leaders Speak of Force to Keep Taiwan "Chinese"' (8 Mar. 2005); NYT, 'China Denies "Taiwan" Law on Secession is a "War Bill"' (14 Mar. 2005).

245 ICB, 'Iran Nuclear', crisis 439; NYT, 'Iran's President Says "Israel Must be Wiped Off the Map"' (27 Oct. 2005); NYT, 'Cheney Warns of "Consequences" for Iran on Nuclear Issue' (9 Mar. 2006); NYT, 'Threats Rattle at Nuclear Meeting on Iran' (9 Mar. 2006); NYT, 'Bush Won't Rule out Nuclear Strike against Iran' (18 Apr. 2006).

246 Similar caution at generalisations is expressed by Alexander L. George and William E. Simons (eds.), *The Limits of Coercive Diplomacy* 268 (2nd edn, 1994).

247 See above, chapter 4, at p. 111: 'Practice is consistent if in the period under consideration it follows a recurring pattern, such that firm expectations of behaviour have formed.'

One step towards differentiation concerns the theory that state silence amounts to approval. As stated in chapter 4, much depends on the analyst's theory of customary law. If state silence is coded as approval, open threats of the kind examined in this chapter by and large could be argued to be compatible with the UN Charter because a majority of states almost always stand aloof. The case studies indicate, however, that state reactions are determined by a host of factors, many of which have nothing to do with legal considerations. It is plausible, to name an example, that the bulk of nations in the world simply did not care about what happened between Uganda and Kenya in the 1970s since none but the Cold War antagonists could accrue any benefits from voicing dissent. The British ultimatum against Israel was only partly public and embedded in a larger war setting that made third-party singling out of threats unlikely. The same holds for Korea and Kashmir. In contrast, in 'high flying' cases such as the Turkish missile crisis, the Moroccan march, Kosovo or Iraq, these constraints did not operate. The 'silence equals consent' thesis is not plausible in this context.

It may then be right to conclude that, on the balance, state practice revolves around two questions in order to determine the lawfulness of open threats. The first question is whether the threat brandished, under the circumstances of the time, was *credible* and thus sufficiently serious and dangerous to raise the shared risk of armed conflict. A threat is credible when it is rational to carry it out,[248] or at least if it appears plausible that it is carried out when facing an 'irrational' threatener (although the appearance of irrationality is, in a sense, again rational for the uncertainty it instils). Military preponderance and capability provide the basis for a credible threat, and so does the increase of the political stakes by openly and consistently declaring a readiness to use force. Idi Amin's moody declarations were not the mark of a well-planned course of action, and Kenya's grip on Uganda's oil supply proved a highly effective countermeasure. The Chinese border ultimatum in 1965, too, was judged as largely empty policy stunt. This is not true of NATO threats against Yugoslavia or UK-US threats against Iraq. The 'outlier' is the Korean War, which is exceptional in respect to the fact that the UN was in effect a warring party. Overall, the credibility test performs well as an explanatory variable for communal reaction.

248 Franck C. Zagare and D. Marc Kilgour, 'Deterrence Theory and the Spiral Model Revisited', 10 J. Theo. p. 59–87 (1998), at 63.

The second question is whether the course of action taken by the threatening state was a genuine attempt to *manage a pre-existing crisis*. This is an extenuating element, which states seem to have applied to the 1948 British ultimatum to rein in Israeli advances into Egypt at a time when the UN Security Council had called for a ceasefire. The Council was also involved in Iraq in 2003 and Yugoslavia in 1999. Third parties then well understood, although acknowledged with reluctance, that military pressure could have the short-term advantage of avoiding armed conflict altogether. Yet in the way the threats were employed, the USA failed the test in Iraq in 2003, while there remain doubts for Yugoslavia in 1999. From this diagnosis one may infer that extenuation only applies, if at all, when the UN Security Council has actively identified the need to induce compliance with collectively formulated demands. The 'honest broker' in such a context, there is some reason to believe, is not faulted. (However, there is no honest broker if there is no pre-existing crisis to intervene for.[249])

The two criteria provide some guidance to explain third-party reaction in the face of open threats to extract concessions. The common wisdom that threats are met with indifference is false. As noted, the UN Charter took roots in an era when Germany and Japan's coercive diplomacy formed the prelude to World War II, and where collective action was necessary to bring their ambitions to a halt. There is little evidence in the cases examined that states, as of principle, have wished to change this frame of mind at any time since 1945. The next chapter will show whether the same criteria hold for a new set of historical cases that focus on demonstrations of force.

[249] See in analogy article 25(2)b; ILC *Articles of State Responsibility*, GAOR Supp. 10, A/56/10 (annex to A/RES/56/83, 12 Dec. 2001).

6 Demonstrations of force

> I wish it were possible to convince others, with words, of what we now find it necessary to say with guns and planes: Armed hostility is futile. Our resources are equal to any challenge. Because we fight for values and we fight for principles, rather than territory or colonies, our patience and our determination are unending.
>
> President Lyndon B. Johnson, *Speech at Johns Hopkins University*, 7 April 1965, referring to US military operations in Vietnam[1]

Deeds more than words

This chapter will examine state and UN practice as it applies to demonstrations of force: cross-border displays of military capability signalling resolve to use force for political ends, usually to compel or to discourage. In chapter 4, demonstrations of force were defined as follows:

> Where state A, in the form of non-routine military deployments, build-ups, manoeuvres, tests or other militarized acts signals preparedness and resolve to use armed force on a particular issue under dispute with state B. The initiation of militarised acts in a period of high tension is a firm indication that a demonstration of force is at play.[2]

Demonstrations of force may take a great variety of forms. For example, a state may send missile-bearing ships towards the coastline of another state, or may 'exercise' military jets as an immediate signal of its non-toleration of a particular move. Its armies may serve to communicate resolve by parading along a border or by simulating a particular scenario of military encounter with its rival state. Weapon tests of any kind, particularly those exhibiting the acquisition of

[1] Quoted from Anders Breidlid, Fredrik Chr. Brogger, *et al.*, *American Culture: An Anthology of Civilization Texts* 351 (1996).
[2] See above, chapter 4, at p. 113.

superior military technology, do not fail to raise concern among rivals. Finally, force can also be demonstrated by using it; some 'border incidents' and retaliatory acts may be understood as being more about implying the further use of force than about imposing material damage or redressing a previous wrong. These are acts of force, but whether they also constitute a demonstration of force depends on whether the action in question had been designed to convey a signal that more force might be forthcoming in foreseeable circumstances.

With the possible exception of weapon tests, all such activities were understood in the interwar period to be 'measures short of war' and of doubtful legality.

What the cases in this chapter have in common is that the demonstration of force is the instrument to convey foreign policy. Words may accompany the demonstration, but the presence of military might is intended to convey a more potent message. While it is difficult to draw a clear line between military exercises, alerts and troop movements that are peaceful from those that are aggressive, it appears that twenty-eight international crises since 1945 (representing 25 per cent of the total) have included unilateral demonstrations of force in one form or another, and fall remarkably clearly into this category. These form the basis for this chapter. The remaining cases fall within a quasi-self-defensive, tit-for-tat, two-sided context and thus belong in the next chapter.

'Actions', as the saying goes, 'speak louder than words'. If so, we can expect that states, despite the ambiguity of some actions, will display more sensitivity to demonstrations of force than to verbal threats. Thomas Schelling notes:

> ... words are cheap, not inherently credible when they emanate from an adversary, and sometimes too intimate a mode of expression. The action is more impersonal, cannot be 'rejected' the way a verbal message can, and does not involve the intimacy of verbal contact. Actions also prove something; significant actions usually incur some cost or risk, and carry some evidence of their own credibility ... actions tend to be irrevocable, and the fact that action occurred proves that authority is behind it.[3]

Demonstrations of force carry more credibility and are more serious than most verbal messages.[4] The expectation, therefore, is that condemnation will be more readily forthcoming.

[3] Thomas C. Schelling, *Arms and Influence* 150 (1966).

[4] One might add that in distinction to a verbal threat, a demonstration of force is easier to call off. Since no demands have been clearly formulated and militarised acts often

That said, ambiguity is a particularly acute problem of demonstrations of force. Governments often deny making a threat; sometimes that denial is genuine, sometimes not. For example, a genuine error occurred in 1982 when the USSR misinterpreted NATO's extensive nuclear exercise, *Able Archer*, as a genuine preparation for a strike, and responded by putting its forces onto high alert.[5] On the other hand, the US naval exercises in the Gulf of Sidra in 1981 ostensibly held on a routine basis were a barely concealed attempt to impress upon Libya that its territorial claim over the Gulf would be rebutted.[6] There is an inherent ambiguity about all land, sea, and air exercises, deployments and tests since there is little doubt that they are accepted between nations whose relations are on a completely peaceful footing, while in other situations the claim of innocence is false. On the eve of World War I, Lord Grey, Britain's Foreign Secretary commented retrospectively on German military build-ups:

> The distinction between preparations made with the intention of going to war and precautions against attack is a true distinction, clear and definite in the minds of those who build up armaments. But it is a distinction that is not obvious or certain to others ... Germany would be specially prone to attribute to others motives and views that we have entertained ourselves. Each Government, therefore, while resenting any suggestion that its own measures are anything more than defence, regards similar measures of another Government as preparation for attack.[7]

The question, then, is how states have attempted in practice to separate the wheat from the chaff.

USSR–Turkey (Turkish Straits, 1946)

During the opening trumpeting of the ideological partition between East and West after World War II, the USA and the USSR engaged in several trials of strength along the perimeters of the territories of Soviet-occupied Eastern Europe, the Balkans and the Middle East. In 1946, the USA viewed the Italian and Yugoslav bids for Trieste, the Greek civil war and the Iranian troop-withdrawal crisis as concerted

run under the cover of normality, there is no loss of face to withdraw forces to previous positions.

[5] ICB, 'Able Archer', crisis 344. [6] ICB, 'Gulf of Syrte I', crisis 330.

[7] Lord Edward Grey, *Twenty-five Years: 1892–1916* vol. I, 91 (1925).

instances of Soviet expansionism. Another trial of strength took place at the time over the Turkish Straits, connecting the Black Sea and the Mediterranean.[8] This waterway through the Dardanelles, the Sea of Marmara and the Bosporus was of paramount strategic importance both for the USSR, to secure its ports in the Black Sea and to gain access to the eastern Mediterranean, and for the USA and UK, to keep the USSR at bay and away from their Middle Eastern sphere of influence.[9]

Under the 1936 Montreux Convention, Turkey retained exclusive military control over the Turkish Straits.[10] It was authorised to close them to warships when it was at war or threatened by aggression. Due to Turkey's neutrality during World War II, the fact that it had control over the passage raised calls for a revision of the Straits regime in the immediate post-war period.[11] In March 1945, the USSR rescinded the Russo-Turkish friendship treaty. A year later, in 1946, it openly sought revision of the terms of the Montreux Convention, in order to challenge Turkey's exclusive role as guardian of the Straits, simultaneously entertaining territorial claims to parts of the Caucasus. At that time, some 400,000 Soviet troops were distributed along parts of the Soviet border with Turkey and Turkish fear of an aggressive move by the USSR had grown to such an extent that it maintained its military presence at high - and costly - levels of readiness throughout the year.[12]

In a note issued on 7 August 1946, the USSR demanded renegotiation of the Straits regime such that Soviet forces would share responsibility over its defence, in order to prevent their utilisation, as it explained, 'by other countries for aims hostile to the Black Sea powers'.[13] Simultaneously, there were reports of large-scale troop movements in Transcaucasia and Bulgaria, and of naval exercises in the Black Sea.[14]

[8] ICB, 'Turkish Straits', crisis 111; Jonathan Knight, 'American Statecraft and the 1946 Black Sea Straits Controversy', 90 PSQ 451–75 (1975); Anthony R. de Luca, 'Soviet-American Politics and the Turkish Straits', 92 PSQ 503–24 (1977), at 516–20; Süleyman Seydi, *The Turkish Straits and the Great Powers: From the Montreux Conventions to the Early Cold War 1936–1947* 227–42 (2003).

[9] William R. Keylor, *A World of Nations* 16 (2003).

[10] *Convention Regarding the Regime of the Straits, and Protocol*, 28 LNTS 12 (20 Jul. 1936).

[11] de Luca, 'Soviet-American Politics', at 507–10.

[12] Seydi, *The Turkish Straits*, at p. 228; NYT, 'Turkey To Keep Army Mobilized' (10 Aug. 1946).

[13] The USSR also sent copies of the note to the UK and the USA: see 1946 FRUS vol. VII, 827–9; NYT, 'Russian Note Asks Share in Defense of Turkish Straits' (13 Aug. 1946).

[14] de Luca, 'Soviet-American Politics', at 516.

This raised concern in the USA and UK, as they took the note to mean not only that the USSR wished to build a military base at the Dardanelles,[15] but also that the USSR's bid for joint guardianship would entail military occupation of Turkey and its conversion into a vassal state.[16] The joint UK-US response was to provide Turkey with verbal and physical support:[17] on 20 August, President Truman authorised the sending of all destroyers of the Twelfth Fleet and the aircraft carrier *Franklin D. Roosevelt* to proceed to the eastern Mediterranean in addition to reinforcements by the existing naval forward presence.[18]

With this backing, Turkey, within a short period of time, flatly rejected the USSR's demand. The Turkish government expressed willingness to participate in a conference to revise the Montreux Convention with all the original signatories, but would not countenance a bilateral deal with the USSR alone.[19] This prompted a second note from the USSR, milder in tone than the first, but warning that it considered 'military measures in the Straits together with any non-Black Sea power' as 'directly contradictory to the interests of the Black Sea states' and that the defence of its own coastlines was its essential interest.[20] This was, of course, referring to the US naval reinforcements. The USA replied to this note in a firm and assertive manner: on 11 October, the State Department explained 'in the most friendly spirit' that 'should the Straits become object of attack or threat of attack by an aggressor, the resulting situation would be a matter for action on the part of the Security Council of the United Nations'.[21] In full awareness of the USSR's command of the Security Council veto, US Secretary of State

15 *The Ambassador in Turkey (Wilson) to the Secretary of State* (8 Aug. 1946), 1946 FRUS vol. VII, 830.

16 de Luca, 'Soviet-American Politics', at 518; NYT, 'British Alarmed Over Dardanelles' (18 Aug. 1946); See further *The Acting Secretary of State to the Secretary of State, at Paris* (15 Aug. 1946), 1946 FRUS vol. VII, 840–2.

17 NYT, 'Acheson Hints U.S. is Firm on Straits' (17 Aug. 1946); NYT, 'U.S. Note on Straits' (22 Aug. 1946).

18 Knight, 'American Statecraft', at 467, 472.

19 NYT, 'Ready to Discuss Straits, Turkey Says' (15 Aug. 1946); NYT, 'Turkey Rejects Demands of Russia on the Straits' (24 Aug. 1946). See also NYT, 'Text of Turkey's Reply to Soviet Union on Straits' (25 Aug. 1946).

20 NYT, 'Russia Warns Turks to Shun Outsider's Aide in Key Straits' (29 Sep. 1946).

21 NYT, 'U.S. Note to Russia on the Dardanelles' (12 Oct. 1946). This note had been sent by US Secretary of State Dean Acheson to the Soviet Chargé already on 19 August: see *The Acting Secretary of State to the Soviet Chargé (Orekhov)*, 1946 FRUS vol. VII, 847–8. But the note was repeated on 8 October, see *Acting Secretary of State to the Ambassador of the Soviet Union (Smith)*, 1946 FRUS vol. VII, 874.

Dean Acheson wrote this note as an alternative way of stating that the USA was not giving the USSR a free hand in the Middle East, and that advances in regional hegemony would be resisted – but to what degree remained a matter of strategic ambiguity.[22] Eventually tensions abated, as the USSR announced in late October 1946 its intention not to hold a conference to revise the Montreux Convention.[23]

In this early Cold War crisis, the prohibition of military threats included in the Charter of the recently formed United Nations was not invoked by any party. Apart from a passing remark by Turkey in the General Assembly,[24] the UN did not become involved, and neither did any third-party state other than the UK and the USA. These strategic partners aligned themselves with Turkey and succeeded in seeing off the USSR's plans for a military presence in the Dardanelles. The USSR, however, was alone in criticising the concentration of US forces in the eastern Mediterranean. It asserted on radio and in the *Pravda* that the choice of location for military exercises and the US tendency to distribute its forces in foreign ports had 'nothing in common with the ideals of the U.N., nor can it serve to remove the threat to the peace'.[25] Yet the Soviet government stopped short of filing a formal protest with the US ambassador in Moscow.[26]

It would appear that what was at issue was not so much whether there had been a demonstration of force, but rather the question of whether or not the demonstrations of either side had grown to intolerable proportions. There was no common answer to this question. The problem of the Turkish Straits was treated as a regional problem, the solution of it being cast into the middle of growing US–Soviet antagonism. Information about the troop movements of both sides was largely unpublicised, news coverage of them was lacking or confined to rumour. Both powers, too, exercised restraint. US warships were not overtly concentrated around the Dardanelles, but were dispersed; Soviet demands for the renegotiation of the Montreux Convention were not formulated in compelling terms, and its naval exercises in the Black

22 Knight, 'American Statecraft', at 467. 23 ICB, 'Turkish Straits', crisis 111.
24 NYT, 'Turk's U.N. Speech Taken as Defiance on Straits Demand' (27 Oct. 1946).
25 Knight, 'American Statecraft', at 468.
26 Knight, 'American Statecraft', at 468, reports that Soviet Ambassador Gromyko denounced the *Roosevelt* cruise during a conference in Paris and also within the Security Council. What remains certain is that the USSR did not send a formal complaint to the USA or the Security Council at any time during the events.

Sea, too, were not staged directly off the coast of Turkey. Confronted with a firm US response, the USSR chose not to push further.

In short, on their own the actions of neither the USSR nor the USA sufficed to arouse the kind of alarm that should have triggered a UN response. But with the adversaries concerned, the UN would have been paralysed under even graver circumstances. There is little, therefore, that may be extracted from this case as a lesson for present purposes, apart perhaps from the observation that in the eyes of the protagonists themselves the creation of tensions leading to open war was actively contemplated and considered, but not (yet) judged as being imminent.

India–Portugal (Goa, 1961)

After the British withdrawal from India in 1947, Salazar Portugal rejected all requests from India to hand over its colonial possessions on its west coast. Portugal had possessed Goa, its main presence in the subcontinent, ever since Goa's conquest in 1510, and the Portuguese government, viewing the territory not as a colony but as an integral part of the Portuguese state, stubbornly refused to heed any UN calls for Goan decolonisation and self-determination.[27] In 1955, Portugal crushed an initial Indian attempt at unification by force of arms,[28] and by 1961 hopes for Lisbon voluntarily to change its colonial policy had faded; a sense of frustration courted nationalist sentiments in favour of militant action.[29] At the same time, the Portuguese being distracted by troubles in Angola seemed to open a window of opportunity for New Delhi to act with regard to Goa.[30]

[27] Sources on this case study are: ICB, 'Goa II', crisis 190; 1961 UNYB 129–32; Quincy Wright, 'The Goa Incident', 56 Am. JIL 617–32 (1962); Rosalyn Higgins, *The Development of International Law Through the Political Organs of the United Nations* 187–8 (1963); B. M. Kaul, *The Untold Story* 290–307 (1967); Arthur G. Rubinoff, *India's Use of Force in Goa* (1971); Thomas M. Franck, *Nation Against Nation: What Happened to the UN Dream and What the US Can Do About It* 53–8 (1985); A. Mark Weisburd, *Use of Force: The Practice of States Since World War II* 35–7 (1997); Thomas M. Franck, *Recourse to Force: State Action Against Threats and Armed Attacks* 114–17 (2002); Christine Gray, *International Law and the Use of Force* 53, 57 (2nd edn, 2004). See also the (unfortunately deeply coloured) world press records reproduced in National Secretariate for Information, *The Invasion and Occupation of Goa in the World Press* (1962).

[28] ICB, 'Goa I', crisis 151.

[29] Rubinoff, *India's Use of Force*, at p. 73; The ICJ's ruling *Case concerning Right of Passage over Indian Territory (Portugal v. India), Merits*, 1960 ICJ Rep. 6 (12 Apr. 1960), too, did not indicate any UN-propelled action to steep up pressure on Portugal.

[30] NYT, 'Goan Extremists Exploiting Troubles in Angola' (21 May 1961).

Two previously Portuguese enclaves, Dadrá and Nagar Aveli, had been seized by crowds of Indians in 1954, and on 14 August 1961 India constitutionally integrated them into its territory.[31] On that occasion, Prime Minister Jawaharlal Nehru gave a speech in parliament in which he indicated a shift of policy by warning that he could no longer rule out the possible use of force to bring Goa into its rightful place under Indian control and that no government would be permitted passage through Indian territory to reach the two enclaves that had just been formally annexed.[32] Hints of a seizure of Goa by India continued to be publicised throughout the following months.[33]

At the end of November, in circumstances that are not entirely clear, Portuguese defence forces from the island of Angediva, ten miles south of Goa, fired at an Indian passenger steamboat and shot an Indian fisherman. Anxious about reported plans for an Indian retaliation, the minuscule Portuguese armed forces present in the colony began to swell their ranks on the Goan border at Majali,[34] while the Governor of Goa, Vasalo do Silva, declared a state of emergency.[35] Following the Angediva incident, Nehru came under increasing domestic pressure to act: although to India the value of Goa was purely symbolic, public opinion was strongly in favour of Portugal finally abandoning its territorial possessions on the subcontinent.[36]

On 6 December, Indian officials declared that as a 'precautionary measure', New Delhi had sent troops to the Goan border to areas that were 'threatened by aggressive maneuvers of Portugal'. It was said that the situation was being re-examined daily and further action stood in balance.[37] By 8 December, Nehru stated that the situation had become 'intolerable' and that India would take some form of action if Portugal did not hand Goa over.[38] Events had steered Nehru into a position with few options open to him. That same day, Portugal made the charge in

31 NYT, 'Annexation Approved' (15 Aug. 1961).

32 NYT, 'Nehru Threatens Force on Goa; Bars Portuguese from 2 Areas' (18 Aug. 1961).

33 NYT, 'Nehru Warns Lisbon' (24 Oct. 1961).

34 NYT, 'Shot Kills Indian Fisherman' (26 Nov. 1961); NYT, 'Lisbon Scores Nehru' (27 Nov. 1961); NYT, 'Goa Build-up Reported' (30 Nov. 1961).

35 NYT, 'State of Emergency Reported' (1 Dec. 1961).

36 NYT, 'India Expected to Press Portugal to Yield Some Land Near Goa' (1 Dec. 1961).

37 NYT, 'India is Weighing Force to Win Goa' (7 Dec. 1961). The alleged Portuguese provocations seem not to have taken place. See Wright, *The Goa Incident*, at p. 621; Rubinoff, *India's Use of Force*, at pp. 85–7.

38 NYT, 'Goa's Liberation Pledged by Nehru' (8 Dec. 1961).

the Security Council that the Indian military build-up near Goa posed a threat to peace, and accused India of 'unprovoked aggression' and of conducting a campaign of threats and intimidation designed to annex Goa by force.[39] Nehru in turn, citing unprovoked Portuguese raids into Indian territory, declared on 11 December that his patience was exhausted.[40] A force of 30,000 Indian troops had by now been amassed along the Goan border, while the aircraft carrier *Vikrant*, along with a cruiser and five frigates, had installed a sea blockade around the tiny colony.[41] On 12 December, do Silva ordered the evacuation of women and children from Goa and adamantly pledged to defend Goa 'to the last'.[42] Indian jet fighter planes flew over Goa on the 14th.[43] Delhi's intention to seize Goa by force was now clearly revealed, and Lisbon's refusal to yield was reconfirmed.

British and US ambassadors to New Delhi tried to persuade Nehru not to resort to force. Brazil made a public plea to that effect. President Kennedy, in addressing both Nehru and Salazar, urged them to renounce military action.[44] UN Secretary-General U Thant, too, sent cables to both men, requesting them not to allow the situation to deteriorate and to negotiate in order to reach a peaceful solution.[45] Reconsidering, Nehru twice postponed India's 'D-Day'.[46] But as things stood, it was politically untenable for Nehru to withdraw troops without any progress being made towards freeing Goa from Portuguese control.[47] On the night between 17 and 18 December, Indian forces rolled into Goa, Damão and Diu, meeting feeble resistance.[48] Thirty-six

[39] NYT, 'Portugal Charges India Perils Peace' (9 Dec. 1961).

[40] NYT, 'Nehru Issues Warning' (12 Dec. 1961).

[41] NYT, 'U.S. Urged to Make Study' (12 Dec. 1961). Reports of the Portuguese forces varies, as widely as between 3,500 and 12,000. However, there is no doubt that Goa did not have a chance in repelling a determined Indian advance to take over the territory. Portuguese forces were already depleted due to engagements in Africa.

[42] NYT, 'Goan Evacuation of Women Begins' (13 Dec. 1961).

[43] NYT, 'Indians Fly Over Goa' (15 Dec. 1961). See also charges of further over-flights contained in Portugal's letter to the Security Council, SCOR Supp. S/5029 (16 Dec. 1961).

[44] NYT, 'Kennedy Sends Pleas to Nehru and Sukarno Not to Use Force' (15 Dec. 1961). See also NYT, 'Rusk Meets Aides' (18 Dec. 1961).

[45] NYT, 'Thant Sends Plea on Goa to Nehru' (17 Dec. 1961).

[46] Kaul, *The Untold Story*, at p. 299.

[47] See the estimate of the US Department of State, *Memorandum From the Assistant Secretary of State for Near Eastern and South Asian Affairs (Talbot) to Acting Secretary of State Ball* (12 Dec. 1961), 1961 FRUS vol. XIX, 153.

[48] NYT, 'Troops Clash in Goa' (18 Dec. 1961).

hours later, all opposition had been overcome and the 451 years of Portuguese rule over Goa had come to an end.[49]

The invasion of Goa revealed a deep division of opinion among UN members. What had their reaction been to the Indian troop build-up prior to the use of force? In the ten days preceding the invasion, Portugal had made several efforts to secure the attention of the Security Council.[50] It said that the 'concentration of military forces, naval, land and air, can only find explanation in the Indian objective of violent conquest of a foreign territory by force of arms', that Indian accusations against it were 'designed ... to arouse an emotional climate calculated to justify premeditated aggression' and finally, that 'such aggression constitutes a grave threat to peace and security'.[51] Yet apparently in order to await further developments, Portugal stopped short of asking the Council to convene and take action to halt the impending Indian march into Goa.[52]

That changed markedly on the day of the invasion. Portugal now called upon the Security Council to order an immediate ceasefire and the withdrawal of Indian troops.[53] The debate within the Council exposed a split within it, two opposing camps disagreeing over the legitimacy of India's action.[54]

On the one hand, Portugal's NATO allies – the USA, the UK, France and Turkey – as well as Nationalist China, Ecuador and Chile, held that New Delhi had done wrong; that while its demand for Portugal to leave Goa might have been right, the use of force in pursuit of that end could not be justified. At a NATO ministerial conference on an earlier occasion, NATO member states had made it clear to Portugal that no material aid would be forthcoming and that collective defence

[49] Casualties assessments range between thirty-nine and seventy-five. See Rubinoff, *India's Use of Force*, at p. 93; Kaul, *The Untold Story*, at p. 305.

[50] SCOR Supp. S/5016 (8 Dec. 1961); SCOR Supp. S/5018 (11 Dec. 1961); SCOR Supp. S/5028 and S/5029 (16 Dec. 1961).

[51] SCOR Supp. S/5016 (8 Dec. 1961).

[52] *Memorandum From the Assistant Secretary of State for Near Eastern and South Asian Affairs (Talbot) to Acting Secretary of State Ball* (12 Dec. 1961), 1961 FRUS vol. XIX, 154. On 4 October, however, the Portuguese representative had accused India of 'threats of aggression': see GAOR A/PV.1025, referred to in SCOR S/PV.987, at para. 16 (18 Dec. 1961).

[53] SCOR Supp. S/5030 (18 Dec. 1961). See the Council debates in SCOR S/PV.987 (18 Dec. 1961); S/PV.988 (18 Dec. 1961).

[54] The Security Council was composed as follows: Ceylon, Chile, Nationalist China, Ecuador, France, Liberia, Turkey, the United Arab Republic, the UK, the USSR and the USA. Only these eleven members took part in the deliberations.

obligations under NATO did not extend to overseas possessions.[55] 'Doubtless India would hold', US ambassador Adlai Stevenson reasoned, 'that its action is aimed at a just end. But, if our Charter means anything, it means that States are obligated to seek a solution of their differences by peaceful means, are obligated to utilize the procedures of the United Nations when other peaceful means have failed'.[56] The seven states that supported Portugal's position accordingly called for an immediate ceasefire to stop ongoing Indian advances, and demanded the withdrawal of Indian troops to re-establish the *status quo ante*. However, a resolution introduced to that end was defeated by a Soviet veto.[57]

On the other hand, the representatives of Asian and African states in the Security Council – Ceylon, Liberia, the United Arab Republic – joined by the USSR, took an opposing stance, in support of India. For these four, the use of force could not be artificially separated from the issue of colonialism: India was entitled to liberate Goa from foreign oppression. Turning the tables, Ceylon's ambassador Malalasekera remarked that it was the Portuguese build-up of forces in Goa that was to blame, and that: 'The Security Council cannot but also note that such a build-up was inconsistent with the desire to seek settlement of the issue on peaceful lines.'[58] A counter-resolution in support of India, rejecting the Portuguese claim of aggression and calling it to cooperate with India in the liquidation of its colonial possessions, was defeated by the same division of seven to four.[59]

With the Security Council in a deadlock, the USA considered taking the matter to the General Assembly in a revival of the 1950 'Uniting for Peace' mechanism. But an informal poll among the Assembly members conducted by Adlai Stevenson brought to light the fact that most Asian and African countries, allied in the NAM, would not support a resolution condemning one of its leading members.[60] As a two-thirds majority was necessary for this purpose, and Asian-African states already filled half of the 104 member seats in the General Assembly at that time, this

[55] NYT, 'Goa Resists Move' (18 Dec. 1961); NYT, 'Rusk Tells India of U.S. "Regrets"' (19 Dec. 1961).

[56] SCOR S/PV.987 (18 Dec. 1961), at para. 76.

[57] 1961 UNYB 131. The draft was supported by the USA, UK, France, Turkey, China (Taiwan), Ecuador and Chile, and rejected by Ceylon, Liberia, the United Arab Republic and the USSR.

[58] SCOR S/PV.987 (18 Dec. 1961), at para. 139.

[59] 1961 UNYB 131.

[60] Franck, *Nation Against Nation*, at p. 56.

ended the USA's initiative within the UN.[61] According to the patchy records available, apart from the states already mentioned, those who sided with Portugal were Brazil,[62] India's enemy Pakistan,[63] and the PRC, which fought a border conflict in the north of the subcontinent.[64] India, on the other hand, gained overt support from Morocco,[65] South Africa, Northern Rhodesia, Mozambique and Portuguese Guinea.[66] On 19 December, the General Assembly overwhelmingly condemned Portugal for non-compliance with its obligation to report on activities in her colonies; the vote was ninety to three (Portugal, Spain, South Africa), with two abstentions (Bolivia and France).[67] The minority within the Security Council represented the majority in the General Assembly.

Clearly, there was no expression of support towards Portugal for the loss of its colony; the only sympathy for Salazar was regret that India had not refrained from the use of force. Conversely, the support of India by African and Asian states was easily explained by the championing of anti-colonialism and their conclusion that the use of force was acceptable, if no viable alternative was available to bring Western domination to an end.[68] Many members of the NAM (founded in September 1961 by Tito),[69] had, after all, acquired their independence because the international system had given currency to the legitimacy of self-determination and the end of colonial imperialism. Portuguese rule was especially resented in Africa; at an Indian-sponsored, four-day seminar on Portuguese colonialism in October, African leaders had passionately tried to persuade New Delhi to occupy Goa by force in order to bring the Portuguese empire to a point of collapse.[70] In Asia, Indonesia actively contemplated the use of force to eject the Dutch from New Guinea. The USSR, antagonising the USA, signified its approval of these states, to

61 NYT, 'Soviet Veto Cited' (20 Dec. 1961). 62 SCOR Supp. S/5034 (18 Dec. 1961).

63 Rubinoff, *India's Use of Force*, at p. 98.

64 NYT, 'Red China Backs India on "Recovering" Goa' (20 December 1961); NYT, 'China Equates Goa With Taiwan' (21 Dec. 1961).

65 NYT, 'Rabat Backs New Delhi' (19 Dec. 1961).

66 NYT, 'Africa Nationalists Praise Indian Action' (20 Dec. 1961).

67 A/RES/1699 (XVI) *Non-compliance of the Government of Portugal with Chapter XI of the Charter of the United Nations and with General Assembly resolution 1542 (XV)* (19 Dec. 1961). The resolution had been proposed by India on 9 August 1961, 1961 UNYB 427–8.

68 Antonio Cassese, *Self-determination of Peoples: A Legal Reappraisal* 198 (1995).

69 On the NAM see Peter Wiletts, *The Non-Aligned Movement: The Origins of a Third World Alliance* (1978).

70 Rubinoff, *India's Use of Force*, at pp. 80–2.

advance its bid for power and leadership among the newly formed majority in the General Assembly.

The story of the takeover of Goa can be interpreted in a variety of ways. Not just one, but many, principles endorsed by the UN were on trial. Some were openly debated, while others, although considered quietly, were no less important. India was a democracy, Portugal a dictatorship. Goa was a Western colony, while its inhabitants were of Indian origin. For more than a decade India had, to no avail, sought ways of making Portugal release territory that India believed belonged to it by right. Force had been used only reluctantly, and the invasion had resulted in only a few casualties. There is of course much worthy of comment on all these points: for example, that India did not demand a Goan plebiscite, and that the colony's 650,000 Christian inhabitants felt no eagerness to join India or, indeed being largely agnostic, to stay with Portugal.[71] Perhaps, too, the Goan apple had been bound to fall, and so the use of force had actually been unnecessary. All these factors shaped the international response to India's troop build-up and the eventual seizure of Goa in December 1961.

As for the threat of force, it seems reasonable to assume, without challenging the evidence available, that states did not entertain any doubts *per se* that the Indian troop build-up encircling the Portuguese colony was in conflict with article 2(4) of the UN Charter; the ambassador of Ceylon, taking sides with India, even postulated that the Portuguese troop build-up was to blame for the first inconsistency with the Charter. Instead, the discussion revolved around the issue of justification; whether, as the majority of states held, Indian recourse to coercive measures was excusable in light of decolonisation and self help. A consistent pattern emerges that a number of states urged for moderation on both sides and space to be made for diplomatic compromises. The pleas for restraint issued by President Kennedy and UN Secretary-General U Thant illustrate the pre-eminence given by some UN members to withholding condemnation in favour of mediation and avoidance of the use of force.

USSR–Czechoslovakia (Prague Spring, 1968)

Early 1968 brought a major shift within Czechoslovak politics as Alexander Dubček became leader of the Communist party. His 'action

[71] NYT, 'Behind the Goa Crisis' (16 Dec. 1961).

programme', published on 8 April, sought to reform Czechoslovakia along more liberal economic and political lines, steering the country along a more independent course towards 'socialist democracy', a feature of which was relaxed censorship of the press. The USSR deeply resented Dubček's plans for reform, fearing the spread of liberalisation to other socialist countries and thus a decline of Soviet influence in Eastern Europe. An open letter from Prague on 27 June (the 'Two Thousand Words' manifesto), which called for the acceleration of Czechoslovak democratisation and criticised the conditions inside the Czechoslovak Communist party prior to the January reforms, added a sense of urgency to the USSR's perceived loss of control; after Yugoslavia in 1948 and Hungary in 1956, there should not be another upheaval. Urgent and intense negotiations between Prague and Moscow ensued, resulting in the Bratislava agreement of 3 August. In it, the Warsaw Pact members, with the exception of Romania, affirmed their allegiance to Marxism-Leninism and proletarian internationalism.[72]

As differences became more pronounced in the spring of 1968, the USSR decided to suppress any further steps towards liberal reform, and step up pressure against Czechoslovakia. Russian press reports grew more outspoken in their criticism of Czechoslovakia, in July likening its political direction to that of Hungary in 1956.[73] Czech officials were ordered to meetings of the Communist leadership. By early May, Warsaw Pact troops had already started staging major manoeuvres along the Czech border in East Germany and Poland. A Soviet division was reported to be moving westwards across southern Poland. While these movements had been announced previously, they turned out to be larger in scale than anticipated, and were inconsistent with the previous postponement of such manoeuvres as a concession to Czechoslovakia's concern that these might be construed as an ominous sign of intervention.[74] Western analysts concluded at the time that Moscow was pursuing a policy of 'decisive half-measures', exercising

72 2004 ICB 'Prague Spring', crisis 227; Peter Calvocoressi, *World Politics 1945–2000* 309–13 (8th edn, 2001); Franck, *Recourse to Force*, at pp. 73–5; Franck, *Nation Against Nation*, at pp. 71–5; Weisburd, *Use of Force*, at pp. 224–7.

73 NYT, 'Stormclouds Over Prague' (13 Jul. 1968); NYT, 'Moscow Continues to Press Prague' (28 Jul. 1968).

74 NYT, 'Russian Soldiers Said to be on Move Near Czech Line' (10 May 1968); NYT, 'Hostile Intent Dismissed' (11 May 1968); NYT, 'Pressure on Prague' (11 May 1968).

the 'right level of threat' to give pause, yet avoiding a blatant threat that could inflame anti-Soviet sentiments in Czechoslovakia.[75]

When these initial steps led to no success in reining back Czechoslovakia's move towards liberalisation, Moscow announced that joint military exercises would be held on Czech soil in June. Apparently Czechoslovakia had agreed to this, partly to allay suspicions that its plans for reform were designed to challenge its adherence to the Warsaw Pact alliance.[76] So in early June, Soviet army forces rolled though the Czech countryside, in the midst of deliberate uncertainty in Czechoslovakia about their size and possession of offensive weaponry, and in no hurry to leave.[77] After the publication of the Two Thousand Words manifesto, Moscow issued accusations of 'counter-revolutionary forces' in Prague and kept postponing the date of withdrawal of Soviet troops.[78] Additional manoeuvres were held in July.[79] By the end of that month, the air pregnant with foreboding, West Germany cancelled its own scheduled manoeuvres on the Czechoslovak border area so that it could not be construed as participating in a secret scheme for secession from the Warsaw bloc.[80] In the run-up to the Bratislava talks, the USSR switched to clear indications that 'time was running out' and that there would be no compromise on the reversal of Prague's liberal reforms. A warning was issued that Soviet forces were increasing their readiness for combat.[81] Simultaneously, the USSR increased its troops in Poland.[82] The Bratislava conference first made the appearance of having successfully deflected an actual military intervention; Soviet troops left Czechoslovak territory. However, they remained along its borders, and on 20 August invaded Czechoslovakia with approximately ten divisions, each 12,000 to 15,000 strong. Dubček was personally coerced to consent to the Russian invasion, laying the way for the USSR to claim

[75] NYT, 'Moscow Takes "Decisive Half-Measures"' (12 May 1968).
[76] NYT, 'Red Troops to Hold Games on Czech Soil' (25 May 1968).
[77] NYT, 'Soviet Tanks Join Maneuvers in Czechoslovakia' (5 Jun. 1968); NYT, 'Prague Nervous on Soviet Troops' (11 Jul. 1968); NYT, 'Soviet Troop Withdrawal Halted in Czechoslovakia' (15 Jul. 1968). See on charges of uncertainty NYT, 'Czechs Demand a basic Revision of Warsaw Pact' (16 Jul. 1968), where the Soviet force was estimated to be 16,000 soldiers, accompanied by 4,500 vehicles, seventy tanks and forty airplanes.
[78] NYT, 'Anti-Red Threat Seen by Pravda in Czech Appeal' (12 Jul. 1968).
[79] NYT, 'Soviet is Holding Army Maneuvers Near Slovak Line' (24 Jul. 1968).
[80] NYT, 'Bonn Shifts Maneuvers away from Czech Line' (25 Jul. 1968); NYT, 'War of Nerves' (25 Jul. 1968); Calvocoressi, *World Politics*, at p. 311.
[81] NYT, 'Time Running Out, Moscow Cautions' (29 Jul. 1968).
[82] NYT, 'Movements in Poland' (30 Jul. 1968); NYT, 'Soviet Reported Widening Troop Build-up in Poland' (31 Jul. 1968).

that its actions were lawful under the cloak of invitation.[83] The Soviet ambassador to the UN, Yakov Malik, put forward the justification on 21 August:

> The armed units of the Socialist countries, as is known, entered the territory of the Czechoslovak Socialist Republic on the basis of the request of the Government of this state, which applied to the allied governments for assistance, including the assistance with armed forces, in view of the threats created by the external and internal reaction to the Socialist system and to the statehood established by the constitution of Czechoslovakia.[84]

And alluding to alleged USA interference in Czechoslovakia and the right to individual and collective self-defence of the Socialist countries as counter-response:

> The Soviet Government has repeatedly warned that the attempts of the imperialist reaction to interfere into the domestic affairs of the Czechoslovak Socialist Republic and into the relations between the Socialist countries will not be tolerated and will meet with a resolute rebuff.[85]

Endorsing that statement a few months later, the Warsaw Pact members declared at the USSR's behest the Brezhnev doctrine, which asserted the right to intervene to suppress counterrevolutionary forces adverse to socialism within the perimeters of the communist orbit. In October, the now obedient Czech leadership signed a treaty permitting Russian troops to be stationed in Czechoslovakia in undefined numbers.[86]

Western response to the USSR's gradual tightening of the screw against Prague was muted. To those of an optimistic frame of mind, the major policy thrust of this policy would be to avoid throwing fuel onto the flames, in the hope that matters could still turn to the better. To a pessimist, the silence of states indicated mere indifference, notwithstanding the fact that parallels to Munich had become painfully apparent. Expressing the pervasive sense of indignation, British Member of Parliament Sir Fitzroy Maclean wrote to *The Times* of London on 25 July:

> Today Czechoslovakia is once more threatened with armed aggression. It seems scarcely conceivable that, in such a situation, no word of warning should be

[83] George Nolte, *Eingreifen auf Einladung: Zur völkerrechtlichen Zulässigkeit des Einsatzes fremder Truppen im internen Konflikt auf Einladung der Regierung* 271–3 (1999).
[84] SCOR S/PV.1441 (21 Aug. 1968), at para. 3. [85] *Ibid.*
[86] Calvocoressi, *World Politics*, at p. 312.

uttered by any Western statesman, that the matter should be referred neither to the Security Council nor the General Assembly of the United Nations.[87]

What Maclean demanded occurred in wake of the Soviet invasion, when members of the Security Council and the General Assembly starkly condemned Moscow's action.[88] A proposed Security Council resolution by Denmark and co-sponsored by Brazil, Canada, France, Paraguay, the United States, the United Kingdom and Senegal considered:

> ... that the action taken by the Government of the USSR and other members of the Warsaw Pact in invading the Czechoslovak Socialist Republic was a violation of the United Nations Charter, and, in particular, of the principle that all Members shall refrain in their international relations from the threat or use of force against the territorial integrity or political independence of any State; ...

and further, to:

> ... condemn the armed intervention of the USSR and other members of the Warsaw Pact in the internal affairs of Czechoslovakia and call upon them to take no action of violence or reprisal that could result in further suffering or loss of life, forthwith to withdraw their forces, and to cease all other forms of intervention in Czechoslovakia's internal affairs.[89]

The draft resolution received ten votes in favour, but, to no one's surprise, was shipwrecked as a result of the Soviet veto.[90] While the military manoeuvres in Czechoslovakia had not evoked an international response, the invasion itself caused the communal resentment over the Soviet conduct to spill over, at least rhetorically. As US President Johnson noted, the excuses offered by the USSR were 'patently contrived'. A truthful criticism, yet ringing hollow in the light of the USA's own record of interventions in the Dominican Republic in 1965 and Cuba in 1961. Disenchanted with the UN, the USA did not even consider taking the issue to the General Assembly, since it considered that the non-aligned states would not move in such a way as to

[87] NYT, 'Echoes of Munich' (26 Jul. 1968).
[88] Franck, *Recourse to Force*, at pp. 73–5. Weisburd, *Use of Force*, at pp. 224–6.
[89] 1968 UNYB 300. See the Security Council debates clearly in disfavour of the USSR, SCOR S/PV.1441 (21 Aug. 1968); S/PV.1442 (22 Aug. 1968); S/PV.1443 (22 Aug. 1968); S/PV.1445 (24 Aug. 1968).
[90] 1968 UNYB 302.

antagonise the USSR.[91] In the Assembly, numerous speeches condemned the USSR, but no resolution was passed.[92]

The question for this study is whether the overwhelming protest filed against the invasion of Czechoslovakia extended to the demonstrations of force preceding it. As in the Moroccan case discussed in the previous chapter, coercion also produced a tangible legal product: the treaty signed in October permitting Russian troops to be stationed within Czech territory.[93] In the same way, the right to self-determination was on trial, together with the principles of the UN Charter on the use of force.[94] The theatrical debate in the Security Council occupied five full days, yet it revolved around not the threat, but the actual use of force, invasion and infringement of sovereignty. Protest was lacking during the days prior to the invasion. At the same time, it is clear that the silence of third-party nations was not an expression of approval – that much may plausibly be inferred from the reactions to the invasion – but was actually the withholding of public expression of opinion for political convenience. Western governments did not want to imperil the delicate process of *détente* that had held out the promise of normalised relations and the successful conclusion of arms-control talks. The lesson from the USSR's use of force against Hungary in 1956 had been that condemnation, while politically face-saving, was fruitless. The USA, too, had its hands full in Vietnam, where the Tet Offensive of February 1968 was troubling the Johnson administration. It partially relied on a *quid pro quo* for its policy in Vietnam and in Latin America. Silence, therefore, was not tantamount to approval, but, by any measurement undertaken, constituted dissent suppressed because of overriding considerations of *Realpolitik*.

Colombia–Nicaragua (San Andrés Islands, 1979–1980)

On 12 December 1979, six months after the Sandinista guerrilla movement had toppled the authoritarian Somoza regime in Nicaragua, the

91 Franck, *Nation Against Nation*, at p. 74.

92 GAOR A/PV.1677 (2 Oct. 1968); A/PV.1679 (3 Oct. 1968); A/PV.1681 (4 Oct. 1968); A/PV.1682 (4 Oct. 1968); A/PV.1684 (7 Oct. 1968); A/PV.1685 (8 Oct. 1968); A/PV.1686 (8 Oct. 1968); A/PV.1687 (9 Oct. 1968); A/PV.1688 (9 Oct. 1968); A/PV.1689 (10 Oct. 1968); A/PV.1690 (10 Oct. 1968); A/PV.1691 (11 Oct. 1968); A/PV.1692 (11 Oct. 1968); A/PV.1694 (14 Oct. 1968); A/PV.1696 (15 Oct. 1968); A/PV.1697 (16 Oct. 1968); A/PV.1701 (21 Oct. 1968); A/PV.1702 (22 Oct. 1968); A/PV.1703 (22 Oct. 1968); A/PV.1705 (23 Oct. 1968).

93 Stuart S. Malawer, 'Imposed Treaties and International Law', Cal. WILJ 1–178 (1977), at 99–100.

94 1868 UNYB 300.

new national government revived claims of sovereignty over the San Andrés Archipelago, an island chain located close to its eastern coastline and the archipelago's surrounding continental shelf of the Costa Atlántica.[95] Nicaragua did this by extending its maritime limits to 200 miles, thus engulfing the archipelago, speculated to be rich in natural resources.[96]

The USA had owned the islands between 1919 and 1928. In an effort to improve its relations with Bogotá over the loss of Panama, it had ceded the archipelago to Colombia on 24 March 1928 by way of the Bárcenas Meneses-Esguerra Treaty, formally signed between Colombia and the then US-controlled Nicaragua.[97] In 1979, however, a 1972 treaty between the USA and Bogotá to fortify the latter's title on the archipelago still awaited US ratification. In a White Paper of 4 February 1980, Nicaragua, while pledging to consider no use of force and signalling a willingness to negotiate, declared that this treaty was null and void due to duress. It argued that at the time Nicaragua had been occupied by the USA, had so been under pressure and had therefore been unable to make good its claim on the archipelago.[98]

Colombia, which administered the San Andrés islands as part of its national territory, flatly rejected Nicaragua's claims as well as refusing to take part in any negotiations on the matter. Colombia considered its territorial title, which it traced back to a Spanish royal order of 1803, as irrefutable. The President of Colombia, Julio César Turbay Ayala, swiftly ordered the dispatch of three surface warships and a submarine, along with the nation's Mirage squadron and an additional 500 marines, to

[95] Sources: ICB, 'Columbia–Nicaragua', case 310; NYT, 'One-Time Pirate Isles Caught in a Latin Tug-of-War' (15 Dec. 1980); Institute for the Study of Conflict, *Annual of Power and Conflict 1980–1981* 181 (1981); Henry W. Degenhardt, *Maritime Affairs – A World Handbook: A Reference Guide to Maritime Organizations, Conventions and Disputes and to the International Politics of the Sea* 212–13 (1985); Gerhard Drekonja-Kornat, 'Der Kolumbianisch-Nicaraguanische Streit um den San Andrés-Archipel', 16 Verf. & R. Übersee 163–80 (1983).

[96] Anonymous, 'Future Petroleum Provinces Are Many in Gulf of Mexico-Caribbean Area', 78 Oil & Gas J. 216–26 (20 Oct. 1980).

[97] Drekonja-Kornat, 'Der Kolumbianisch-Nicaraguanische Streit', at 169. The *Bárcenas Meneses-Esguerra Treaty* is reprinted in Enrique Gaviria Liévano (ed.), *Nuestro Archipiélago de San Andrés y el Tratado con Nicaragua* 265–366 (2001).

[98] Latin Am. Wkly Rep., 'Colombia Enraged by Nicaragua's Revived Caribbean Claims' (4 Jan. 1980); FBIS (Latin America), 'Daily Report: D'Escoto Comments On Colombian Treaty Renunciation' (11 Feb. 1980). See also NYT, 'One-Time Pirate Isles Caught in a Latin Tug-of-War' (15 Dec. 1980).

reinforce the garrison on San Andrés and step up patrols.[99] This made it clear that Colombia was willing to resist any attempt at repossession of the islands by force.[100] Reports, too, of collusion by Cuban mercenaries infiltrating the islands had supposedly led Bogotá to demonstrate this resolve.[101] Nicaragua, with its approaches to negotiation stifled and, more importantly, its victorious alliance plagued by other political quarrels, shelved its claim over the archipelago. Nicaragua had temporarily been able to hold out promises of friendly relations to both the USA and Cuba, but the political chaos in neighbouring El Salvador all too soon set the new Reagan administration against the Sandinistas.[102] The US Congress, now entertaining an interest in establishing a military base on the San Andrés Islands and wishing to draw a clear line against the Marxist 'menace' in the Caribbean, eventually, in July 1981, ratified the 1972 Vásquez Saccio treaty, quietly supporting Colombia's position in the dispute.[103]

While the Carter administration had, in January 1980, urged for a judicial solution to the territorial dispute, Nicaragua's Caribbean and Latin American neighbours had little to say about Colombia's demonstration of force. Their reactions, if any, focused on the validity of territorial title, which they felt belonged to Nicaragua.[104] Colombia reportedly took its case to the Third UN Conference on the Law of the Sea (which had been convened since 1973 to bring about a constitution governing the oceans), but to no avail.[105] Neither the Organization of American States (OAS) nor the UN was appealed to in order to address concerns of regional security.[106]

99 FBIS, 'Daily Report (Latin America), Government to Build Military Base on San Andres Island' (5 Feb. 1980).

100 *Annual of Power and Conflict 1980–1981*, at p. 181.

101 FBIS (Latin America), 'Daily Report: Agents Search for Cuban Mercenaries on San Andres' (11 Feb. 1980); FBIS (Latin America), 'Daily Report: San Andres Island Residents Denounce Cuban Interference' (12 Feb. 1980); FBIS (Latin America), 'Daily Report: Cuba Allegedly Intervened' (13 Feb. 1980).

102 Keylor, *A World of Nations*, at p. 271.

103 Drekonja-Kornat, 'Der Kolumbianisch-Nicaraguanische Streit', at 171, 173; Latin Am. Wkly Rep., *Rift Looms as Colombia Recalls Managua Envoy* (15 Feb. 1980).

104 See FBIS (Latin America), 'Daily Report: "International Powers" Side with Nicaragua in Cay Issue' (11 Feb. 1980).

105 Degenhardt, *Maritime Affairs*, at p. 213. In addressing the UN General Assembly, Colombia's Foreign Minister Diego Uribe Vargas on 10 October 1980 asserted that '*los titulos de Colombia ... son irrefutables y no admiten discución alguna* [the rights of Colombia ... are irrefutable and unquestionable]'. Quoted from Drekonja-Kornat, 'Der kolumbianisch-nicaraguanische Streit', at 170 n. 20.

106 The *Latin America Weekly Report*, 'Rift Looms as Colombia Recalls Managua Envoy' (15 Feb. 1980) observed on Nicaragua's options: 'Nicaragua has few cards to play in

Several factors could have contributed to the fact that the issue was ignored by these international fora. For one thing, there was no palpable likelihood that Nicaragua would try to recapture the archipelago by force and raise tensions to a level that would have called for a concerted effort at preventive diplomacy. Colombia's show of determination and of military strength occurred within the confines of territory that it had administered for over fifty years. Its actions were of the order primarily to preclude, not provoke, confrontation. The UN may therefore be forgiven for not having cast its vote on the implications of the incident on the UN Charter's regime on force. Yet the fact remains that Colombia's military entrenchment of its territory did not prompt critical comments. In December 2001, Nicaragua formally filed a case against Colombia before the ICJ, reviving its territorial claim over the San Andrés Archipelago.[107]

USA–Libya (Gulf of Sidra, 1981)

During the eight years of the Reagan presidency, USA-Libyan relations were especially poor. Tripoli's support for terrorism and the USA's attempts, by means of coercive diplomacy, to make it forego that support formed the major theme of several hostile encounters.[108] Libya's territorial claims over the Gulf of Sidra during that period provided fertile ground for one of them.

the conflict, and has limited its actions to delaying safe-conducts for 90-odd right-wing refugees in the Colombian embassy in Managua. If Colombia refuses to discuss the matter, there is little Nicaragua can do, even if its argument that the 1928 treaty was signed under duress, during the US military occupation, were to be accepted as valid. Colombia, with a growing energy gap, will be all the more determined not to relinquish its grip on islands which might have substantial oil deposits in the surrounding waters.'

107 *Territorial and Maritime Dispute (Nicaragua* v. *Colombia), Application Instituting Proceedings*, 2001 ICJ Rep. 1 (6 Dec. 2001). Nicaragua asserts that fishing vessels of its nationals in 1994 were 'repeatedly intercepted and captured by Colombian patrol boats in areas as close as 70 miles off the Nicaraguan coast in the course of a dispute over sovereignty claims over islands'. It also points out the disparity of naval powers significantly in favour of Colombia, and that Nicaragua was in no position to defend itself effectively. However, Nicaragua did not ask the ICJ to decide on a possible violation of the UN Charter. It confined itself to have the Court decide over the sovereignty of the islands and the maritime boundaries.

108 Tim Zimmerman, 'Coercive Diplomacy and Libya', in Alexander L. George and William E. Simons (eds.), *The Limits of Coercive Diplomacy* 201–28 (1994). See also Bruce W. Jentleson, 'The Reagan Administration and Coercive Diplomacy: Restraining More than Remaking Governments', 106 PSQ 57–82 (1991); Claudia Wright, 'Libya and the West: Headlong into Confrontation?', 58 Int. Aff. 13–41 (1981–2).

In 1973, Libya had publicly claimed much of the Gulf of Sidra as its territorial waters and had subsequently decreed a 'line of death', a straight line connecting the two opposite ends of the Gulf, the crossing of which would invite a military response.[109] This claim was generally rejected, since the line extended Libya's territorial waters to 200 miles from its coast, far beyond the twelve miles considered the international norm.[110] The USA challenged this directly by declaring that its ships would continue to regard all areas beyond a distance of three nautical miles from the coast as international waters. During the next few years, the USA repeatedly conducted military manoeuvres to assert its claim of access to the Gulf. However, President Carter then suspended military exercises as a response to the Iranian hostage crisis.[111]

But the newly elected President, Ronald Reagan, changed course. At his direct order,[112] his administration announced on 12 August 1981 that the US Sixth Fleet would hold manoeuvres in the Gulf of Sidra on 18 and 19 August.[113] Libya responded with a full military alert the same day, accusing the USA of violating Libya's territorial waters. On 20 August, a dogfight over the Gulf of Sidra ensued: according to the USA, two of its F-14s jets destroyed two Libyan Sukhoi-22 fighters sixty miles off Libya's coast after having been shot at. Libya, on the other hand, said that eight F-14s had attacked two of its fighters that had been on a routine mission.[114] After the incident, the USA warned Libya against retaliation, saying that it would use force if Libya attacked US aircraft or ships involved in the Sixth Fleet exercise.[115] Those exercises, however, ended on the following day without further incident.

Libya made vigorous protests against both the US naval presence and the shooting down of its Sukhois. It said that the US military manoeuvres constituted part of a pattern of military threats, and that US vessels and aircraft had manoeuvred into a position of preparation for an imminent raid upon the northern parts of Libya.[116] Libyan leader Muammar Qaddafi declared that Libya was ready to defend its

[109] Sources: ICB, 'Gulf of Syrte I', crisis 330; Steven R. Ratner, 'The Gulf of Sidra Incident of 1981: A Study of the Lawfulness of Peacetime Aerial Engagements', 10 Yale JIL 59–77 (1984); Weisburd, *Use of Force*, at pp. 289–90.

[110] Ratner, 'Gulf of Sidra', at 73 n. 67. [111] *Ibid.*, at 66.

[112] NYT, 'Reagan Wraps Up a Week Marked by Buoyancy' (23 Aug. 1981).

[113] Ratner, 'Gulf of Sidra', at 62.

[114] NYT, 'Qaddafi, Condemning U.S., Vows to Defend Sidra Gulf' (20 Aug. 1981). For a detailed account see Joseph T. Stanik, *El Dorado Canyon: Reagan's Undeclared War With Qaddafi* 51–6 (2003).

[115] ICB, 'Gulf of Syrte I', crisis 330. [116] Ratner, 'Gulf of Sidra', at 67, 71.

territorial waters even if doing so meant 'bilateral war with the United States or a third world war' and that the US naval manoeuvres were part of a 'premeditated plan to launch military aggression against Libya and to invade it'.[117] In a letter to the Security Council, Libya condemned the aerial intrusion of the two US jets as a 'provocative terrorist attack' infringing its territorial sovereignty.[118] In turn, the USA said that it had previously announced the exercises, that they were routine and that the incident actually constituted an unprovoked attack by Libya.[119] However, President Reagan then told the press that he had deliberately ordered the manoeuvres in order to challenge Libya's claim to the disputed waters.[120] Nonetheless, the crisis ended abruptly with the orderly termination of the naval exercises. Neither the USA nor Libya requested further action from the Security Council.[121]

Although the UN was not involved in the crisis, condemnatory remarks castigating the USA were not in short supply. Acting through the League of Arab States and the Gulf Cooperation Council, all Arab states except Egypt and the Sudan criticised the behaviour of the USA.[122] The Islamic Conference stated that the USA had disregarded international law and had engaged in a muscle-flexing exercise, jeopardising peace in the region.[123] Officials of the Organization of Petroleum Exporting Countries (OPEC), meeting on 19 August to discuss petroleum prices, chose not to comment on the US–Libyan aerial confrontation, but there were public calls to demonstrate Arab unity and to impose sanctions on the USA by charging higher oil prices.[124] Other countries also strongly criticised the USA. The fifty-three members of the Organization of African Unity (OAU) denounced the USA for promoting the 'policy of cowboys' in a 'wanton act of aggression', constituting a 'provocative act of undeclared war'.[125] The NAM equally

[117] NYT, 'Qaddafi, Condemning U.S., Vows to Defend Sidra Gulf' (20 Aug. 1981).
[118] SCOR Supp. S/14636 (20 Aug. 1981). See further SCOR Supp. S/14642 (25 Aug. 1981).
[119] SCOR Supp. S/14632 (19 Aug. 1981). [120] ICB, 'Gulf of Syrte I', crisis 330.
[121] On 6 October, however, Libya wrote a letter to the president of the General Assembly, in which it referred to the wide condemnation of the USA. See 1981 UNYB 361; GAOR A/C.1/36/3 (7 Oct. 1981).
[122] 1981 UNYB 361; SCOR Supp. S/14638/Rev.1 (21 Aug. 1981).
[123] Ratner, 'Gulf of Sidra', at 73 n. 65.
[124] *Facts On File World News Digest*, 'U.S. Navy F-14s Down Two Libyan Jet Fighters; Incident Occurs over Disputed Waters' (21 Aug. 1981); NYT, 'OPEC Remains Divided on Unifying Base Prices' (20 Aug. 1981).
[125] FBIS (Middle East) 'Daily Report: Middle East and South Asia Review, Libyan-U.S. Clash' (24 Aug. 1981).

condemned US actions as constituting a 'threat as well as a flagrant violence against [all] non-aligned countries in the region'.[126] The Reagan administration asserted to the press that the reactions of most nations had privately been supportive, but that the wide publicity of the incident had compelled many Middle Eastern and Third World nations to issue at least mild statements of rebuke.[127] However, such mild statements came only from Europe, and even there the reaction was lukewarm, showing only slight approval. Europe's foreign ministry aides supported the firm stance of the USA against Libya, but suggested unease over the apparently increasing signs of an aggressive US foreign policy.[128] The UK said that it supported the US position that Libya had no territorial rights over the Gulf of Sidra, but it regretted the incident and made clear its belief that the USA had deliberately invited confrontation. Italy, France and Germany made similar comments.[129] The USSR, a major supplier of weapons to Libya, but sceptical of its territorial claims, stood back, choosing not to take sides.[130]

Clearly this time, a majority of states resented US intervention, disregarding the widely held view that Libya was wrongfully claiming the Gulf of Sidra as its own. Criticism did not therefore flow from a perceived violation of sovereign title over territory. Rather, the view was that the Reagan administration had deliberately cornered Libya and thus set the scene for a confrontation. In the eyes of many, the naval manoeuvres and, more importantly, the actual use of force against the jets, indicated that the USA was willing to use its military might in furtherance of its Libya policy, which was to isolate and undermine Qaddafi's rule and retaliate for suspected involvements in terrorist acts.[131] At the same time, condemnation of US actions was partly shaped by the desire, particularly among Arab nations, to create a united front against US interventionism in the Middle East. No rebuke of Qaddafi's harsh warnings was heard, and neither was any enquiry made into the exact circumstances of the air battle. To be sure, US

126 Ratner, 'Gulf of Sidra', at 73 n. 65.

127 NYT, 'U.S. Action: Sign to Libya' (21 Aug. 1981).

128 NYT, 'Western Europe Expressing Favor and Unease' (21 Aug. 1981); *Facts On File World News Digest*, 'U.S. Navy F-14s Down Two Libyan Jet Fighters; Incident Occurs Over Disputed Waters' (21 Aug. 1981).

129 NYT, 'Western Europe Expressing Favor and Unease' (21 Aug. 1981).

130 NYT, 'U.S. Action: Sign to Libya' (21 Aug. 1981); NYT, 'Western Europe Expressing Favor and Unease' (21 Aug. 1981).

131 Wright, 'Libya and the West', at 13–19.

credibility was not held in high esteem, yet as soon as the crisis was over, the matter was considered closed and not worthy of any further response.[132]

USA–Nicaragua (MiG-21s, 1984)

Another sore spot of US foreign relations during the 1980s was the deepening involvement of the USA in Nicaragua. Soon after the Sandinistas had toppled the Somoza dictatorship in 1979, the White House under Ronald Reagan began to regard Nicaragua's leftist rebellion movement as a Soviet satellite state in the making. Managua's suspected ties to Cuba and the USSR, and its support for revolution in El Salvador, were perceived as a direct threat to US national security. Reagan and his advisors soon decided that in order to 'roll back' communism from the northern hemisphere, the Sandinista regime had to go. In 1983 and 1984, the CIA and the US military provided covert training and logistical support to anti-Sandinista mercenaries stationed in Honduras and Costa Rica: they laid mines in Nicaragua's ports, destroyed its main oil terminals, bombed its principal airport, conducted inland air raids and stepped up pressure by staging military exercises off its coast. Against this background, a crisis erupted on 6 November 1984.[133]

On that day, election day in the USA for Ronald Reagan's second term, intelligence reports suggested to the White House that a Soviet cargo ship, the *Bakuriani*, was en route from the Black Sea to Nicaragua carrying Soviet MiG-21 jets for the Sandinista regime in what appeared to be the USSR's first direct delivery of a major military system to Nicaragua.[134] Intelligence about it was circumstantial, relying as it did on the unique shape of twelve crates on the freighter that were said to fit MiG-21 aircrafts, and the freighter's 'suspicious' avoidance of the Panama canal. When the concern of the US administration was leaked to the press, Nicaragua promptly rejected the accuracy of the intelligence,

[132] This changed in the second Gulf of Sidra crisis in 1986. See Christopher Greenwood, 'International Law and the United States Air Operation Against Libya', 89 WVa LR 933–60 (1986–7).

[133] ICB, 'Nicaragua MIG-21s', crisis 354; 1984 UNYB 206–12; George P. Shultz, *Turmoil and Triumph: My Years as Secretary of State* (1993).

[134] NYT, 'Nicaragua Said to Get Soviet Attack Copters' (7 Nov. 1984); Mary Desjeans and Peter Clement, 'Soviet Policy Toward Central America', 36 Proc. Acad. PS 223–34 (1987), at 225.

saying that it had not ordered any jet fighters and that none were on their way to it.[135] The USSR, in response to a US enquiry, made the same assurance.[136] The next day, on 7 November, the *Bakuriani* arrived in Nicaragua's Pacific coast port of Corinto.

The delivery of Soviet fighter planes to the regime in Managua had previously been an item on the agenda of US-Soviet relations. US Secretary of State George Shultz had privately informed the USSR Ambassador Gromyko in 1982 that such delivery would be 'unacceptable' to the USA and would be regarded as an 'unfriendly act'.[137] In diplomatic parlance, that meant that the USA was ready to use force, and indeed the US President himself had at the time agreed on a plan to 'take them out' if fighter planes were brought to Nicaragua.[138] In a revival of that policy, Shultz now renewed the warning to the USSR that the USA would not tolerate the delivery of MiG fighter jets to Nicaragua, and, speaking to the press, said that although he knew of no plans of an invasion of Nicaragua, MiGs in Nicaragua would 'create an unacceptable situation' and that he could not foretell what might lie ahead in the next few days.[139] Statements by other US officials indicated that the delivery of advanced fighter jets to Nicaragua would constitute an intolerable change in the balance of military forces in Central America, and that such aircraft would give Nicaragua 'the ability to attack nearby nations' that lacked sophisticated air defence systems.[140] President Reagan himself iterated in a press conference that if Nicaragua took delivery of advanced aircraft, which were 'absolutely unnecessary to them', this would 'indicate that they are contemplating being a threat to their neighbours here in the Americas'.[141]

In the meantime, a Crisis Pre-Planning Group met on 7 November to consider the military options.[142] Amid rising speculation of a possible

[135] NYT, 'Nicaragua Says No Jet Fighters are being Sent' (8 Nov. 1984); NYT, 'Nicaraguan Says Soviet Ship Carried One or Two Military Copters' (9 Nov. 1984).

[136] NYT, 'Shultz Indicates Soviet has Denied Shipping Fighters' (9 Nov. 1984).

[137] Shultz, *Turmoil and Triumph*, at p. 311 n. 6.

[138] Shultz, *Turmoil and Triumph*, at 345, 424.

[139] NYT, 'Shultz Indicates Soviet has Denied Shipping Fighters' (9 Nov. 1984).

[140] NYT, 'U.S. Warns Soviet It Won't Tolerate MIGs in Nicaragua' (8 Nov. 1984).

[141] NYT, 'Transcript of President's News Conference on Foreign and Domestic Issues' (8 Nov. 1984). A high-ranking official stated in a television interview with CBS that 'if the Reagan Administration were to verify the fact that ships were carrying such aircraft towards Nicaragua it might consider a surprise attack to destroy them'. Quoted from SCOR S/PV.2562 (9 Nov. 1984), at para. 10. For further statements see paras. 11–14, 26.

[142] Shultz, *Turmoil and Triumph*, at p. 424; NYT, 'Military Moves Considered' (10 Nov. 1984).

US invasion of Nicaragua, the administration's major response was to increase the number and the visibility of military exercises that the Pentagon was conducting in the Gulf of Fonseca, opposite the Honduran port of Amapala and the Salvadorian anchorage at La Union, as well as drills in the Caribbean Sea – only some of which had been announced earlier – with seventeen and twenty-five warships respectively.[143] Low-altitude SR-71 surveillance overflights, emitting sonic booms, over Nicaraguan territory were intensified.[144] The freighter *Bakuriani* was kept under specific surveillance by two navy frigates and a C-130 aircraft circling above the port of Corinto.[145]

While each of these acts independently could have been said to have been part of military routine in US-Nicaraguan relations, when combined, and added to the USA's hard-line rhetoric, they fed the fear that a US invasion of Nicaragua was imminent.[146] Rumours about troop movements, special alerts at US military bases and constant reconnaissance flights matched the template of preparation for war. Moreover, a year earlier, in October 1983, the USA had stated, when its navy encircled Grenada, that it did not intend to invade the island – only to proceed to do precisely that.[147] Reports during the Presidential campaign had also leaked from unconfirmed congressional and Pentagon sources that the White House had formulated contingency plans for a post-election, all-out assault against the regime in Managua.[148]

Alarmed, Nicaragua put its military forces on alert and made preparations for the defence of the capital.[149] President-elect Daniel Ortega Saavedra made the accusation that the Reagan administration had artificially drummed up a crisis to pave the way for premeditated military action, and that it was the right of Nicaragua to procure weapons for the

[143] NYT, '25 U.S. Warships in the Caribbean' (9 Nov. 1984); SCOR S/PV.2562 (9 Nov. 1984), S/PV.2562, at paras. 19–23; NYT, 'Off Puerto Rico, a "Normal" Exercise' (10 Nov. 1984).

[144] SCOR S/PV.2562 (9 Nov. 1984), at paras. 7, 9; NYT, 'Nicaragua Can't Vote Away Pressures' (11 Nov. 1984); NYT, 'Sonic Booms Shake Cities in Nicaragua the Fourth Day' (12 Nov. 1984).

[145] SCOR S/PV.2562 (9 Nov. 1984), at para. 8.

[146] *Council On Hemispheric Affairs, News and Analysis*, 'Reagan Nicaragua Strategy: on the Threshold of Intervention' (8 Nov. 1984).

[147] Franck, *Recourse to Force*, at pp. 86–8; Weisburd, *Use of Force*, at pp. 234–8 (the Grenada invasion was universally condemned).

[148] Council on Hemispheric Affairs, News and Analysis, 'Reagan Administration Taking Two-Track Approach on Nicaragua: Talk Peace, Prepare for War' (30 Aug. 1984).

[149] NYT, 'Nicaragua Puts Forces on Alert for a U.S. Invasion' (13 Nov. 1984).

defence of the revolution.[150] On 9 November, Nicaragua requested an emergency meeting of the UN Security Council,[151] which convened at 8 p.m. the same day, to discuss the matter of 'the very serious situation created by the escalation of acts of aggression, the repeated threats and new acts of provocation fostered by the U.S. government'.[152]

Citing the military activity around Nicaragua's borders, and the intervention in Grenada as evidence for the USA's tendency to use force, Ambassador Chamorro Mora explained that:

> . . . all these military actions, the threatening statements by members of the Reagan Administration, including the President himself, and the acts of aggression of which we are victims every day and which are being stepped up – all of these things lead us to fear constantly a United States military intervention, and even more so in the present circumstances.[153]

He stated that the US government had deliberately leaked information about the supposed jet delivery 'to prepare the climate for a direct military attack against our territory and establish conditions conducive to the participation of United States troops in large-scale aggression'.[154] Yet despite these allegations, Nicaragua introduced no resolution to the Security Council for a symbolic vote, nor did any other Council member, apart from the USA, comment on the accusations. Representative Richard Schifter's best retort to Nicaragua's indictment was that the alleged threat of invasion, like previous ones made by Nicaragua, was 'totally without foundation',[155] adding that Nicaragua's own involvement in its neighbouring countries should not be forgotten.[156] The Council meeting ended after two hours of fruitless debate.

So, too, did the whole crisis, which turned out to be the result of a false alarm. It simply dissolved as new intelligence reports confirmed on that same day that the *Bakuriani* had indeed been carrying no jets on board.[157] In fact, the USSR had made it fairly clear earlier that it would

150 NYT, 'Sandinista Accuses Reagan' (11 Nov. 1984); NYT, 'Nicaragua Vows to Resist U.S.' (14 Nov. 1984).

151 SCOR Supp. S/16825 (9 Nov. 1984).

152 SCOR S/PV.2562 (9 Nov. 1984). The Council was composed as follows: China, Egypt, France, India, Malta, the Netherlands, Nicaragua, Pakistan, Peru, Ukrainian Soviet Socialist Republic, the UK, the USA, the USSR, Upper Volta and Zimbabwe.

153 SCOR S/PV.2562 (9 Nov. 1984), at para. 25.

154 *Ibid.*, at para. 33. 155 *Ibid.*, at para. 46. 156 *Ibid.*, at para. 49.

157 NYT, 'Managua Held Unlikely to Get Advanced Jets' (10 Nov. 1984); NYT, 'Officials Doubt Soviet Freighter Contains MIG's' (10 Nov. 1984).

not donate any planes, and the Sandinistas had no money to purchase them.[158] On 12 November, the US State Department issued a categorical statement that the USA did not intend to invade Nicaragua, although military steps to block off Soviet future or pending military supply shipments were further considered.[159] An invasion of Nicaragua never took place.

In this case of US military pressure against Nicaragua, if the silence of third-party states in the Security Council on 9 November were to be construed as acquiescence of US actions, this would be misleading. This is not to explain away the fact that no state chose to inject a remark in the US-Nicaraguan debate, or that Nicaragua had obviously thought the matter not worthy of proposing a condemnatory Council resolution. Rather, Nicaragua's call for a Council session has to be seen in the light of its by then habitual practice to keep the Security Council constantly informed of the tensions in its neighbourhood since the early 1980s, occasionally summoning a meeting, and on some occasions asking for a resolution that would compel the USA to save its skin by a lone veto against a critical Council majority. Thirteen of the same Council members that met in November, with the UK abstaining, had after a heated debate on 29 March that year voted in favour of a Nicaraguan resolution that condemned the USA for the mining of Nicaragua's ports. Another twenty-one states had then joined the Council debate to lend the resolution further political support.[160] The Reagan administration, if it had ever entertained such an aspiration, had lost any chances of winning the Council majority to its side long before the MiG-21 issue came to the table.[161] A majority of states had already, before November 1984, condemned US policy towards Nicaragua.

Nicaragua continued, after 9 November, as it had previously done, to provide meticulous information to the Security Council about US airspace violations and other activities in the days. Criticism of US policy became more overt as it became clear that no jets had been delivered, but US considerations of military responses lingered on. On 15 November, the USSR shed its previous low-profile approach and declared publicly: 'In the USSR, the U.S. actions are seen as a crude violation of international law, as a manifestation of state terrorism, as

[158] NYT, 'Managua Held Unlikely to Get Advanced Jets' (10 Nov. 1984).

[159] *Guardian*, 'Arms Cargo War of Words Rumbles On' (15 Nov. 1984).

[160] 1984 UNYB 207–9; SCOR S/PV.2525, SCOR S/PV.2527 to S/PV.2529 (30 Mar.–4 Apr. 1984).

[161] Franck, *Nation Against Nation*, at p. 246.

an encroachment of the rights of the Nicaraguan people', and further that the USA had engaged 'in a frenzied campaign of threats' backed up by large shows of military force.[162] On 19 November, the NAM, representing ninety-nine of the then 159 UN members, joined ranks with Nicaragua and adopted a *communiqué* which stated that the 'latest developments, particularly those manifested in the form of intensified aerial and naval actions, in flagrant violation of the airspace and territorial waters of Nicaragua, increase the dangers of a regional war' and that the movement 'demanded the immediate cessation of all hostile actions and threats' against Nicaragua.[163] The OAS, too, showed signs of unease with a policy that held the potential of derailing the fragile Contadora peace process, a process initiated by it and aimed at the demilitarisation of Central America. US 'maneuvers aimed at weakening or frustrating' the group's peace efforts were expressly criticised by Mexico.[164] In sum, the US argument that Nicaragua's imminent receipt of Soviet jets necessitated a deterrent demonstration of force was rejected as either fraudulent or unsubstantiated.

The Reagan administration, it was widely speculated, emboldened by its landslide victory in the elections, had exploited faulty intelligence reports to the fullest in order to shore up public support on the pretext of coercive action against Nicaragua.[165] Nicaragua had no air force, and its airspace was under complete control by the USA. Later in November, the news arrived that the ICJ had accepted jurisdiction of the case brought by Nicaragua against the USA,[166] and in 1986 the Court rejected the contention that US action had largely been justified by collective self-defence for El Salvador. It did not, however, as explored earlier in chapter 3, consider the naval manoeuvres and overflights to be an unlawful threat of force.

USA–Libya (Rabta controversy, 1989)

During the final weeks of Reagan's second term, in January 1989, Libya and the USA became embroiled in yet another hostile encounter.[167] US

162 NYT, 'Russians Accuse U.S. of Seeking to Meddle in Nicaraguan Affairs' (16 Nov. 1984).
163 1984 UNYB 211; SCOR Supp. S/16835 (19 Nov. 1984).
164 NYT, 'U.S. Faulted at Talks on Latin Peace Treaty' (14 Nov. 1984).
165 NYT, 'The MIG's Are Coming!' (18 Nov. 1984).
166 NYT, 'World Court Acts to Overrule U.S. in Nicaragua Case' (27 Nov. 1984).
167 ICB, 'Libyan Jets', crisis 386.

intelligence reports in September 1988 suggested that Libya had embarked on the production of chemical weapons at a plant near the desert town of Rabta, sixty kilometres south of Libya's capital, Tripoli.[168] US officials estimated that the completed plant would be capable of churning out some 80,000 lbs of nerve gas per day.[169] Chemical weapons from Rabta, the USA feared, could end up in terrorist hands or being used against Israel in the Middle East.

The Reagan administration swiftly notified Libya that it knew the Rabta plant was designed to produce chemical weapons and that it had to be dismantled.[170] At the same time, the White House did not hide from the public that it would not 'rule out' a military strike to destroy the plant if necessary.[171] Libya denied the charges and said that the plant under US scrutiny was a pharmaceutical factory.[172] Qaddafi insisted that the story about the Rabta plant was fabricated, and constituted merely a pretext to initiate military action against himself and his country.[173] Iran and Syria also accused the USA early on of preparing an attack and pledged their support for Libya.[174] A Saudi Arabian offer to mediate between Libya and the USA in order to avoid a confrontation was rejected by the Reagan administration.[175]

Worries over a possible strike against Rabta grew with two events at the turn of the year. First, on 21 December 1988, Pan American flight 103 exploded over Lockerbie, Scotland, causing the deaths of 257 passengers, most of whom were US citizens. British and US investigators speculated that the terrorist bombing had a Libyan or Iranian origin.[176] Second, on New Year's Day 1989, a US naval task force headed by the aircraft carrier USS *John F. Kennedy* and composed in addition of two cruisers, two destroyers, five frigates and an amphibious group with 2,000 marines, departed from Cannes and held manoeuvres in the

[168] Shultz, *Turmoil and Triumph*, at p. 244.
[169] *Economist*, 'The Duel Over Rabta' (7 Jan. 1989).
[170] NYT, 'U.S. Spurns Saudis on Libya Mediation' (7 Jan. 1989).
[171] NYT, 'Reagan Confers With Allies on Libya Plant' (22 Dec. 1989).
[172] NYT, 'Libya Offers to Allow Inspection of Chemical Plant but U.S. Balks' (31 Dec. 1989). On Libya's defence and further developments see Ronald Bruce St John, *Libya and the United States: Two Centuries of Strife* 159–62 (2002).
[173] NYT, 'U.S. Says Libya Moves Chemicals for Poison Gas away from Plant' (4 Jan. 1989).
[174] NYT, 'Attacks and Accusations: The U.S.-Libya Bitterness' (5 Jan. 1989).
[175] NYT, 'U.S. Spurns Saudis on Libya Mediation' (7 Jan. 1989)
[176] On 31 December 1988, ten days after the attack, these suspicions were not yet backed up by clear evidence. See NYT, 'Pan Am Blast: An Inquiry In Hot Pursuit' (1 Jan. 1989). However, Libyan involvement was later substantiated: see Fiona Beverage, 'The Lockerbie Affair', 41 Int. & Comp. LQ 907–20 (1992).

central Mediterranean some 200 kilometres off the coast of Libya. On 4 January two US F-14 fighters shot down two Libyan, Soviet-made MiG-23s over international waters, 110 kilometres off the Libyan coast north of Tobruk.[177] The USA claimed that the Libyan jets had intercepted the F-14's on a regular patrol from the *John F. Kennedy*, that the Libyans had displayed hostile intent by attempting to manoeuvre into firing positions and that the US pilots, after repeated attempts at evasion, had acted in self-defence. It also maintained that the downing of the Libyan MiGs had nothing to do with the suspect chemical plant and that the incident had taken place too far away for Qaddafi to believe that an immediate attack on the installation was to be carried out. Libya responded that its planes had been on a routine flight, were unarmed and the USA had carried out a 'premeditated attack', Qaddafi vowing that he would meet 'challenge with challenge'.[178] A day after the aerial clash, the *John F. Kennedy* group moved on to Haifa, Israel, where it was scheduled for a visit before returning home to the USA. Another battle group, led by the nuclear-powered carrier USS *Theodore Roosevelt*, was dispatched to take over guard duty in the Mediterranean.[179] No attack on the suspect chemical plant took place in the final days of the Reagan administration.

Many states viewed the US presence off the Libyan coast sceptically, despite the fact that, this time undisputedly, US forces were stationed in international waters. The Co-ordinating Bureau of non-aligned countries issued a *communiqué* on 3 January, a day before the aerial incident, in which it made the point that US threats and media campaigns had preceded the 1986 attacks against Libya. It warned that the current campaign might serve as a pretext for launching 'fresh acts of aggression' against that country.[180] The sending of the *Theodore Roosevelt* battle group – described by the USA as a routine deployment – also aroused concern among European NATO allies that the Reagan administration was preparing a military strike.[181] Only the UK, Canada and the Netherlands had accepted the US evidence about Rabta, while other

177 For a detailed account see Stanik, *El Dorado Canyon*, at pp. 228–31.
178 NYT, 'U.N. Meeting Asked' (5 Jan. 1989); NYT, 'Qaddafi Vows to "Meet Challenge With Challenge"' (5 Jan. 1989).
179 NYT, 'U.S. Says Tape Shows Missiles on Libyan Jet' (6 Jan. 1989); NYT, 'Bonus From Clash: Intelligence' (6 Jan. 1989).
180 1989 UNYB 155; SCOR Supp. S/20369 (3 Jan. 1989).
181 NYT, 'Clash off Libya Arouses Concern in Europe' (6 Jan. 1989).

European states had not, and therefore advised against a military solution.[182]

The aerial incident on 4 January brought these wider concerns over US foreign policy to the fore. Accusing the USA of aggression, Qaddafi had called for an emergency session of the UN Security Council on the same day.[183] Diplomatic responses, accustomed to the frequency of US-Libyan confrontations, dispassionately condemned the USA. The twenty-member Arab League announced on the day of the incident that the Arab nations felt 'solidarity with Libya against the American attack' and that the incident would sever US-Arab relations and damage the Middle East peace process.[184] On 5 January, the NAM, too, promptly condemned the attack and demanded that the USA withdraw its forces from the area.[185] The USSR accused the USA of 'state terrorism' and 'political adventurism', while only the UK's veto saved the USA from a EU statement that failed to support the US version of events.[186] Little was to be expected from any US attempts to convince the non-Western Security Council members otherwise, since the aerial dogfight had already been discounted, in the crowded Security Council debate of 5 to 11 January.[187] What was on trial there was the US Libya policy, in which the aerial engagement was seen as another ominous sign for US readiness to take out the Rabta chemical plant.[188]

The Libyan representative to the UN therefore accused the USA of assembling a fleet to attack Libya, and stated that the fighter clash was a 'premeditated prelude to a large-scale aggression in striking economic and military installations' in Libya.[189] Condemnations were forthcoming by other members of the Arab League and the Non-Aligned Movement. Several resolutions were drafted that, in order to secure maximum support, gradually reduced their condemnation of the

[182] NYT, 'Reagan, Qaddafi and the Death Cloud' (8 Jan. 1989). [183] 1989 UNYB 156.
[184] NYT, 'U.N. Meeting Asked' (5 Jan. 1989).
[185] 1989 UNYB 156; SCOR Supp. S/20377 (5 Jan. 1989). [186] ICB, 'Libyan Jets', crisis 386.
[187] The US administration produced several pieces of evidence that the Libyan jets had been armed and that the US Tomcats had not invited combat. However, in July 1988 a US Navy warship in the Strait of Hormuz had accidentally shot down an Iranian commercial airliner over the Persian Gulf, killing 290 passengers. The US administration then had argued that the Navy commander had mistaken the airbus for an Iranian F-14 but, and due to that erroneous assumption, had been within his rights to open fire. As in 1981, US credibility was at a low. See NYT, 'Action is Defended' (4 Jul. 1988); NYT, 'Aviation Experts Assess the Incident' (4 Jul. 1988).
[188] SCOR S/PV.2835–2837 (5–6 Jan. 1989), SCOR S/PV.2839–2841 (9–11 Jan. 1989). Twenty-nine states participated in the discussion without the right to vote.
[189] NYT, 'Russians at U.N. Say Moscow had Urged Restraint by U.S.' (6 Jan. 1989).

USA.[190] A third draft on 11 January, sponsored by Algeria, Colombia, Ethiopia, Malaysia, Nepal, Senegal and Yugoslavia, had the Council 'deplore' the downing of the two Libyan planes, while calling on the USA to suspend military manoeuvres off the Libyan coast. The resolution also proposed that parties should refrain from the use of force, should exercise restraint, and should resolve their differences by peaceful means.[191] In what US representative Herbert Okun described as a 'better than expected' outcome, the draft was rejected by nine votes to four (Canada, France, the UK and the USA), with two abstentions (Brazil and Finland).[192] The next day, an emergency meeting of the Arab League and the Islamic Conference nonetheless condemned US aggression.[193]

In short, the US policy against Libya was widely resented, and its military presence off the Libyan coast and the aerial showdown were seen as evidence for its eagerness to use force against Rabta. Non-Western countries considered the use of force to be unacceptable, while Western countries considered it unwise to employ it. The withdrawal of US forces from the vicinity of Libya, it was held, would remove the potential for confrontation. Only Israel, which stood at risk of a Libyan attack with chemical weapons, welcomed the arrival of the *John F. Kennedy* in Haifa on its last stop before heading back to Norfolk, Virginia.[194] With what appears to be some sensitivity to Libya's successes in the Council, the USA cancelled on 11 January its previously announced plans to hold aerial manoeuvres near Libya scheduled for 16 and 17 January.[195]

Whether the negative response of the international system to the posture of the US forces in the Mediterranean is approximate to their legal views is hard to tell. With regard to the aerial incident on 4 January, it is clear that condemnation did not flow from an impartial reading of the facts. No state seemed inclined to verify whether the US' version of events stood on firmer ground than Libya's. On the other

[190] NYT, 'Softer Tone at U.N. on Libya Incident' (10 Jan. 1989); NYT, 'U.N. Resolution on Dogfight Softened Again' (11 Jan. 1989).

[191] 1989 UNYB 156; S/20378 (11 Jan. 1989). It also called on the USA and Libya to cooperate with the Secretary-General in bringing about a peaceful settlement of their differences.

[192] 1989 UNYB 157; NYT, 'U.S. and Allies Veto U.N. Move on Libyan Planes' (12 Jan. 1989).

[193] 1989 UNYB 157.

[194] Stanick, *El Dorado Canyon*, at p. 229.

[195] NYT, 'U.S. Halts Navy Maneuvers that Libya Calls Provocative' (12 Jan. 1989).

hand, it is possible to read the majority opinion as one that condemned the USA for maintaining a coastal presence off Libya that from experience would inevitably provoke another clash among unequal rivals, and that the USA should shoulder most of the responsibility for the incident. In this sense, the naval exercises by the USA and its use of force against the Libyan MiGs, combined with the USA's publicised ambiguity over its military cards, stood as witness to the US inclination to use force against Libya in general and the chemical plant at Rabta in particular. This was despite the fact that the USA kept a naval presence of thirteen ships in the Mediterranean at all times.[196] As in 1981, the highest priority in the minds of many governments might have been opposition to the USA and the signalling of solidarity with a fellow Arab or non-aligned state.[197]

Iraq–Kuwait (sanctions defiance, 1994)

On 2 October 1994, an Iraqi force of an estimated 40,000 to 50,000 troops began to head towards its southern border and on 7 October stationed itself in close proximity to Kuwait. More troops were scheduled to arrive, to accumulate to a total of 70,000 soldiers, combined with Republican Guard divisions and accompanied by armoured personnel carriers and 700 tanks.[198] This troop build-up was strongly reminiscent of the events in 1990 when Iraqi military preparations had led directly to the invasion of its southern neighbour on 2 August. Two further facts rendered the 1994 mustering of troops ominous to outside observers: first, in the previous week Iraq had warned that it would 'retaliate' if the Security Council, at its next scheduled meeting on 10 October, decided to renew economic sanctions. Iraq condemned US insistence on retaining sanctions, the oil embargo especially, that had crippled the nation's economy since their imposition in August 1990.[199]

[196] NYT, 'Bonus from Clash: Intelligence' (6 Jan. 1989).

[197] While the USA clearly did not receive any support for a military solution to the Rabta problem, it did succeed in making its European allies think more seriously about its concerns over Libyan chemical weapons, if only because Washington might prove 'nutty' enough to go in and hit Qaddafi. So too, it is said, did Qaddafi lower his profile on international terrorism for the next two years. See NYT, 'Using Force Against Libya?' (11 Jan. 1989).

[198] NYT, 'Keeping the Iraqis Back' (11 Oct. 1994). The number of soldiers that arrived at the Kuwait border is not precisely known. Reports varied from 60,000 to 80,000. The estimate of 70,000 derives from the *New York Times* article cited.

[199] S/RES/661 (6 Aug. 1990).

Second, in defiance of orders from the Security Council,[200] Iraq still refused to acknowledge the sovereignty of Kuwait and had recently begun to refer to it again as Iraq's 'nineteenth province'.[201]

US President Clinton reacted swiftly and firmly on 8 October by giving the green light to *Operation Vigilant Warrior*. The USA would deploy additional troops into the Persian Gulf area.[202] The aircraft carrier *George Washington* was ordered to move from the Adriatic into striking distance in the Red Sea, along with an Aegis cruiser equipped with Tomahawk missiles. A contingent of 16,500 marines from the Diego Garcia military base set sail from the Indian Ocean. In a White House press conference, Clinton said that these were precautionary steps and that he would not permit Baghdad to intimidate the UN into raising the sanctions. 'It would be a grave mistake for Saddam Hussein', he emphasised, 'to believe for any reason that the United States had weakened its resolve on the same issues that involved us in that conflict just a few years ago'.[203] US troops scheduled to arrive in the Gulf the next day totalled 36,000;[204] the lessons of 1990 learnt, the commitment of the USA to defend Kuwaiti territorial integrity was not to be misunderstood a second time. The UK also dispatched a battalion of Royal Marines, two warships and Tornado aircraft to double its presence in the Gulf, and France sent a warship. In the meantime, Iraqi officials denied any intention to invade Kuwait and insisted that since Iraq was a sovereign and peaceful state, it had 'all the rights to move its troops within its territories and borders'.[205]

That claim convinced no one. Syria, Egypt, Saudi Arabia and the Persian Gulf Emirates swiftly condemned Iraq's military build-up, and Jordan, which had formerly supported Saddam Hussein in 1990, now sided with Kuwait.[206] On 11 October, the EU issued a statement urging Iraq to withdraw its troops from the border region and to refrain from

200 S/RES/687 (3 April 1991).

201 NYT, 'U.S. Sends Force as Iraqi Soldiers Threaten Kuwait' (8 Oct. 1994).

202 US deployment before October was about 12,000 troops, some eighty planes and not sufficiently numbered to resist an invasion. See NYT, 'Pentagon Moving a Force of 4,000 to Guard Kuwait' (9 Oct. 1994).

203 NYT, 'U.S. Sends Force as Iraqi Soldiers Threaten Kuwait' (8 Oct. 1994). In telephone calls on 10 October, Clinton received support from the UK, France, Russia, Egypt and Turkey for 'quick and vigorous military measures to defend Kuwait' if necessary. They also agreed to oppose Iraq's attempt to press the UN to lift economic sanctions. See NYT, 'Clinton Sees No Pullback and Sends More Planes' (11 Oct. 1994).

204 NYT, 'Force May Double' (9 Oct. 1994).

205 NYT, 'Pentagon Moving a Force of 4,000 to Guard Kuwait' (9 Oct. 1994).

206 NYT, 'Arab States Withholding Their Support for Baghdad' (11 Oct. 1994).

confrontation.[207] A statement made by Senegal on the same day and transmitted to the Security Council branded Iraqi troop movements as 'unacceptable' and 'unjustifiable'.[208] On 12 October, the six members of the Gulf Cooperation Council – Saudi Arabia, Kuwait, Bahrain, Qatar, Oman and the United Arab Emirates – not only condemned Baghdad but also committed themselves to paying the costs of deploying US forces to the Gulf.[209] Even Libya, not a friend of the USA, criticised Iraqi troop movements.[210]

Kuwait had raised the alarm at the Security Council as early as 6 October.[211] On Saturday 15 October, thirty minutes before midnight, the Council unanimously passed resolution 949, which had been sponsored by Argentina, France, Oman, Rwanda, the UK and the USA.[212] In it, Iraq's troop concentrations were condemned in no light terms.

Acting under Chapter VII of the Charter of the United Nations, [the Security Council] 1. Condemns recent military deployments by Iraq in the direction of the border with Kuwait; 2. Demands that Iraq immediately complete the withdrawal of all military units recently deployed to southern Iraq to their original positions; 3. Demands that Iraq not again utilize its military or any other forces in a hostile or provocative manner to threaten either its neighbours or United Nations operations in Iraq; 4. Demands therefore that Iraq not redeploy to the south the units referred to in paragraph 2 above or take any other action to enhance its military capacity in southern Iraq; 5. Demands that Iraq cooperate fully with the United Nations Special Commission; 6. Decides to remain actively seized of the matter.[213]

[207] Mentioned by the Spanish delegate in the Security Council, SCOR S/PV.3438 (15 Oct. 1994), at 8.

[208] 1994 UNYB 458; SCOR Supp. S/1994/1881 (11 Oct. 1994).

[209] 1994 UNYB 458; SCOR Supp. S/1994/1162 (12 Oct. 1994); NYT, 'Six Gulf Nations Pledge to Repay Much of U.S. Costs and Back Efforts to Contain Iraq' (13 Oct. 1994).

[210] NYT, 'Reversing Gulf War Stand, King Hussein Condemns Iraq' (12 Oct. 1994).

[211] 1994 UNYB 457; SCOR Supp. S/1994/1137 (6 Oct. 1994). The Council was composed as follows: Argentina, Brazil, China, Czech Republic, Djibouti, France, New Zealand, Nigeria, Oman, Pakistan, Russian Federation, Rwanda, Spain, the UK and the USA. Following informal consultations among the Council members, its president was authorised on 8 October to state on the Council's behalf that it had received 'with grave concern' reports 'that substantial numbers of Iraqi troops, including units of the Iraqi Republican Guard, are being redeployed in the direction of the border with Kuwait' and reaffirmed its commitment to the sovereignty and territorial integrity of Kuwait. See SCOR S/PV.3435 (8 Oct. 1994). Kuwait joined the discussion of the Council on 15 October and Iraq on 17 October.

[212] SCOR S/PV.3438 (15 Oct. 1994), at 4; NYT, 'Security Council Condemns Iraqi's Threat Against Kuwait' (16 Oct. 1994).

[213] S/RES/949 (15 Oct. 1994).

This in effect meant the creation of a buffer zone in which Iraqi surface troops would be excluded from southern Iraq.[214] Equally clearly, the Council squarely put Iraq into the category of norm-breaker. The presence of Iraqi troops amounted to a threat of force in violation of the UN Charter, while Iraq's assertion that it was acting within its sovereign rights was flatly rejected. As the British president of the Council Sir David Hannay stated:

> The Iraqi Government has tried to justify its behaviour by speaking of its sovereign right to deploy its troops wherever it likes within its territory. But Article 2, paragraph 4, of the Charter of the United Nations requires all Members to refrain 'from the threat or use of force against the territorial integrity or political independence of any state.' Four years ago similar Iraqi troop movements led to the invasion of Kuwait. On this occasion Iraqi artillery and tanks were deployed in positions pointing towards and within range of Kuwait, with ammunition at the ready. Let us be clear: this action was a threat to Kuwait and represented a breach of the provisions of the Charter of the United Nations.[215]

Other countries such as the Czech Republic,[216] Spain,[217] Argentina,[218] Pakistan[219] and Kuwait openly criticised Iraq but made little legal reference.[220] Russia seemed to draw a distinction between unlawfulness according to article 2(4) and threats to peace triggering the authority of Chapter VII. The Council met on 17 October, during which the Russian representative Kozyrev mounted a rescue attempt for Iraq and suggested that the country's manoeuvres had been pre-announced to some states and that Iraq had not really entertained thoughts to invade Kuwait.[221] To this, US Ambassador to the UN Madeleine Albright retorted sharply that the threat against Kuwait had been very real,[222] and in response to the statement by Iraq's representative Tareq Aziz, she declared: 'Words are cheap. Actions are the coin of the realm.'[223] Whatever credibility Iraq could summon among the Security Council members, it stood on unstable ground in claiming peaceful intent. If its offensive posture was a bluff this backfired, since there was now less willingness to ease economic sanctions than before, whereas

214 NYT, 'U.S. Offers Plan to Avoid Threat from Iraq Again' (13 Oct. 1994). (In addition to the already unilaterally imposed no-fly zones.)
215 SCOR S/PV.3438 (15 Oct. 1994), at 11.
216 *Ibid.*, at 6. 217 *Ibid.*, at 8. 218 *Ibid.*, at 10. 219 *Ibid.*, at 11. 220 *Ibid.*, at 13.
221 SCOR S/PV.3439 (17 Oct. 1994), at 2. 222 *Ibid.*, at 7. 223 *Ibid.*, at 18.

earlier, France, China and Russia had considered adopting a softer line favouring first steps to the relaxation of sanctions.[224]

Perhaps Nizar Hamdoon, the Iraqi Ambassador to the UN, had in that realisation already announced a troop withdrawal to rearward positions on 10 October.[225] But US intelligence during the subsequent few days suggested that not all armed forces had retreated and that units of the Republican Guard showed no signs of moving to the north, remaining near Nasiriya. Mistrustful, the USA therefore continued with its plans for deployment.[226] Reports of Republican Guard units starting to leave the border area eventually appeared on 15 October, when the Security Council voted on the proposal for the US resolution.[227] After the passing of resolution 494, Iraq declared a willingness to comply with UN demands,[228] and on 10 November its National Assembly formally declared recognition of the sovereignty of Kuwait.[229] That declaration, signed by Saddam Hussein, terminated the 1994 Gulf crisis, while economic sanctions remained in place unaltered.[230]

For the White House, condemnation in October by a unified Security Council was not enough: the US objectives were to find a way to make Iraq withdraw its troops permanently, and also to find ways of avoiding a costly redeployment into the Gulf in the future. The military buffer zone was part of that idea. Under no circumstances, it was thought, should Saddam Hussein be allowed to use his military arsenal in a show of desperation to negotiate the conditions of sanctions relief and imperil the unity of the Security Council. Russia had already preferred to negotiate with Iraq and, to the USA's dismay, had come up with proposals to trade the partial lifting of sanctions with Iraqi recognition of Kuwaiti sovereignty.[231] No such concessions were acceptable to the Clinton administration.

In the light of these considerations, the White House wanted to send a deterrent message as forcefully as possible. Therefore, resolution 949 declared at the outset that the Council was 'Determined to prevent Iraq from resorting to threats and intimidation of its neighbours and the

[224] NYT, 'Iraq's Reckless Ploy' (11 Oct. 1994).
[225] NYT, 'Cites Duty In Gulf' (11 Oct. 1994).
[226] NYT, 'U.S. Forces Continue to Pour into Gulf' (13 Oct. 1994).
[227] NYT, 'Perry Reports Elite Iraqi Army is Set to Retreat' (16 Oct. 1994).
[228] NYT, 'Iraq Signals Acceptance of U.N. Move' (17 Oct. 1994).
[229] NYT, 'Iraqis to Accept Kuwait's Borders' (11 Nov. 1994).
[230] NYT, 'U.N. Council Decides to Keep Economic Sanctions on Iraq' (15 Nov. 1994).
[231] NYT, 'Russia and Iraq Work out Plan to Ease Gulf Tension' (14 Oct. 1994).

United Nations' and 'that it will consider Iraq fully responsible for the serious consequences of any failure to fulfil the demands in the present resolution'.[232] Madeleine Albright accordingly warned that the USA was prepared to take punitive action against Iraq if the draft resolution of 15 October demanding Iraqi troop withdrawal failed: 'let me assure this Council that pursuant to the resolutions of this Council and Article 51 of the United Nations Charter, my Government will take appropriate action if Iraq fails to comply with the demands of this resolution'.[233] Other statements to the press made by President Clinton and Secretary of Defense William Perry, the latter during a visit in Kuwait, made it unmistakably clear that the USA would use force to compel Iraqi troops to abandon their positions.[234] Now that its military forces had arrived in the desert, the USA was inclined to make use of them. Several military exercises, including a simulated B-1 and B-2 bombing of targets in southern Iraq, underlined verbal assurances.[235] A move by Russia to criticise the US presence along the lines that it was creating 'a dangerous situation' failed to gain support.[236] Eventually, in early November, orders to leave the Gulf area were received.[237] The US demonstration of resolve had undoubtedly become an effective strategic deterrent to another Iraqi deployment, not merely one to hasten the return to base in October 1994. It seems that the vast majority of states clearly understood that rationale and accepted it. In the light of Iraq's previous use of force in 1990 and the US role in responding to it, the present show of strength by the USA appeared either as an act endorsed by the Security Council or the right to assist Kuwait in collective self-defence.[238]

232 S/RES/949 (15 Oct. 1994).

233 SCOR, S/PV.3438 (15 Oct. 1994), at 6. See also NYT, 'U.S. Is Demanding a Quick U.N. Vote on Iraqi Pullback' (15 Oct. 1994); NYT, 'U.S. Warns Iraq to Complete Pullout' (15 Oct. 1994). For a defence of the US position in regard to the 1998 Iraqi weapons inspections defiance see Ruth Wedgwood, 'The Enforcement of Security Council Resolution 687: The Threat of Force Against Iraq's Weapons of Mass Destruction', 92 Am. JIL 724–8 (1998).

234 NYT, 'U.S. Warns Iraq to Complete Pullout' (15 Oct. 1994).

235 NYT, 'Marines Stage Desert Exercise in Show of Force' (14 Oct. 1994); NYT, 'U.S. Jets Fly Dry Runs on Iraq Targets to Show "We're Here"' (18 Oct. 1994). See also NYT, 'Iraq Condemns Plan for U.S. War Games' (1 Nov. 1994), where Iraq branded US B-1 and B-2 bomber exercises scheduled over Kuwait and southern Iraq as a 'provocative military action' and a 'flagrant violation and a reckless disregard of the sanctity of international law'.

236 NYT, 'U.S. Criticizes a Russian Aide at U.N. on Iraq' (18 Oct. 1994).

237 NYT, 'Officials Say U.S. to Cut Forces in Haiti and Kuwait' (7 Nov. 1994).

238 The US claim that it acted under implied authority of the Security Council did not receive the same support in other instances. The imposition and enforcement of

It is interesting to compare diplomatic responses to the preludes to the Iraqi invasion of Kuwait four years previously in July 1990.[239] At that time, Iraqi troop concentrations – very similar, as it turned out, to those of 1994 – prepared to make a move across the border. But in 1990, Saddam Hussein's overt threats to extract greater compliance with OPEC oil quotas were in alignment with the desire clearly stated by the two other major powers of the Gulf, Saudi Arabia and Iran, to make Kuwait and the United Arab Emirates curb their excessive oil production and raise oil prices. Many officials of the thirteen nations of OPEC, while concerned by Iraq's open sabre-rattling, were privately pleased by the tough stance taken by Iraq against notorious spoilers of oil prices.[240] Diplomatic protests had been few, and slow in coming. Arab nations, such as Egypt, preferred to try the diplomatic track to defuse tensions, while outsiders would treated Iraq's militarism as a mainly Arab affair.[241] The apparent success of Iraq in pushing Kuwait and the United Arab Emirates back into line with other OPEC members might have also raised expectations that Saddam Hussein, having achieved his goal, would forgo preliminary plans for attack.[242] But in 1994, the situation was different, and the readiness of other states to condemn Iraq was disproportionably higher.

no-fly zones in 1991–2 or the 1993 bombing of Baghdad raised concerns over the extent of unilateral liberties on the use of force against Iraq. See Jules Lobel and Michael Ratner, 'Bypassing the Security Council: Ambiguous Authorizations to Use Force, Cease-Fires and the Iraqi Inspection Regime', 93 Am. JIL 124–55 (1999), at 132–3; Dino Kritsiotis, 'The Legality of the 1993 US Missile Strikes on Iraq and the Right of Self-Defence in International Law', 45 Int. & Comp. LQ 162–77 (1996); Christine Gray, *International Law and the Use of Force* 264–7 (2nd edn, 2004).

[239] For reports of events in 1990 see NYT, 'Iran Threatens Emirates and Kuwait on Oil Glut' (18 Jul. 1990); NYT, 'Iraq Speaks of Act of War' (19 Jul. 1990); NYT, 'Iraq Deploys Troops Near Kuwait Border Amid Dispute on Oil' (24 Jul. 1990).

[240] NYT, 'OPEC Meets Today; Talks Are Clouded by Iraq's Threat to Kuwait' (25 Jul. 1990).

[241] The USA, however, modestly signalled its willingness to support the UAE and Kuwait and defend the flow of oil through the Strait of Hormuz by force if necessary. See NYT, 'U.S. Deploys Air and Sea Forces After Iraq Threatens 2 Neighbors' (25 Jul. 1990); NYT, 'Congress Backs Curbs Against Iraq' (28 Jul. 1990).

[242] NYT, 'OPEC in Agreement to Raise Oil Price by Cutting Output' (28 Jul. 1990). Iraq's interest was to have its vast Kuwaiti debts forgiven, which it had accumulated during the Iran-Iraq war, and its long-standing territorial claim over its mineral-rich neighbour were overlooked. With the invasion in 1990, Baghdad's designs for a dominant regional role in control of a substantial chunk of its oil resources became more apparent. See Keylor, *A World of Nations*, at p. 402.

Conclusions

What, then, constitute the criteria of unlawfulness in the light of state practice since 1945? There is evidence that demonstrations of force are considered as a serious matter – more serious than verbal threats – resulting in a palpable difference in the degree of state reactions. Demonstrations of force tend to be inherently the more credible threat. Indeed, as the US Ambassador to the UN Madeleine Albright asserted in the Security Council: 'Actions are the coin of the realm.'[243] The more recent examples in this study – the US naval demonstrations in Libya in 1981 and 1989, the involvement of the USA with Nicaragua in 1984 and the Iraqi troop concentrations against Kuwait in 1994 – were all condemned. The debate over India's encirclement and eventual seizure of Goa was fought over the justification of it, not over whether it had passed the threshold of article 2(4). It is plausible, too, that states viewed the USSR intimidation of Czechoslovakia in 1968 as wrongful, despite widespread silence until the Soviet tanks eventually rolled into Czechoslovakia's capital. The two cases to which reaction was patently absent were the Turkish Straits incident in 1946 and the Colombian fortification of the San Andrés Islands in 1979–80; it is conceivable, apart from the imperfections of the international system to detect and react to infringements of the law, that the actions undertaken fell below the threshold of violation, and that, in view of the comparatively low-key naval arrangements, the military actions did not amount to a breach of article 2(4). They fell short of raising the shared risk of armed conflict to serious levels.

In line with the second criterion proposed in the last chapter, the US show of strength in the Persian Gulf in response to the Iraqi troop build-up in 1994 attracted no condemnation from other nations because it was judged as an effort in *crisis management*. A cautious reading of the facts suggests that the UN Security Council quietly endorsed US actions that served to impress upon Baghdad the strength of its resolution. In contrast, the Security Council flatly rejected the Iraqi contention that its sovereign rights entitled it to unrestricted military activities within its own territory.

There is further evidence that is indicative of states being keenly aware of the first criterion identified in the last chapter, that the political uses of peacetime military activities may *credibly* imply hostile

[243] SCOR S/PV.3439 (17 Oct. 1994), at 18.

intent. First, nearly all military exercises that take place outside the borders of a state or that involve firing of ordnance are announced in advance, both at military-to-military level and between ministries of states. Even internal exercises that could be detected and misconstrued as hostile, such as missile test launches or large troop concentrations, are normally communicated abroad.[244] This, it may be understood, is a safety measure, but it serves the equally important task of removing the erroneous suspicion that military activities are a prelude to the actual use of force.[245] The establishment of military buffer zones fulfils the same function.[246] Military exercises are banned altogether in the Antarctic and in outer space.[247]

Second, in introducing Exclusive Economic Zones in the 1982 Law of the Sea Convention (UNCLOS III),[248] Bangladesh, Brazil, Cape Verde, India, Malaysia, Pakistan and Uruguay declared that in their understanding military exercises or manoeuvres within the Exclusive Economic Zone would be illegal unless previous consent had been given by the coastal state concerned. Germany, Italy, the Netherlands and the UK, on the other hand, opposed that claim.[249] The bone of contention, however, was not whether foreign warships were able to threaten

[244] Personal communication with Lt Cr Scott Tait, US Navy (16 Nov. 2004). Warnings by virtually all nations are duplicated in the US and UK notification services, due to universal subscription. See 'Notices to Airmen', at http://www.faa.gov/ntap/index.htm, and 'Notices to Mariners, at http://www.ukho.gov.uk/amd/weeklyNms.asp.

[245] Such confidence- and security-building measures emerged in Europe with the *Final Act of the Conference on Security and Co-operation in Europe (Helsinki Final Act)*, 14 ILM 1292 (1 Aug. 1975). See for an overview of the numerous regional and bilateral notification arrangements Steve Tulliu and Thomas Schmalberger, *Coming to Terms with Security: A Lexicon for Arms Control, Disarmament and Confidence-Building* 135–64 (2004). See on prior notification duties in general Frederic L. Kirgis, *Prior Consultation in International Law: A Study of State Practice* (1983).

[246] Surya P. Subedi, *Land and Maritime Zones of Peace in International Law* 77–81 (1996); Sydney D. Bailey, 'Nonmilitary Areas in UN Practice', 74 Am. JIL 499–524 (1980).

[247] Article 1 *Antarctic Treaty*, 402 UNTS 71 (1 Dec. 1959); article 4 *Treaty on Principles Governing the Activities of States in the Exploration and Use of Outer Space, Including the Moon and Other Celestial Bodies*, 610 UNTS 205 (27 Jan. 1967); article 3 *Agreement Governing the Activities of States on the Moon and other Celestial Bodies*, 1363 UNTS 21 (18 Dec. 1979).

[248] *United Nations Convention of the Law of the Sea*, 1833 UNTS 3 (10 Dec. 1982).

[249] See http://www.un.org/depts/los/. See further B. A. Boczek, 'Peace-time Military Activities in the Exclusive Economic Zone of Third Countries', 19 Ocean Dev. & IL 455–68 (1988); B. A. Boczek, 'Peaceful Purposes Provisions of the United Nations Convention on the Law of the Sea', 20 Ocean Dev. & IL 359–89 (1989); S. Rose, 'Naval Activity in the Exclusive Economic Zone: Troubled Waters Ahead', 21 Ocean Dev. & IL 71–103 (1990); R. R. Churchill and A. V. Lowe, *The Law of the Sea* 171, 426–8 (3rd edn, 1999).

shore-based territory – that aspect was common ground – but the requirement of consent by the coastal state.[250] Similarly, with regard rights of passage for warships, the Convention declares in articles 19 and 39 that any ship or aircraft exercising the right of transit or passage must refrain from threatening or using force against the coastal state concerned. If those words are to have any meaning, this, too, indicates that signatory states understood, as is recognised among military professionals, that warships and fighter aircraft can pose a threat of force through their very presence.[251]

Overall, practice since 1945 fortifies the view that shows of force – on land, on sea or in the air – may indeed amount to a threat of force in the sense of article 2(4), quite independently of where they are performed. The important lesson is that demonstrations of force suffice to signal the readiness to use force which is in general condemned by states. There is no necessity for the threat to be embedded in the context of a specific demand, or, for that matter, a specific deadline for response. At the same time, the practice of notification of military exercises, along with a maritime regime that acknowledges military uses of the oceans, also proves that a large percentage of such exercises are widely accepted as lawful.[252]

The perennial question, then, remains how demonstrations of force may be distinguished from regular drills, routine exercises and ordinary test firings that do not violate the UN Charter. In 1998, for example, North Korea accused the US of escalating tensions by 'amassing the latest type of war equipment in south Korea under the pretext of a threat of a fictitious "preemptive strike" ' and by the 'reorganization of the [Eighth and Third Armies] following the reinforced deployment of state-of-the-art military equipment in south Korea'.[253] It referred to the

250 Ken Booth, *Law, Force, and Diplomacy at Sea* 138 (1985).

251 Standard texts on naval operations, however, are patently oblivious of article 2(4) in their discussion of maritime law, while being outspoken and clear-minded about the role of a nation's navy to project power ashore. Instead of many see Bernard H. Oxman, 'International Law and Naval and Air Operations at Sea', in Horace B. Robertson, Jr (ed.), *The Law of Naval Operations*, 64 US Nav. War. CIL Stud. 18–37 (1991), at pp. 30–1; Ondolf Rojahn, 'Naval Demonstration', 3 Enc. Pub. IL 526–7 (1997); Günter Hoog, 'Naval Manoeuvres', 3 Enc. Pub. IL 527–8 (1997).

252 The standard derivative of the freedom of military uses is article 87 *UNCLOS III*. See Booth, *Diplomacy at Sea*, at pp. 82–4; Churchill and Lowe, *The Law of the Sea*, at pp. 426–8.

253 SCOR Supp. S/1998/264 (24 Mar. 1998). See for a discussion of the *Team Spirit* exercises Matthew A. Myers, 'Deterrence and the Threat of Force Ban: Does the UN Charter Prohibit Some Military Exercises?', 162 Mil. LR 132–79 (1999).

US' persistent 'policy of aggressive power' subverting efforts to achieve lasting peace in the region and provoking counter-measures on the part of North Korea. It also stigmatised a joint military exercise with the Chinese army to assist US preparations for war.[254] Conversely, North Korea, also in 1998, fired a new Taepodong-1 missile over Japan that demonstrated its ability to deliver (nuclear) payloads over a longer range, possibly as far as the USA.[255] A second round of missile launches on 4 July 2006 (American Independence Day), which included a Taepodong-2 firing,[256] seems to have at least partially pursued the same purpose, together with a first nuclear weapon test explosion on 9 October 2006.[257]

In the eight cases examined, militarised acts served a specific foreign policy objective vis-à-vis a particular state beyond the requirements of traditional training. Military manoeuvres in and around Czechoslovakia exceeded the norm in numbers, frequency, and intensity. The deployment of Iraqi forces to its southern border could not conceivably fall under the rubric of routine, nor could the scale of US troop movements around Nicaragua be justified under the cover of normal military procedure. The test, it appears, is whether militarised acts, first, are non-routine, second, are of an unusual intensity and, third, can be credibly said to convey, by their timing and location, a message of force with regard to a specific interstate dispute. As this involves technical assessment, good judgment will have to rely on military officers to decipher the operational elements in question.[258] On the political level, it is conceivable that a *prima facie* identification of hostile intent could be defused by positive and public assurances that none was intended. Most importantly, however, is the insight that whatever the limits are that determine the distinction between permissible and impermissible

[254] SCOR Supp. S/1998/264 (24 Mar. 1998).

[255] NYT, 'North Korea Fires Missiles over Japanese Territory' (1 Sep. 1998); NYT, 'North Korea Draws Anger with Test of a Missile' (2 Sep. 1998); NYT, 'North Koreans Declare They Launched a Satellite, Not a Missile' (5 Sep. 1998).

[256] NYT, '6 Missiles Fired by North Korea; Tests Protested' (5 Jul. 2006); NYT, 'U.N. Council, in Weakened Resolution, Demands End to North Korean Missile Program' (15 Jul. 2006); S/RES/1695 (15 Jul. 2006); SCOR S/PV.5490 (15 Jul. 2006). See for an appraisal Frederic L. Kirgis, 'North Korea's Missile Firings', *ASIL Insights* (Jul. 2006), http://www.asil.org/insights/2006/07/insights060724.html.

[257] NYT, 'N. Korea Reports 1st Nuclear Arms Test' (9 Oct. 2006); S/RES/1718 (14 Oct. 2006); SCOR S/PV.5551 (14 Oct. 2006); see for an appraisal Andreas L. Paulus and Jörn Müller, 'Security Council Resolution 1718 on North Korea's Nuclear Test', *ASIL Insights* (Nov. 2006), http://www.asil.org/insights/2006/11/insights061103.html.

[258] Booth, *Diplomacy at Sea*, at p. 146.

peacetime military activities, it is put into effect in state practice, and as such 'accepted as law'.[259] The determination of whether a demonstration of force has occurred must start out from the basis that a legal appraisal, however difficult, must tread the straight and narrow path between breach of and compliance with the UN Charter.

259 Article 38(1)(b) *Statute of the International Court of Justice*, 39 Am. JIL Supp. 215–9 (1945) (26 Jun.1945).

7 Countervailing threats or: threats in self-defence

Two narratives

There are few other principles in international law that have been as fully enshrined by governments as the right to act in self-defence and in accordance with the requirements of national security. Virtually all states assert that their resort to force is justified under the rubric of article 51 of the UN Charter.[1] As any military officer knows, all use of force carries with it a deterrent effect. Force inevitably includes the threat of further force and raises the stakes for future encounters. If deterrence were lawful under all circumstances, it would follow that all use of force – and, for that matter, all threat of it – would be justified under its terms. Obviously no state has argued that the prerogatives of defence are unlimited, and so they are subject to regulation. The question is to what extent.[2]

As shown in chapter 2, there are two rival historical narratives that both appear to make sense in practice. One is the deterrence model, which provides cogent explanations for the fortunate non-occurrence of World War III in the twentieth century and, in a sense, for order and stability. This model also suggests that World War II might have been averted had Hitler been faced with sterner and more timely resistance.[3] The second narrative is the spiral model. It is powerful in suggesting that World War I was sparked because the intricate blocks of military alliances had failed, and the readiness for and anticipation of war in and of itself had led to the war's outbreak. Following the assassination of Archduke Franz Ferdinand by Serbian nationalists on

[1] Christine Gray, *International Law and the Use of Force* 95 (2nd edn, 2004).
[2] Oscar Schachter, 'Self-Defense and the Rule of Law', 83 Am. JIL 259–77 (1989).
[3] Donald Kagan, *On the Origins of War and the Preservation of Peace* 414–15 (1995).

28 June 1914, the Austrian ultimatum against the Serbian government triggered the commencement of the war that the major European powers had fatally thought of as inevitable.[4] That this series of terrible human failures had led Europe to stumble into war was the lesson Neville Chamberlain, as one of the architects of Munich, tried to apply to Germany, but the agreement reached ended in complete and utter failure.

Seeking to implement the lessons from the past, the signatories of the UN Charter at the end of World War II determined, first, that the system of antagonistic alliances which had so patently failed to prevent World War I would have to be replaced by a collective system of universal membership of Wilsonian transparency, and, second, that future aggressors would have to be deterred, and if deterrence failed, fought into submission by force of arms. Individual members would have to seek the peaceful solution to disputes, and force was only permissible unilaterally if faced with an attack and until the Security Council took action. In short, although theory did not inform the thinking of delegates in 1945 as it could today in envisioning a post-war order, they sought to reconcile two – mutually exclusive? – models of reality. On the spiral side was the installation of universal membership and a plea for self-restraint; on the deterrence side, the reliance on collective and self-defensive military action. In what respects, if at all, communal judgment has changed since the founding of the UN Charter, and how that reflects upon the title to self-defence, is the subject of this chapter.

According to the traditional reading of the UN Charter, article 2(4) contains merely the prohibition of an initial threat. As soon as one state breaks this rule, the victim state is entitled to respond with a counter-threat, authorised as self-defence. A distinction is maintained at all times between aggressor and victim. Whether this predisposition of the law has changed since 1945 is empirically falsifiable by checking the reactions from other states. If only one party can be right, international response should be lop-sided, favouring the side which has not issued the initial threat. If the underlying facts are unclear and the aggressor-victim distinction is indiscernible, international response should acknowledge all threats from all sides, since none can be proven wrong in invoking the right to self-defence.

[4] Barbara W. Tuchman, *The Guns of August* 1–72 (1962).

USA–PRC (Seventh Fleet, 1950)

When, in December 1949, Chiang Kai-shek and his followers retreated to the island of Taiwan (at the time called Formosa), they did so in order to escape the People's Liberation Army (PLA).[5] Two months earlier, Mao Zedong had proclaimed in Tiananmen Square the establishment of the People's Republic of China (PRC). Determined to extend his control over the entire country, he made no secret of his intention to invade Taiwan and root out the last traces of Nationalist China for good. Although Chiang Kai-shek hoisted the Republic of China (ROC) flag in Taiwan, proclaiming Taipei its temporary capital until a military comeback would enable him to retake the mainland,[6] most observers expected Chiang's government to fall sooner or later. The USA initially showed no interest in supporting him in his final stand, and US officials expected an invasion of Taiwan by the PRC sometime in 1950.[7]

However, when war broke out on the Korean peninsula on 25 June 1950, it became politically untenable for the USA to allow a communist victory over Chiang. President Truman responded promptly, by authorising, on 27 June, US forces to fight alongside South Korean troops against North Korea and by ordering the Seventh Fleet, consisting of more than twenty ships and manned by around 8,000 navy personnel, to proceed into the Taiwan Strait. He demanded that Chiang Kai-shek suspend all military operations there.[8] The aid provided to South Korea received the blessing of the UN Security Council on 7 July, but the deployment of the Seventh Fleet was a unilateral US undertaking ordered without international consultation.[9] Five out of eleven members of the Council had already recognised Mao's regime in Beijing at the expense of Chiang's in Taipei, which made it difficult to gain formal approval for action in defence of Taiwan even at a time when the

[5] NYT, 'Chinese Nationalists Move Their Capital to Formosa; Now Plan a Guerrilla War' (9 Dec. 1950).

[6] ICB, 'Korean War I', crisis 132.

[7] NYT, 'Formosa Invasion Seen Set by Spring' (21 Dec. 1949); NYT, 'Fall of Formosa Expected, Says U.S.' (4 Jan. 1950).

[8] Dean Acheson, *Present at the Creation* 406 (1969); *The Secretary of State to the Embassy of China* (27 June 1950), 1950 FRUS vol. VII 188. The Seventh Fleet was put under strict orders not to enter the territorial waters of either Taiwan or mainland China: see NYT, 'U.S. Planes Keeping Watch Off Formosa' (16 Jul. 1950). Furthermore, commercial vessels were allowed free passage. There was no naval blockade of either side. See 1950 UNYB 296.

[9] S/RES84 (7 Jul. 1950).

Soviet Union was not occupying its seat in the Security Council to wield its veto in support of the PRC.[10]

US action, however, was couched in terms of Chapter VII of the UN Charter, not as collective self-defence. On 27 June, Truman explained to the US public that in view of the events in Korea, the communist world was now evidently ready to invade independent nations and that under these circumstances the occupation of Taiwan by communist forces would pose a direct threat to the security of the Pacific and to US forces there. He continued:

> Accordingly, I have ordered the Seventh Fleet to prevent any attack on Formosa. As a corollary to this action, I am calling upon the Chinese Government on Formosa to cease all air and sea operations against the mainland. The Seventh Fleet will see that this is done. The determination of the future status of Formosa must await the restoration of security in the Pacific, a peace settlement with Japan or consideration by the United Nations.[11]

Ernest Gross, the US Ambassador to the UN, would later explain that the deployment of the Seventh Fleet was 'an impartial neutralizing act . . . designed to keep the peace'.[12] This sums up the public stance of the Truman administration.[13]

For Beijing, however, US action was nothing less than an unjustified interference with its internal affairs, designed to prevent the liberation of Taiwan. From that point onwards, the PRC's plans for an invasion of Taiwan were rendered deeply hazardous because the Seventh Fleet was patrolling the area. Worse, this confirmed the communist party's fear that the overarching strategic goal of the USA was to encircle China from Taiwan, Indochina and Korea.[14] The assertions of even-handedness made by the White House were, moreover, discredited in part by General MacArthur, who, honouring Chiang Kai-shek's offer to contribute Nationalist troops to Korea, paid a visit to Taipei in July and fulsomely declared to the press that the USA would stand shoulder to shoulder with Taiwan to repel invasion attempts from the mainland.[15]

10 NYT, 'Austin Denies Aggression; Calls Peiping Charge False' (26 Aug. 1950).

11 *Statement Issued by the President* (27 Jun. 1950), 1950 FRUS vol. VII, 202–3.

12 SCOR S/PV.474 (25 Aug. 1950), at 6–9.

13 In 1953, the USA under Eisenhower/Foster Dulles officially changed policy from a maintaining a ceasefire to allowing Taiwanese attacks against the mainland.

14 Chen Jian, *China's Road to the Korean War: The Making of the Sino-American Confrontation* 129 (1994).

15 William R. Keylor, *A World of Nations* 194 (2003). For US motives to send the Seventh Fleet see Edwin C. Hoyt, 'The United States Reaction to the Korean Attack: A Study of

Mao Zedong was infuriated. A day after Truman's speech, the PRC Foreign Minister Zhou Enlai branded the USA's interposition of the US Navy as 'aggression against the territory of China, and a total violation of the United Nations Charter', asserted further that 'Taiwan is part of China [and] will remain unchanged forever ... All the people of our country will certainly fight to the end single-mindedly to liberate Taiwan from the grasp of the American aggressor'.[16] In repeated statements Chinese leaders made repeated assurances notwithstanding the presence of the Seventh Fleet they were determined to invade Taiwan. To lend credibility to these words, the PLA began to build up a troop presence in Fujian and Chekiang provinces across the strait from Taiwan, assembling over 100,000 soldiers and an invasion fleet in ostensible preparations for an attack.[17] Taiwan, observing the concentrations of PRC forces along the mainland coast, responded with general mobilisation.[18] In July, PLA troops began the shelling of the Nationalist-held islands of Quemoy and Amoy, regarded as key defence outposts of Taiwan, but were repulsed by the better equipped Nationalists.[19] The USA decided to stay out of the fight, reasoning that their President's guarantee of protection made on 27 June extended only to the islands of Taiwan and the Pescadores and, further, that no request from Taipei for military assistance had been received.[20] By September, the start of the northeast monsoon storms over the East China Sea had rendered an invasion that year extremely difficult.[21]

Unknown to foreign governments, however, the Chinese communist leadership had, in response to the appearance of the Seventh Fleet, already decided at the end of June to put the Taiwan campaign on hold.[22] Instead it shifted focus onto Korea. This became self-evident on 19 October when the troops that had been assembled along the Taiwan

the Principles of the United Nations Charter as a Factor in American Policy-Making', 55 Am. JIL 45–76 (1961), at 66–70. The sending of the fleet was designed, *inter alia*, as a bargaining chip to exchange withdrawal of the fleet against recognition of a unified, non-communist Korea.

16 Quoted from Hoyt, 'Reaction to the Korean Attack', at 69. See also NYT, 'Red China Assails U.S. "Aggression"' (30 Jun. 1950).

17 NYT, 'Red Air Strength Built Up in China' (21 Jul. 1950).

18 NYT, 'Formosa is Ready in Case of Invasion' (16 Jul. 1950).

19 NYT, 'Red China's Guns Open Barrage on Quemoy, Nationalists Say' (23 Jul. 1950); NYT, 'Formosa Still Worries U.S. Despite Subsiding of Debate' (28 Jul. 1950); NYT, 'Mao Seems Determined on Formosan Invasion' (30 Jul. 1950).

20 NYT, 'U.S. Navy not to Aid Quemoy Fight a Chinese Red Invasion' (25 Jul. 1950).

21 NYT, 'Winds Over Formosa' (23 Sep. 1950).

22 Jian, *China's Road to the Korean War*, at p. 130.

Strait crossed the Yalu river on the border of China and North Korea and so initiated the second phase of the Korean War. The Seventh Fleet, however, remained in the Taiwan Strait for as long as that war endured.

International reaction was at first muted. Apart from some reservations expressed by Great Britain and India, and some initial approval for Truman's speech through diplomatic channels by France, the Netherlands, Belgium and Taiwan itself, there was no third-party discussion until 14 August, when the PRC formally filed a complaint to the UN Security Council.[23] The PRC maintained that the arrival of the Seventh Fleet and US Air Force contingents in Taiwan had constituted direct armed aggression against the territory of China;[24] the USA rebutted the argument, stating that it had no secret designs for Taiwan and that its actions were motivated impartially, to preserve peace and security in the area.[25] The Chinese complaint, sponsored by the USSR in the form of two resolutions condemning the USA and calling for the withdrawal of its forces,[26] eventually progressed as far as a vote in the Council, even though this took place no earlier than 27 November.[27] By then, Chinese communist troops had entered the Korean War. The two draft resolutions were promptly defeated by nine votes to one (USSR), with India abstaining.[28]

The USSR had also proposed that the question of the Seventh Fleet should be included on the agenda of the fifth session of the General Assembly.[29] During the debate, the USSR repeated that: 'United States armed intervention in the internal affairs of China had been accompanied by the threat of the use of armed force against the only legitimate Chinese Government, in gross violation of the sovereignty and political independence of China.'[30] Its draft resolution condemned US action,[31] but was outmanoeuvred on 7 December. On that day, France

23 Hoyt, 'Reaction to the Korean Attack', at 69; *The Ambassador in France (Bruce) to the Secretary of State* (27 Jun. 1950), 1950 FRUS vol. VII, 203; *The Ambassador in The Netherlands (Chapin) to the Secretary of State* (27 Jun. 1950), 1950 FRUS vol. VII, 206–7; *The Ambassador in Belgium (Murphy) to the Secretary of State* (27 Jun. 1950), 1950 FRUS vol. VII, 207–8.

24 1950 UNYB 287; SCOR Supp. S/1715 (14 Aug. 1950); Hoyt, 'Reaction to the Korean Attack', at 69.

25 1950 UNYB 287; SCOR Supp. S/1716 (25 Aug. 1950).

26 The PRC representative introduced the Chinese proposal in the Security Council, while an almost identical Soviet proposal had been introduced earlier. See 1950 UNYB 289, 293; SCOR Supp. S/1757 (2 Sep. 1950); SCOR Supp. S/1921 (28 Nov. 1950).

27 1950 UNYB 291–2.

28 1950 UNYB 292–4. SCOR S/PV.526 (28 Nov. 1950).

29 1950 UNYB 294; GAOR Supp. A/1375 (20 Sep. 1950).

30 1950 UNYB 296.

31 1950 UNYB 295; GAOR Supp. A/C.1/637 (27 Nov. 1950).

proposed that the First Committee should accord priority to a discussion of the Chinese intervention in Korea and that it should start consideration of it immediately.[32] The French proposal was adopted by the Committee by forty-two votes to five, with four abstentions. Hence no further action was taken and the Russian complaint was silently buried by the majority of the Assembly.[33]

The outcome of the votes in both the General Assembly and the Security Council strongly suggests that the interposition of the US navy, although having been ordered without UN approval, was approved of under the circumstances prevailing – namely, that the legal status of Taiwan was not beyond doubt, and further, that the US-imposed ceasefire was one that denied access, but was not intended to conquer territory. Although many governments had feared that the stance of the administration might draw China into the Korean War, they were not prepared to condemn it as a violation of the UN Charter, at least not in the definite terms of an 'invasion' of Taiwan that Beijing claimed but evidently did not yet control.[34]

The diplomatic responses of third-party states could be read in different ways. First, as a rejection of mainland China's primary argument that the USA had violated article 2(4). If so, from the perspective of the UN majority, the deployment of the Seventh Fleet, while problematic, did not violate the no-threat rule. Second, responses could be read as an intervention rendered lawful by prior Chinese approval. If Taipei was still accepted as the government that was representative of the whole of China, its consent to US presence was valid for both sides of the Taiwan Strait. Most states at least seemed to agree that the status of Taiwan was unclear to an extent that made the precautionary defence of it acceptable and non-aggressive. Third, it was conceivable that the US action was one of collective self-defence. If the Taiwan Strait was taken as a *de facto* international boundary between two separate Chinas, then it could be taken that as the PRC had threatened invasion from the very start in December 1949 a deterrent interposition of naval forces was lawful. These issues being left unresolved, the vote in the UN could equally well be taken to mean that while the threat of force was undeniable, it was justified in the broader context of Taiwanese effective territorial independence. Finally, one must not lose sight of the fact that international response, however unanimous, followed in the context of the ongoing

[32] 1950 UNYB 296; GAOR A/PV.408 (7 Dec. 1950). [33] 1950 UNYB 297.
[34] Hoyt, 'Reaction to the Korean Attack', at 72.

Korean War. By late October 1950, UN votes cast against mainland China were votes cast against its armed intervention on the Korean peninsula. In view of the disastrous consequences for UN forces caused by the entry of the PRC into the war, impartial judgment on the lawfulness of US action in the East China Sea could not be expected.

Pakistan–India (Kashmir, 1951)

The first clash between the newly independent states of Pakistan and India ended in a ceasefire brokered by the UN in January 1949. A so-called Line of Control was established that divided Jammu and Kashmir along entrenched battle fronts, India occupying two-thirds and Pakistan one-third of the disputed territory, while a UN observer group monitored the ceasefire.[35] In the summer of 1951, India protested against a number of Pakistani border ambushes and raids in violation of the ceasefire line, accusing Karachi, in a letter to the UN Security Council on 30 June, of 'fanatical warmongering propaganda' justifying the suspicion of 'a planned program calculated to lead, if unchecked, to an outbreak of hostilities between the two countries'.[36] In early July, the State Minister of India declared that unless Pakistan took immediate steps to prevent ceasefire violations in Kashmir, 'responsibility for graver consequences' would be set 'squarely on its shoulders'.[37] Pakistan rejected these claims on the grounds that there was nothing unprecedented or extraordinary about the alleged incidents in view of the lengthy history of border complaints between the two countries. Pakistan said that since January 1949, it had filed 492 border incidents, and India 392.[38] On 7 July, however, Pakistan ordered a brigade to take up position within fifteen miles of the Kashmir district of Poonch.[39] This military move, along with growing evidence of political instability in Pakistan and reported calls for *jihad* among the wider public, led Prime Minister Nehru to respond on 10 July with an order to move Indian troops to the Punjab border and to Jammu and Kashmir. Leave for Indian army officers was cancelled.[40]

[35] ICB, 'Kashmir I', crisis 119; Josef Korbel, 'The Kashmir Dispute After Six Years', 7 Int. Org. 498–510 (1953).

[36] SCOR Supp. S/2225 (30 Jun. 1951). On details on the raids complained of see SCOR Supp. S/2233 (5 Jul. 1951) and NYT, 'Indians Complain To U.N. On Kashmir' (4 Jul. 1951).

[37] NYT, 'Pakistan is Accused of Kashmir Violation' (2 Jul. 1951).

[38] NYT, 'India Again Files Kashmir Charges' (7 Jul. 1951).

[39] ICB, 'Kashmir I', crisis 119. [40] *Ibid.*

Pakistan's principal response, made on 15 July, was to inform the press that 90 per cent of India's troops (an estimated 400,000 men) were now concentrated within easy striking distance of the border, and that Pakistan would not allow itself to be intimidated or influenced by any threat of force. It was now, Prime Minister Liaquat stated, 'for the world to judge India's aggressive designs'.[41] In a telegram sent on the same day, he requested Nehru 'to remove the threat to the security of Pakistan created by the forward move of your armed forces'.[42] Pakistan informed the Security Council that:

> ... heavy concentrations of Indian armed forces are taking place in East Punjab and in Jammu and Kashmir. As a result of these troop movements, the bulk of the Indian army is now concentrated against Pakistan borders. In particular, all its armoured formations have been moved forward within easy striking distance of West Pakistan. This constitutes a grave threat to the security of Pakistan and to international peace.[43]

To this, Nehru asserted in rebuttal that Indian troops had taken defensive positions, simultaneously accusing Pakistan of waging a 'propaganda campaign filled with threats of war'. However, Nehru also issued the assurance that he had no intention of launching an attack.[44] Having little faith in these words, Karachi sent out four battalions of the Pakistan National Guard on 27 July to reinforce its army on the border.[45]

While the rhetoric on both sides was accusatory in form, the UN was actively involved not as judge but as mediator. During the precarious state of affairs of summer 1951, it entertained the hope that the still-young Kashmir conflict could be settled speedily if a Kashmiri plebiscite were to be manufactured. To that end, UN representative Frank Graham mediated between India and Pakistan, urging both to demilitarise in the border area, as a necessary step to defuse the crisis. His report to the Security Council was completely non-partisan.[46] The Security Council, too, practised impartiality. It passed a resolution in November acknowledging Graham's work and refused to accept the allegations that Pakistan and India had previously raised in the Council.[47] Eventually,

[41] NYT, 'Pakistan Protests Indians on Border' (16 July 1951).
[42] SCOR Supp. S/2245 (15 Jul. 1951). [43] *Ibid.*
[44] NYT, 'Nehru Says Troops Mass for Defense' (17 Jul. 1951).
[45] NYT, 'Pakistan Invites India Peace Talks' (27 Jul. 1951).
[46] SCOR Supp. S/2375 (15 Oct. 1951). [47] S/RES/96 (10 Nov. 1951); 1951 UNYB 345.

after a further series of accusatory exchanges, tensions gradually abated when the two governments found they could agree on a partial withdrawal of their forces.[48]

Whilst a variety of factors may be said to have resulted in the relative silence of the international system to the Indo-Pakistani troop manoeuvres and war rhetoric, it seems that the impartial lead of the Security Council in mediation was of paramount importance. For it to have taken sides would have effectively destroyed the perception of its role as an honest broker. Neither of the parties formally requested a Council decision, and in recognition of the Council's preferred approach to the conflict, no other state - and none of the superpowers in particular - intervened on their behalf. Moreover, while it was plain for all to see that India and Pakistan threatened each other, the facts regarding the origins of initial provocation remained shrouded in obscurity. In light of these factors, it appears in 1951 the attitude of states to mutual threats of force is best described as incorporating two rationales: first, detachment from the strict application of article 2(4) and its distinction between aggressor and victim; second, condemnation of one side and favour of the other could jeopardise the successful management of a crisis.

Iraq–Iran (Shatt-al-Arab, 1969–1975)

The Shatt-al-Arab ('Shore of the Arabs') is the waterway formed by the merging of the Tigris, Euphrates and Karun rivers, flowing 204 kilometres southwards to the Persian Gulf. The final 102-kilometre stretch of the Shatt forms the present-day boundary between Iran and Iraq. Dispute over the boundary has been a constant source of conflict for several centuries. For Iraq, the Shatt represented its only functional access to the sea: its own coast had no port. For Iran, the Shatt provided access to the oil ports of Abadan, Khorramshahr and Khosrowabad, and was a crucial outlet for its navy.[49] The latest of a series of diplomatic accords had in 1937 provided that the water's edge on the Iranian side was to serve as the boundary between the two countries, not, as Tehran desired, the median line of the waterway, in adoption of the more

48 ICB, 'Kashmir I', crisis 119.

49 ICB, 'Shatt-al-Arab II', crisis 234; 1969 UNYB 245–6; Elihu Lauterpacht, 'River Boundaries: Legal Aspects of the Shatt-al-Arab Frontier', 9 Int. & Comp. LQ 208–36 (1960), at 226; S. H. Amin, 'The Iran-Iraq Conflict: Legal Implications', 31 Int. & Comp. LQ 167–88 (1982), at 173.

customary *Thalweg* principle. At the same time, the agreement provided free navigation rights for trade purposes and, to a limited extent, shared control and maintenance of the waterway.[50] The treaty notwithstanding, the boundary dispute remained unresolved and in 1959 its escalation pushed both countries to the brink of war.[51] In 1980, this dispute proved pivotal to the outbreak of the Iran-Iraq war.[52] A further hostile encounter occurred between 1969 and 1975 against the background of Britain's anticipated withdrawal from the region, scheduled for 1971.

Ruptures in relations between Iraq and Iran appeared when Iraq's Baathist party came to power in July 1968 and decided to take a tougher stance in defence of its territorial prerogatives.[53] On 15 April 1969, the Deputy Foreign Minister of Iraq informed the Iranian ambassador to Baghdad that Iraq considered the Shatt al-Arab as part of its territory; Iranian vessels should cease flying the Iranian flag upon entry into the estuary, and Iran should withdraw any naval personnel on board such ships. Iraq warned that if its demands were not met, it would 'not permit in future any ship which sails to the ports of Iran to enter the Shatt-al-Arab'.[54] Iran took from the meeting that Iraq, breaking with previous policy, was now willing to use force to assert exclusive authority over the Shatt-al-Arab.[55]

On 19 April, Iran publicly responded that since Iraq had not honoured its obligations under the 1937 treaty, Iran considered it 'as abrogated, valueless and null and void in accordance with the principles of international law'.[56] Iran justified its withdrawal on the grounds that the agreed joint administration of the Shatt had never been forthcoming, that the *clausula rebus sic stantibus* applied, and that its signature to the 1937 treaty had been made under duress by the British colonial rule of the time. So Iran would no longer accept terms falling short of the median-line principle.[57] Iran's Deputy Foreign Minister warned

[50] *Boundary Treaty and Protocol Concerning the Shatt-al-Arab Waterway*, 190 UNTS 4423 (4 Jul. 1937); J. M. Abdulghani, *Iraq & Iran: The Years of Crisis* 116–18 (1984).
[51] ICB, 'Shatt-al-Arab I', crisis 172. [52] ICB, 'Onset Iran-Iraq War', crisis 317.
[53] NYT, 'Iraq Presses Dispute Over Iran' (19 May 1969).
[54] Quoted from Abdulghani, *The Years of Crisis*, at p. 118.
[55] Amin, 'The Iran-Iraq Conflict', at 173.
[56] Quoted from Abdulghani, *The Years of Crisis*, at p. 119.
[57] 1969 UNYB 245; Abdulghani, *The Years of Crisis*, at pp. 118–19; Amin, 'The Iran-Iraq Conflict', at 173–4; Hussein Sirriyeh, 'Development of the Iraq-Iranian Dispute, 1847–1975', 20 J. Cont. Hist. 483–92 (1985), at 485–6.

that any violation of Iran's sovereign rights would be met with full retaliation.[58] Two days later, on 20 April, Iraq rejected Iran's assertion and claimed the right to take legal and legitimate counter-action.[59]

On 22 April, in an overt demonstration of resolve, the 1,176-ton Iranian merchant ship *Ebn-i-Sina* proceeded through the Shatt into the Persian Gulf, escorted by Iranian jet fighters and heavily armed naval vessels – the first Iranian vessel flying Iran's flag to pass through the Shatt since the onset of the crisis.[60] Meanwhile, both countries strengthened their fortifications along the river bank, putting artillery, heavy tanks and anti-aircraft units onto full alert. Iran had concentrated its troops around Khorramshahr and Abadan; Iraqi forces had been placed on alert at the port of Basra.[61] Iraq, however, did not attempt to block the passage of the *Ebn-i-Sina*. Then three days later, the freighter *Arya Far*, escorted by four gunboats, also passed the Shatt-al-Arab with Iranian flags flying, yet met no resistance.[62] Tensions remained high in the subsequent weeks as Iranian freighters sustained their use of the Shatt and both parties continued to fortify their military positions against the possibility of a conflict erupting, but no shots were fired.[63] Partly because of its troop commitments in Syria, Jordan and the north to fight the Kurds, Iraq compensated for its lack of military response by maltreating and evicting thousands of Iranians resident in Iraq, and by banning the import of Iranian goods.[64] At the same time, Iran continued with its covert supply of arms to the Kurds fighting Iraqi forces in the north. Relations between Iraq and Iran continued to deteriorate.

Worries over a possible Iran-Iraq war produced agitation in neighbouring countries. Jordan, Kuwait, Saudi Arabia and Turkey all made attempts to mediate. From the ministerial meeting in late May of the Central Treaty Organization (CENTO) in Tehran there emerged a *communiqué* signed by Iran, Pakistan, Turkey, the UK and the USA

[58] ICB, 'Shatt-al-Arab II', crisis 234.
[59] ICB, 'Shatt-al-Arab II', crisis 234; Abdulghani, *The Years of Crisis*, at 119.
[60] Rouhollah K. Ramazani, *The Persian Gulf: Iran's Role* 44 (1972).
[61] ICB, 'Shatt-al-Arab II', crisis 234; Amin, 'The Iran-Iraq Conflict', at 175; NYT, 'Iranian Ship Sails On Disputed River' (23 Apr. 1969).
[62] NYT, 'Iran Plans 2D Test in Dispute with Iraq' (25 Apr. 1969); NYT, 'Iranian Ship Challenges Iraq' (26 Apr. 1969); NYT, 'Iran Rejects Iraqi Protest' (26 Apr. 1969).
[63] NYT, 'Iran Warns U.N. Tension is Rising on Iraq Border' (10 May 1969); NYT, 'Iranian Anger in Border Issue Grows' (19 May 1969); NYT, 'Iran Presses Dispute with Iran' (19 May 1969); Abdulghani, *The Years of Crisis*, at pp. 121–2.
[64] Abdulghani, *The Years of Crisis*, at p. 121; Ramazani, *The Persian Gulf*, at p. 44.

which disclosed that the dispute had been discussed.[65] However, no state chose to support claims advanced by either side regarding the lawfulness of their territorial titles or, for that matter, those of the ominous concentrations of troops along the Shatt-al-Arab.

Both Iraq and Iran brought their case to the attention of the UN Security Council. In a letter dated 29 April, Iraq accused Iran of illegally abrogating the 1937 Boundary Treaty and stated that Iran had stationed a massive disposition of troops, and naval and air force units along the Iraqi border. Iraq also made the accusation that some of these troops had violated Iraqi sovereignty and – making clear reference to the passage of the escorted freighters – had 'engaged in acts that constituted a serious intervention in Iraq's right to exclusive administration of the Shatt-al-Arab'.[66] The representative of Iran refuted this by explaining, *inter alia*, that it was Iraq that had first used threats to enforce its demands regarding navigation of the Shatt-al-Arab should Iran fail to comply with them. Iran's reactions, he said, were a 'minimum exercise of its sovereignty', and Iran's stationing of troops was no more than 'a response to threatening military movements by Iraq'.[67] Meanwhile, Iran was, he stated, prepared to conclude a new treaty with Iraq under which 'the sovereign rights of both nations would be safeguarded'.[68] While statements on the 1937 treaty and claims over sovereignty prevailed, Iraq complained on 11 July that Iran was continuing its demonstration of force in the Shatt-al-Arab.[69] In the same letter, Iraq offered to refer all disputes concerning the application of the Boundary Treaty to the ICJ and to abide by its decision.[70] But Iran declined the offer, on the grounds that it could not accept the validity of the Treaty as a starting point for settlement of the dispute.[71]

Despite continual accusations by the foreign ministers of both states, and with concentrations of troops continually being reported to the Secretary-General in the succeeding years, neither side formally

[65] ICB, 'Shatt-al-Arab II', crisis 234. CENTO was formerly known as the *Middle East Treaty Organization* or *Baghdad Pact* until in 1959 Iraq walked out of the organisation. Members were Turkey, Iran, Pakistan and the UK. The USA joined the conference as a member only of the military and economic committees of the pact. See NYT, 'CENTO Ministers Focus on Mideast' (27 May 1969).

[66] 1969 UNYB 245; SCOR Supp. S/9185 (29 Apr. 1969).

[67] 1969 UNYB 245; SCOR Supp. S/9190 (1 May 1969).

[68] 1969 UNYB 245; SCOR Supp. S/9200 (9 May 1969).

[69] 1969 UNYB 246; SCOR Supp. S/9323 (11 Jul. 1969).

[70] *Ibid.*

[71] 1969 UNYB 246; SCOR Supp. S/9425 (2 Sep. 1969).

requested action by the Security Council.[72] Only five years later, in 1974, when recurring skirmishes and clashes along the frontier escalated, did Iraq request an urgent meeting, and file a complaint about the Iranian military build-up and its violations of Iraqi territorial sovereignty. Iraq stated that:

> The situation on the frontier is deteriorating rapidly as the Iranian aggression continues and heavy massing of Iranian troops on the borders is still in progress … Iranian forces at different levels are concentrated on the border area and continue their military actions, openly violating Iraqi territory in a planned manner while Iranian air force fighters violate Iraqi air space threatening Iraq's national security and sovereignty.[73]

Iran in turn accused Iraq of cross-border attacks and demanded compensation for losses incurred.[74] Yemen, the United Arab Emirates and Libya joined the Council debate. They contended that 'Iran's aggression against Iraqi border posts could be regarded as an escalation of tension and an invitation to large-scale hostilities'.[75] On 28 February, the Council reached the consensus that a special UN representative should be appointed to investigate the conflict, and by way of a presidential statement it called on the parties 'to refrain from all military action and from any move which might aggravate the situation'.[76]

UN special envoy Luis Weckmann-Muñoz not only revealed that Iraq and Iran were relying on incompatible sets of maps without knowledge of the discrepancies, but he also persuaded both sides to agree on a ceasefire, the withdrawal of their forces from the border and the total avoidance of any hostile action against each other.[77] The Security Council, in resolution 348, fully endorsed these steps by a vote of fourteen to zero (China abstaining).[78] Following further UN mediation efforts, the two governments met in Istanbul in August 1974 to resolve

[72] ICB, 'Shatt-al-Arab II', crisis 234; 1974 UNYB 253.

[73] SCOR Supp. S/11216 (12 Feb. 1974). [74] SCOR Supp. S/11218 (12 Feb. 1974).

[75] 1974 UNYB 253; See SCOR S/PV.1763 (20 Feb. 1974) for statements of Yemen, the UAE and Libya.

[76] SCOR Supp. S/11229 (28 Feb. 1974), at para. 2; SCOR S/PV.1764 (28 Feb. 1974). The Security Council was composed as follows: Australia, Austria, Byelorussian SSR, Cameroon, China, Costa Rica, France, Indonesia, Iraq, Kenya, Mauritania, Peru, the USSR, the UK and the USA.

[77] *Report of the Secretary-General on the implementation of the consensus adopted by the Security Council on 28 February 1978*, reprinted in Supp. S/11291 (20 May 1974); Abdulghani, *The Years of Crisis*, at p. 125.

[78] S/RES/348 (28 May 1974). S/PV.1770 (28 May 1974).

their differences at the highest level. But the agreement they reached, while creating a basis for mutual understanding, fell short of a comprehensive settlement. Hostilities resumed after the talks ended, both sides blaming the other for breaking the ceasefire.[79] However, tensions finally eased in June 1975 with the signing of the Algiers Agreement, whereby Iraq conceded to Iran the application of the *Thalweg* principle to the Shatt-al-Arab. In return, Iran pledged to cease its support of Kurdish resistance in the north of Iraq.[80]

Overall, the UN took the role of impartial mediator and acted only within the limits mandated by the contending parties. However, when pushed to make a decision, the Security Council's response was one of virtually unanimous denial of legitimacy. It flatly refused its seal of approval to the actions of either side, suggesting that it judged both Iranian and Iraqi troop build-ups in a critical light and did not approve of them as measures of lawful self-defence.

Greece–Turkey (continental shelf, 1976)

Greece and Turkey made competing claims over territorial waters, air traffic control and the continental shelf in the Aegean Sea.[81] Turkey, having boosted its confidence two years earlier by its seizure of northern Cyprus in July 1974, openly resented that the islands immediately facing Turkey's continental coast belonged to Greece. Turkey had issued numerous statements about potential territorial aggrandisement that had caused Greece to fear military action.[82] In the year of the invasion, Turkey had already dispatched the survey ship *Candarli* into disputed waters of the Aegean Sea to conduct magnetometric

79 1974 UNYB 255; Abdulghani, *The Years of Crisis*, at p. 125.

80 Abdulghani, *The Years of Crisis*, at pp. 126, 152–77, 244–9. For a brief discussion of the treaty considering duress see Stuart S. Malawer, 'Imposed Treaties and International Law', Cal. WILJ 1–178 (1977), at 102–4.

81 ICB, *Aegean Sea I*, crisis 272; Peter Calvocoressi, *World Politics 1945–2000* 285–6 (8th edn, 2001).

82 Andrew Wilson, 'The Aegean Dispute', 155 *Adelphi Papers* (1979), at 7 fn. 16: 'On 13 January Turkish Prime Minister Irmak told the Innya Municipal Council: "Half the Aegean is ours. Let the whole world know that this is so ... We know how to crush the heads of our enemies when the prestige, dignity and interests of the Turkish nation are attacked."' And on 19 January the Foreign Minister, Mr Essenbel, was quoted in *Cumhuriyet* as saying: 'The policy followed by the growing Turkey to safeguard her interest in the Aegean has to be different from the policy of the Turkey of 50 years ago ... The reason for this is not only a reaction to Greece's Great Idea policy. Turkey is not the Turkey of 1923 after the Lausanne treaty. It is a growing Turkey.'

studies in preparation for oil-drilling. A force of thirty-two warships had escorted the *Candarli* in the face of strong protest from Athens.[83] In turn, Greece had reinforced its naval fortifications near the Turkish coast, thereby compromising its obligations under the Treaties of Lausanne and Paris.[84] As the following crisis unfolded in 1976, both governments experienced pressure from their right-wing opposition, and the popular voice became passionately excited.[85]

On 15 July 1976, the Prime Minister of Turkey, Süleyman Demirel, announced that another research vessel, the MTA *Sizmik I*, would, before the end of the month, prospect for oil near the Greek island of Thasos, the sensitive area of the Greek discoveries three years earlier.[86] After the ship had set sail from its Turkish port, Greece publicly informed NATO (of which Turkey was also a member) that it would use force if necessary to prevent the ship entering Greek waters. Turkey retorted that it would deem any interference with the *Sizmik* as an act of piracy.[87] On 29 July, Greece dispatched several warships to patrol the area, persuading the *Sizmik* to avoid the area under dispute and return to Turkey on 4 August.

However, Turkey promptly announced that the ship was scheduled for another voyage.[88] The *Sizmik* left Canakkale for the disputed area on 6 August, flanked by a Turkish minesweeper and military aircraft, and prospected for three days on the continental shelf near Lesbos.[89] Greece immediately filed a complaint and dispatched its navy to monitor the movements of the *Sizmik* closely. Both countries put their troops into a state of advanced readiness and patrolled the Aegean by air and sea.[90]

On 10 August, Greece sought an urgent meeting of the UN Security Council and simultaneously initiated proceedings before the ICJ. It cited a threat to peace and security caused by what it saw as repeated Turkish violations of Greek sovereign rights over the Aegean continental shelf.[91] In the Council, the Greek Foreign Minister, Dimitrios Bitsios, accused Turkey of 'provocative acts', warning that 'a mere accident might suffice to lose control of the situation'.[92] In reply, the Turkish Minister made the charge that the Greek request for a Council meeting

83 Wilson, 'The Aegean Dispute', at 6. 84 *Ibid.*, at 7. 85 *Ibid.*
86 *Ibid.*, at 7–8. 87 NYT, 'Oil on the Waters' (28 Jul. 1976).
88 NYT, 'Turkish Research Vessel Interrupts Aegean Cruise' (5 Aug. 1976).
89 Wilson, 'The Aegean Dispute', at 8.
90 NYT, 'Turks Alert Army after New Protest by Greece on Ship' (10 Aug. 1976).
91 1976 UNYB 320.
92 NYT, 'Greece, In U.N., Cautions Turkey on Aegean Moves' (13 Aug. 1976).

was a 'propaganda exercise', and that its claim on the continental shelf was designed to turn the Aegean Sea, which is dotted with Greek islands, into a 'Greek lake'.[93] The Greek Minister refuted his point with the argument that it was Turkey which entertained ambitions to annex Greek islands in the Aegean. As proof, he submitted statements by Turkish leaders to the Council.[94]

While the *Sizmik* returned unmolested to Turkey on 15 August, it was scheduled to carry out a third round of seismic studies in September, and duly carried these out undisturbed.[95] The return of the *Sizmik* to port and the reopening of negotiations then brought the crisis to an end.[96]

The response of the UN and third-party states to the 1976 Aegean confrontation were unanimously geared towards impartial advancement of conciliation. The USA was allied to both countries and urged them to show restraint and to refrain from any resort to force.[97] The USSR supported that view, sending a diplomatic note to both governments;[98] inflammatory acts should cease and the parties should be brought to the negotiation table. The Security Council adopted resolution 395 by consensus, calling upon the parties to 'exercise the utmost restraint in the present situation' and 'to do everything in their power to reduce the present tensions in the area so that the negotiating process may be facilitated'.[99] This was the universal theme that ran through Council discussion.[100]

The ICJ, on the other hand, rejected the indication of provisional measures, and also jurisdiction at a later stage, on formal grounds.[101]

93 NYT, 'Greek and Turkish Ministers Clash in U.N. over Aegean Issue' (14 Aug. 1976).
94 *Ibid.* 95 NYT, 'Aegean Survey Ship Returns to Turkey' (16 Aug. 1976).
96 Wilson, 'The Aegean Dispute', at 33.
97 NYT, 'Turks Alert Army after New Protest by Greece on Ship' (10 Aug. 1976); NYT, 'Kissinger in Plea for Peaceful Greek-Turkish Solution' (11 Aug. 1976).
98 NYT, 'Soviet Urges Restraint' (15 Aug. 1976); NYT, 'Turkey's Vessel to Stay in Aegean' (17 Aug. 1976).
99 S/RES/395 (25 Aug. 1976), at paras. 1–2; 1976 UNYB 321–2; NYT, 'U.N. Calls for Greek-Turkish Talks' (26 Aug. 1976).
100 SCOR S/PV.1953 (25 Aug. 1976). The Security Council was composed as follows: Benin, China, France, Guyana, Italy, Japan, Libya, Pakistan, Panama, Romania, Sweden, Tanzania, the UK, the USSR and the USA.
101 *Aegean Sea Continental Shelf Case (Greece* v. *Turkey), Request for the Indication of Interim Measures of Protection*, 1976 ICJ Rep. 6 (11 Sep. 1976); *Aegean Sea Continental Shelf Case, Jurisdiction of the Court*, 1978 ICJ Rep. 3 (19 Dec. 1978); Leo Gross, 'The Dispute Between Greece and Turkey Concerning the Continental Shelf in the Aegean', 71 Am. JIL 31–59 (1977); Richard T. Robel, 'The Aegean Sea Continental Shelf Case', 18 Harv. JIL 649–75 (1977).

Greece had asked the Court to declare as an interim measure, *inter alia*, that Turkey should 'abstain from all measures likely to react prejudicially upon the execution of any judicial decisions given in these proceedings and abstain from any sort of action which may aggravate or extend the present dispute between Greece and Turkey'.[102] Turkey should be reminded of its obligations under articles 2(4) and 33 of the UN Charter.[103] But the Court found, by a vote of twelve to one, that according to article 41 of the ICJ Statute, the rights of Greece were not in enough danger to do irreparable prejudice to its case on the merits, which was concerned not with violations of the UN Charter but with the delimitation of the parties' rights over the continental shelf.[104]

To the international observer, the 1976 Aegean dispute presented itself as follows: Greece, still struggling with a two-year-old return to democratic rule and all too conscious of its failure to prevent Turkey's invasion of Cyprus, felt compelled to stand firm in defence of its claim to the continental shelf.[105] Meanwhile Turkey, militarily dominant, could not resist escalating the situation by sending an escorted vessel three times into disputed waters, the implied message clearly being the strengthening of its own title to the shelf and its natural resources.[106] Greece sought to compel the Turkish vessel to leave the Aegean; Turkey sought to deter Greece from any interference with the ship's presence. The international system responded with the dictum: exercise self-restraint and refrain from fuelling the flames any more. This, it may be understood, constituted a tacit rejection of either side having the right to threaten force in self-defence.

Syria–Jordan (Arab League summit, 1980)

Ties between Arab nations became strained in September 1980 with the onset of the Iran-Iraq war. Syria and Libya sided with Iran, while Jordan

102 *Request for Interim Measures*, at para. 15(ii).

103 *Request for Interim Measures*, at para. 34. The Court affirmed the applicability of the UN Charter to the dispute in paras. 35 and 41, but elaborated no further.

104 *Request for Interim Measures*, at para. 46. The submission of Greece is reproduced in *Jurisdiction of the Court*, at para. 12.

105 NYT, 'Cyprus, Oil And The Aegean' (6 Aug. 1976).

106 Wilson, 'The Aegean Dispute', at 8. At the time of the crisis, Turkey's army was 470,000 troops strong, while Greece had 145,000 troops at its disposal (*ibid.*, at 3). The discrepancy between fighting ships (124:72) and combat aircraft (303:259), however, was less severe.

openly supported Iraq. The Arab world, never noted for its unity, stood on either side of a divide.[107]

Syria and Jordan were particularly at odds with one another. Syria accused Jordan of harbouring members of the Moslem Brotherhood, a terrorist organisation fostering opposition against Syria's President, Hafez al-Assad. Syria demanded that Jordan's support for the Brotherhood cease. Syria also resented Jordan's moderate tone vis-à-vis Israel: according to Damascus, Amman should have no authority to negotiate with Israel, least of all as a substitute for the Palestine Liberation Organization (PLO). And finally, due to the differences between the two countries over the Iraq-Iran war, Syria desired it to be understood that it would not allow Jordan to provide military support for Baghdad; President Assad of Syria chose to deliver this message to King Hussein of Jordan through demonstration of force.[108]

A three-day summit meeting of the Arab League scheduled to take place in Jordan contained the potential of isolating the Syrians from a newly formed pro-Iraqi axis. Syria announced that it would boycott the summit and ordered armoured units to take positions along the Syria-Jordan border near Al Mafrak on 25 November 1980.[109] Alarmed, Jordan immediately put its forces on full alert, cancelled all leave and concentrated such of its army as was available to confront the Syrians at the border.[110] By the first week of December some 30,000 Syrians and 24,000 Jordanians, supported by 1,000 tanks, stood eyeball to eyeball in readiness for military onslaught.[111] King Hussein of Jordan announced in a thirty-minute speech that the rallying of Syria's forces was a 'clear threat', and that, while Jordan hoped that 'logic and reason and a sense of responsibility will prevail', it was prepared to fight with all its strength to 'defend every inch' of Jordanian soil.[112] In the meantime, Israel, Syria's ancient enemy, announced that it would not 'stand idly by' if Syria invaded Jordan.[113] By the end of the month, amid reports of

[107] ICB, 'Jordan-Syria Confrontation', crisis 319; NYT, 'Arab Nations: 2 Camps Now' (29 Nov. 1980).

[108] *Newsweek*, 'Syria and Jordan Square Off' (15 Dec. 1980); *Economist*, 'The War That Wasn't, Maybe' (6 Dec. 1980).

[109] NYT, 'Syria Announces Boycott of Arab Summit Meeting' (23 Nov. 1980); NYT, 'Syrians Said to Move Troops Close to Jordan as Arab Leaders Confer' (27 Nov. 1980).

[110] NYT, 'Syrians Said to Move Troops Close to Jordan as Arab Leaders Confer' (27 Nov. 1980).

[111] ICB, 'Jordan-Syria Confrontation', crisis 319.

[112] NYT, 'Jordanian Ruler Cautions Syrians Against Invasion' (28 Nov. 1980).

[113] NYT, 'Syrians Said to Move Troops Close to Jordan as Arab Leaders Confer' (27 Nov. 1980).

a continued troop build-up even though the summit had come to its end as scheduled, the Syrians warned that they were prepared to defend 'national and security interests by all available ways and means'.[114] It was, however, not clear to foreign governments precisely what those interests were.

In response to the efforts at mediation made by Saudi Arabia, Syria finally produced a list of twenty-one demands but simultaneously began to withdraw its troops from the border zone.[115] Jordan rejected the demands,[116] but tensions nonetheless eased to the point where both sides rolled back their military presence to pre-crisis positions.[117] In a final warning, however, that Syria meant business, Syrian jets carried out cross-border attacks against suspected terrorist strongholds on Jordanian soil.[118]

Syria's military build-up and Jordan's similar response, while discussed in the corridors of the UN in private, never reached formal deliberation in any of its principal bodies.[119] Of the Middle Eastern countries it was Iraq that offered Jordan military assistance.[120] President Carter of the USA, to which Jordan had appealed to speed up the delivery of arms that had been previously ordered, urged both sides to calm down, and also warned Syria not to attack.[121] Despite the somewhat muted international reaction, a reading of news sources suggests that Jordan had gained sympathy among its Arab neighbours; participants in the Arab League summit would not honour Syria's troop build-up with a response, and in indication of this proceeded with their conference as planned. It may be speculated that they sympathised with Jordan not only because they endorsed King Hussein's Middle East policy but also because they tacitly agreed that Jordan's defensive posture was right and legitimate; overall, Jordan had exercised moderation, indulging in almost no war rhetoric, but had simply mobilised such forces as were required for its military defence. No state objected to that posture, and accordingly the diplomatic note from the

114 NYT, 'Syria Warns Jordan Troops May Attack Sanctuaries of Foes' (30 Nov. 1980).

115 NYT, 'Syria Gives Jordan List of 21 Demands' (3 Dec. 1980).

116 NYT, 'Jordan Rejects Syria's Conditions for Removing Troops from the Border' (4 Dec. 1980).

117 NYT, 'Syria Said to Agree to Troop Pullback' (5 Dec. 1980); NYT, 'Jordan and Syria Say They're Pulling Back' (11 Dec. 1980).

118 NYT, 'Syria Said to Raid Foe's Jordan Bases' (14 Dec. 1980).

119 NYT, 'U.N. Session's Feat: No Namibia Action' (22 Dec. 1980).

120 NYT, 'Hussein Urges U.S. to Speed Delivery of Arms for Jordan' (2 Dec. 1980).

121 *Ibid.*

USA was in favour of Jordan. Perhaps as a result of this, Israel's single announcement that it might interfere, as much as the subtle hint at action by the USA, evoked no diplomatic remark.

PRC–Vietnam (Spratly Islands, 1988)

Territorial claims over the Spratly and Paracel Islands in the South China Sea, rich in minerals but uninhabited, have been longstanding, and made by no less than six powers surrounding that body of water: Vietnam, the PRC, Taiwan, Malaysia, Brunei and the Philippines. By 1987, the historic rivalry between Vietnam and China, focusing on Cambodia, had begun to result in a hardening of attitudes and bellicose posturing about the Spratlys.[122] By early 1988, near-clashes between the naval forces of the two states had become frequent occurrences. China publicly asserted the right to 'survey, study and patrol' the islands and their surrounding waters,[123] but in the eyes of China's maritime neighbours this was little other than a claim to sovereign title through effective control; it looked like becoming a repetition of the Chinese occupation of the Paracel Islands that had resulted from a Sino-Vietnamese clash in 1974.[124]

To enforce its claim, Beijing dispatched its navy, seized the two coral reefs Chu Thap and Chau Vien, and asserted its authority over Vietnamese shipping.[125] North Vietnam defended its opposing bid by demanding the withdrawal of all Chinese warships and by warning that China would have to 'answer for all consequences of its wrong-doings'.[126] China retorted on 26 February that Vietnam 'must take full responsibility for all the consequences' if it obstructed 'China's legitimate activities' in the Spratlys.[127]

On 14 March 1988, Chinese naval ships patrolling the vicinity of the Spratlys intercepted three Vietnamese freighters carrying supplies to small Vietnamese army outposts stationed in disputed waters. A half-hour

[122] ICB, 'Spratly Islands', crisis 384.

[123] Chen Jie, 'China's Spratly Policy: With Special Reference to the Philippines and Malaysia', 34 Asian Surv. 893–903 (1994), at 898. Chinese policy to evict intruders by force found a formal form in 1992, when the Chinese National People's Congress adopted a law on the country's territorial sea and contiguous zone.

[124] A. Mark Weisburd, *Use of Force: The Practice of States since World War II* 272–3 (1997).

[125] Michael Bennett, 'The People's Republic of China and the Use of International Law in the Spratly Islands Dispute', 28 Stan. JIL 425–50 (1992), at 427; Monique Chemillier-Gendreau, *Sovereignty Over the Paracel and Spratly Islands* 46 (2000).

[126] UPI, 'Vietnam Threatens China over Disputed Islands' (27 Feb. 1988).

[127] ICB, 'Spratly Islands', crisis 384.

exchange of gunshots ensued, each side accusing the other of firing the first shot. Two Vietnamese ships were destroyed, three of their sailors reportedly killed and seventy-four listed missing.[128] In the following weeks, both sides stepped up their military presence. Mutual accusations and undisguised threats ensued.[129] North Vietnam authorised an extensive military exercise in May, designed to simulate an anticipated battle against PRC naval forces in the Spratlys. China in turn held its own exercises in June, reportedly simulating a tactical nuclear attack. Yet during the course of the summer, the heat of the crisis moderated to a mere simmer with reduced risk of a further clash.[130]

For Western spectators, this Sino-Vietnamese confrontation over the Spratlys was taken as a conflict between two communist countries, so calling for no intervention. In 1974 South Vietnam had still been pro-Western, but in 1988 this was one communist regime quarrelling with another. By sending its navy to the Spratly islands, the PRC, in the military ascendant, laid claim to its share of the area's rich resources. Its establishment of a quasi-maritime exclusion zone meant that it was inclined to use force against intruders. Vietnam, whose presence and sovereign title the PRC directly challenged, resisted, but with no success. China's chief aim, it was further speculated, was to increase its pressure on Vietnam so that it would withdraw its army from Cambodia, which was supported by China.[131] The USA, for once, remained explicitly neutral between the disputants, and so did the UN. The Association of Southeast Asian Nations (ASEAN), too, stood aloof.[132]

Those who reacted, albeit not judicially, were competing claimants. Malaysia, Vietnam, the Philippines and Taiwan had already established a partial presence on the Spratlys, all relying on being able to exercise effective control to advance their claims. North Vietnam had entered the Spratly dispute just after the PRC had seized the Paracels from the faltering regime in South Vietnam.[133] In response to the events in early

128 Wash. Post, 'Vietnamese, Chinese Ships Exchange Fire' (15 Mar. 1988); *Guardian*, 'China Protests at Hanoi Attack' (15 Mar. 1988); NYT, 'Hanoi Seeks Talks With Beijing' (18 Mar. 1988); Marko Milivojevic, 'The Spratly and Paracel Island Conflict', 31 *Survival* 70–7 (1991), at 70.

129 *Guardian*, 'Island Clash Looms Again' (6 Apr. 1988).

130 ICB, 'Spratly Islands', crisis 384.

131 *Economist*, 'Five-handed Poker in the Spratlys' (21 May 1988).

132 Taiwan CNA, 'U.S. Takes No Position on Disputed Spratly Islands' (15 Mar. 1988).

133 Robert Catley and Makmur Keliat, *Spratlys: The Dispute in the South China Sea* 25–31 (1997). The claimants' common plan to fortify their claims has been to establish a physical presence.

1988, and following the dictates of *Realpolitik* thereto, the Philippines warned both Vietnam and China not to intrude into the area it claimed, while Malaysia and Taiwan either increased their patrols or reinforced their garrisons around the islets they claimed.[134] In contrast to South Vietnam in 1974, Vietnam did not take its verbal protest to the Security Council; the new communist government, politically isolated, held less confidence in the Council than had its predecessor.[135] There was no Security Council consideration of the March incidents, because neither Vietnam nor China requested this.

What little learning may be gleaned from the Sino-Vietnamese encounter in March 1988 is that for all practical purposes no state expressed any enthusiasm for either side, neither confirming nor rejecting the proposition that recourse to counter-threats was the appropriate means to reinforce claim and counterclaim. That was of no concern to rivals who were already fighting on other fronts: the PRC was actively supporting Cambodia against Vietnamese occupation at the time.[136] The flare-up of tensions in mid-March may thus be seen as merely symptomatic of the previously demonstrated willingness to employ force in a different location. In this light, to issue a diplomatic statement must have appeared of questionable value for third-party states with no stakes in the Spratlys.

PRC–Taiwan (Lee Teng-hui, 1995–1996)

On 22 May 1995, the Clinton administration acceded to pressure from Congress and approved a visa to permit the President of Taiwan, Lee Teng-hui, to attend his graduate school reunion at Cornell University the following June.[137] The decision reversed some twenty-five years of US policy not to permit contacts between US and Taiwanese high-level leaders, and it stood squarely in breach of assurances that had previously been made to mainland China. Officials in Beijing were concerned that Lee's 'vacation diplomacy' would, if successful in rallying support on US soil for a Taiwanese declaration of independence, push

[134] ICB, 'Spratly Islands', crisis 384.

[135] 1974 UNYB 188, 1085; Weisburd, *Use of Force*, at pp. 272–3; Suisheng Zhao (ed.), *Across the Taiwan Strait: Mainland China, Taiwan, and the 1995–1996 Crisis* (1999).

[136] Ronald C. Cima, 'Vietnam in 1988: The Brink of Renewal', 29 Asian Surv. 64–72 (1989), at 69.

[137] NYT, 'Aides to Clinton Say He will Defy Beijing and Issue Visa to Taiwan's President' (22 May 1995).

Taipei's campaign for statehood to an intolerably high level. The Chinese leadership considered the reversal of US policy ominous, especially in the light of, first, Taiwan's impending presidential elections in March 1996, in which Lee Teng-hui was hoping to become the first democratically elected leader of the island and, second, the scheduled 1997 handover of Hong Kong.[138] Earlier in 1995, China had to no avail tried to persuade Taiwan to accept reintegration into mainland China by offering a guarantee of autonomy similar to that being granted to Hong Kong. At the same time, Beijing had for years reserved the right to use force to suppress any unilateral Taiwanese declaration of independence.

China responded to Lee's three-day visit in early June by cutting short the scheduled Sino-US diplomatic exchanges, recalling its ambassador from Washington, and by announcing on 18 July that it would conduct a week-long series of missile tests and military exercises in the Taiwan Strait.[139] These were intended to bring home a firm message to both Taiwan and the USA: the USA was to make formal commitment to China's One-China policy and US encouragement of Taiwanese independence could drag it into a war that the PRC was willing to wage should Taipei declare formal independence.[140] During this first phase, the PRC launched between 21 to 28 July a handful of M-9 surface-to-surface missiles off the coast of Taiwan's Pengchaiyu Island. The M-9 missiles were suitable, because they were capable of carrying nuclear warheads and Taiwan possessed no defence against them.[141] Taiwan, however, responded a few days later with its own missile and naval exercises.[142] Lee announced that Taiwan would not be suppressed by outside forces.[143] To this the PRC answered between 15 and 25 August with a live artillery simulation of a naval blockade of Taiwan and a military response appropriate to a hypothetical US intervention.[144] The island, defiant, in turn carried out missile tests and simulated

138 ICB, 'Taiwan Straits IV', crisis 415; Robert S. Ross, 'The 1995–96 Taiwan Strait Confrontation: Coercion, Credibility, and the Use of Force', 25 Int. Sec. 87–123 (2000).

139 NYT, 'Angered Over Taiwan, China Recalls its Ambassador in U.S.' (17 Jun. 1995).

140 Ross, 'Taiwan Strait Confrontation', at 94; NYT, 'China Asks Clinton to Reaffirm Policy on Taiwan's Status' (13 Jul. 1995).

141 NYT, 'Taiwan Reports Nearby Firing of 4 Test Missiles by China' (24 Jul. 1995); NYT, 'Sound and Fury in East Asia' (23 Aug. 1995).

142 Ross, 'Taiwan Strait Confrontation', 96.

143 ICB, 'Taiwan Straits IV', crisis 415.

144 Ross, 'Taiwan Strait Confrontation', at 97; NYT, 'China War Games Viewed as Tactic to Press Taiwan' (19 Aug. 1995).

military opposition in October.[145] The USA also would not relinquish its support for Taiwan.

The PRC, concerned about Lee's encouragement of domestic public opinion for independence, and also about its own failure to extract a concession from the USA, chose to raise the stakes in October and again in November with more extensive military exercises.[146] This time the climax of the extensive 'high-tech war game' of destroyers, bombers, and nuclear submarines conducted by the People's Liberation Army (PLA) was personally attended by Jiang Zeming, and the exercise was clearly aimed to impress upon the Taiwanese public that China's territorial integrity would be preserved; voters should not reward Lee for his mainland policy in the parliamentary elections in December, nor, certainly, in the first presidential elections to be held on 23 March 1996.[147]

In late January and through February, the PLA amassed more than 100,000 troops in the province of Fujian.[148] This time the USA issued a warning of serious consequences if hostilities should break out, yet on 7 March the PRC pushed ahead with its plans and fired three M-9 missiles into waters near Taiwan.[149] The Clinton administration, its credibility in the Asian Pacific and Taiwan challenged, issued another warning that its national interests were at stake and that it was ready to demonstrate its military capability for that purpose.[150] The US Secretary of Defense, William Perry, ordered the deployment of the *Independence* battle group to waters east of Taiwan and the *Nimitz* carrier group to the Philippine Sea, near enough at hand for rapid relocation to the Taiwan Strait.[151] Ignoring this, the PRC conducted another M-9 missile test on 13 March and, between 18 and 25 March, carried out joint air, ground and naval exercises, approaching to within ten nautical miles of the Taiwanese islands.[152] Despite these indications of belligerence, a cooling-off phase

[145] Ross, 'Taiwan Strait Confrontation', at 101. [146] *Ibid.*, at 102. [147] *Ibid.*

[148] *Ibid.*, at 106.

[149] *Ibid.*, at 108. NYT, 'Beijing Steps up Military Pressure on Taiwan Leader' (7 Mar. 1996); NYT, 'Chinese, in a Move to Alarm Taiwan, Fire Test Missiles' (8 Mar. 1996); NYT, 'War Games off Taiwan to Expand, China Says' (10 Mar. 1996).

[150] Ross, 'Taiwan Strait Confrontation', at 109; NYT, '"Ambiguity" on Taiwan' (12 Mar. 1996); NYT, 'U.S. Sending More Ships to Taiwan Area in Warning to China' (11 Mar. 1996); NYT, 'China Warns U.S. to Stay Out of Taiwan Feud' (12 Mar. 1996).

[151] Ross, 'Taiwan Strait Confrontation', at 110; NYT, 'Gunboat Diplomacy, '96 Model' (17 Mar. 1996); NYT, 'China Warns U.S. to Keep Away from Taiwan Strait' (18 Mar. 1996); NYT, 'Off Taiwan, U.S. Soldiers Are Unworried' (19 Mar. 1996).

[152] Ross, 'Taiwan Strait Confrontation', at 111; NYT, 'China Says Maneuvers Will Last Through Taiwan's Elections' (16 Mar. 1996).

in cross-Strait relations commenced when Lee emerged victorious in the Taiwanese presidential elections and the PRC ceased its military manoeuvres. Although these had delivered the indisputable message that China would resist independence by force, the PRC's attempt to influence the Taiwanese elections in its favour had backfired.[153]

The communal response to this Taiwan-Strait crisis was relatively muted. During the days following the election, the EU parliament showed approval to Taiwan for the vote. Some members of the EU parliament indicated to the press their delight that the people of Taiwan had been 'undaunted by Beijing's saber-rattling' and were 'able to choose their future national leader based on their own free will and wisdom in a peaceful atmosphere'.[154] Five Central American countries – Costa Rica, El Salvador, Guatemala, Honduras and Nicaragua – went further, condemning the PRC's military exercises in the Taiwan Strait and reaffirming their support for Taiwan.[155] On the other hand, it appears that Russia gave Beijing support by declaring unequivocal adherence to the One-China principle,[156] while South Korea withheld criticism of the PRC's missile tests in a conscious effort not to sever its fragile ties with North Korea (for which it relied on mainland China).[157] Whether any of the views expressed are legal views is doubtful. The fact is that the states which condemned the PRC most forcefully were the Central American countries with whom Taiwan had previously traded substantial development aid for political support.[158] The opinions of European representatives in Brussels seem less related to the retaliatory cross-Strait military exercises than to the successful establishment of

[153] NYT, 'Taiwan's Leader Wins its Elections and a Mandate' (24 Mar. 1996); NYT, 'China is Offering High-Level Talks to Taiwan Leader' (25 Mar. 1996); NYT, 'Clinton Pleased by Easing Tension' (26 Mar. 1996); NYT, 'Tensions Seen as Receding as China Ends War Games' (26 Mar. 1996).

[154] FBIS (Taipei CNA), 'Daily Report: European Parliament Members Laud Election' (25 Mar. 1996).

[155] FBIS (Taipei CNA), 'Daily Report: Central American Leaders to Attend Inauguration' (23 Mar. 1996); FBIS (Taipei CNA), 'Daily Report: Central American Nations "Strongly Oppose" PRC Threats' (23 Mar. 1996). See also earlier FBIS (Taipei CNA), 'Costa Rican Communiqué Condemns PRC Missile Tests' (12 Mar. 1996).

[156] FBIS (Beijing Xinhua), 'Daily Report: Russia Says Taiwan "Inalienable" Part of China' (21 Mar. 1996).

[157] FBIS (Seoul Yonhap), 'Daily Report: Reaction to PRC-Taiwan Situation Analyzed' (13 Mar. 1996).

[158] NYT, 'Taiwan Issue Held U.N.'s Attention' (27 Sep. 1996); Dennis V. Hickey, 'U.S. Policy and Taiwan's Bid to Rejoin the United Nations', 37 Asian Surv. 1031–43 (1997), at 1034.

a democracy. With that established, the international response in general seems to have been aligned with political alliances that had been formed earlier, to the extent that, for all practical purposes, legal motives were absent, at least with regard to article 2(4) of the UN Charter. The only legally relevant inference may be that the majority of non-participant states, by overtly welcoming the Taiwanese elections in defiance of military pressure, on the balance viewed China as the wrongful *agent provocateur*.

The motives for this reaction can only be guessed. For one thing, the legal status of Taiwan remained highly controversial. The legality of any Chinese recourse to force hinged upon whether or not article 2(4) of the UN Charter applied to the *de facto* regime of Taiwan – a question to which none of the reactions provided an answer.[159] It may be noted that Taiwan had sought to mobilise the UN General Assembly to give it limited recognition in accordance with the September 1995 model of parallel representation of divided countries. A handful of states voted in favour, yet the remaining 165 members of the Assembly showed no inclination to vote – even in favour of discussing the creation of a study committee to address the matter.[160] Even during the run-up to Taiwan's first democratic elections, no major state other than the USA was willing, in the face of massive tit-for-tat demonstrations of force in the Taiwan Strait, to shield Taiwan from pressure imposed by the PRC.

Instead, the lesson impressed upon all states, and on the USA in particular, was that the problem of Taiwan should not be resolved but merely managed, and that if this renegade island received too much foreign support, it could, calling upon military commitments, plunge China and the USA into a war that nobody really wanted.[161]

[159] On the legal status of Taiwan and the applicability of the non-use of force principle see Jonathan I. Charney and J. R. V. Prescott, 'Resolving Cross-Strait Relations between China and Taiwan', 94 Am. JIL 453–77 (2000); Jianming Shen, 'Sovereignty, Statehood, Self-determination, and the Issue of Taiwan', 15 Am. UILR 1101 (2000); Anne Hsiu-An Hsiao, 'Is China's Policy to Use Force Against Taiwan a Violation of the Principle of Non-Use of Force in International Law?', 32 New Eng. LR 715 (1998); Glenn R. Butterton, 'Signals, Threats, and Deterrence: Alive and Well in the Taiwan Strait', 47 Cath. ULR 51 (1997).

[160] 1995 UNYB 1428; NYT, 'Taiwan Again Tries to Join U.N., and Again China Bars Door' (21 Sep. 1995). The supporting states were: Burkina Faso, the Central African Republic, Costa Rica, Dominica, the Dominican Republic, Grenada, Guinea-Bissau, Guatemala, Nicaragua, Niger, Panama, Saint Lucia, Saint Vincent and Grenadines and Swaziland.

[161] See for a look at US official policy in response to Taiwan's 1999 announcement that it would depart from the One-China principle and regard cross-Strait relations as henceforth 'state-to-state' Sean D. Murphy, 'Contemporary Practice of the United

Indeed, although the events of 1995–6 were not perceived by the USA as an immediate risk, the scale of China's military commitment raised concerns that the Taiwan issue had become such a test of Chinese pride that the danger of war had become acute, even in the face of US military supremacy.[162] Ever since the Chinese nationalists had seized Taiwan in 1949, the dispute over its status under international law had been treated by other countries as an exclusively Sino-US affair. It is therefore not surprising that the three parties embroiled in the 1995–6 crisis were left to play out their trial of strength among themselves, while the wider East Asian neighbourhood quietly hoped that no accidental shot would force the area into open hostility.

ROK–DPRK (submarine incident, 1996)

On 18 September 1996, a military submarine from the Democratic Peoples Republic of Korea (DPRK) ran aground near the South Korean coastal city of Kangnung, about sixty miles south of the demilitarised zone. South Korea (ROK) reported the incident to the Security Council on 23 September. It said that detailed pictures of Kangnung Airport, the Yongdong Power Plant and other facilities had been taken by the North Koreans, and it believed that part of the aim of the mission had been to assassinate VIPs attending a national athletic competition due to take place in Chunchon. It further condemned the intrusion as a flagrant violation of the 1953 armistice agreement and declared that it amounted to an act of war.[163] In the course of a large-scale search operation that lasted several weeks, South Korean soldiers hunted down and shot several of the submarine crew members who were trying to escape to the north.

The DPRK informed the Security Council that the lightly armed submarine had been on a routine training exercise when engine problems had forced it to go aground.[164] Faced daily with the news of

States Relating to International Law', 93 Am. JIL 879–912 (1999), at 896. The USA refused to take sides for Taiwan as the PRC threatened a forceful response if it officially declared independence or otherwise hindered unification.

162 See on the military stakes Ross, 'Taiwan Strait Confrontation', at 108. During the crisis, the PRC did in fact promise that it did not plan to invade Taiwan this time. See NYT, 'China Signals U.S. That it Will Not Invade Taiwan' (13 Mar. 1996). However, earlier it had indicated that it had completed plans for a 'limited attack' after the presidential election, see NYT, 'As China Threatens Taiwan, it Makes Sure U.S. Listens' (24 Jan. 1996).

163 1996 UNYB 265; SCOR Supp. S/1996/774 (23 Sep. 1996).

164 1996 UNYB 265; SCOR Supp. S/1996/768 (23 Sep. 1996).

yet another of its submarine crew tracked down by South Korean forces, the DPRK government demanded the immediate and unconditional return of the submarine, its still-living crew and the dead. On 27 September, it added that if its demands were not met, it would be forced to take 'strong countermeasures' and retaliate. To demonstrate its resolve, North Korea forwarded to the Security Council a report of an emergency meeting of its political parties and social organisations that it held on 26 September. A decision was adopted on countermeasures to be taken against what the DPRK called the provocative misuse of the submarine incident by the South to aggravate confrontation and drive the peninsula to the brink of war.[165] Further, as a consequence of the rising tensions for which it held Seoul responsible, the possibility of an attack on the South could not be excluded if it became necessary.[166]

South Korea rebutted this accusation, stating that the incident reflected a clear pattern of DPRK military provocation and was part of a wider scheme not only to dismantle the armistice agreement but also to destabilise South Korea.[167] It also brought to the attention of the Security Council a resolution of its National Assembly wherein it called on the international community (1) to take a serious view of the Korean situation, (2) to cooperate in restraining the DPRK from further acts of provocation, (3) to urge it to abandon its irrational goal of communising the Republic by force and immediately to cease acts of provocation and (4) to respond positively to the Republic's initiatives to build a genuine national community on the Korean peninsula.[168] A South Korean military spokesman indicated to the media that as a consequence of the incident, the government might reactivate joint military exercises with the USA.[169] On 1 October, the President of South Korea, Kim Young Sam, also made it clear that he would 'reconsider' all assistance that the South was giving to the North and warned that his armed forces were ready to respond to a military attack;[170] North Korea would have to apologise before peace talks or humanitarian aid could be continued.[171]

[165] 1996 UNYB 266; SCOR Supp. S/1996/800 (27 Sep. 1996).
[166] NYT, 'North Korea Threatens South Over Killing of Soldiers of Sub' (28 Sep. 1996).
[167] 1996 UNYB 266; SCOR Supp. S/1996/824 (3 Oct. 1996).
[168] 1996 UNYB 266; SCOR Supp. S/1996/847 (23 Sep1996).
[169] NYT, 'Another North Korean Infiltrator is Killed' (1 Oct. 1996); NYT, 'North Korea Delivers Warning in Sub Incident' (3 Oct. 1996).
[170] NYT, 'North Korea Delivers Warning in Sub Incident' (3 Oct. 1996).
[171] ICB, 'North Korean Submarine', crisis 420.

At this point, the USA under President Clinton intervened as mediator with the aim of bringing the parties back to the negotiation table. After three weeks of intense negotiations in New York between State Department negotiator Mark Minton and a senior official of North Korea's Foreign Ministry, Li Hyong Chol, the DPRK formally apologised on 29 December for the submarine incident, expressing 'deep regret' for the incursion and for 'the tragic loss of human life'.[172] On the following day, South Korea returned to North Korea the remains of the twenty-four crew members killed during the crisis.[173]

Deliberation, reaction and results were handled almost entirely behind closed doors. The Security Council had convened informally already on 20 September. But while listening to both parties, it chose not to act or take a public position until 15 October, when it authorised its President to make a public statement on its behalf.[174] Referring to the submarine incident, he said that the armistice agreement should be fully observed and that 'no action should be taken that might increase tension or undermine peace and stability on the Korean peninsula' and even-handedly encouraged both sides 'to settle their outstanding issues by peaceful means through dialogue, so that peace and security on the peninsula will be strengthened'.[175]

In short, the Security Council chose to let the USA handle the matter while the parties were about to come to an agreement by themselves, and thought it wiser to remain in the background. No other state made a public effort to stigmatise North Korean threats of war or decry South Korea's bellicose response. But while the international response was low key, those states that acted – South Korea and the USA – did so vigorously. As a result of the submarine incident, all diplomatic initiatives came to a halt. Humanitarian aid to North Korea was frozen. The agreed construction of the two light-water nuclear power plants by the US-ROK-Japanese consortium, KEDO, was suspended.[176] South Korea relentlessly hunted down the shipwrecked sailors, and suggested that

172 NYT, '"Deep Regret" Sent by North Koreans' (30 Dec1996); NYT, 'U.S. Reports Foes Willing to Discuss Peace' (31 Dec. 1996).

173 ICB, 'North Korean Submarine', crisis 420.

174 SCOR S/PV.3704 (15 Oct. 1996); S/PRST/1996/42 (15 Oct. 1996). In 1996 the Security Council was composed of the following states: Botswana, Chile, China, Egypt, France, Germany, Guinea-Bissau, Honduras, Indonesia, Italy, Poland, South Korea, Russia, the UK, and the USA.

175 S/PRST/1996/42 (15 Oct. 1996).

176 Chris. S. Mon., 'US Sighs Relief as North Korea Apologizes, Agrees to Talks' (2 Jan. 1997).

it would seek to reactivate the highly contentious *Team Spirit* military exercises with the USA (a move that the USA had not approved). These measures together were aimed at putting strong pressure onto North Korea to withdraw its demands.

The submarine crisis came at a time when several other diplomatic events were taking place in the Korean peninsula, raising tensions to an acute level. US-North Korean relations were facing tremendous problems as the 1994 Agreed Framework started to fall apart. US officials were scrambling to rescue the painstakingly negotiated deal to build two nuclear power reactors in North Korea in exchange for an end to the North's secretive nuclear weapons programme.[177] A severe famine was taking its toll on the civilian population of North Korea, making it desperate for action. Meanwhile, US and South Korean forces, already under stress from the constant threat of invasion through the massive troop and missile deployments along the demilitarised zone, became even edgier as a result of unconventional manoeuvres recently carried out by North Korean AN-2 aircraft, old biplanes reportedly capable of flying beneath radar defences. This all added a sense of urgency to the ever-tense standoff in the divided nation in which North Korea had notoriously threatened the South and the USA with all-out war.[178] Within the context of highly charged mutual accusations, the demands by North Korea to have the submarine and its crew returned under the threat of severe 'countermeasures' did not make matters significantly worse. And as with Taiwan, third-party states preferred to leave the thorny issue of Korean affairs to the major actors involved. What emerged from the Security Council was, however, a reprimand that urged both parties to refrain from trumped-up charges and hostile acts, and may be

[177] Ashton B. Carter and William J. Perry, *Preventive Defense: A New Security Strategy for America* 123–42 (1999).

[178] USN & World Rep., 'A Korean Style of Chicken' (21 Oct. 1996). For example, as recently as 26 April 1996, in a meeting with US Deputy Secretary of State Thomas Hubbard, the Vice Chairman of North Korea's external economy commission threatened that if the USA did not provide food aid and technological assistance to North Korea, the people of South Korea and Japan could fall victim to four nuclear missiles. Conversely, between 28 October and 10 November 1996, the USA and South Korea held the annual 'Foal Eagle' military exercise. North Korea condemned the exercise as a 'replica of the "Team Spirit" joint military manoeuvres', and an attempt to increase military tension on the Korean Peninsula. See further Matthew A. Meyers, 'Deterrence and the Threat of Force Ban: Does the UN Charter Prohibit Some Military Exercises?', 162 Mil. LR 132–79 (1999).

understood to have stated that it saw no reason to accord to either side the right to threaten the use of force.

Conclusions

In four of the cases examined – Pakistan-India in 1951, Iraq-Iran in 1969, Greece-Turkey in 1976 and North Korea-South Korea in 1996 – the Security Council called on all parties to exercise restraint and undertake no action that might increase tension or undermine peace and stability. In these cases, distinction between victim and aggressor was not relevant, and it appears that a large proportion of the international community worked on the understanding that a chain of threats and counter-threats was symptomatic of a spiral of escalation that should be broken. In those four cases, an analogy to the series of events leading to the outbreak of World War I is valid. It is important to state that all of these belong within the category of chronic and protracted conflicts, in which escalation is to be expected as a result of previous experience of confrontation between the parties involved.[179] The communal silence with regard to the Taiwanese-PRC tit-for-tat of military exercises in 1995–6 appears as anomaly in so far as no Security Council criticised the parties even-handedly, although the conflict was certainly a protracted one. This may be explained, although with limited confidence, by referring to the contentious status of Taiwan and the involvement of two permanent veto powers, both of which for all practical purposes barred the Security Council from taking up any position.

The remaining cases present themselves in a different, less consistent, manner. The theme of deterrence is discernible in some of them. The international system may be said to have tolerated the US maritime interposition between Taiwan and the PRC in 1950 and in 1995–6. Applying the criteria developed in the last two chapters, we may argue that US policy in Taiwan, although far from completely impartial, was nonetheless designed for preventative rather than offensive ends. That is, it is credible that US forces in the Taiwan Strait helped deter (or 'neutralise') the danger of a cross-Strait violent encounter. The theme of deterrence could also conceivably have found its way into third-party appraisal of Jordan's signalled readiness to defend itself in 1980. Syria appeared as the aggressor, and Jordan was entitled to take measures for its own protection within the bounds of

[179] For a list of protracted conflicts see below annex, table 2, at pp. 318–19.

military necessity; the measures taken by Jordan were never excessive. Finally, the Sino-Vietnamese clash over the Spratly Islands in 1980 is more or less unclassifiable in terms of this analysis. The protagonists were left by their neighbouring nations to play their strategies out purely on the level of military power. It may be argued that there was no external judgment of this incident, and therefore it cannot be taken to either confirm or reject our hypothesis.

Although it can hardly be said that results are free from speculation, there are good grounds on which to conclude that both the deterrence and spiral themes figure in post-Charter practice. States rely on these themes in order to judge the permissibility or otherwise of countervailing threats. True tit-for-tat behaviour, as frequently practised between constant rivals, is not rewarded, and as such, not justified under the terms of article 51 of the UN Charter. At the same time, an attempt at genuine deterrence, aimed to preclude the use of force, combined with the implementation of a policy of mere negation and no retaliatory counter-charge, is tolerated. Here then, is acknowledgement that the cost of ignoring serious and malevolent threats is disproportionately higher than that of nipping such threats in the bud. An example of a deterrent threat is the ill-fated French Maginot Line, which fulfilled its purpose inasmuch as at the outset of World War II no German invasion force attempted to breach it. On the other hand, the defence of personal or national prestige, or influence, and the urge to respond to ill-defined putative dangers, are not motives approved of in principle by the international system.

Together, the cases examined may be taken as revealing a pattern in which threats and counter-threats are judged not so much by a victim-aggressor scheme but through the question of what effect a further threat of force will have on the course of conflict: the answer to this will create the distinction between the spiral and deterrence themes. Governments tend to base their diagnoses, as do gamblers betting on a competitive event, on the past record of the participants. There is little reason to believe that players will change their behaviour entirely if the latest decades of conflict have brought no change.[180] The hypothesis expressed in chapter 4, i.e., that states are not willing to apply the

[180] The results of this chapter support the view that the general reputation of a state or government is less important than the reputation and experience acquired bilaterally between different actors. See Jonathan Mercer, *Reputation and International Politics* 24 (1996).

self-defence clause to parties to protracted conflict, gains confirmation. The examples of Turkey-Cyprus in 1997–8 and Iraq-Kuwait in 1994 in the previous chapters illustrate, amid other ample evidence, the heightened sensitivity accorded to threats issued between long-standing enemies.[181]

One might object that the reluctance of states to take sides in some conflicts and their preference to call for restraint is not a result of any historical analogy: instead the frequent obscurity of the facts constitutes the reason why the victim-aggressor distinction is not upheld. If the threatener cannot be identified, the offence of initiating the threat of force cannot be attributed to any party. However, there is no reason why international law should not operate within the framework of facts being nebulous, such that the threat of force – initial or reciprocal – is impermissible for the precise reason that the facts cannot be established or that they are inappropriate for bringing the victim-aggressor distinction into play. States have not qualified their criticisms with the remark that they were predicated on the proof of detailed circumstances. On the contrary, it seems more accurate to maintain that they refuse to adjust their beliefs based on the exposition of such facts as are presented to them by the parties. In both US-Libya cases, for example, governments did not pay attention to the US contention that its pilots had acted in self-defence.

The description of state practice of this type must also be kept separated from the debate, yet unresolved among scholars of international relations, as to whether it is the deterrence or the spiral model that is more accurate in explaining state behaviour in general. All that we can say is that governments make the distinction in practice, and that international law, reflecting consensus, must be understood in recognition of this.

[181] The Security Council follows the same logic in many more examples. See, *inter alia*, its resolution S/RES/1172 (6 Jun. 1998) as a reaction to the first nuclear tests of Pakistan and India in 1998. The Council urged both parties to 'exercise maximum restraint and to avoid threatening military movements, cross-border violations, or other provocations in order to prevent an aggravation of the situation'; resolutions S/RES/1322 (7 Oct. 2000) and S/RES/1397 (12 Feb. 2002), adopted by votes of 14 to 1 and 14 to 0 (with one abstention), critical of Israeli actions against Palestinians.

8 Findings and conclusions

The previous chapters have scrutinised article 2(4) from four perspectives: (1) historical, (2) contextual, (3) judicial and (4) empirical. In terms of international law, these are the *travaux préparatoires*, general interpretation, case law and subsequent state practice. How do the four perspectives fit together? What are the common denominators? Which interpretation should prevail? In appraising all the accumulated facts, we shall assemble the pieces of the puzzle; a brief stock-take of the knowledge acquired will help in that task.

General stock-taking

The point of departure was the historical development of the no-threat rule and its strategic, political and intellectual underpinnings. In 1945, the signatories at San Francisco, informed by two world wars, wove two themes together into the UN Charter. On the one hand, they created a system of collective security of universal membership, free from mutually exclusive alliances, which relied on joint action in order to preserve post-war order, as they envisioned it, against future aggressors. The 'lesson of Munich' was that aggressors had to be resisted in a timely manner and with determination. The threat of collective military action was designed to work as a deterrent. This first communal tier was complemented by the right of states to take individual action in self-defence. The right of self-defence combined with the duty to retain forces ready for collective action meant that the maintenance of arms by individual UN members was accepted. Following the logic of deterrence, and as a matter of military necessity, readiness to resist aggressors was an integral feature of even the world aspired to by the Charter.

On the other hand, the newly devised prohibition of threats and the use of force expressed the will to brush aside old formalism and to bring into the UN Charter's strict ban on force the measures that had previously been known as 'short of war'. Following the logic of military strategy of the time, failure to disarm, preparations for war, mobilisation, ultimata, blockades, unwarranted military reprisals and even warmongering were the sort of actions that in the minds of governments showed aggressive intent. A state displaying any such belligerence was acting unlawfully and would, under Chapter VII of the Charter, merit collective action against it. The duty to refrain from any such actions was placed hand in hand with the duty, enshrined in article 2(3), to seek settlement of disputes only through peaceful means and at the expense of all measures relying on military strength. It was these two extremes – lawful deterrence against aggression and unlawful threat of aggression – that bounded the broad intent of those who drafted the UN Charter. But the Charter did not say specifically how action taken by states between the two extremes ought to be judged, nor, above all, which forms of military coercion fell under the rubric of permissible deterrence and which under the rubric of unlawful threat of force.

In hindsight, the drafters left unresolved an inherent tension: the UN Charter required the preservation of order through a state of readiness, yet at the same time it prohibited readiness as a mark of aggression. This was not conducive to the effectiveness of a legal system relying on objective standards. While aggressive or defensive intent was a clear, unambiguous concept of a state preparing for hostility, there was nothing that could inspire confidence in its neighbours that one course was clearly being pursued in preference over another. In 1945, judgment was won in favour of the victorious allies and against the defeated Axis powers, against whom the Charter quietly reserved military action in article 107. After both World Wars, the odium of aggressor was squarely placed on Germany, and later on Germany and Japan. While this provided a sweeping distinction between aggressor and defender, it was antithetical to principles of universality and thus legally incongruent.[1] It could only mean that the dual scheme governing military threats, tested against the widening gulf between

[1] The bias against former enemy states is, to some extent, still discernible today in the international response to 'rogue' nations: states such as Iraq and North Korea were more readily condemned by the Security Council for troop concentrations (Iraq 1994) or missile tests (DPRK 2006) than other states. See S/RES/949 (15 Oct. 1994) and S/RES/1695 (15 Jul. 2006).

the Cold War antagonists, would not operate as originally hoped for. In addition to that, a disabled Security Council, commensurate reliance on unilateral measures of protection and the advent of military technology enabling instantaneous destruction, meant that the immediate post-war security environment did not bode well for article 2(4). Laborious attempts to define 'aggression' in the subsequent years, with recurring moves to include the threat of aggression, led nowhere.

Within the framework of 1945, a series of interpretations of article 2(4) presented themselves. As explored in chapter 2, interpretation could help to stand the no-threat principle on better defined ground but, at the same time, widely contradictory results were possible. A first conceptual crossroads was as to whether the formula 'threat or use of force' used by the Charter could be split in two; that is, whether the no-threat duty was a *sui generis* duty, clearly standing independent from the legality of the contemplated use of force. This duality, if adopted, meant one of two things. First, it could mean that military threats were lawful in scenarios where the use of force was not. This could be achieved by arguing that the threat, as against the use, of force could serve the Charter's peace objective through deterrence and that it more readily fulfilled the requirement of proportionality. Second, duality could, on the other hand, mean that military threats were illicit even when recourse to force would not have been so, namely, in situations of self-defence. This view also derived from the Charter's peace objective, but followed the different reasoning that it could best be served if counter-threats, despite their implicit reference to self-defence, were considered impermissible. A *sui generis* interpretation could be made to tighten or relax the requirements of article 2(4).

Three other avenues have been explored. Another interpretation sought a direct link to the obligation to create peaceful settlement of disputes contained in article 2(3), making it possible to clothe the no-threat rule in reverse terms, i.e., the positive duty of states to remove even the *semblance* of military pressure in negotiating with one another. This interpretation provided a powerful method of dealing with the notorious ambiguity of threats: an ambiguous threat would now be presumed unlawful in principle, the removal of ambiguity being part of the duty incurred on states by virtue of article 2(4) and (3). On the other hand, it was possible – but not to be recommended – to argue that in order for a threat to be unlawful, it needed to be *imminent*, quasi in corollary to the ostensible permission of forceful action in anticipation of an armed attack stated within article 51. A final view provided that article 2(4) was best described to require *coercion*, the essence of which was that a state would threaten force if compliance with specific demands was not forthcoming. Threats would thus be defined by their strategic utility.

The ICJ did not consider any of the above in formulating three decisions pertaining to the threat of force. In what may be called the most nuanced judgment, the Court declared in the *Corfu Channel* case that the UK had been entitled to deter Albania from firing against British ships passing through the channel,[2] but not to demonstrate such force 'for the purpose of exercising political pressure' on Albania.[3] The judges took into account the fact that the British mission was limited to assert the right of innocent passage while exercising considerable self-restraint. However, in its 1986 *Nicaragua* judgment, the Court simultaneously rejected, on the one hand, the US accusation of the illegality of Nicaragua's 'militarization' and, on the other, Nicaragua's own allegation that US military pressure against it amounted to a threat of force. The first it rebuffed as a matter of legal principle, the second, without specifying, as a matter of the overall circumstances in which US-Honduran military manoeuvres had been held.[4] A third and final opportunity for the Court to develop article 2(4) arrived with the General Assembly's request for an advisory opinion on nuclear weapons. In it, the ICJ stated two things. First, it determined that the threat and the use of force were to be bracketed together in the sense that the unlawfulness of the former was predicated on the unlawfulness of the latter.[5] It rejected the view that they had separate meanings. Second, the Court held that *de lege lata*, nuclear deterrence for purely self-defensive reasons and to secure the very survival of a state was potentially justified but ultimately beyond the Court to determine.[6] Whether that was a licence to legality depended on whether the ageing *Lotus* principle, according to which sovereign freedom of action is presumed, applied to the facts of the case. The advisory opinion seemed to characterise deterrence in terms of self-defence, implying that the

2 *Corfu Channel Case (United Kingdom* v. *Albania), Merits*, 1949 ICJ Rep. 4 (9 Apr. 1949), at para. 30.
3 *Corfu Channel, Merits*, at para. 35.
4 *Military and Paramilitary Activities in and Against Nicaragua (Nicaragua* v. *USA), Merits*, 1986 ICJ Rep. 14 (27 Jun. 1986), at paras. 227, 269.
5 *Legality of the Threat or Use of Nuclear Weapons (Advisory Opinion)*, 1996 ICJ Rep. 226 (8 Jul. 1996), at para. 47.
6 *Nuclear Weapons Advisory Opinion*, at para. 2E of the *dispositif*.

possession of nuclear weapons was in itself a threat of force requiring justification.[7]

While the Nuremberg and Tokyo judgments had clearly assigned criminal responsibility for the compelled submission of Czechoslovakia and French Indochina as aggression or preparation for aggression, the case law of the ICJ treated the issue of threat of force evasively. Nothing more can be reaped than was sown by the Court. Regrettably, at no point did the judges justify their decisions with any exposition of arguments. Furthermore, their findings are not reconcilable with one another. In the *Nuclear Weapons* opinion, the implication was that nuclear capacity was sufficient to pass the threshold of article 2(4), while the *Nicaragua* judgment asserted sovereign freedom in all matters of armament. In the *Nicaragua* context, the Reagan administration had openly declared its aim to exercise political pressure against Nicaragua. This was exactly the criterion that the *Corfu Channel* judgment had formulated as a test for illegality. These internal contradictions and the lack of transparency in reasoning meant that the contribution of the ICJ could not satisfactorily serve to solve the threat puzzle.

The examination of post-Charter state practice was designed to prompt more conclusive answers. Such an examination is not only necessary because other means of defining the law have yielded no certainty, but also because there is a need to know whether state perceptions have shifted – not because of second thoughts, but in view of important changes as to the ways in which interstate conflicts are conducted in the modern era. Some of these changes have already been mentioned, such as the advance in military technology that allows instant use of force without time-consuming mobilisation, and reliance on nuclear deterrence between the principal antagonists of the Cold War. There have been other changes, as well. Since 1945, there has been no major war between the major industrialised nations. Instead, not only have civil wars been prevalent, but also conflicts last longer, are more limited and have less definite results. The 'decisive battle', as defined by Karl von Clausewitz, has become a rarity, while outcomes of conflict often labour under the latent danger of renewed hostilities.[8] The end of the Cold War merely brought these trends more to the fore. It was therefore necessary to investigate whether the original

[7] *Ibid.*, at para. 48.

[8] Illustrative Holger Herwig, Christian Archer, *et al.*, *Cassell's World History of Warfare* 549–78 (2003).

parameters of unlawfulness have altered, or, in less revolutionary terms, have lived through constructive refinement – not by formal accord, but through states consistently appraising related sets of circumstances in the same manner. This was put to an empirical test through taking a random sample of twenty-four comparative case studies.[9]

It is appropriate to make a brief mention of a critically important preliminary finding: out of the nearly 200 member states of the UN today, only a handful react by actually filing protests against, or conveying their approval of, potential violations of the UN Charter. It turns out that, at least in threat-related cases, the assumption that silence equals approval is empirically false.[10] The Latin adage *qui tacet consentire videtur* may have its merits in bilateral and municipal settings, but it is not adequate in the context of multilateral obligations. As is known from the field of psychology, responsibility shared tends to result in shirking. The concept of *erga omnes* obligation may be designed to make the breaches of article 2(4) of the UN Charter an offence to all, but obviously states are affected in different ways – as victims, allies, dependents, neighbours or historical kin.[11] If the empirical survey shows anything, then it is that often states keep their opinions to themselves due to their own short-term concerns that are devoid of any worry about the *legal* implications of silence: such concerns include loyalty to allies, lack of relevance for national purposes and the calculation that 'getting involved', particularly against powerful states, is more costly than 'staying out'. Even genuinely selfless concerns may advise silence. Brownlie reports, for example, that during the period of operation of the League of Nations, states consciously refrained from

[9] Two cases were hand-picked: NATO-Yugoslavia 1999 and USA and UK-Iraq 2002–3. For details see above, chapter 4, at pp. 119–21.

[10] The cases in the present study suggest that international responses have become more common. In the immediate post-war period, third-party reactions were rare and hardly channelled through institutions. It was a period dominated by the Cold War antagonists and their respective spheres of influence. A differently composed UN General Assembly from the 1960s onwards and the rise of the Non-Alignment Movement changed this, starting to voice a different view than that of the Security Council and its most influential members.

[11] On obligations to the international community as a whole see James Crawford, *The International Law Commission's Articles on State Responsibility: Introduction, Text and Commentaries* 242–5 (2002), in reference to the *Barcelona Traction, Light and Power Company, Limited (Belgium* v. *Spain), Second Phase*, 1970 ICJ Rep. 3 (5 Feb. 1970), at para. 33; Maurizio Ragazzi, *The Concept of International Obligations* Erga Omnes (1997); Christian J. Tams, *Enforcing Obligations* Erga Omnes *in International Law* (2005).

condemnation because they felt that this would merely serve to unduly expose the League's inaction.[12] In the context of military threats, governments seem to recognise that the UN best serves its objectives if it wears the hat of mediator whose impartiality is appropriate in situations where room for negotiation remains and recourse to force has not yet been decided upon. Interference by third parties would only render the task of the UN (or another honest broker) more difficult. In short, silence is not intended to reward transgression, but simply means, as it does in other contexts, abstention. This, of course, strongly affects the legal appraisal of state practice, and it is only correct to inform the reader that it is based on that premise.

A further caveat needs to be mentioned. It is in the nature of any comparative study on a relatively small-*n* basis that sweeping generalisations cannot be relied upon. It is routinely a difficult business to gauge the attitudes and motives of states, and there is no question that historical cases, like all cases, have to be read in the context of the facts surrounding them. Often the attitude of individual states can only be inferred. Often reality is not as clear-cut as hoped for. But by filtering out a host of factors co-determining international reaction and by distilling commonalities, it is possible to arrive at a number of conditional, theory-guided and context-dependent generalisations about the permissibility of predefined types of state conduct.[13]

What, then, are the legal duties that the UN Charter imposes on states? We can now survey the principal empirical findings and combine them with the results of previous analysis. The case studies serve the purposes of determining, first, the threshold of article 2(4) and, second, under what circumstances, once that threshold has been passed, there could be legal justification for violation of it.

Criteria for violation

The strongest form of unlawful threat is the *ultimatum*. Under the state of war doctrine prior to 1945, an ultimatum intended to bring about the formal condition of war was considered to be a violation of international law. Today the ultimatum, freed from the anachronistic

[12] Ian Brownlie, *Use of Force by States*, at p. 59 (1963).

[13] See further above, chapter 4, at p. 113. Similar in regard to lessons on coercive diplomacy Alexander L. George and William E. Simons (eds.), *The Limits of Coercive Diplomacy* 268 (2nd edn, 1994).

requirement of such formalism, is characterised by objective standards. It means that another state is faced point-blank with a 'last clear chance', the unequivocal promise that unless it complies with a specific demand, the use of force will result. The state issuing the threat will normally instil a sense of urgency.[14] There is no need here to seek a detailed definition of the ultimatum, because in practice states assess legality based on less stringent criteria, to the point where the classic ultimatum is entirely enclosed by broader parameters of illegality. The historical trend has marked a departure from the subjective state of war doctrine, still popular in the first half of the twentieth century, to more objective and comprehensive criteria in the modern era.

Overall, state practice since 1945 has converged into a single, overarching credibility test: *does a state credibly communicate its readiness to use force in a particular dispute?* A threat is credible when it appears rational to implement it, when there is a sufficiently serious commitment to run the risk of armed encounter. A calculated expectation is created that an unnamed challenge might incur the penalty of military force; no certainty is required as to whether force really will be used, or under what conditions it will be triggered or that there be an urgent and imminent danger of its deployment. Daniel Webster's 'Caroline' formula of 'instant, overwhelming' necessity of self-defence that 'leaves no choice of means and no moment of deliberation'[15] is not transposable to article 2(4). Nor does a threat, to be described as such, have to be tied to specific demands and a tight deadline for a reply. All that matters is that the use of force is sufficiently alluded to and that it is made clear that it may be put to use.[16] On the other hand, a threat will not be perceived or even recognised without there being, so to speak, a peg of dispute on which to hang the expectation of the use of force. A threat that contains no reference to a particular dispute, no issue to create pressure against and no element of coercion usually appears meaningless. These are all lessons that the political scientists support for the simple reason that,

[14] Variants of the same definition are common among political scientists. See George and Simons, *The Limits of Coercive Diplomacy*, at p. 274.

[15] Letter from Daniel Webster to Lord Ashburton (6 Aug. 1842), reprinted in John Bassett Moore, *A Digest of International Law as Embodied in Diplomatic Discussions, Treaties and Other International Agreements*, vol. II, 412 (1906).

[16] In this sense, state practice seems to lean on an interpretation of the UNC which combines the obligation of refraining from threats with the one to peaceful settlement. However, the hypothesis cannot be appropriately tested.

as states understand, threats are best assessed according to their effectiveness in international affairs.

More specifically, chapter 5 suggested that in addition to the classic ultimatum, *open, explicit or verbal indications* of the use of force, such as those often relayed to the general public or through diplomatic channels, may qualify as being credible. The Turkish 1997–8 warning that it would take out Cypriot missiles in the event of their deployment was credible, and so too, undoubtedly, was the diplomatic *communiqué* of NATO member states against Yugoslavia in 1999. However, some public statements, for example, Uganda-Kenya in 1976, elicited less international reaction. Here the credibility criterion is helpful, suggesting that inflammatory speeches alone do not often generate in and of themselves much anticipation of the actual use of force. There is some requirement for specific language in formulating demands and consequences of defiance, hence the tendency of explicit threats to be directed towards the extraction of a specific concession. Moreover, theory informs us that a state may render credible its verbal threats in two ways. First, the government can openly commit itself to carrying out a threat to a domestic audience, thus increasing the political costs of a bluff.[17] Second, it may put its international reputation on the line by declaring to other governments its willingness to use force. The line drawn for all to see involves more 'face' than does one communicated privately, is harder to reverse and cannot be denied.[18] The reliance on what governments say, and to whom, is a proposition that fits easily into international law. It goes without saying that the almost integral confidence of general international law in the validity of official declarations and statements of all sorts makes the relevance of verbal threats clear without the need for a move into belligerent action.[19]

Chapter 6 revealed that a threat need not be explicit. In fact, the evidence is stronger for a *demonstration of force* to constitute a violation of article 2(4). This may be surprising, because the threat is primarily

[17] James Fearon, 'Domestic Audiences and the Escalation of International Disputes', 88 Am. PSR 577–92 (1994); James Fearon, 'Signaling Foreign Policy Interests: Tying Hands Versus Sinking Costs', 41 J. Conf. Resol. 68–90 (1997).

[18] Anne Sartori, 'The Might of the Pen: A Reputational Theory of Communication in International Disputes', 56 Int. Org. 121–49 (2002).

[19] The Ihlen declaration and the French nuclear tests moratorium readily come to mind. See *Legal Status of Eastern Greenland (Denmark* v. *Norway), Merits*, 1933 PCIJ Rep. Series A/B No 53 (5 Apr. 1933), at para. 70; *Nuclear Test Cases (Australia & New Zealand* v. *France), Merits*, 1974 ICJ Rep. 253 (20 Dec. 1974), at para. 43–9.

implied, generated through apprehension, and not spoken aloud, and thus is presumably less apparent. Yet, the credibility of a demonstration as a threat is established more readily through the physical presence of military authority. Demonstrations of force are costly, indicate commitment and governments take the calculated risk that events may spin out of their control.[20] The present study assumed that any *militarised* act would qualify as a demonstration of force, such as military deployments, troop build-ups, manoeuvres or tests, provided that they signal readiness and resolve to use armed force on a particular issue at dispute with another state. The case studies confirm the validity of this assumption to a significant degree. However, there is a qualification of great importance. Not all militarised acts amount to an unlawful demonstration of force in violation of article 2(4). In the cases examined, the assertions that militarised acts were conducted without hostile intent or on a routine mission were refutable on the grounds that they were evidently non-routine, suspiciously timed, scaled-up, intensified, geographically proximate, staged in the exact mode of a potential military clash and easily attributable to a foreign policy message. For the Turkish Straits crisis in 1946, the evidence was not strong enough; with regard to the Iraqi troop concentrations along the Kuwaiti border in 1994, however, no state accepted the argument that Iraqi troops were conducting routine exercises. Thereby state practice suggests a more sophisticated view of military build-ups than that achieved by the ICJ in the *Nicaragua* case. Sovereignty over territory cannot provide a flimsy justification for concentrations of troops that cause neighbouring countries to take up defensive positions. It needs to be emphasised, however, that under the criteria listed above, the majority of military exercises and manoeuvres are conducted under perfectly lawful conditions. The duty of states to announce exercises in advance, established through a host of international instruments, would not be explainable otherwise, and between good neighbours a threat through militarised actions is almost never perceived. Again, a resolve to use force can be plausibly relayed only in the context of a dispute between author and victim state. The difficulty lies not in determining whether demonstrations of force violate article 2(4); the

[20] Thomas C. Schelling, *Arms and Influence* 150 (1966); Fearon, 'Signaling Foreign Policy Interests'; Branislav L. Slantchev, 'Military Coercion in Interstate Crises', 99 Am. PSR 533–47 (2005).

problem is how they are to be distinguished from unsuspicious conduct. Again, the credibility criterion is to be recommended.

A further finding is that the *actual use of force*, too, may occasionally constitute a threat of force. In many cases the label 'threat' is more accurate. The dichotomy of threat and use, as suggested by the formulation of article 2(4), is misleading. Although the threat and the use of force are conceptually different, that does not mean that they exclude each other in the field. For example, in the US-Libya clashes in the 1980s, the aerial dogfights were judged as merely symptomatic of the US naval presence off Libya's coast, and states were critical of the USA primarily because it signalled that more force, larger in scale and directed against targets on the mainland, could be forthcoming. Many more incidents involving limited use of force, such as border clashes, retaliatory strikes or naval blockades, are best described as examples of coercive diplomacy.[21] This is no idle finding. It means that the modes of engagement between combatants on the 'micro-level' are not necessarily or exclusively relevant in determining infringements of article 2(4). Condemnation of the USA in 1980 and 1989 was not based on whether or not, as a matter of fact, Libyan jets had fired first and US jets had responded in self-defence; instead, the impression was that whatever the details of the incident, the superior US deployment had inappropriately invited a clash in order to demonstrate US fire-power. In the Iran-Iraq border dispute over the Shatt-al-Arab in 1969, the opposing parties turned out to have relied on maps showing differing border demarcations; both sides therefore saw themselves as victims of border attacks. But the real issue was the deployment of troops in over-close proximity to one another along the border. In both cases, the threat of force 'narrative' superseded the use of force 'narrative', whose conditionality on first shot, location over sovereign territory or sufficient gravity was deemed inadequate to describe the real issues at stake. The same reasoning applies to PRC-Vietnam in 1995–6, Pakistan-India in

[21] As for blockades, authors already have expressed difficulties in judging whether there was a use of force involved or not. See e.g. the Egyptian blockade of the Gulf of Aqaba and the Strait of Tiran on the eve of the 1967 Israeli-Arab War: see Malcolm Shaw, *International Law* 1029 (5th edn, 2003). Similar problems of categorisation apply, e.g., to the 'defensive quarantine' of Cuba in 1962, the Indian blockade of Goa in 1961 or the establishment of maritime exclusion zones in the Falklands/Malvinas War in 1982. Israel had argued in 1967 that the Egyptian blockade amounted to an armed attack, which is highly doubtful. There can be little doubt, however, that the establishment of a maritime exclusion zone displays hostile intent and implies that force will be used against intruders.

1951, India-Portugal in 1961, USA-DPRK in 1950 and Morocco-Spain in 1975. In judging a specific case, it is therefore imperative to enquire whether the diagnosis of a threat of force beyond the occurrence of actual violence alters the legal appraisal. This is particularly important if one holds that the margin between a violation of article 2(4) and an 'armed attack' according to article 51 is narrow and thus would soon entitle one participant to self-defensive action. The actual use of force may well be immaterial occasionally in view of the threat of force posed by the other side.

If a threat may also be construed as such, even when only implied, do 'excessive' *levels of armament* or the 'militarisation' of a country qualify as a breach of article 2(4)? Limitations on armaments have traditionally been imposed by victorious nations after a major war. Such arrangements formed the point of departure for both the League of Nations Covenant and the UN Charter, but they have become rare in the post-war world, the last one being imposed on Iraq in 1991 through resolution 687.[22] From the scarce evidence available, it seems that the defiance of disarmament obligations is treated under the rubric of Chapter VII threats to peace rather than under article 2(4). No government has argued that Iraq was in violation not only of Security Council resolutions but also of the UN Charter's ban on threats. Outside the context of post-war settlement, the picture appears largely permissive. The current arms control and partial weapons ban regime indicates that in the absence of specific treaty obligations, governments in principle retain the right to acquire whatever weapons, and in whatever quantity, they desire. Even in the case of nuclear weapons, acquisition may run counter to obligations under the Non-Proliferation Treaty, but for now, acquisition does not of itself appear to constitute a threat of force.[23] Since nations are free to withdraw from disarmament treaties, it is problematic to judge breaches of treaty obligations as violations of a peremptory norm.[24] Moreover, the signatories of the UN Charter

22 S/RES/687 (8 Apr. 1991); David J. Bedermann, 'Collective Security, Demilitarization and "Pariah States"', 13 Eur. JIL 121–38 (2002).

23 See above, chapter 3, at pp. 79–82, in discussion of the *Nuclear Weapons Advisory Opinion*. However, the acquisition of nuclear weapons may constitute a threat of force if other criteria for violation are met. See e.g. the international response to the nuclear tests of India and Pakistan in 1998 (which in the case of Pakistan also signalled to the world that it had acquired nuclear weapons), S/RES/1172 (6 Jun. 1998); S/PV.3890 (6 Jun. 1998); 1998 UNYB 321–2.

24 Contrary to Michael Bothe, 'Friedenssicherung und Kriegsrecht', in Wolfgang Graf Vitzthum (ed.), *Völkerrecht* 589–667 (3rd edn, 2004), at p. 600, who argues that the

conceded to member states the right to bear arms for collective and self-defensive purposes. Military strength, however unevenly distributed, is a generally acknowledged feature of the present international system. In order to breach article 2(4), a state must go further: it must actively attempt to intimidate through specific threats, troop concentrations or displays of force that remove any doubt of non-hostile intent. Under these circumstances, the threat becomes both targeted and visible as an effort to exercise military pressure.[25] From time to time, governments have criticised the acquisition of weapons systems, on the grounds that they disrupt military balance to their disadvantage. In the reaction to the deployment of Soviet nuclear missiles in Cuba in 1962, US President John F. Kennedy famously declared:

> Neither the United States of America nor the world community of nations can tolerate deliberate deception and offensive threats on the part of any nation, large or small. We no longer live in a world where only the actual firing of weapons represents a sufficient challenge to a nation's security to constitute maximum peril. Nuclear weapons are so destructive and ballistic missiles are so swift that any substantial increased possibility of their use or any sudden change in their development may well be regarded as a definite threat to peace.[26]

There are other cases. Turkey, too, argued in 1997 that the Cypriot purchase of surface-to-air missiles was unduly upsetting the military balance of the region, and the USA in 1986 claimed that the delivery it suspected of Soviet combat jets to Nicaragua posed a threat to its Central American neighbours. Yet in all these cases international reaction, like the invokers of the UN Charter themselves, couched and evaluated the claim of disruptive action in the language of Chapter VII. In invoking a right to take countermeasures, there was no suggestion that the other party had violated article 2(4). There is the added conceptual

violation of disarmament obligations may amount to an unlawful threat of force. The withdrawal of North Korea from the Non-Proliferation Treaty (NPT) in January 2003, however, indicates that this view is not plausible. The NPT does not have customary status. See Frederic L. Kirgis, 'North Korea's Withdrawal from the Nonproliferation Treaty', *ASIL Insights* (Jan. 2003), http://www.asil.org/insights/insigh96.htm.

25 By a similar token, the formation of *military alliances* does not amount to a breach of article 2(4). The acceptance of regional arrangements under Chapter VIII of the UN Charter would not make sense otherwise. If in breach of article 2(4), they would be invalidated by article 52 of the *Vienna Convention on the Law of Treaties*, 1155 UNTS 331 (23 May 1969). There is no indication that states entertain that view.

26 President John F. Kennedy, *Radio and Television Report to the American People on the Soviet Arms Buildup in Cuba*, 47 Dept. St. Bull. 715–20 (22 Oct. 1962).

difficulty that the alleged military balance is rarely much of a balance and that in the final analysis there is no useful distinction to be made between who is threatening whom.[27] Cuba possessed no nuclear weapons, whilst the USA did. Vis-à-vis the Soviet Union, the USA had already lined up missiles along the Russian border. Turkey enjoyed complete air superiority over Cyprus. And Nicaragua did not even have an air force. For all practical reasons, a breach of article 2(4) requires more than the ownership of arms. This may be seen as the mark of an international legal system that no longer contains the concept of designated 'enemy states', and whose claim to universality renders deeply problematic any distinction merely based on the identity of buyers of military hardware.

Criteria for justification

According to the general scheme of the UN Charter, there are two sources that may render a violation of article 2(4) legal: recourse to self-defence and authorisation by the UN Security Council.

The first and clearest scenario is a threat of force in response to an armed attack. Article 51 entitles the victim state to threaten and deploy force as a countermeasure. It may threaten its attacker with increased firepower to compel discontinuation of an attack, or to terminate hostilities altogether by means of a ceasefire. There is no ambiguity of the law in this respect.[28]

However, the more relevant question in practice is whether states are free to reciprocate threats when no armed attack has actually occurred. We have seen that states essentially draw upon two historical analogies to answer that question. The first analogy comes from August 1914, where the 'dynamics of mutual alarm'[29] forced the hand of policy-makers into war. The second analogy is to the events of September 1938, where appeasement of Hitler only intensified his thirst for further concessions. Two seemingly incompatible policy prescriptions followed: either to exercise self-restraint because threats are best left

[27] On the rationale to rely on the threat to peace theme see Abram Chayes, *The Cuban Missile Crisis: International Law and the Rule of Law* 62–6 (1974); Richard N. Gardner, 'Neither Bush Nor the "Jurisprudes"', 97 Am. JIL 585–90 (2003), at 587.

[28] On the validity of treaties brought about by the threat of force see Stuart S. Malawer, 'Imposed Treaties and International Law', Cal. WILJ 115, 156–8 (1977) and below, chapter 9, at pp. 285–89.

[29] Schelling, *Arms and Influence*, at p. 221.

unanswered or to issue a counterthreat in as timely and decisively a manner as possible. Rather than treating the spiral and deterrence themes as opposites, states have treated them as complementary. In judging the permissibility of countervailing threats, they first assess the *characteristics of crisis* in order to decide which theme is applicable. What effect will a further threat have on the course of conflict? Will it be likely to prevent or provoke hostilities?

In a first set of cases, states have indicated that no party is entitled to proceed with a further threat, no matter whether or not an enquiry into the facts would validate a reference to self-defence. States worry about the dynamics of escalation. They also worry about the possibility that minor irritations could be used by either side as a pretext for military retaliation. Communal condemnation is calibrated to the fact, symptomatic of many conflicts, that the *aggressor-victim distinction*, on which article 51 relies, is essentially inadequate. These characteristics are most usual for *protracted conflicts*, where the parties already have a record of escalation and where neither of them has acquired the strength to decide the conflict in its favour. If one party has the advantage of overwhelming military preponderance, the threats involved will appear lopsided and the escalation analogy does not apply. This legal scheme for protracted conflicts will easily be rejected by some as abrogating the 'inherent' right to self-defence within UN Charter law. The right to self-defence will always override the obligation of self-restraint if 'national security' so requires. Quite simply, however, UN practice does not support that claim. There is, moreover, not so much of a revolutionary touch to an interpretation that favours self-restraint: it falls in line with the format of the UN Charter's analogous dictate, ambiguously described by the ICJ in its *Nicaragua* decision, that a state is not allowed to use force in response to an intervention that falls short of an armed attack.[30]

[30] Commonly referred to as the 'Nicaragua gap'. See *Military and Paramilitary Activities in and Against Nicaragua (Nicaragua v. USA), Merits*, 1986 ICJ Rep. 14 (27 Jun. 1986), at para. 195. See further Terry D. Gill, 'The Law of Armed Attack in the Context of the Nicaragua Case', 1 Hague YBIL 30–58 (1988); Yoram Dinstein, *War, Aggression and Self-Defence* 173–6 (2001). The Court upheld the 'Nicaragua gap' in its recent *Oil Platforms* case: see *Oil Platforms Case (Islamic Republic of Iran v. United States of America), Merits*, 2003 ILM 1334–485 (6 Nov. 2003), at paras 51–64; Dominic Raab, '"Armed Attack" After the Oil Platforms Case', 17 Leid. JIL 719–35 (2004), at 724–33. The Court also seems to have been guided by the concept in its *Case Concerning Armed Activities on the Territory of the Congo (Democratic Republic of Congo v. Uganda), Merits*, 2006 ILM 271–395 (19 Dec. 2005), at para. 165.

In a second set of cases, states accept the proposition that the use of threats is justified in order to provide an effective preventative measure against the threat of an armed attack. This is what the ICJ acknowledged in its *Corfu Channel* judgment when it stated that the UK could not be held to be at fault for the minimum-deterrent measure it undertook to ensure the safety of its ship and crew. A strictly defensive threat made in order to deter an attack is lawful. Thus in contrast to countervailing threats in such cases as Pakistan-India in 1951, Iraq-Iran in 1969–75 or Greece-Turkey in 1976, Syria's troop build-up in response to Jordan's prior deployment in 1980 appeared legitimate. The French Maginot Line could not have been anything other than a precaution set up against a German assault. Article 51 operates in its classical disposition: aggressor and victim are readily discernible, and there is a meaningful distinction to be made between the initiator of and the responder to a crisis. At the very least, a state is entitled to repeat the statement within article 51 that it will resist an armed attack. However, state practice indicates that the margins of legality are narrow. Threats that are genuinely self-defensive will normally revolve around denial and deterrence, not compellence. There is no *carte blanche* for counter-threats to acquire a tinge of provocation, the purpose of which is not to deflect military pressure but to extract concessions in kind, above abstention from the use of force.[31]

In short, the overriding objective of prevention of war has been evident since 1945. Forbearance is rewarded, whilst brinkmanship, the act of seeking advantage by a signalled willingness to push a dangerous situation to the limit, is condemned. Governments recognise the special function of threats as markedly distinct from the use of force, to achieve results without resort to military conflict. What is more, states recognise that the path of coercive diplomacy is associated with the substantial risk of misperception, cognitive traps, pretexts for premeditated actions and limited control, together creating a situation that could easily escalate into war.[32] At the same time, they recognise

[31] Out of the twenty-four case studies, compellence turned out to be the far more popular strategy. Only in six cases (PRC-USA 1950, Turkey-Cyprus 1997–8, Colombia-Nicaragua 1984, Iraq-Kuwait 1994, USA-PRC 1950, Syria-Jordan 1980) did one of the parties involved practice deterrence.

[32] Recast in the terminology of international law, this means that the requirements of proportionality and necessity are applied strictly. A threat is unnecessary if it goes beyond self-defence. It is disproportional if the expected risks of a further threat are the outbreak or intensification of war itself.

that the attempt to deter aggression is legitimate, and that sometimes the line between attacker and attacked is as clear as the UN Charter presumes; clearly, UN law does not dictate the repetition of appeasement. The distinction between lawful and unlawful conduct is a fine line to draw, but the lesson is that the drawing of it is desired by states, as shown by their practice since 1945. Categorisation, they say, does not hinge so much on the details of confrontation as on the characteristics of a crisis. Through this, uncertainty over the occasion on which a particular rule applies is adequately resolved and the goals of the UN Charter are met. The temptation to define justification exclusively according to the template of self-defence, however well-intended and theoretically meritorious, should be resisted. It has been long abandoned in practice. This is to be welcomed, because in the majority of conflicts the contingency of self-defence on crystal-clear facts bars UN Charter law, and to some degree UN organs trapped in the victim-aggressor frame, from any contribution to crisis management.[33] Abandonment of the self-defence contingency could, for example, make it easier for international courts to issue interim measures of protection in cases where sporadic hostilities are attended by nebulous facts.

The theme of prevention of war also runs through Chapter VII Security Council authorisations. The Council has never to date initiated or explicitly authorised formal sanctions in response to a threat of force according to article 2(4) of the UN Charter, and neither has the General Assembly done so under the 'Uniting for Peace' procedure. The Security Council probably came closest to authorising sanctions in 1994, when it strongly condemned Iraqi troop concentrations along the border of Kuwait. But even then, it did not formally authorise deterrent countermeasures or any other form of penalty in order to persuade Iraq to withdraw its troops. The question, then, most relevant in practice is whether military threats are nonetheless permissible in situations where the intent to manage a crisis is genuine but not formally approved by the UN. This is the thorny question of implied and *ex post facto* authorisation.[34] Whatever one's beliefs about the matter, the

[33] On the notion of crisis management and international law see Hanspeter Neuhold, *Internationale Konflikte: Verbotene und erlaubte Mittel ihrer Austragung* 258–66 (1977).

[34] Jules Lobel and Michael Ratner, 'Bypassing the Security Council: Ambiguous Authorizations to Use Force, Cease-Fires and the Iraqi Inspection Regime', 93 Am. JIL 124–55 (1999); Ruth Wedgwood, 'The Enforcement of Security Council Resolution 687: The Threat of Force Against Iraq's Weapons of Mass Destruction', 92 Am. JIL 724–8 (1998).

evidence suggests that states show greater tolerance to threats in such a context than they do with regard to the use of force. UN members are more tolerant to quasi-Chapter VII threats for two reasons. First, because they are reluctant to shield the target state from pressure to comply and, second, because they believe that threats may indeed serve the purposes of war prevention. Approval is strongest when the intervening state interposes itself between contending parties and seeks to deter the use of force by one of them. The rationale of collective self-defence assists in legitimising the action taken; it is markedly weaker when the intervening state has co-authored the conditions of crisis.[35]

Accordingly, states tolerated the deployment of US troops in the Persian Gulf in 1994 to deter a second invasion of Kuwait. Sensibly, they did not object to the British interposition between Israel and Egypt in 1948, a measure designed to bring the Israeli campaign to a halt (but, in contrast to 1994, not covered by the right to collective self-defence). International reaction can be explained equally well in the Taiwan Strait cases and, to a lesser extent, with regard to joint military pressure against Yugoslavia in 1999 and Iraq in 2002. The latter case clearly illustrates that there is no authority of governments to proceed with military threats on the self-judging basis that Chapter VII needs to be invoked and peace restored or defended. Rather, the Security Council, while agreeing in November 2002 to put pressure on Iraq, made it clear that it wanted to retain authority over the subsequent course of action. In 1948, too, the Security Council had actively demanded a ceasefire between Israel and Egypt. It had actively demanded compliance with its resolutions vis-à-vis Iraq in 1994 and Yugoslavia in 1999. In short, a careful reading of the cases, with the possible exception of Taiwan, demonstrates that the Security Council's seal of approval must at least be plausible, and that in order to avoid the onset of war itself the threat of force is apparently the trigger required to facilitate the success of diplomatic efforts.[36] That, of course, is playing with fire. But there is no explaining away the fact that state practice reveals a pattern whereby

[35] See the similarly to the concept of necessity as a circumstance precluding wrongfulness, article 25 *Articles on State Responsibility*, A/56/10 (annex to A/RES/56/83, 12 Dec. 2001), reprinted and commented in James Crawford, *The International Law Commission's Articles on State Responsibility: Introduction, Text and Commentaries* 178–86 (2002).

[36] A possible addendum would be approval by the General Assembly in observance of the 'Uniting for Peace' procedure. There being no such case in my case pool, there can be no validation or falsification of this hypothesis in this study.

the unilateral threat of force finds limited accommodation under the umbrella of collective action designed to manage a crisis.

Reviewing the grounds for justification, one may conclude that states have not abandoned article 51 and Chapter VII as sole sources of legitimacy, but that they have fine-tuned some of their traditional content. Impetus for adjustment stemmed from the changed nature of conflicts and the underlying facts leading to the outbreak of those conflicts. The law of justification for military threats accounts for the early 'fog of war', a fertile ground for crises to spiral out of control. The idea of shared responsibility for conflicts, an idea alien to statesmen in the first half of the twentieth century, has taken hold.[37] Through reliance on different types of crises, the tension inherent in the Charter between threat against aggression and threat of aggression, unresolved in 1945, found adequate relief. As a corollary, there has also been a shift in understanding that the aims pursued with coercion do matter beyond the strait-jacket of self-defence. Threats narrowly designed and for ends determined as legitimate by the collective decision-making process of the Security Council – to what degree is uncertain – appear to be permissible.[38]

Changes in the law

Has the law changed since 11 September 2001?[39] In the immediate aftermath of the attacks on Washington, DC and New York, the Security Council and the General Assembly unanimously pledged their support

[37] For the Cold War superpowers, that realisation took hold through the Cuban missile crisis. The nuclear dimension was, however, understood early on to transform military strategy. Hence Bernard Brodie's observation in 1946 that the purpose of having a military establishment had now shifted from winning wars to averting them. See Bernard Brodie, 'Implications for Military Policy', in Bernard Brodie (ed.), *The Absolute Weapon: Atomic Power and World Order* 70–110 (1946), at p. 76. See for an account James A. Nathan, *Soldiers, Statecraft, and History: Coercive Diplomacy and the International Order* 131–56 (2002).

[38] On the legitimising function of the Security Council see the interesting study by Eric Voeten, 'The Political Origins of the UN Security Council's Ability to Legitimize the Use of Force', 59 Int. Org. 527–57 (2005).

[39] See for a discussion on the use of force level Christine Gray, *International Law and the Use of Force* 159–94 (2nd edn, 2004); Steven R. Ratner, '*Jus ad Bellum* and *Jus in Bello* after September 11', 96 Am. JIL 905–21 (2002); Michael Byers, 'Terrorism, the Use of Force and International Law after 11 September', 51 Int. & Comp. LQ 401–14 (2002); Sean D. Murphy, 'Terrorism and the Concept of Armed Attack in Article 51 of the UN Charter', 43 Harv. JIL 41–51 (2002); See further the symposia published in 'Agora: Future Implications of the Iraq Conflict', 97 Am. JIL 553–642 (2003) and 97 Am. JIL

for self-defensive measures.[40] Since 2001, the USA has issued threats against Iraq, Afghanistan, Syria, Iran and North Korea. It has fought two major wars in suit of those attacks.[41] Could the unanimous support of UN members immediately after the terrorist attacks mean that states agreed instantaneously to a new standard whereby the justification for a threat of force was made broader? Could it be argued that states are now entitled to use military threats against 'rogue regimes' suspected of harbouring terrorists or themselves entertaining designs to use catastrophic terrorism?[42]

One must be careful to remain methodologically consistent. This study took as a frame of enquiry the period from 1945 to the present, a research design intended to expose the wider trends that have shaped the second half of the twentieth century. In applying this time frame, it is not possible to change gear and seek to derive new law with the certainty of time-honoured practice.[43] If law was determined purely on an *ad hoc* consensual basis, there would be no need for the UN Charter. All that can be investigated is whether there was a marked break in diplomatic reactions that render plausible the claim of changed law.

The touchstone for the policy of pre-emption was the run-up to war and eventual conflict waged against Iraq in 2002–3. In chapter 5 it was shown that the international community reacted to the threat of force against Iraq ambiguously. In autumn 2002, it was possible for the USA and the UK to convince Security Council members that in order to deflect the outcome of war, Iraq needed to feel the weight of a united Council front. Pressure included the 'stick' of a Security Council authorising UK-US military action.[44] This narrow consensus, however, soon evaporated as it became clear that the two allies were intent on invading Iraq despite ongoing weapons inspections; the 'carrot' of non-invasion no longer was credible. Criticism of continued UK-US preparation for and implementation of the invasion of Iraq in spring 2003 was strong and overwhelming. This being global reaction, there is

803–72 (2003); 'Symposium: 'A War Against Terrorism': What Role for International Law? US and European Perspectives', 14 Eur. JIL 209–378 (2003).

40 S/RES/1368 (12 Sep. 2001); A/RES/56/1 *Condemnation of Terrorist Attacks in the United States* (12 Sep. 2001); Gray, *Use of Force*, at pp. 164–5.

41 Gray, *Use of Force*, at pp. 184–6.

42 See on the US doctrine of pre-emption *The National Security Strategy of the United States of America*, (19 Sep. 2002), http://www.whitehouse.gov/nsc/nss.html.

43 See above, chapter 4, at pp. 110–11. 44 S/RES/1441 (8 Nov. 2002).

not much indication that the law governing the threat of force underwent substantial revision: the dilemma of shielding a notorious norm-breaker through overt condemnation of unilateral action designed to induce compliance remains identical to that faced in previous crises. Similar unease over the threat (as distinct from the use) of force accompanied the NATO-led military pressure on Yugoslavia in 1999. The same dilemma of choosing between the desiderata of inducing compliance and the prevention of war seems to have guided the thinking of the state majority. Iraq in 2002–3 does not fall out of line with previous state practice, and this may be taken to indicate that the perception of UN members has not gone through a radical transformation, as is purported by some.

On another level, the question is also one as of whether the historical analogies have changed: from World Wars I and II (the spiral and deterrence model) to 11 September 2001. A preliminary survey suggests this is not the case; decisively perhaps, 9/11 is about a *casus belli*, whereas the two World Wars are about a *narrative* on the prudence of threats in certain situations. It is difficult to see how the 'war against terror' could provide a viable alternative for governments to think about the values and dangers of threats in the context of international conflicts. In this chapter, the reluctance of states to accord one another too much freedom in assessing and acting upon perceived dangers to their national security has also been identified. Freedom of action has too often opened a chasm allowing the making of subjective claims and counter-claims that experience shows us tend to lead, in self-fulfilling prophecy, to war.[45] It is not bound to make the international system any safer.[46] From the perspective of international law, a universal standard, applicable to all, that permits mutually exclusive claims of pre-emption can be neither a healthy nor an equitable prescription for order. That is the lesson of post-Charter practice, and one that the international judge, in faithful observance of the sources of law, cannot ignore.[47]

[45] Seminal Robert Jervis, *Perception and Misperception in International Politics* (1976).

[46] Against Anne-Marie Slaughter, 'Chance to Reshape the U.N.', Wash. Post (13 Apr. 2003); Lee Feinstein and Anne-Marie Slaughter, 'A Duty to Prevent', 83 F. Aff. 136–51 (2004); Michael J. Glennon, 'Why the Security Council Failed', 82 F. Aff. 16–35 (2003).

[47] Concurring Gardner, 'Neither Bush Nor the "Jurisprudes"', at 588. Kant's categorical imperative is obviously of help here: 'Act only according to that maxim by which you can at the same time will that it should become a universal law.'

The regulation in a nutshell

The legal regulation of the threat of force in the UN Charter may be summarised as follows: to begin with, the no-threat principle has a *sui generis* character to some extent independent of the regulation of actual force. The utility of threats for states is quite different; in the minds of decision-makers, a threat is successful if it obviates the use of force.

In order for there to be a violation of article 2(4), a state must *credibly communicate its readiness to use force in a particular dispute*. A threat is not credible when its implementation is not a real danger. A threat with no reference to a dispute will not be perceived as one. But creating the expectation that even an unnamed challenge might incur the use of force is sufficient; it is not required that certainty exists that force will be used, that it is imminent or that it be framed within specific demands and deadlines. What matters is that the use of force is sufficiently alluded to and thereby increases the shared risk of military encounter. The form of communication is irrelevant; specifically, article 2(4) outlaws (1) explicit promises to resort to force and (2) demonstrations of force, the latter defined as any militarised act that reveals hostile intent; and (3) the use of force may also constitute a threat of force if the purpose of a military operation is to signal that more force may be forthcoming. In judging a specific case, it is imperative to examine whether the diagnosis of a prior threat of force by one side does or does not alter the overall legal appraisal.

A state is justified in issuing a counterthreat in self-defence, first, when it is exposed to an ongoing armed attack or, second, if its threat is designed to prevent such an attack by way of deterrence. But this is not the case between states involved in a protracted conflict, where the distinction between aggressor and victim implied by article 51 of the UN Charter does not hold good; in this case neither side is entitled to make a threat in response. The overarching dictate is one of self-restraint, to avoid escalation into or within armed conflict. Actions undertaken must be in proportion and necessary within that context. Exceptionally, a threat of force may find justification under Chapter VII of the UN Charter beyond the explicit authorisation of the Security Council. Provided that there is genuine international concern over the course of a crisis, threats of force narrowly designed to manage that crisis along the lines of collectively determined goals by the Security Council appear to be lawful. This, it seems, is a concession to the insight that threats may from time to time serve UN diplomatic efforts and the purposes of prevention of war. However, justification will usually fail if the threatening state itself has created the crisis in question.

It follows from the above that states may, within the same conflict, simultaneously be engaged in making unlawful threats of force. The rules regulating the actual use of force presume that there is always an aggressor and victim, and thus that the actions of one party (the victim) are sanctioned by law, whereas those of the other party (the aggressor) are not.[48] With regard to the threat of force, this is different: the self-defence clause does not operate in settings of protracted conflict, and therefore there may be several norm-breakers at a time if threats are issued. Given that two-thirds of all interstate crises are connected to protracted conflicts, this is a significant qualification.[49]

The law thus identified, the goal of the final chapter is to examine what lies beyond the strict question of legality. This is not intended to be a comprehensive analysis, but merely an attempt to understand the sub-structure of the no-threat rule, how it may facilitate the settlement of disputes and why states behave the way they do.

[48] The 'Nicaragua gap' (see above, n. 30) allows for the possibility that state A uses force in violation of article 2(4) but falls short of an armed attack. In this case, the forceful response by state B would also be unlawful because it is not justified by article 51. Moreover, the customary requirements of necessity and proportionality, or a binding Security Council resolution, may also lead to situations where the use of force by both parties to a conflict are unlawful. But these are all conceptual exceptions.

[49] There is the further possibility that, in the setting of a non-protracted conflict, the threat of state A is intended to deter the initial threat of state B, but the threat of state A is physical, communicated through the actual use of force. Under such a scenario, both threats are unlawful. The fact that the use of force of state A is *also* qualified as a threat of further use of force (e.g. in case of a surgical air strike) does not, in the absence of an armed attack upon it, justify its use of actual force as a (*per se* lawful) deterrent counter-threat.

9 Epilogue: the law in operation

Reappraising article 2(4)'s blind spot

What do the results of chapter 8 imply for the regime of force? The present study was started with the aim not only of exploring the legal meaning of the no-threat principle but also of arriving at some conclusions on how it operates in practice: by operation I mean qualities that are assets for states in their international dealings with one another, so that UN Charter law serves its primary objective - peaceful settlement of disputes and the avoidance of major war.

An early theory, expressed in chapter 1, was that little legal impact on state behaviour could be expected for the simple reason that the no-threat rule has remained poorly understood, grossly underdeveloped and rarely invoked. Operation of the law implies that a rule may be appealed to positive effect. It also, intuitively, pre-conditions that the operation of law is understood by relevant actors. Rules cannot have instrumental effect unless they are communicated to relevant actors, and these actors are legal advisors, judges and academics assisting governments in their decision-making process. If these members of the 'invisible college of international lawyers'[1] practise omission, then, surely, the UN and individual states can hardly be blamed for not relying on it.[2]

[1] Oscar Schachter, 'The Invisible College of International Lawyers', 72 Nw. ULR 217–26 (1977–8). See further Nicholas G. Onuf, 'Law and Lawyers in International Crises', 29 Int. Org. 1035–53 (1975).

[2] For the impact of legal considerations on the political organs of the UN see Oscar Schachter, 'The Quasi-Judicial Role of the Security Council and the General Assembly', 58 Am. JIL 960–5 (1964).

Omission accordingly appears to be the mark of practice. Violations happen recurrently; in this study's compilation, states were embroiled in over a hundred crises since 1945 in which two or more parties engaged in military threats against one another, and in many cases the threats involved were not justified and thus unlawful. While such transgressions of article 2(4) provide no proof that the UN Charter has no effect, it is more telling to observe that only in very few of these instances have states actively asserted or defended a right to threaten with force. The Security Council, the political organ mandated for preventive diplomacy, has never taken substantial action in response to a threat of force by a member state. It condemned South Africa in 1986 for threatening its neighbours during repeated battles involving Angola and Namibia,[3] and it scolded Iraq's southward troop concentrations in 1994.[4] But there was no collective action under Chapter VII of the UN Charter. Symptomatic of a state of oblivion, too, is the case law of the ICJ, whose judges, while defending the non-use of force principle in their decisions, have felt palpable unease with the concept of threat of force. Even more tellingly, litigating parties have presented facts to the Court involving potential infringements of the no-threat principle, but then dropped that charge in the course of writing their final submissions.[5] All in all, this is not the record one would hope for a principle that forms part of the UN Charter's central mission to prevent the use of force between states. Rather, the record appears as testimony to the painful conclusion that article 2(4) has been stillborn.

But, as reasoned in chapter 1, this might be the wrong conclusion. It has been simply assumed – wrongfully, it was argued – that there was nothing to invoke on behalf of the no-threat principle, the status of which may have been judged as even more lamentable than the rest of article 2(4). In the absence of a universal understanding of the intentions of the drafters, the case law, state practice and underlying rationale on the threat of force it could hardly be expected that governments would often invoke it – hence the prescription to increase awareness, a task that could best be met by sharpening article 2(4)'s determinacy and by fortifying that determinacy with solid proof – proof from the drafting history, subsequent state practice and so on. Oblivion could be overcome.

[3] S/RES/581 (13 Feb. 1986); see also S/RES/326 (2 Feb. 1973). [4] S/RES/949 (15 Oct. 1994).
[5] See above chapter 8, at pp. 65–8 for a brief survey of such cases.

One objection to this is that no matter how well it defines the obligations of states, the Charter cannot work as a restraint if the members themselves do not accord it the necessary authority. As the British government commented in an early memorandum on the UN idea:

> In actual fact there was never any doubt, in the cases in which the League of Nations was concerned, as to the identity of the aggressor, though sometimes as to the character of the provocation to aggression. States, it is true, adapted their actions and procedure to the language and resolutions adopted at Geneva and later to the Pact of Paris. But in no case were the real intentions and motives of the aggressive State concealed from the Governments of the other members of the League or from public opinion.[6]

Ultimately, the lack of effective action was due not to 'any defect in the Articles of the Covenant but to the lack of will on the part of other States, and notably the Great Powers involved, to go to war with the recalcitrant State'.[7] The ban on threats could be said to face similar problems; even when transgressions of the UN Charter could be quickly detected, states might simply not be willing to act against them.

And yet, the surprising characteristic of state practice is that nations pay tribute to the no-threat principle without directly invoking it. As shown, there is no lack of occasions when they file protests, condemn or register complaints over conduct that they deem impermissible in the broad UN Charter context. When they are consistent in their attitude to the same class of events, this is legally relevant as it sheds light on what standards the majority of states wish to live by. A puzzling question results. Given that the no-threat rule was underdeveloped for all this time, dim in the collective mind of the 'invisible college' and affiliate government branches, would states have acted all that differently in the absence of formal Charter law? The objective here is not to call the validity of previous findings into question – they are founded on the agreed standards of finding the law – nor to adopt an Austinian positivism denying the very existence, or relevance, of law in the international sphere. Rather, the objective is to explore how the ban on

6 *Tentative Proposals by the United Kingdom for a General International Organisation, Memorandum B: The Pacific Settlement of Disputes, The Question of Guarantees and the Conditions in Which Action Should be Taken for the Maintenance of Peace and Security. Copy transmitted by the British Embassy to the Department of State on 22 July 1944*, 1944 FRUS vol. I, 684.

7 *Tentative Proposals by the United Kingdom*, at 683.

threats may still be of assistance in an international system that has yet to develop a solid enforcement machinery. That is not strictly a legal question, but, at the end of the day, it is all about law: only when the operation of UN law outside the courtroom is well understood can efforts bear fruit to make it more relevant.

Robert Ellickson's Shasta County

In 1986, Robert Ellickson published an article in the *Stanford Law Review* in which he presented the results of a richly detailed investigation into how ranchers and farmers in Shasta County, located at the northern end of California's Central Valley, resolved disputes arising from trespass by stray cattle.[8] What started as hypothesis testing of Ronald Coase's Nobel prize-winning law and economics theorem (and more specifically, its famous farmer-rancher parable)[9] ended up as an analysis of how social norms emerge and operate among private landowners.

Several findings of Ellickson's seemingly exotic research provide fertile ground for present purposes. For one thing, it turned out that residents of Shasta County, including local enforcement authorities, were uninformed about the modalities of animal trespass law even though trespasses were frequent throughout the region.[10] Just as most government officials never read an international law textbook or entertain much awareness of article 2(4) 'part two', so Shasta County cattlemen never read legal regulations. Animal trespass law consisted of an interweaving of English common law and newer federal legislation dealing with open-range and closed-range areas, 'fencing out' rules resulting in different degrees of liability for livestock.[11]

But ranchers and farmers in Shasta County instead solved trespass conflicts, as Ellickson reports, in allegiance to rudimentary social norms wholly independent of formal legal entitlements,[12] not 'in the shadow of law' but rather beyond that shadow.[13] Formal law had

[8] Robert C. Ellickson, 'Of Coase and Cattle: Dispute Resolution Among Neighbors in Shasta County', 38 Stan. LR 623–87 (1986). Five years later, Ellickson published an expanded version of his thesis in a book. See Robert C. Ellickson, *Order Without Law: How Neighbors Settle Disputes* (1991). For a comparable and seminal study see Elinor Ostrom, *Governing the Commons: The Evolution of Institutions for Collective Action* (1990).

[9] Ronald H. Coase, 'The Problem of Social Cost', 3 JL & Econ. 1–23 (1960).

[10] Ellickson, 'Of Coase and Cattle', at 667–71. [11] *Ibid.*, at 659–67.

[12] *Ibid.*, at 673. [13] *Ibid.*, at 672.

changed during the period he examined, but the informal norms that neighbours had worked out among themselves had not.[14] These were footed on good neighbourliness, the distillation of what ranchers and farmers considered morally right. In a first tier, owners of livestock were responsible for acts of their animals, but minor damages were tolerated on a reciprocal 'live and let live' basis. Because residents expected to deal with one another over longer periods of time, they exercised self-restraint and withheld demands for compensation in return for future favours.[15] In a second tier, defectors who did not pay tribute to the overarching principle of good neighbourliness could be resisted. Self-help measures ranging from negative gossip, threatening sanctions and eventually hurting stray cattle became acceptable.[16]

Landowners in Shasta County evidently show parallels to states in the international system. Both groups are organised horizontally and under largely self-reliant conditions. The local sheriff, the UN Security Council, is rarely active. The number of neighbours is relatively small and interactions with these are frequent and enduring. Nations usually do not change their neighbours, and they have a lot of business going on with each other that make them face each other on a regular basis. In regard to the no-threat rule, governments interact not unlike California landowners in the sense that they, too, may be said to act upon crudely hewn out standards of conduct that need not be congruent with the law, especially if applied to specific cases. The black letter of the law is of limited importance; what matters are the underlying principles and their rationale. This being so, one is pushed to the question: if an informal social code of conduct took precedent over legal regulation, then how did that second-level norm framework come into being? How did social order without law emerge?

While Aristotle would have argued that people are by nature sociable and thus inclined to organise themselves in community structures, Thomas Hobbes and other social contract theorists contended instead that social norms were the outcome of an agreed escape from what Hobbes famously called the 'State of Nature' – war among all against all in the absence of governmental authority.[17] Social order, Ellickson concluded, emerged in Shasta County through a set of circumstances that in the 1950s political scientists realised are quintessentially game theoretic: what each player wants to do depends on what he or she

[14] *Ibid.*, at 654. [15] *Ibid.*, at 672–6. [16] *Ibid.*, at 676–85.
[17] Thomas Hobbes, *Leviathan*, part I, chapter 17 (1968) [1651].

thinks the other is going to do,[18] in this case, enriched by the setting that a game is not a one-shot affair but repeats itself among the same actors over time. Players then cooperate on a self-enforcing, tit-for-tat strategy up to the moment when they are crossed, in which case they apply 'eye-for-an-eye' remedies.[19] Hence the two-tiered approach of landowners in California. Ellickson concluded:

> To achieve order without law, people must have continuing relationships, reliable information about past behavior, and effective countervailing power. Recast in the vocabulary of game theory, some basic variables in social structure are the numbers of players involved in an inning of a game, the number of innings in which current players may expect to encounter each other, the time span within which the players expect those innings to occur, the quality of the players' information, and the distribution of power among the players. Legal rules can influence all these attributes of social structure and thereby promote – or impede – informal cooperation.[20]

The important insight is that the emergence of informal cooperation does not bar law from a meaningful role. It can do what traditionally is its assigned purpose: solve disputes through judicial process. But it can also, and this is what game theory supports, positively influence the way actors deal with one another, to the effect that bad outcomes of the Hobbesian 'State of Nature' may be converted into good ones even when there is no *Leviathan* to enforce rules that are to the agreed benefit of all.[21]

Fostering cooperation

Assuming that the Ellickson's logic is transposable to the international world, how do states fare under the UN Charter? This section presents

[18] James D. Morrow, *Game Theory for Political Scientists* 1 (1994).

[19] Ellickson, *Order Without Law*, at pp. 149–55. See for the tit-for-tat strategy Robert Axelrod, *The Evolution of Cooperation* (1984). See also the symposium on cooperation in security affairs 38 World P. 1–254 (1985).

[20] Ellickson, *Order Without Law*, at p. 284 (footnotes omitted). Similarly Charles W. Kegley Jr and Gregory A. Raymond, 'Normative Restraints on the Use of Force Short of War', 23 J Peace Res. 213–27 (1986).

[21] For a first debate in international law on the relevance of game theory see John K. Setear, 'An Iterative Perspective on Treaties: A Synthesis of International Relations Theory and International Law', 37 Harv. ILJ 139–229 (1996), and the response by Michael Byers, 'Response, Taking the Law out of International Law: A Critique of the "Iterative" Perspective', 28 Harv. ILJ 201–5 (1997). For a historical placement of the debate see Harold Hongju Koh, 'Why Do Nations Obey International Law?', 106 Yale LJ 2599–659 (1997), at 2630–4. See further Edna Ullmann-Margalit, *The Emergence of Norms* (1977).

five interrelated hypotheses as to how the no-threat principle may be said to operate under these terms.

First, as mentioned in chapter 2, there is an added value for rules to be spelt out as clearly as possible, such that a state's violation of the rule is easily detected and made accountable.[22] One reason why the beliefs of farmers and ranchers in California did not correspond with the law was that the rules were too complicated. Good fences indeed make good neighbours:[23] there is a qualitative difference when the boundaries of neighbours are well demarcated and thus the act of transgression is beyond reasonable doubt. In this regard, article 2(4) fulfils the prerequisite of a straightforward, no-frills rule. It soberly dictates 'do not threaten with force'. But the meaning of that phrase is at present too easily lost in the thicket of real-life cases and too much hampered by the standard interpretation of the right to self-defence. The accumulation of too many 'Ifs' benumbs the law when it should sting.

Second, not only can clear legal trip-wires be helpful in avoiding disputes, but law also serves by providing a common ground for the *accepted and established order*. That order is a mental construct, a point of reference by which players assess the appropriateness of each others' conduct. In Shasta County, that was the principle of good neighbourliness. In the UN world, it is the similar principle of peaceful cooperation, in which the UN organisation is pictured as 'a centre for harmonizing the actions of nations'.[24] That is the starting point, and the maxim not to threaten with force (or use it) appears as one of its natural corollaries. To act according to what good neighbours should do informed the thinking of Shasta County landowners. To act according to the aspired outcome of non-violence also shapes the expectations of governments. That may appear as an appeal to ethics or morals, but it is not only 'fair' to entertain such expectations; it is also rational for selfish reasons.[25] In the ideal state of cooperation, all participants are better off. There is no need to fight. States may reap the 'peace dividend' and engage in mutually beneficial exchange of goods, services, knowledge, and so on. Therefore, it is a sound strategy to try to see, offer cooperation for a start, and then reciprocate if it

[22] On determinacy see Thomas M. Franck, 'Legitimacy in the International System', 82 Am. JIL 705–59 (1988). For the same from a game theory perspective see Thomas C. Schelling, *Arms and Influence* 132 (1966).

[23] Robert Frost, *Mending Wall* (1914), quoted from the *Oxford Dictionary of Quotations* 295 (4th edn, 1992).

[24] Article 1(4) UNC.

[25] Axelrod, *The Evolution of Cooperation*, at pp. 3–24.

fails.[26] Quite intuitively, then, only when the other side defects can there be fall-back justification for one's own defection.[27] Only when faced with an armed attack may there be recourse to armed self-defence. In the threat realm, this carries particular weight under the rubrics of provocation and escalation. *Self-restraint* becomes a virtue.[28] Thus Robert Kennedy reports of the Cuban missile crisis:

> With some trepidation, I argued that, whatever validity the military and political arguments were for an attack [against Cuba] in preference to a blockade, America's traditions and history would not permit such a course of action. Whatever military reasons he and others could marshal, they were nevertheless, in the last analysis, advocating a surprise attack by a very large nation against a very small one. This, I said, could not be undertaken by the U.S. if we were to maintain our moral position at home and around the globe. Our struggle against Communism throughout the world was far more than physical survival – it had as its essence our heritage and our ideals, and these we must not destroy ... The strongest argument against all-out military attack, and one that no one could answer to his [Kennedy's] satisfaction, was that a surprise attack would erode if not destroy the moral position of the United States throughout the world.[29]

States see virtue in self-restraint to the extent that it developed into an ethical standard. It is, so to speak, the true opposite pole to the still frequently invoked term 'aggression', which implies hot-headed, unbridled and reckless pursuit of aims by force. States recognise that whenever possible no oil should be poured onto a fire and that quick, self-judged deployment of threats are best avoided. From the bystander perspective, too early countermeasures in too forcible a manner raise

26 *Ibid.*, at p. viii.

27 In this sense, it may be noted, a state that breaks the law while submitting extenuating circumstances in its defence is indeed upholding the primary rule of cooperation. This supports the ICJ's dictum that: 'If a State acts in a way prima facie incompatible with a recognized rule, but defends its conduct by appealing to exceptions or justifications contained within the rule itself, then whether or not the State's conduct is in fact justifiable on that basis, the significance of that attitude is to confirm rather than to weaken the rule.' See *Military and Paramilitary Activities in and Against Nicaragua (Nicaragua* v. *USA), Merits*, 1986 ICJ Rep. 14 (27 Jun. 1986), at para. 186.

28 For an interesting analysis on the benefits of self-restraint on the international security level see Janice Gross Stein, 'Reassurance in International Conflict Management', 106 PSQ 431–51 (1991).

29 Robert F. Kennedy, *Thirteen Days: A Memoir of the Cuban Missile Crisis* 30, 39 (1969). See further Abram Chayes, *The Cuban Missile Crisis: International Law and the Rule of Law* 38–40 (1974), discussing the same passage.

doubts about who deserves support. Accordingly, farmers in Shasta County took care not to take self-help measures that could be misunderstood or deliberately construed as acts of initial aggression.[30] On the eve of World War I, France ordered a ten-kilometre withdrawal of its troops from the German border to make clear beyond doubt, above all to the half-committed UK, who was the first to cross the French and Belgian border, who was the attacked and who the attacker.[31] Robert Axelrod reports another striking example from World War I: during the trench warfare, whole battalions facing each other informally agreed to hold fire during bad weather, holidays and in the early morning while food was supplied. In addition, soldiers started to shoot past each other under the – often successful – condition of reciprocity.[32] There is a rational incentive to exercise self-restraint. It represents a community interest, and it is necessary for states to invoke justifications which are acceptable to as many peers as possible to achieve as much support as possible if they trespass the codex.[33] Whether all this is the work of law, ethical convictions or rational calculation may not be all that important. All that matters is that UN Charter law and state practice reflects the same wisdom to positive effect. It provides a point of reference to coordinate mutual expectations and to measure defection.[34]

Third, article 2(4) may provide parties in crisis a *face-saving way out*. As Thomas Schelling writes:

> One of the great advantages of international law and custom, or an acknowledged code of ethics, is that a country may be obliged *not* to engage in some dangerous rivalry when it would actually prefer not to but might otherwise feel obliged to for the sake of bargaining reputation ... One of the values of laws, conventions, or traditions that restrain participation is that they provide a graceful way out.[35]

[30] Ellickson, *Order Without Law*, at p. 216.

[31] Barbara W. Tuchman, *The Guns of August* 84 (1962).

[32] Axelrod, *The Evolution of Cooperation*, at pp. 73–87. The commitment problem of 'cheating' on agreements is not as relevant here because it is a repeated game situation. Axelrod accordingly reports that no cooperation was possible when soldiers were ordered to conduct a raid (at 82–3). The real-life relevance of repeated games chips away some of the persuasiveness of John Herz's famous security dilemma. See John Herz, 'Idealist Internationalism and the Security Dilemma', 20 World P. 157–80 (1950); Robert Jervis, *Perception and Misperception in International Politics* 58–116 (1976).

[33] Schachter, 'The Quasi-Judicial Role of the Security Council and the General Assembly', at 962.

[34] On the concept of 'focal points' seminal Thomas C. Schelling, *The Strategy of Conflict* 111–13 (1960).

[35] Schelling, *Arms and Influence*, at p. 120 (emphasis in original).

If one of the functions of law is to promote rather than to substitute informal cooperation, then it may serve that purpose by providing viable means of settling disputes without recourse to the threat or use of force. Again escalation worries play a role. If the dictate of law is to refrain from countervailing threats even when faced with threats or minor uses of force, there is at least a platform from which non-action may be rewarded with increased international support and, occasionally, to fend off domestic pressure. In the 1976 Greek-Turkish dispute over the continental shelf, public opinion in both countries was pushing hard for an aggressive policy. Similar to how international adjudication is said to help government officials justify a foreign policy outcome to domestic audiences in declaring that not they, but an independent judiciary, decided the merits of a dispute,[36] the no-threat principle gives governments cover against pressure from inside and, perhaps just as importantly, against the loss of personal 'face' or 'honour'. It can provide avenues for adversaries silently to agree on a tie, and thus informally to cooperate not to engage in a test of nerves. If one accepts the notion that some crises are spawned by exogenous events (such as the shooting of an Indian fisherman near Goa in 1961, or Taiwanese moves to independence) that compel governments to respond, there is a strong case to devise methods that minimise the mutual risk of things getting out of hand.[37] In this sense, international law is relevant in building mechanisms for crisis-defusing and to avoid headlong confrontations as far as possible. An interpretation of article 2(4) that diminishes its conditionality on self-defence promotes the operation of law in this respect because the dictate not to threaten the use of force, the 'way out', is clearer between long-term adversaries.

Fourth, as game theory suggests, informal cooperation works best if defection can be effectively reciprocated or, to apply a cruder term, 'punished'. Therefore, there is room for deterrence. Article 51 of the UN Charter accommodates deterrence not as a policy of first choice but as a necessary evil. Too much deterrence renders the costs of escalation fatal and, in the nuclear age, apocalyptic. No deterrence, on the other hand, invites cheating. In this sense, the plea for self-restraint and the concession that everyone may, so to speak, keep a loaded shotgun are not

[36] Todd L. Lee and Paul K. Huth, 'Legitimizing Dispute Settlement: International Legal Rulings as Domestic Political Cover', 100 Am. PSR 219–34 (2006); John Collier and Vaughan Lowe, *The Settlement of Disputes in International Law* 7 (1999).
[37] Schelling, *Arms and Influence*, at p. 121.

incompatible; they are complimentary. However, self-restraint takes precedence in as much as there is an expectation that actors should start with friendly conduct and that aggression by others is subject to some solid proof. Because 'eye for an eye' behaviour, once it has started, is bound to climb the escalation ladder, the plea of self-restraint persists even when the first bullet has travelled across the fences. Since self-restraint receives support by third parties, a state practising forbearance can score points in the international community that a 'tough' player that always follows 'eye for an eye' strategy cannot. The more states become dependent on one another in political, economic or military terms, the more the goodwill of other states and international organisations will be relevant.

Finally, international law is highly relevant in providing a platform on which important outcomes of informal negotiations will be built and from which further cooperation may proceed.[38] By defining the circumstances when agreements are valid, it provides for the *stability of treaties*.[39] Article 52 of the Vienna Convention on the Law of Treaties, entitled 'Coercion of a State by the threat or use of force' provides that:

> A treaty is void if its conclusion has been procured by the threat or use of force in violation of the principles of international law embodied in the Charter of the United Nations.[40]

Duress was an issue in at least six of the twenty-four cases examined, either because that was the objective of military pressure or because parties raised the claim that previous treaties relevant to the dispute were invalid.[41] This is to show the pervasive character of the problem,

[38] James Crawford, 'Negotiating Global Security Threats in a World of Nation States: Issues and Problems of Sovereignty', in James Crawford, *International Law as an Open System: Selected Essays* 95–121 (2002), at p. 95.

[39] On their function in crisis settings see the interesting study by Christopher Gelpi, 'Crime and Punishment: The Role of Norms in Crisis Bargaining', 91 Am. PSQ 339–60 (1997).

[40] Article 52 *Vienna Convention on the Law of Treaties*, 1155 UNTS 331 (23 May 1969). See the International Law Commission's commentary at 1966 YBILC vol. II, at 246–7. And further: Harmut Brosche, *Zwang beim Abschluss völkerrechtlicher Verträge* (1974); Stuart S. Malawer, 'Imposed Treaties and International Law', Cal. WILJ 1–178 (1977); H. G. de Jong, 'Coercion in the Conclusion of Treaties: A Consideration of Articles 51 and 52 of the Convention on the Law of Treaties', 15 Neth. YBIL 209–47 (1984); Michael Bothe, 'Consequences of the Prohibition of the Use of Force: Comments on Arts. 49 and 70 of the ILC's Draft Articles on the Law of Treaties', 27 ZaöRV 507–19 (1967).

[41] See USSR-Turkey 1946, USSR-Czechoslovakia 1968, Iran-Iraq 1969–75, Morocco-Spain and Algeria 1975, Nicaragua-Colombia 1979–80 and NATO-Yugoslavia 1999. On the

which obviously has implications for the central notions of consent and sovereign equality in international law.[42] Article 52 of the Vienna Convention refers to article 2(4) of the UN Charter.

In drafting the Vienna Convention, the International Law Commission dodged the controversy whether, as some commission members had held, non-military pressure (such as the 'strangling' of an economy) would also invalidate a treaty.[43] It stated that the 'precise scope of the acts covered by this definition should be left to be determined in practice by interpretation of the relevant provisions of the Charter'.[44] The controversy continued among governments during the Vienna Conference, but article 52 remained unchanged.[45] If the aim of the Vienna Convention is to guarantee freedom of consent, the concern of ignoring non-military forms of coercion is well founded. According to the ICJ in 1973 in the Anglo-Icelandic *Fisheries Jurisdiction* case, the applicable test is whether an agreement was 'freely negotiated by the interested parties on the basis of perfect equality and freedom of decision by both sides'.[46] That is an adoption of the free consent approach. Nonetheless, the result of the specific reference to the UN Charter is that the no-threat rule virtually alone shoulders the considerable burden of determining under what conditions an accord is invalid under article 53 of the Vienna Convention.[47] The more precise the conditions of failure, the better agreements can be negotiated to avoid that result.

latter see *Legality of Use of Force (Yugoslavia* v. *Belgium et al.), Application*, 1999 ILM 950–62 (29 Apr. 1999), submissions; see further *Verbatim Records*, CR/99/14 (10 May 1999) and CR/99/25 (12 May 1999).

42 Malawer, 'Imposed Treaties', at 156; de Jong, 'Coercion in the Conclusion of Treaties', at 222.

43 Bothe, 'Consequences of the Prohibition', at 511–12.

44 1966 YBILC vol. II, at 246. It is to be noted that the threat of other than physical injuries was considered a ground for invalidity if directed against a representative of a state: see article 51 VCLT.

45 In compromise, the Conference drafted and issued a *Declaration on the Prohibition of Military, Political or Economic Coercion in the Conclusion of Treaties*, A/Conf.39/26 (23 May 1969). The Conference '*solemnly condemns* the threat or use of pressure in any form, whether military, political, or economic, by any state in order to coerce another state to perform any act relating to the conclusion of a treaty in violation of the principles of the sovereign equality of States and the freedom of consent'. For a brief account see de Jong, 'Coercion in the Conclusion of Treaties', at 245–7; Ian Sinclair, *The Vienna Convention on the Law of Treaties* 177–81 (2nd edn, 1984).

46 *Fisheries Jurisdiction Case (United Kingdom* v. *Iceland), Jurisdiction*, 1973 ICJ Rep. 14 (25 Jul. 1974), at para. 24. See above, chapter 3, pp. 66–7.

47 This was a novelty. See the survey of the literature contained in the commentary to the *Draft Convention on the Law of Treaties*, 29 Am. JIL Supp. 1148–61 (1935) of the

There are some obviously unresolved issues. Article 75 of the Vienna Convention retains the validity of obligations under treaties 'which may arise for an aggressor State in consequence of measures taken in conformity with the Charter of the United Nations with reference to that State's aggression'.[48] Only unlawful *vis compulsiva* by an aggressor 'to consolidate the fruits of his aggression'[49] invalidates a treaty. A threat or use of force that finds justification under Chapter VII or article 51 of the UN Charter mends the flaw of coercion. This may make 'all the difference in the world'[50] and smooth out all wrinkles in the legal realm, but it immediately collapses on entering practical territory. This is so because it leads back to the Kafkaesque question of who threatened first, and if force was used, by whom first, and if first use and first threat stemmed from different sources, to whom to assign the odium of aggressor. For a majority of protracted conflicts, that enquiry leads nowhere. It would mean that the legal status of many international ceasefires, truces, armistices, boundary and (by now rare) peace treaties concluded since 1945 are potentially void – but there is no way of telling for sure.[51] There is thus some serious questioning warranted whether a rigid one-to-one application of the UN Charter, particularly under a traditional reading, is advisable for the law of treaties.[52] Is the attacked nation really free to impose any condition on the attacker? Does not the fact suffice that tired parties of a prolonged conflict agree to cease hostilities? It is not the point here to provide a definite answer,

Harvard Law School; Malawer, 'Imposed Treaties', at 156; de Jong, 'Coercion in the Conclusion of Treaties', at 244.

48 ILC members thought it 'essential to avoid the impression that an aggressor State is to considered as completely *exlex* with respect to the law of treaties' and that there was a danger of 'one party unilaterally characterizing another as an aggressor for the purpose of terminating inconvenient treaties'. With that in mind, article 75 was formulated in 'entirely general terms'. See further 1966 YBILC vol. II, at 268; Malawer, 'Imposed Treaties', at 158–9, commenting on the unhappy 'reference to' formula.

49 Sir Humphrey Waldock, *Second Report on the Law of Treaties*, 1963 YBILC vol. II, at 36, 52, quoted by Yoram Dinstein, *War, Aggression and Self-Defence* 38 (3rd edn, 2001).

50 Waldock, *Second Report on the Law of Treaties*, at p. 36.

51 The status of peace treaties terminating civil wars is a separate, equally problematic issue. See Christine Bell, 'Peace Agreements: Their Nature and Legal Status', 100 Am. JIL 373–412 (2006). On the prevalence of peace agreements in general see Lotta Harbom, Stina Högbladh and Peter Wallensteen, 'Armed Conflict and Peace Agreements', 43 J. Peace Res. 617–31 (2006).

52 Similar Bothe, 'Consequences of the Prohibition', at 513, who proposes that only such treaties are 'procured' by the threat or use of force if they were 'directly intended to bring about the treaty or if the treaty is aimed at maintaining a situation which was created by an illegal use of force'.

and there is certainly merit to the point that some treaties, even peace treaties, should not acquire the approval of law. The 1938 Munich agreement was void, all can agree. But there is further investigation needed under what conditions withholding approval makes sense.[53] There is some leeway for a more calibrated approach under the UN Charter by arguing that some settlements, however imperfectly negotiated, are forged along the lines of conflict prevention and quasi-Chapter VII authorisation described in chapter 8. More than in other scenarios, an *ex post facto* approval is plausible.[54] UN Charter goals are met under more informal terms to provide practical means to terminate hostilities.[55] Evidently, in applying military pressure against Yugoslavia in the mid-1990s to engineer the Dayton agreement, many could be convinced that it did serve a just cause, and indeed, applying the criteria of Security Council legitimising fleshed out earlier, there is reason to support the application of the principle *pacta sunt servanda.* Formally, however, resolutions 1244 (Kosovo) and 687 (Iraq) are the only instances where the Security Council in effect imposed peace treaties.[56]

There is also the question, barely contemplated, whether article 52 through customary law does not apply to treaty-akin situations, that is, whenever concessions procured by the threat of force have legal significance. As discussed earlier, the 'consent' for military occupation procured by the threat of force does not pardon the breach of article 2(4).[57] The suppression of unilateral declarations is another, less clear

[53] A consideration that occupied writers as early as Grotius and Vattel. See the Harvard commentary to the *Draft Convention on the Law of Treaties*, at 1148–51. It begins: 'Writers on international law appear to be unanimous in the opinion that, *with the possible exception* of treaties of peace which are often imposed by a victorious belligerent upon a State which has been defeated in war, freedom of consent by the parties is an essential condition of the validity of a treaty' (emphasis added).

[54] The *League Covenant* expressly reserved the League Assembly the 'advisory' authority to revise treaties 'whose continuance might endanger the peace of the world' in article 19. The UN General Assembly is said to have retained that authority, and more so of course the Security Council. See Malawer, 'Imposed Treaties', at 42–51, 107–15.

[55] Malawer, 'Imposed Treaties', at 156–8.

[56] 1244 (10 Jun 1999); S/RES/ 687 (8 Apr. 1991); Thomas M. Franck, 'Lessons of Kosovo', 93 Am. JIL 857–60 (1999). The number of peace agreements that the UN Security Council *helped to negotiate* or *endorsed ex post facto* is significantly larger; for an up-to-date list of peace agreements concluded since 1989 see US Institute of Peace, http://www.usip.org/library/pa.html.

[57] See above, chapter 1, p. 18; Ian Brownlie, *International Law and the Use of Force by States* 88, 410–23 (1963); for details see George Nolte, *Eingreifen auf Einladung: Zur völkerrechtlichen Zulässigkeit des Einsatzes fremder Truppen im internen Konflikt auf Einladung*

example. It is a controversial issue with regard to entities such as Taiwan, whose status under international law remain ambiguous for the very reason that military intervention is the Damocles sword for all political flirting with formal independence. At issue is a much broader item, the legal maxim *ex injuria non jus oritur* – a right cannot arise from a wrong.[58] There, too, enquiry is warranted.

Lessons for the regime of force

The above sections suggest that the main pillars of the UN Charter and states' subsequent practices fall into place with a 'natural' conception of social order that overall favours cooperation over confrontation; in this regard customary law is probably identical to the UN Charter law. Law and social order pay tribute to one another, intricately interwoven and complexly self-arranged to form a stable whole. In Robert Jervis' definition, a security regime is the set of 'those principles, rules and norms that permit nations to be restrained in their behavior in the belief that others will reciprocate'.[59] Article 2(4) of the UN Charter fulfils these conditions. It embodies, in the final analysis, the communal insight that the pursuit of short-term interests by confrontation is potentially self-destructive. The UN Charter's security regime does not, therefore, stand or fall with action or inaction of the Security Council.

The role of international law, and in particular of the no-threat rule in times of crisis, is more subtle. If ranchers and landowners of Shasta County provide any viable lesson for the international world, the promotion of cooperation is achieved by maintaining a close-knit society, where states' best strategy – for legal, ethical or utilitarian reasons – is to rely on the goodwill of each other. The law of the UN Charter, as it is elaborated by states through their practice, helps to structure expectations to that effect and provides a framework of procedures and institutions that will offer avenues for crisis defusing. The dictum of

der Regierung (1999). Specifically on the Stimson doctrine see Stephen C. Neff, *War and the Law of Nations: A General History* 296, 321 (2005); Robert Kolb, *Ius Contra Bellum: Le Droit International Relatif au Maintien de la Paix* Mn. 91–101 (2003).

58 1953 YBILC vol. II, at 148 (H. Lauterpacht); de Jong, 'Coercion in the Conclusion of Treaties', at 244; Bothe, 'Consequences of the Prohibition', at 508. Probably taking different perspectives Bruno Simma, 'NATO, the UN and the Use of Force: Legal Aspects', 10 Eur. JIL 1–22 (1999); Antonio Cassese, '*Ex Iniuria Ius Oritur*: Are We Moving towards International Legitimation of Forcible Humanitarian Countermeasures in the World Community?', 10 Eur. JIL 23–30 (1999).

59 Robert Jervis, 'Security Regimes', 36 Int. Org. 357–78 (1982), at 357.

self-restraint, the possibility to build on stable agreements and the enhanced reference function of clearly formulated and workable rules appear most relevant. In advocating any changes to the law of force, one should consider carefully how these expectations are transformed to impair or improve informal cooperation.[60]

At the same time, it is necessary to see the limits of what law can do. The UN Charter is no sprinkling of holy water for the security worries of governments. For these worries to fade, and thus to render threats obsolete in the eyes of decision-makers, the ordering ideas of the international system need to undergo substantial reconfiguration. Some changes are taking place: the age of territorial conquest is over; the notion of balance of power has been in decline; human rights and accompanying notions of justice are gaining momentum; the number of democracies has increased. But international law cannot, for example, make unequal powers equal such that the tit-for-tat strategy will lead to workable results (and one cannot be sure whether that would really follow). All it can do, to follow up on the example, is lay the groundwork for equality and, as such, the concepts of universality and equality of states are assets in providing the vehicle for cooperation to succeed and for states gradually to lower their guard.

[60] Robert Axelrod and Robert O. Keohane, 'Achieving Cooperation under Anarchy: Strategies and Institutions', 38 World P. 226–54 (1985), at 234.

Annex

Threats of force 1945–2003

Table 1. *Threats of force 1945–2003 in chronological order*[1]

ICB	Crisis	Duration	Events	Type	PR
111	Turkish Straits†	1946	The USSR demanded a revised international regime for the Turkish straits, underlined by naval manoeuvres in the Black Sea and troop concentrations in the Caucasus. The USA responded in kind.	B	2
115	Marshall Plan	1947	The USSR delivered an ultimatum calling upon Czechoslovakia to rescind its acceptance to participate in the Marshall Plan talks in Paris.	A	2
123	Berlin Blockade	1948–49	After the Western Allies had announced their plan to integrate their occupation zones in Germany, the USSR erected a blockade sealing off Berlin.	B	2
128	Sinai Incursion†	1948–49	After the Israeli invasion of the Sinai during the Israeli war of independence, the UK issued an ultimatum in response to Egypt's plea for help.	A	2

[1] *Abbreviations*: (A) Explicit threats, excluding counter-threat scenarios; (B) Demonstrations of force, excluding counter-threat scenarios; and (C) Explicit threats or demonstrations of force exclusively in counter-threat scenarios. The type C threats are subdivided in explicit (CA) and demonstrated (CB) types. Protracted conflicts (PR), following Brecher and Wilkenfeld, are characterised by three levels: (1) Non-protracted conflict; (2) Non-long-war protracted conflict; and (3) Long-war protracted conflict. Crises denoted with a (†) are one of the twenty-four cases examined in detail. The names used for the crises in the table may differ from the ones used in the chapters of this book.

Table 1. (*cont.*)

ICB	Crisis	Duration	Events	Type	PR
131	Soviet Bloc–Yugoslavia	1949–51	Displeased with Yugoslavia's independent trajectory under Tito, the USSR issued an ultimatum that was perceived as a possible prelude to invasion and was accompanied by a show of force. Yugoslavia responded with its own military manoeuvres and a forces alert.	CB	1
132	Korean War I†	1950	In response to the North Korean invasion of South Korea, the USA sent troops to repel the attack but also interposed the 7th fleet between Taiwan and the PRC to dissuade a Chinese attack on Taiwan.	CB	3
133	Korean War II†	1950–51	After South Korea's crossing of the 38th parallel, US General MacArthur issued two ultimata against North Korea demanding unconditional surrender. The PRC in turn assured the USA that a crossing of the 28th parallel would bring China into the war.	A	3
135	Punjab War Scare I†	1951	India and Pakistan mirrored troop concentrations along the border to assert their claim over the Punjab.	CB	2
140	Korean War III	1953	In response to and during a new PRC-North Korean offensive, US Secretary of State Dulles threatened the PRC with the possible use of tactical nuclear weapons to break the deadlock in Korea, and, once an armistice was signed, to deter any resumption of the war.	A	3
142	Trieste II	1953	Upon the announcement of Allied plans to withdraw troops from Trieste and leave it to Italian governance, Yugoslavia underlined its protest by calling its military reserves and moving warships to the area.	B	2
145	Dien Bien Phu	1954	Before the fall of the French fort at Dien Bien Phu at the hands of the communist-led Vietminh, France appealed to the USA and the UK for military aid and threatened a strong military response.	CA	2
146	Taiwan Strait I	1954–55	After the PRC's bombing of Quemoy and Matsui and retaliatory Taiwanese air-strikes against the mainland, the USA sent its 7th fleet into the Taiwan Strait. In	CB	2

Table 1. (*cont.*)

ICB	Crisis	Duration	Events	Type	PR
			December 1954 Taiwan and the USA signed a defence pact, leading to another clash and US help in fortifying the two islands.		
152	Suez Nationalisation War	1956–57	Upon proclaiming the nationalisation of the Suez Canal, France and the UK asserted control over the Canal by force in a joint campaign with Israel. Called upon for aid, the USSR declared its willingness to use force if the situation was not rectified, warning that the UK, France and Israel stood under the threat of Soviet nuclear missiles. The three states yielded, while the USA asserted it would not stand by idly in case of an attack.	CA	2
153	Qalqilya	1956	Following the Iraqi statement that it was ready to send troops to Jordan if requested to do so by Jordan, Israel responded by declaring that in such an event it would retaliate. Jordan declared that Iraqi forces would not enter Jordan at that time but would do so if Israel attacked.	CA	2
154	Poland Liberalisation	1956	Worried about internal shifts in Polish leadership, the USSR put divisions on alert and ordered troop movements along the East German border.	B	2
166	Taiwan Strait II	1958	Upon the massing of PRC military forces near Quemoy and Matsu and their subsequent bombing, the USA moved its reinforced 7th fleet into the area and strongly implied that it would intervene if Quemoy were invaded, possibly with nuclear weapons. In return, the USSR stated that an attack on the PRC would be seen as an attack on the USSR.	CA	2
168	Berlin Deadline	1958–59	The USSR underlined its proposal for the future of West Berlin with the assurance that a Western attempt to force its way into the city by land would lead to war.	A	2
173	Rottem	1960	Tipped off by the USSR about supposed troop build-ups, Egypt began secret troop manoeuvres across the Suez Canal, which were mirrored by Israel.	CB	2

Table 1. (*cont.*)

ICB	Crisis	Duration	Events	Type	PR
178	Central America–Cuba II	1960	An exile invasion of Nicaragua was said to originate from Cuba. The latter protested against US naval presence in the area, in support of Nicaragua.	B	1
180	Pathet Lao Offensive	1961	An offensive by Pathet Lao troops prompted the USA to warn the USSR and North Vietnam that support for the offensive would increase the probability of war. US forces were subsequently ordered into Laos. Thai forces were readied to repel an attack by the Pathet Lao.	CB	2
181	Bay of Pigs	1961	During an attempted invasion of Cuba by US-trained exiles, the USSR warned the USA of a possible chain reaction and reasserted Soviet support to Cuba to repel the attack. The USA in turn declared that it would act to protect the hemisphere in case of military intervention by an outside force.	CA	2
183	Kuwait Independence	1961	Upon the granting of independence by the UK to Kuwait, Iraq threatened military action to nullify Kuwait's independence on the basis that it was an integral part of Iraq. Kuwait called on the UK for help, which rapidly built up a military presence.	CA	2
190	Goa II†	1961	India had persistently demanded the end of Portugal's rule over Goa. Prior to Indian troops entering Goa, Portugal protested against an Indian military build-up and the imminence of an attack to the UN Security Council.	B	1
192	Taiwan Strait III	1962	Alarmed by Taiwanese announcements of an invasion of the mainland, supposedly with US support, the PRC responded with a troop build-up in Fukien province.	CB	2
196	Cuban Missiles	1962	The USA imposed a maritime blockade against Soviet shipments bound for Cuba after learning about a secret nuclear missiles programme on the island. The USA indicated eventually that time was running out and that it would take the missiles out by force if they were not dismantled.	A	2

Table 1. (*cont.*)

ICB	Crisis	Duration	Events	Type	PR
202	Cyprus I	1963–64	In response to announced Cypriot plans to change the newly independent state's Constitution in ways seen by Turkey to disadvantage the Turkish minority on the island, Turkey threatened to intervene in Cyprus if the Constitution was altered in any way. Troop deployments followed after an outbreak of fighting between Greek and Turkish Cypriots. Greece pledged itself to intervene if Turkey did so. Several threats were subsequently exchanged along with clashes.	CA	2
216	Kashmir II†	1965–66	A Pakistani-instigated uprising in Kashmir led to forceful exchanges with India and an eventual Indian invasion of Pakistan. During the war, the PRC issued an ultimatum against India that unless it dismantled all military bases near the Chinese border and stopped all incursions into China, it would intervene.	A	2
218	Rhodesia's UDI	1965–66	Zambia gave white-dominated Rhodesia a final warning not to declare independence unilaterally. The communal response was one of non-recognition of Rhodesia.	A	2
222	Six Day War	1967	In response to force mobilisations, the withdrawal of UNEF troops from Sinai and an Egyptian blockade of the port of Eilat, Israel launched a pre-emptive strike against Egypt. Egypt retaliated, and Jordan and later Syria also became involved. The USSR responded by threatening action unless Israel halted operations at once. The USA responded with an immediate order to change the course of its 6th Fleet to the Syrian coast, signalling that it was prepared to resist Soviet intervention.	CB	2
224	Pueblo	1968	Upon the seizure of the *USS Pueblo* by North Korean forces in its territorial waters, the USA called up army and air force reservists and dispatched its aircraft carrier *Enterprise* into the Sea of Japan, demanding the return of the ship and its crew.	CB	2

Table 1. (*cont.*)

ICB	Crisis	Duration	Events	Type	PR
227	Prague Spring†	1968	The invasion of Czechoslovakia was preceded by several warnings by the USSR, reinforced by troop movements along the border.	B	1
231	Ussuri River	1969	During several border clashes between the PRC and the USSR over the Ussuri river, the USSR threatened to bomb China's nuclear facilities situated several thousand miles away in the remote province of Xinjiang.	A	1
233	EC-121 Spy Plane	1969	The North Korean shooting down of a US reconnaissance plane triggered a crisis for the USA, which subsequently deployed a strong naval force into the Sea of Japan.	B	2
234	Shatt-Al-Arab II†	1969–75	Iraq regarded the Shatt-al-Arab as part of its territory and requested ships flying Iran's flag to lower their flag when entering the estuary. Furthermore, no Iranian nationals were to be aboard. If the demands were not met, Iraq would use force. Iran warned that any violation of Iran's sovereign rights would be met with full retaliation, concentrating its forces and putting its navy on full alert, an action mirrored by Iraqi forces.	CA	2
242	Bangladesh	1971	The secession of East Pakistan to become the state of Bangladesh put India and Pakistan at war. Both the USA and the USSR moved their military in symbolic support of their respective allies.	B	2
254	Cod War I	1973	Iceland's unilateral extension of its territorial waters was detrimental to UK fishing interests. The UK responded to firing on British trawlers with the dispatch of Royal Navy ships. At Iceland's request, the USSR engaged in a special naval exercise as a warning signal to the UK.	CB	1
255	October–Yom Kippur War	1973–74	During the Yom Kippur war, both the USSR and the USA declared their readiness to intervene with force, including nuclear force, to defend their allied states. Both also positioned their military strategically. The USSR	CA	2

Table 1. (*cont.*)

ICB	Crisis	Duration	Events	Type	PR
			delivered an ultimatum to the USA to make Israel stop its military actions in Suez.		
259	Mayaguez	1975	A US-registered cargo ship, the *Mayaguez*, was seized off Cambodian coastal waters by the Khmer Rouge. Following demands for the return of the ship and crew and the unsuccessful threat to use force if necessary, the USA intervened militarily.	CA	2
261	Moroccan March†	1975–76	Morocco threatened to march 350,000 civilians into Western Sahara for its annexation, and to use force if it encountered resistance.	A	3
262	Belize I	1975	A movement of troops and patrol boats near the Belize border and a declaration by Guatemala that it intended to annex Belize led the UK (as colonial power) to dispatch additional forces to strengthen the British garrison in Belize.	CB	1
266	Uganda Claims†	1976	Ugandan claims to Kenyan territory caused a crisis for Kenya. Uganda stated that it would consider engaging Kenya in a war in order to recover disputed territory.	A	1
269	Iraq Threat	1976	An Iraqi troop concentration on its border with Syria caused a crisis for Syria, which was engaged in the Lebanese civil war. Syria responded by moving a military division from the Golan Heights to the Iraqi border.	CB	1
272	Aegean Sea I†	1976	The Greek-Turkish dispute over the Aegean continental shelf flared up with a Turkish vessel prospecting for oil. Greece threatened military retaliation if Turkey violated its jurisdiction in the Aegean and proceeded with a significant forces deployment, while Turkey accompanied its vessel with a minesweeper and military aircraft.	CA	2
274	Poplar Tree	1976	After a scuffle between forces of the UN Command and the North Korean army, US soldiers were killed in the attempt to prune a poplar tree along the DMZ. The USA demanded that the DPRK accept	CB	2

Table 1. (*cont.*)

ICB	Crisis	Duration	Events	Type	PR
			responsibility for the casualties, pledge non-repetition, and punish those who perpetrated the attack, supporting its demand with a series of visible military measures and placing its forces on a Defcon 3 state of alert. 'Operation Paul Bunyan' resulted in a massive show of force for a group of soldiers pruning a poplar tree.		
275	Syria Mobilisation	1976	As Syrian forces pushed toward southern Lebanon as part of its intervention in that country's civil war, Israel responded by concentrating infantry and tanks along its northern border with Lebanon.	CB	2
279	Belize II	1977	Guatemalan claims to Belize caused a second crisis for the UK. Guatemalan troops were deployed to the Belize border area, and reservists were called up, following which the UK dispatched air, infantry, and naval forces to within two miles of Guatemala's border to dissuade an attack.	CB	1
287	Beagle Channel I	1977–78	Chile and Argentina contested the ownership of three islands in the Beagle channel, resulting, after unfruitful negotiation, in mutual preparations for a military confrontation.	CB	1
294	Nicaragua Civil War II	1978–79	Fighting broke out between Nicaragua and Costa Rica after an alleged invasion by Costa Rican guerrilla forces aimed against Nicaragua's dictator Samosa. During the course of hostilities, Somoza threatened to invade Costa Rica if it continued to assist the guerrillas.	CA	1
295	Beagle Channel II	1978–79	The second Beagle Channel crisis was triggered by Argentina's call-up of 50,000 reservists. To this and troop movements, with minor clashes, Chile responded by sending troops to the border and cancelling naval manoeuvres with the USA and Peru. Later Chile put 45,000 troops on full alert.	CB	1
297	Angola Invasion Scare	1978	Reports of a South African troop build-up and of an invasion triggered a crisis for	CB	2

Table 1. (*cont.*)

ICB	Crisis	Duration	Events	Type	PR
			Angola. Angola responded with a general mobilisation of the Angolan army.		
309	US Hostages Iran	1979–81	The Iranian students hostage taking of US embassy personnel triggered a crisis for the USA. An initial response included US and British naval manoeuvres in the Arabian Sea.	B	1
310	Colombia–Nicaragua†	1979–81	Colombia rejected negotiations with Nicaragua over longstanding competing claims to the San Andrés Archipelago and reinforced bases in and around the San Andrés Islands and deployed three warships and a submarine to the area.	B	1
311	Raid on Gafsa	1980	An incursion by Libyan-trained Tunisian insurgents against installations in Gafsa triggered a crisis for Tunisia. Heeding Tunisia's call, France dispatched three warships and five submarines to patrol off the Tunisian/Libyan coast. Libya later threatened war against France, and its Parliament demanded that France withdraw its 'invasion force' from Tunisia.	CB	1
314	Libya Threat Sadat	1980	Libya's leader Qaddafi proclaimed Libya's 'alliance with the Egyptian people and army in order to topple treason in Egypt' and urged a *jihad* (holy war) against it. Egypt responded by deploying troops to the region bordering Libya, and by re-imposing martial law regulations, steps that Libya claimed were war preparations.	CB	1
315	Solidarity	1980–81	In response to a widespread Polish workers' strike, three Warsaw Pact members concentrated troops on the Polish border, following the lead of the USSR.	B	2
316	Libya–Malta Oil Dispute	1980	Libyan submarines and a frigate began to harass Malta's oil rig, which responded by placing its minuscule air force on alert. Italy intervened, offering military aid and diplomatic support to Malta in exchange for favourable concessions.	B	1
319	Jordan–Syria Confrontation†	1980	Accusing Jordan of breaking ranks with its Arab allies in the conflict with Israel, and of meddling in its internal affairs,	CB	1

Table 1. (*cont.*)

ICB	Crisis	Duration	Events	Type	PR
			Syria moved its armoured units to positions on the Jordanian border. Military confrontation became ominous, when 30,000 Syrians and 24,000 Jordanians, supported by 1,000 tanks, ended up facing each other.		
321	Chad–Libya V	1981	Following the coming into power of a new transitional government in Chad and a large-scale Libyan military intervention, the announcement of the unification of the two countries led to a harsh exchange of verbal threats between Libya and France. France deployed troops and put its Mediterranean fleet on alert.	CA	2
322	Ecuador–Peru Border III	1981	Accusing each other of initiating several minor incidents, Peru and Ecuador closed their border, mobilised their forces, and suspended commercial flights.	B	2
325	Essequibo II	1981–83	As part of the dispute between Venezuela and Guyana over the Essequibo river and an ongoing 'war of words', Guyana, anticipating a possible attack, held a 10-day military exercise named 'Operation Thunderflash'. Several border incidents were also complained of.	B	1
327	Al-Biqa Missiles I	1981	During the Lebanese civil war, Israeli planes shot down two Syrian helicopters, prompting Syria to deploy ground-to-air missiles in Lebanon. As threatened by Israel's Prime Minister, Israeli planes destroyed the Syrian missile bases. The USSR held joint landing manoeuvres with Syrian forces as an indicator of its willingness to intervene if the crisis threatened to overthrow the Syrian regime.	CB	2
330	Gulf of Sidra I†	1981	During exercises of the 6th Fleet in the Gulf of Sidra (Syrte), which were designed to challenge Libya's territorial claim over the gulf, the USA shot down two Libyan aircraft. It warned Libya against retaliation, threatening to use military force if Libya attacked US aircraft or ships. Libya in turn declared that it was ready to defend its territorial waters even if it led to war with the USA 'or a World War III',	B	1

Table 1. (*cont.*)

ICB	Crisis	Duration	Events	Type	PR
			and said it would attack US nuclear bases in the Mediterranean if the USA intruded into the Gulf again.		
331	Operation Protea	1981	A South African 'hot pursuit' operation called 'Protea' into Angola escalated into a full-fledged interstate crisis. Angola responded with general mobilisation and a threat to deploy 20,000 troops to repel the invaders and to use Cuban forces for that purpose.	CB	2
336	Falklands–Malvinas	1982	Argentina warned that, if an agreement on the islands were not reached shortly, Argentina would resort to 'other means' to resolve the dispute. A group of Argentine civilians raised the Argentine flag in South Georgia, later followed by Argentine troops taking control after less than four hours' combat. In response, the UK installed naval blockades and issued an ultimatum that if Argentine naval forces were still within the maritime exclusion zone, they would be subject to attacks. After heavy casualties on both sides, Argentina formally surrendered.	CA	1
340	Libya Threat–Sudan	1983	Tensions between Libya and Sudan escalated with a visible increase in Libya's military presence, notably air power, near Sudan's northern border, perceived in both Khartoum and Cairo as a Libyan plan to overthrow the Sudanese (pro-Western) regime. The USA signalled resolve to support Sudan by dispatching parts of its forces to the area, as did Egypt.	CB	1
344	Able Archer 83	1983	The Soviet Union misinterpreted NATO's most extensive nuclear exercise, 'Able Archer', as a real preparation for a first strike against it, and put its forces on high alert.	B	2
352	Sino–Vietnam Clashes	1984	Coinciding with Vietnam's military offensive against Thailand, the PRC initiated long-range shelling of Vietnam. During several clashes between the two countries, the PRC criticised the USSR for a display of military support for Vietnam through a landing exercise by Soviet sailors on the Vietnamese coast.	CB	2

Table 1. (*cont.*)

ICB	Crisis	Duration	Events	Type	PR
354	Nicaragua MIG-21s†	1984	Assuming that a Soviet cargo ship was en route to Nicaragua carrying fighter jets for the Sandinista regime, the USA increased the number and visibility of military exercises in Honduras, and in general 'flexed its muscles' on land and at sea in Central America. This show of strength and the accompanying hard-line rhetoric were perceived in Managua as signals of an imminent US invasion.	B	2
356	Expulsion of Tunisians	1985	Libya accused Tunisia of participating in an 'imperialist' anti-Libya plot, triggering a crisis for its neighbour. A build-up of Libyan troops near the border with Tunisia – and Egypt – was reported. Tunisian forces were placed on alert to prevent a possible attack by Libya.	B	1
357	Al-Biqa Missiles II	1985–86	Israel shot down two Syrian military aircraft over Lebanon, according to Israel, after Syrian fighters had threatened Israeli planes on reconnaissance missions over Lebanon. Syria responded by redeploying surface-to-air missiles in several areas. Israel, in turn, warned that the it would respond to the missiles 'whatever the cost'.	CB	2
358	Egypt Air Hijacking	1985	The hijacking of an Egyptian Air flight with apparent backing by Libya led Egypt to put its armed forces on alert, along with a military build-up on its border with Libya, and later to conduct an antiterrorist operation against the hijackers in Malta.	CB	1
362	Chad–Libya VII	1986	Expecting a fresh Libyan offensive against Chad, France warned Qaddafi against an invasion. After Libyan-backed rebels renewed their attacks on government forces, French forces were put on alert, and French commandoes and fighter planes were dispatched. Later French aircraft bombed a rebel airstrip at Qadi-Doum.	CB	2
363	Gulf of Sidra II	1986	Responding to the entry into the Gulf of Sidra (Syrte) of three US naval vessels, Libya fired two missiles on US carrier-based planes, prompting the US planes to	CB	1

Table 1. (*cont.*)

ICB	Crisis	Duration	Events	Type	PR
			attack a Libyan missile ship and a corvette, as well as mounting raids on the radar installations of Libyan batteries at Sidra. The USA warned that its forces would take further action against Libya if necessary. Following a bomb attack in a discotheque frequented by US soldiers in West Berlin, US President Reagan authorised air raids on Tripoli and Benghaz.		
369	Contras II	1986	A crisis for Honduras was triggered by a major Sandinista cross-border military operation against contra bases. In response, Honduran planes bombed Sandinista troops in the border area, with the USA providing logistic support. Honduras threatened Nicaragua with force if the Sandinista troops were not withdrawn, while Nicaragua began military manoeuvres along the border.	CA	2
372	Punjab War Scare II	1987	Concerns of both India and Pakistan began to escalate when the adversary's forces did not return to their bases after substantial military exercises along the Indo/Pakistani border. Both increased the number of soldiers concentrated near their border, each side claiming it was part of routine military exercises in the area.	CB	2
376	Aegean Sea III	1987	Turkey's authorised search for oil off the coast of three Greek islands prompted Greece to declare that its armed forces would 'teach the Turks a very hard lesson' if Turkey continued its 'aggressive acts'. Both put their forces on alert, and Turkey asserted that a Greek act to disturb its oil search mission would be countered by 'unhesitating retaliation'.	CA	2
383	Contras III	1988	A major Nicaraguan offensive against contra camps in Honduras led Honduras to appeal for US military assistance. That granted, Honduran fighter planes bombed Nicaraguan troops operating in the border zone, and Honduras's President threatened further land attacks if Nicaragua's troops were not withdrawn.	CA	2

Table 1. *(cont.)*

ICB	Crisis	Duration	Events	Type	PR
384	Spratly Islands I†	1988	A brief naval battle between China and Vietnam led both sides to upgrade their forces and deploy troops to several contested islands and reefs. Military exercises were held and threats were exchanged. Malaysia and Taiwan also adopted a bellicose stance to defend their claim on the islands.	CB	2
386	Rabta controversy†	1988–89	In response to the Lockerbie incident (with Libya as the suspect) and the suspicion of Libya producing chemical weapons at a factory in Rabta, the USA held manoeuvres in the central Mediterranean, near Libya. Its forces shot down Libyan jet fighters over international waters.	B	1
390	Galtat Zemmour II	1989	Following another Polisario attack, Morocco threatened military intervention in Mauritania if Polisario attacks from its territory continued.	CA	2
392	Kashmir III–Nuclear	1990	After Indian police opened fire and killed 50 pro-independence demonstrators in the Vale of Kashmir, Pakistan and India's stand-off reached new heights with the prospect of employing (then still secret) nuclear weapons. Both countries asserted the defence of Kashmir by force.	CA	2
393	Gulf War	1990–91	Upon the Iraqi invasion of Kuwait, the USA began a massive military build-up in the Gulf region to press for Iraq's compliance with UN resolutions demanding Iraq's withdrawal. Iraq threatened to attack Saudi oil fields, unfriendly Arab states and Israel if UN economic sanctions were to 'strangle' Iraq. With UN Security Council approval, a coalition led by the USA expelled Iraq from Kuwait by force.	CA	2
397	Yugoslavia I: Croatia–Slovenia	1991–92	In response to declarations of independence by Croatia and Slovenia, the federal Yugoslav government responded by calling on the Yugoslav National Army (JNA) to intervene. The ensuing war ended with independence for both Croatia and Slovenia. Before EU recognition, Croatia warned that, unless Serbian 'aggression' against Croatia ceased and the JNA withdrew	CA	2

Table 1. (*cont.*)

ICB	Crisis	Duration	Events	Type	PR
			from Croatia by the end of the month, 'all necessary steps' would be taken to protect the new state.		
401	Nagornyy-Karabakh	1991–92	Nagornyy-Karabakh's wish to independence as a Christian enclave of Muslim Azerbaijan led Azerbaijan to mobilise its armed forces. Armenia replied in kind, and heavy fighting resulted. Turkey threatened Armenia that it would intervene militarily if Armenia's territorial gains were not restored to Azerbaijan. Russia responded by pledging military aid to Armenia if its security were threatened.	CA	1
403	Yugoslavia II: Bosnia	1992–95	Upon Bosnia's declaration of independence, fighting broke out between Bosnian Muslims and Croats on one side, the Yugoslav National Army (the JNA) and Bosnian Serbs on the other. NATO, which provided limited military support for UNPROFOR peacekeepers, issued a series of verbal threats of retaliation, particularly after the bombing of Sarajevo.	A	2
405	Sleeping Dog Hill	1992	Myanmar forces, pursuing rebels near the border with Thailand, occupied the strategic Sleeping Dog Hill in Thai territory. Thailand responded by placing its air force on alert and moving troops to the border. Clashes followed.	CB	1
406	Iraq No-Fly Zone	1992	The USA, France and the UK installed no-fly zones in Iraq below the 32nd parallel in order to protect the Shia population of southern Iraq. This was followed by UK, French and US use of jets to enforce the no-fly zones.	A	2
407	Georgia–Abkhazia	1992–93	The newly independent state of Georgia experienced a crisis with Russia during its prolonged civil war against a separatist movement in Abkhazia, with Russia repeatedly threatening forceful intervention.	A	1
411	Haiti Military Regime	1994	In a strong public statement, US President Clinton announced US willingness to use force against Haiti to obtain an agreement with the military junta that	A	1

Table 1. *(cont.)*

ICB	Crisis	Duration	Events	Type	PR
			had overthrown former President Aristide. With UN approval, the USA sent troops and re-established Aristide with minimal violence.		
412	Iraq Troop Deployment-Kuwait†	1994	Iraq warned that it would retaliate if economic sanctions, especially the oil embargo, continued, and ordered a massive military build-up at Kuwait's border. In response, the USA dispatched troops to the area and assured its readiness to defend Kuwait again. Other countries sent more modest forces. Iraq eventually withdrew its troops. The UN Security Council unanimously passed a resolution condemning Iraq's new threat to the Gulf region.	B	2
415	Taiwan Strait IV†	1995–96	Triggered by a private visit of Taiwan's President Lee Teng-hui to the USA, Chinese military manoeuvres and tests peaked with war exercises off the Taiwan coast in anticipation of Taiwan's first democratic presidential elections.	CB	2
417	Aegean Sea IV	1996	Tension between Greece and Turkey renewed as a Turkish cargo boat ran aground on the disputed island of Imia ('Kardack Rocks'). To reverse a civilian raising of the Turkish flag on the island, Greece deployed its marines, upon which Turkey declared that it could not tolerate a Greek flag on a Turkish island. Warships from both sides armed their missiles around Imia as tensions escalated, with fighter jets chasing each other in the sky over the islet.	CB	2
418	Operation Grapes of Wrath	1996	Israel's response to Hezbollah attacks was an air attack on Hezbollah bases in South Lebanon and targets in Beirut. This retaliation, which catalysed the flight of tens of thousands Lebanese from the south towards Beirut, triggered a crisis for Lebanon. Israel demanded that Lebanon prevent Hezbollah attacks against Israel from its territory.	B	2
420	North Korea Submarine†	1996	In response to a North Korean submarine running aground in South Korea, Seoul initiated a large-scale manhunt for the	CA	2

Table 1. (*cont.*)

ICB	Crisis	Duration	Events	Type	PR
			crew. South Korea warned that its armed forces were ready to respond to a military attack. North Korea in turn demanded that the submarine and crew be returned, threatening 'serious consequences' that could include an attack on the South if they were not.		
421	Zaire Civil War	1996–97	Rwandan and Zaire militias clashed in the course of a rebellion in east Zaire. In the course of events, Rwanda deployed troops to eastern Zaire and warned that it was ready to fight Zaire 'if Zaire brings the war to us'.	CA	1
422	UNSCOM I	1997–98	After Iraq expelled all US inspectors working with UNSCOM, the USA responded with rapid mobilisation of forces in the Persian Gulf and worked to gain support for a military strike against Iraq. While the UK agreed, the other permanent members of the UN Security Council did not. After the negotiation of a 'memorandum of understanding', the USA noted that it would continue to exert military pressure on Iraq until it complied fully with the terms of the new agreement.	A	2
423	Cyprus–Turkey Missile†	1998	Cyprus announced its purchase of Russian surface-to-air missiles. Turkey threatened air strikes if the missiles were installed, which prompted Greece to declare its readiness to intervene to assist Cyprus.	A	2
425	Pakistan Nuclear Tests	1998	India's nuclear tests prompted Pakistan's own nuclear testing shortly after. The crisis terminated when Pakistan announced a unilateral moratorium.	CB	2
427	US Embassy Bombings	1998	The embassy bombings in Nairobi, Kenya, and Dar es Salam, Tanzania, led the USA to demand that Osama bin Laden, suspected chief planner of the attacks, be handed over to them by the Afghan Taliban regime. After denial of that request, the USA launched air strikes against targets in Afghanistan and Sudan.	CA	1

Table 1. (*cont.*)

ICB	Crisis	Duration	Events	Type	PR
428	Syria–Turkey	1998	Turkey issued a 45-day ultimatum against Syria to extradite Kurdish rebel leader Abdullah Öcalan and close down PKK camps in Syria and Lebanon. Turkey had previously declared a right to retaliate against Syria for its 'hostile attitude despite all warnings and efforts and that our patience is about to be exhausted' and had mobilised troops along the Syrian border.	A	1
429	UNSCOM II Operation Desert Fox	1998	After Iraq announced it would stop all cooperation with UNSCOM followed by a short-lived return to cooperation, the USA maintained that it would launch an unannounced military strike if Saddam Hussein violated his latest commitment to work with UNSCOM, a promise that the USA and UK lived up to with a series of air strikes on Iraq.	A	2
430	Kosovo†	1999	NATO issued an ultimatum against Yugoslavia demanding the signing of the proposed Rambouillet agreement to terminate the genocidal crackdown by the Serbs against the ethnic Albanians in Kosovo.	A	2
434	USA–Afghanistan	2001	Following the 9/11 terrorist attacks in the USA, the USA and the UK pledged to take action against all states harbouring or supporting terrorist activities. After a significant military build-up and an unsuccessful ultimatum to hand over prime suspect Osama bin Laden, US and UK forces invaded Afghanistan.	CA	1
435	Indian Parliament Attack	2001–02	After a terrorist attack in India's Parliament, which India ascribed to Pakistani militants, both India and Pakistan placed their military forces on a heightened alert status and escalated troop mobilisation along the Line of Control and the border outside Kashmir, each amassing one million soldiers.	CB	2
436	Kaluchak	2002	After Kashmir militants had attacked the Indian army base in Kaluchak, the Indian government undertook a massive mobilisation of troops along the Line of Control. It announced that it would not negotiate with Pakistan until Pakistan	CB	2

Table 1. (*cont.*)

ICB	Crisis	Duration	Events	Type	PR
			took concrete steps to crack down on militants. During this period, Pakistan also mobilised, and cross-border firing escalated with several civilian deaths reported. Pakistan's President Musharraf made a defiant nationwide address where he said that Pakistan did not want war with India but would respond with full force if attacked.		
437	Myanmar–Thailand	2002	Stray mortar rounds fired by Myanmar troops at Shan rebel positions landed inside Thailand, prompting Thailand to warn that its forces would respond in kind if the shelling continued. Thai troops eventually responded by firing warning shots of artillery into Myanmar and, after the shelling from Myanmar continued, firing at Myanmar positions. On the same day, Shan rebels captured four Myanmar bases, and Myanmar blamed Thailand's artillery support for this outcome. It protested the retaliation and threatened military action against Thai forces.	CA	1
439	Iran Nuclear	2002–	Controversy over Iran's nuclear weapons programme increased with Iranian statements in October 2005 that Israel must be 'wiped off the map' and, in March 2006, that those who wanted to 'violate the rights of the Iranian nation will quickly regret their actions'. The latter declaration followed a day after US Vice-President Dick Cheney had alluded to 'meaningful consequences' if Iran continued with its uranium enrichment activities. At the time of writing, the crisis has not yet come to an end.	CA	1
440	Pankisi Gorge	2002	In September 2002, Russia's President Putin promised military action against Georgia if it did not suppress Chechen rebel activities, particularly those hiding in the Pankisi valley. Georgia referred to the statement as an undisguised threat of force.	A	1
441	Iraq Regime†	2002–03	After repeated warnings, troop concentration in the Persian Gulf and an eventual ultimatum against Saddam Hussein to disarm and give up control	A	2

Table 1. (*cont.*)

ICB	Crisis	Duration	Events	Type	PR
			of Iraq, mainly the USA and the UK launched 'Operation Enduring Freedom', an invasion of Iraq. The UN Security Council had partly endorsed pressure against Iraq through resolution 1441.		
440	North Korea Nuclear II	2002–	Signs that North Korea was continuing its nuclear programme triggered a crisis for the USA and both Koreas. North Korea threatened to renege on the 1953 armistice that ended the Korean War. Four of its jet fighters intercepted a US reconnaissance aircraft in international airspace. The USA bolstered its force in the region by deploying 24 long-range bombers to Guam. US President Bush threatened to use force if diplomacy failed, and North Korea test-fired cruise missiles and a first nuclear bomb.	CB	2
443	Haifa Suicide Bombing	2003	A suicide bomb attack in Haifa by Islamic Jihad prompted Israel to conduct (widely condemned) air strikes against suspected terrorist camps near Damascus. Lending no credibility to the claim that the target had been a Palestinian refugee camp, Israel warned Syria that if it continued to protect terrorist organisations preparing attacks against Israel, Israel would carry out further strikes.	B	2

Source: Michael Brecher and Jonathan Wilkenfeld, *A Study of Crisis* (1997), updated to version 6.0 of January 2006 (http://www.cidcm.umd.edu/icb/). Out of 335 international crises between October 1945 and December 2003, a total of 111 (33.1 per cent) met the case definitions of chapter 4.

Protracted conflicts 1918–2003

Table 2. *Protracted conflicts 1918–2003 by region*

ICB no	Protracted conflict	Duration start-end	Number of int'l crises	In case studies[1]
	Africa			
1.	Angola	1975–88	11	
2.	Chad/Libya	1971–94	8	
3.	Ethiopia/ Somalia	1960–	6	
4.	Rhodesia	1965–80	11	
5.	Western Sahara	1975–	10	261
	Americas			
6.	Costa Rica/ Nicaragua	1918–55	3	
7.	Ecuador/Peru	1935–	5	
8.	Honduras/ Nicaragua	1937–	6	
	Asia			
9.	Afghanistan/ Pakistan	1949–	3	
10.	China/Japan	1927–45	5	
11.	China/Vietnam	1978–	4	384
12.	India/Pakistan	1947–	13	135
13.	Indochina	1946–90	18	
14.	Indonesia	1945–99	8	
15.	Korea[2]	1950–	8	133, 420
	Europe			
16.	Czechoslovakia/ Germany	1938–45	3	
17.	Finland/Russia	1919–61	4	
18.	France/Germany	1920–45	5	
19.	Italy/Albania/ Yugoslavia	1921–53	5	
20.	Lithuania/Poland	1920–81	3	
21.	Poland/Russia	1920–81	4	
33.	Yugoslavia[3]	1991–99	3	429
	Middle East			
23.	Arab/Israel	1947–	27	128
24.	Iran/Iraq	1959–	7	234
25.	Iraq/Kuwait	1961–	5	412
26.	Yemen	1962–79	6	

Table 2. (*cont.*)

ICB no	Protracted conflict	Duration start-end	Number of int'l crises	In case studies
	Multiregional			
27.	East/West	1918–89	21	111, 354
28.	Greece/Turkey	1920–	11	272, 423
29.	Iran/USSR	1920–46	4	
30.	Taiwan Strait	1948–	5	132, 415
31.	World War II	1939–45	24	
32.	Iraq Regime	1992–	5	439
Total			**259**	**16**

Source: Michael Brecher and Jonathan Wilkenfeld, *A Study of Crisis* (1997), at p. 821, and updated to version 6.0 of January 2006, covering the period 1918 to 2003 (http://www.cidcm.umd.edu/icb/). Out of 443 international crises identified in that period, 259 (58.5 per cent) are embedded in a total of 32 protracted conflicts. Sixteen out of twenty-four (two-thirds) of the case studies describe protracted conflicts.

[1] The 'In case studies' column denotes the ICB crisis number of the cases included in the present study.

[2] There is one deviation from the ICB database with regard to crisis 132 (Korean War I). In this table, crisis 132 was classified as belonging to the Taiwan protracted conflict cluster and not to Korea, as the threat in question was concerned with cross-Strait relations.

[3] In lieu of the Spanish Civil War. The new version of the ICB database underwent a change of coding.

Bibliography

Author's note: to save space, the bibliography is limited to books and journal articles cited in the text. It omits official sources, media reports and articles.

Abdulghani, J. M., *Iraq & Iran: The Years of Crisis* (Croom Helm, 1984).

Achen, Christopher H., and Duncan Snidal, 'Rational Deterrence Theory and Comparative Case Studies', 41 World P. 143–69 (1989).

Acheson, Dean, *Present at the Creation: My Years in the State Department* (Norton, 1969).

Akehurst, Michael, 'The Hierarchy of Sources of International Law', 47 Brit. YBIL 273–85 (1974–5).

'Custom as a Source of International Law', 47 Brit. YBIL 1–53 (1976).

Alexandrov, Stanimir A., *Self-Defense Against the Use of Force in International Law* (Kluwer Law International, 1996).

Allain, Jean and John R. W. D. Jones, 'A Patchwork of Norms: A Commentary on the 1996 Draft Code of Crimes Against Peace and Security of Mankind', 8 Eur. JIL 100–17 (1997).

Amer, Ramses, 'The United Nations' Reactions to Foreign Military Interventions', 31 J. Peace Res. 425–44 (1994).

Amin, S. H., 'The Iran-Iraq Conflict: Legal Implications', 31 Int. & Comp. LQ 167–88 (1982).

Ando, Nisuke *et al.* (eds.), *Liber Amicorum Judge Shigeru Oda* (Kluwer Law International, 2002).

Anonymous, 'Future Petroleum Provinces are Many in Gulf of Mexico-Caribbean Area', 78 Oil & Gas J. 216–26 (20 Oct. 1980).

Asrat, Belatchew, *Prohibition of Force Under the UN Charter: A Study of Art. 2(4)* (Iustus, 1991).

Athanasopoulos, Haralambos, *Nuclear Disarmament in International Law* (McFarland & Company, 2000).

Atwood, Susan J., 'From Just War to Just Intervention', 19 New Eng. J. Pub. Pol. 55–75 (2003–4).

Aust, Anthony, *Modern Treaty Law in Practice* (Cambridge University Press, 2000).

Axelrod, Robert, *The Evolution of Cooperation* (Basic Books, 1984).

Axelrod, Robert and Robert O. Keohane, 'Achieving Cooperation under Anarchy: Strategies and Institutions', 38 World P. 226–54 (1985).

Azar, Edward E., Paul Jureidini and Ronald McLaurin, 'Protracted Social Conflict: Theory and Practice in the Middle East', 8 J. Pal. Stud. 41–60 (1978).

Bailey, Sydney D., 'Nonmilitary Areas in UN Practice', 74 Am. JIL 499–524 (1980).

Barker, J. Craig, *International Law and International Relations* (Continuum, 2000).

Bauer, Ekkehard, 'Ultimatum', in Hans-Jürgen Schlochauer (ed.), *Wörterbuch des Völkerrechts* 467–8 (2nd edn, De Gruyter, 1962).

Baxter, R. R., 'Multilateral Treaties as Evidence of Customary International Law', 41 Brit. YBIL 275–300 (1965–6).

Beck, Robert J., 'Munich's Lessons Reconsidered', 14 Int. Sec. 161–91 (1989).

Bederman, David J., 'Collective Security, Demilitarization and "Pariah" States', 13 Eur. JIL 121–38 (2002).

Bell, Christine, 'Peace Agreements: Their Nature and Legal Status', 100 Am. JIL 373–412 (2006).

Bennett, Michael, 'The People's Republic of China and the Use of International Law in the Spratly Islands Dispute', 28 Stan. JIL 425–50 (1992).

Bentwich, Norman and Andrew Martin, *A Commentary on the Charter of the United Nations* (2nd edn, Routledge and Paul, 1951).

Bernhardt, Rudolf, 'Interpretation in International Law', 2 Enc. Pub. IL 1416–26 (1995).

Beverage, Fiona, 'The Lockerbie Affair', 41 Int. & Comp. LQ 907–20 (1992).

Bishop Jr., William W., 'The Corfu Channel Case (Merits)', 43 Am. JIL 558–89 (1949).

Blechman, Barry M. and Tamara Cofman Wittes, 'The Threat and Use of Force in American Foreign Policy Since 1989', in Paul C. Stern (ed.), *International Conflict Resolution after the Cold War* 90–122 (National Academy Press, 2000).

Blix, Hans, *Disarming Iraq* (Pantheon Books, 2004).

Boczek, B. A., 'Peace-time Military Activities in the Exclusive Economic Zone of Third Countries', 19 Ocean Dev. & IL 455–68 (1988).

'Peaceful Purposes Provisions of the United Nations Convention on the Law of the Sea', 20 Ocean Dev. & IL 359–89 (1989).

Bodansky, Daniel, '*Non Liquet* and the Incompleteness of International Law', in Laurence Boisson de Chazournes and Philippe Sands (eds.), *International Law, the International Court of Justice and Nuclear Weapons* 153–70 (Cambridge University Press, 1999).

Booth, Ken, *Law, Force, and Diplomacy at Sea* (Allen & Unwin, 1985).

Borchard, Edwin, 'The Dumbarton Oaks Conference', 39 Am. JIL 97–100 (1945).

Bothe, Michael, 'Consequences of the Prohibition of the Use of Force: Comments on Arts. 49 and 70 of the ILC's Draft Articles on the Law of Treaties', 27 ZaöRV 507–19 (1967).

'Friedenssicherung und Kriegsrecht', in Wolfgang Graf Vitzthum (ed.), *Völkerrecht* 589–667 (3rd edn, Walter de Gruyter, 2004).
Bourquin, Maurice, 'Le Problème de La Sécurité Internationale', 49 Rec. des Cours, vol. III, 473–542 (1934).
Bowett, Derek W., *Self-Defence in International Law* (Praeger, 1958).
'International Incidents: New Genre or New Delusion?', 12 Yale JIL 386–95 (1987).
Bracken, Paul, 'Mobilization in the Nuclear Age', 3 Int. Sec. 74–93 (1978–9).
Brecher, Michael, 'State Behavior in International Crises: A Model', 23 J. Conf. Resol. 446–80 (1979).
Brecher, Michael and Jonathan Wilkenfeld, *A Study of Crisis* (University of Michigan Press, 1997).
Breidlid, Anders, Fredrik Chr. Brogger *et al.*, *American Culture: An Anthology of Civilization Texts* (Routledge, 1996).
Brodie, Bernard (ed.), *The Absolute Weapon: Atomic Power and World Order* (Harcourt, 1946).
Brodie, Bernard, 'Implications for Military Policy', in Bernard Brodie (ed.), *The Absolute Weapon: Atomic Power and World Order* 70–110 (Harcourt, 1946).
Brosche, Harmut, *Zwang Beim Abschluss Völkerrechtlicher Verträge* (Duncker & Humblot, 1974).
Brownlie, Ian, *International Law and the Use of Force by States* (Clarendon Press, 1963).
Burroughs, John, *The (Il)legality of Threat or Use of Nuclear Weapons: A Guide to the Historic Opinion of the International Court of Justice* (Lit, 1997).
Butler, Nicholas Murray, *Across the Busy Years: Recollections and Reflections*, 2 vols. (Scribner, 1939–40).
Butterton, Glenn R., 'Signals, Threats, and Deterrence: Alive and Well in the Taiwan Strait', 47 Cath. ULR 51 (1997).
Buzzini, Gionata Piero, 'Les Comportements Passifs des États et leur Incidence sur la Réglementation de l'Emploi de la Force en Droit International Général', in Enzo Cannizzaro and Paolo Palchetti (eds.), *Customary International Law on the Use of Force: A Methodological Approach* 79–117 (Martinus Nijhoff, 2005).
Byers, Michael, 'Response, Taking the Law Out of International Law: A Critique of the "Iterative" Perspective', 28 Harv. ILJ 201–5 (1997).
Custom, Power and the Power of Rules; International Relations and Customary International Law (Cambridge University Press, 1999).
'Terrorism, the Use of Force and International Law after 11 September', 51 Int. & Comp. LQ 401–14 (2002).
'The Shifting Foundations of International Law: A Decade of Forceful Measures against Iraq', 13 Eur. JIL 21–41 (2002).
book review, 'Recourse To Force: State Action Against Threats And Armed Attacks', 97 Am. JIL 721–5 (2003).

Cahin, Gérard, *La Coutume Internationale et les Organisations Internationales: L'incidence de la Dimension Institutionelle sur le Processus Coutumier* (Editions A. Pedone, 2001).

Calvocoressi, Peter, *World Politics 1945–2000* (8th edn, Pearson Education, 2001).

Cannizzaro, Enzo and Paolo Palchetti (eds.), *Customary International Law on the Use of Force: A Methodological Approach* (Martinus Nijhoff, 2005).

Carter, Ashton B. and William J. Perry, *Preventive Defense: A New Security Strategy for America* (Brookings Institution Press, 1999).

Cassese, Antonio, *Self-determination of Peoples: A Legal Reappraisal* (Cambridge University Press, 1995).

'*Ex Iniuria Ius Oritur*: Are We Moving towards International Legitimation of Forcible Humanitarian Countermeasures in the World Community?', 10 Eur. JIL 23–30 (1999).

Catley, Robert and Makmur Keliat, *Spratlys: The Dispute in the South China Sea* (Ashgate, 1997).

Charney, Jonathan I. and J. R. V. Prescott, 'Resolving Cross-Strait Relations Between China and Taiwan', 94 Am. JIL 453–77 (2000).

Chayes, Abram, *The Cuban Missile Crisis: International Law and the Rule of Law* (Oxford University Press, 1974).

Chemillier-Gendreau, Monique, *Sovereignty Over the Paracel and Spratly Islands* (Kluwer Law International, 2000).

Cheng, Bin, 'United Nations Resolutions on Outer Space: "Instant" Customary Law?', 5 Ind. JIL 23–112 (1965).

Christensen, Thomas C., 'Threats, Assurances, and the Last Chance for Peace: The Lessons of Mao's Korean War Telegrams', 17 Int. Sec. 122–54 (1992).

Chung, Il Yung, *Legal Problems Involved In The Corfu Channel Incident* (E. Droz, 1959).

Churchill, R. R. and A. V. Lowe, *The Law of the Sea* (3rd edn, Manchester University Press, 1999).

Cima, Ronald C., 'Vietnam in 1988: The Brink of Renewal', 29 Asian Surv. 64–72 (1989).

Cimbala, Stephen J., *Coercive Military Strategy* (Texas A&M University Press, 1998).

Coase, Ronald H., 'The Problem of Social Cost', 3 JL & Econ. 1–23 (1960).

Coates, David and Joel Krieger, *Blair's War* (Polity, 2004).

Collier, David and James Mahoney, 'Insights and Pitfalls: Selection Bias in Qualitative Work', 49 World P. 56–91 (1996).

Collier, John and Vaughan Lowe, *The Settlement of Disputes in International Law* (Oxford University Press, 1999).

Corton, Olivier, 'Breach and Evolution of Customary International Law on the Use of Force', in Enzo Cannizzaro and Paolo Palchetti (eds.), *Customary International Law on the Use of Force: A Methodological Approach* 119–44 (Martinus Nijhoff, 2005).

'The Controversies Over the Customary Prohibition on the Use of Force', 16 Eur. JIL 803–22 (2005).

Crawford, James, *International Law as an Open System: Selected Essays* (Cameron May, 2002).

'Negotiating Global Security Threats in a World of Nation States: Issues and Problems of Sovereignty', in James Crawford, *International Law as an Open System: Selected Essays* 95–121 (Cameron May, 2002).

The International Law Commission's Articles on State Responsibility: Introduction, Text and Commentaries (Cambridge University Press, 2002).

The Creation of States in International Law (2nd edn, Oxford University Press, 2006).

Crawford, James and Thomas Viles, 'International Law on a Given Day', in Konrad Ginther *et al.*, *Völkerrecht Zwischen Normativem Anspruch und Politischer Realität: Festschrift für Karl Zemanek zum 65. Geburtstag* 45–68 (Duncker & Humblot, 1994).

D'Amato, Anthony, *The Concept of Custom in International Law* (Cornell University Press, 1971).

Daadler, Ivo H. and Michael E. O'Hanlon, *Winning Ugly: NATO's War to Save Kosovo* (Brookings Institution Press, 2000).

Dahm, Georg, *Völkerrecht*, 2 vols. (W. Kohlhammer, 1960).

Dahm, Georg, Jost Delbrück and Rüdiger Wolfrum, *Völkerrecht*, 2 vols. (2nd edn, de Gruyter, 1988).

Danilovic, Vesna, 'Conceptual and Selection Bias Issues in Deterrence', 45 J. Conf. Resol. 97–125 (2001).

de Chazournes, Laurence Boisson and Philippe Sands (eds.), *International Law, the International Court of Justice and Nuclear Weapons* (Cambridge University Press, 1999).

de Gurmendi, Silva A. Fernández, 'An Insider's View', in Mauro Politi and Giuseppe Nesi (eds.), *The International Criminal Court and the Crime of Aggression* 175–88 (Ashgate, 2004).

de Jong, H. G., 'Coercion in the Conclusion of Treaties: A Consideration of Articles 51 and 52 of the Convention on the Law of Treaties', 15 Neth. YBIL 209–47 (1984).

de Luca, Anthony R., 'Soviet-American Politics and the Turkish Straits', 92 PSQ 503–24 (1977).

Degenhardt, Henry W., *Maritime Affairs – A World Handbook: A Reference Guide to Maritime Organizations, Conventions and Disputes and to the International Politics of the Sea* (Longman Group, 1985).

Delbrück, Jost, 'Proportionality', 3 Enc. Pub. IL 1140–4 (1997).

'Article 24', in Bruno Simma (ed.), *The Charter of the United Nations: A Commentary*, vol. I, 442–52 (2nd edn, Oxford University Press, 2002),

Derpa, Rolf M., *Das Gewaltverbot der Satzung der Vereinten Nationen und die Anwendung Nichtmilitärischer Gewalt* (Athenäum, 1969).

Desjeans, Mary and Peter Clement, 'Soviet Policy Toward Central America', 36 Proc. Acad. PS 223–34 (1987).

Despretz, Patrice, 'Le Droit International et les Menaces d'Intervention de l'OTAN au Kosovo', Act. Droit Int. (Nov. 1998), http://www.ridi.org/adi.

Diehl, Paul F., *A Road Map to War: Territorial Dimensions of International Conflict* (Vanderbilt University Press, 1999).

Dingemann, Rüdiger, *Krisenherde der Welt: Konflikte und Kriege seit 1945* (Westermann, 1996).

Dinstein, Yoram (ed.), *International Law at a Time of Perplexity* (M. Nijhoff, 1989).

War, Aggression and Self-Defence (3rd edn, Cambridge University Press, 2001).

Dorman, Andrew M. and Thomas G. Otte (eds.), *Military Intervention: From Gunboat Diplomacy to Humanitarian Intervention* (Dartmouth, 1995).

Drekonja-Kornat, Gerhard, 'Der Kolumbianisch-Nicaraguanische Streit um den San Andrés-Archipel', 16 Verf. & R. Übersee (1983).

Ellickson, Robert C., 'Of Coase and Cattle: Dispute Resolution Among Neighbors in Shasta County', 38 Stan. LR 623–87 (1986).

Order Without Law: How Neighbors Settle Disputes (Harvard University Press, 1991).

Falk, Richard A., 'Nuclear Weapons, International Law and the World Court: A Historic Encounter', 91 Am. JIL 64–75 (1997).

Fearon, James, 'Counterfactuals and Hypothesis Testing in Political Science', 43 World P. 169–95 (1991).

Threats to Use Force: Costly Signals and Bargaining in International Crises (Berekely, 1992).

'Domestic Audiences and the Escalation of International Disputes', 88 Am. PSR 577–92 (1994).

'Signaling Foreign Policy Interests: Tying Hands Versus Sinking Costs', 41 J. Conf. Resol. 68–90 (1997).

Feinstein, Lee and Anne-Marie Slaughter, 'A Duty to Prevent', 83 F. Aff. 136–51 (2004).

Ferencz, Benjamin B., 'Defining Aggression: Where it Stands and Where it's Going', 66 Am. JIL 491–508 (1972).

Defining International Aggression: The Search for World Peace; A Documentary History and Analysis, 2 vols. (Oceana Publications, 1975).

'Aggression', 1 Enc. Pub. IL 58–65 (1992).

Ferrell, Robert H., *Peace in Their Time: The Origins of the Kellog-Briand Pact* (New Haven: Yale University Press, 1952).

Fitzmaurice, Sir Gerald, 'The Law and Procedure of the International Court of Justice: Treaty Interpretation and Certain Other Treaty Points', 28 Brit. YBIL 1–28 (1951).

Fitzmaurice, Malgosia A., 'The Corfu Channel Case and the Development of International Law', in Nisuke Ando *et al.* (eds.), *Liber Amicorum Judge Shigeru Oda*, vol. I, 119–46 (Kluwer Law International, 2002).

Franck, Thomas M., 'Who Killed Article 2(4)? or: Changing Norms Governing the Use of Force by States', 64 Am. JIL 809–37 (1970).

'The Stealing of the Sahara', 70 Am. JIL 694–721 (1976).

'Of Gnats and Camels: Is there a Double Standard at the United Nations?', 78 Am. JIL 811–33 (1984).
Nation Against Nation: What Happened to the UN Dream and What the US Can Do About It (Oxford University Press, 1985).
'Legitimacy in the International System', 82 Am. JIL 705–59 (1988).
The Power of Legitimacy Among Nations (Oxford University Press, 1990).
Fairness in International Law and Institutions (Oxford University Press, 1995).
'Lessons of Kosovo', 93 Am. JIL 857–60 (1999).
Recourse to Force: State Action Against Threats and Armed Attacks (Cambridge University Press, 2002).
'What Happens Now? The United Nations After Iraq', 97 Am. JIL 607–20 (2003).
Frost, Robert, *Mending Wall* (Ginn and Company, 1914).
Frowein, Jochen A., *Das de Facto-Regime im Völkerrecht: Eine Untersuchung zur Rechtstellung 'Nichtanerkannter Staaten' und Ähnlicher Gebilde* (Heymanns Verlag, 1968).
Gaddis, John Lewis, *The Long Peace: Inquiries Into the History of the Cold War* (Oxford University Press, 1987).
Gardam, Judith, *Necessity, Proportionality and the Use of Force by States* (Cambridge University Press, 2004).
Gardiner, Leslie, *The Eagle Spreads His Claws: A History of the Corfu Channel Dispute and of Albania's Relations with the West 1945–1965* (Blackwood, 1966).
Gardner, Richard N., 'Neither Bush Nor the "Jurisprudes"', 97 Am. JIL 585–90 (2003).
Gazzini, Tarcisio, 'NATO Coercive Military Activities in the Yugoslav Crisis (1992–1999)', 12 Eur. JIL 391–435 (2001).
Geddes, Barbara, 'How the Cases You Choose Affect the Answers You Get: Selection Bias in Comparative Politics', 2 Pol. Analysis 131–50 (1990).
Gelpi, Christopher, 'Crime and Punishment: The Role of Norms in Crisis Bargaining', 91 Am. PSQ 339–60 (1997).
George, Alexander L., *Forceful Persuasion: Coercive Diplomacy as an Alternative to War* (United States Institute of Peace Press, 1993).
George, Alexander L. and Andrew Bennett, *Case Studies and Theory Development in the Social Sciences* (MIT Press, 2005).
George, Alexander L. and William E. Simons (eds.), *The Limits of Coercive Diplomacy* (2nd edn, Westview Press, 1994).
George, Alexander L. and Richard Smoke, *Deterrence in American Foreign Policy: Theory and Practice* (Columbia University Press, 1974).
Gerlach, Axel, *Begriff und Methoden der Intervention im Völkerrecht* (Varia iuris publici, 1967).
Ghebali, Victor-Yves, '*Avaritia et Ambitio* dans les Relations Internationales de l'Entre-guerres: la Gestion des Conflits Internationaux par la Société des Nations', in Michel Porret (ed.) *Guerres et Paix: Mélanges Offerts à Jena-Claude Favez* 715–39 (Georg, 2000).

Gill, Terry D., 'The Law of Armed Attack in the Context of the Nicaragua Case', 1 Hague YBIL 30–58 (1988).
Ginther, Konrad *et al.*, *Völkerrecht Zwischen Normativem Anspruch und Politischer Realität: Festschrift für Karl Zemanek zum 65. Geburtstag* (Duncker & Humblot, 1994).
Gitelson, Susan Aurelia, 'Major Shifts in Recent Ugandan Foreign Policy', 76 Afr. Aff. 359–80 (1977).
Glennon, Michael J., *Limits of Law, Prerogatives of Power: Interventionalism after Kosovo* (Palgrave, 2001).
'Why the Security Council Failed', 82 F. Aff. 16–35 (2003).
'How International Rules Die', 93 Geo. LJ 939–91 (2005).
Gochman, Charles S. and Zeev Maoz, 'Militarized Interstate Disputes 1812–1976: Procedures, Patterns and Insights', 28 J. Conf. Resol. 585–616 (1984).
Goldblat, Jozef, *Arms Control: The New Guide to Negotiations and Agreements* (2nd edn, Sage Publications, 2002).
Gonsiorowski, Miroslas, 'The Legal Meaning of the Pact for the Renunciation of War', 30 Am. PSR. 653–80 (1936).
Goodrich, Leland M., Edvard Hambro and Anne Patricia Simmons, *Charter of the United Nations: Commentary and Documents* (3rd edn, Columbia University Press, 1969).
Gordon, Edward, 'Article 2(4) in Historical Context', 10 Yale JIL 271–8 (1985).
Gray, Christine, 'Bosnia and Herzegovina: Civil War or Inter-State Conflict? Characterization and Consequences', 67 Brit. YBIL 155–97 (1996).
'The Use and Abuse of the International Court of Justice: Cases Concerning the Use of Force After Nicaragua', 14 Eur. JIL 867–905 (2003).
International Law and the Use of Force (2nd edn, Oxford University Press, 2004).
Gray, Colin S., *Military Strategy* (Oxford University Press, 1999).
Greenwood, Christopher, 'International Law and the United States Air Operation Against Libya', 89 WVa LR 933–60 (1986–7).
Grey, Lord Edward, *Twenty-five Years: 1892–1916*, 2 vols. (Frederick A. Stokes Company, 1925)
Gross, Leo, 'The Dispute Between Greece and Turkey Concerning the Continental Shelf in the Aegean', 71 Am. JIL 31–59 (1977).
Grotius, Hugo, *The Law of War and Peace* (Clarendon Press (1925) [1625].
Guicherd, Catherine, 'International Law and the War in Kosovo', 41 *Survival* 19–34 (1999).
Harbom, Lotta, Stina Högbladh and Peter Wallensteen, 'Armed Conflict and Peace Agreements', 43 J. Peace Res. 617–31 (2006).
Harris, D. J., *Cases and Material on International Law* (6th edn, Sweet & Maxwell, 2004).
Harvey, Frank P., 'Practicing Coercion: Revisiting Successes and Failures Using Boolean Logic and Comparative Methods', 43 J. Conf. Resol. 840–71 (1999).
Hemleben, Sylvester John, *Plans for World Peace through Six Centuries* (University of Chicago Press, 1943).

Henkin, Louis, 'The Reports of the Death of Article 2(4) Are Greatly Exaggerated', 65 Am. JIL 544–8 (1971).
How Nations Behave: Law and Foreign Policy (2nd edn, Columbia University Press, 1979).
Herrmann, Richard K. and Vaughn P. Shannon, 'Defending International Norms: The Role of Obligation, Material Interest, and Perception in Decision Making', 55 Int. Org. 621–54 (2001).
Herwig, Holger, Christian Archer *et al.*, *Cassell's World History of Warfare* (University of Nebraska Press, 2003).
Herz, John, 'Idealist Internationalism and the Security Dilemma', 20 World P. 157–80 (1950).
Herzberg, Rolf Dietrich (ed.), *Festschrift für Dietrich Oehler zum 70. Geburtstag* (Carl Heymanns, 1985).
Hickey, Dennis V., 'U.S. Policy and Taiwan's Bid to Rejoin the United Nations', 37 Asian Surv. 1031–43 (1997).
Higgins, Rosalyn, *The Development of International Law Through the Political Organs of the United Nations* (Oxford University Press, 1963).
Problems and Process: International Law and How We Use It (Clarendon Press, 1994).
Hilderbrand, Robert C., *Dumbarton Oaks: The Origins of the United Nations and the Search for Postwar Security* (University of North Carolina Press, 1990).
Hill, Norman, 'Was there an Ultimatum Before Pearl Harbour?', 42 Am. JIL 355–67 (1948).
Hobbes, Thomas, *Leviathan* (Penguin Classics (1968) [1651].
Hoog, Günter, 'Naval Manoeuvres', 3 Enc. Pub. IL 527–8 (1997).
Howard, Michael, 'The United Nations and International Security', in Adam Roberts and Benedict Kingsbury (eds.), *United Nations, Divided World: The UN's Roles in International Relations* 31–45 (Clarendon Press, 1988).
Hoyt, Edwin C., 'The United States Reaction to the Korean Attack: A Study of the Principles of the United Nations Charter as a Factor in American Policy-Making', 55 Am. JIL 45–76 (1961).
Hsiao, Anne Hsiu-An, 'Is China's Policy to Use Force Against Taiwan a Violation of the Principle of Non-Use of Force Under International Law?', 32 New Eng. LR 715–42 (1998).
Hudson, G. F., 'Threats of Force in International Relations', in Martin Wight (ed.), *Diplomatic Investigations: Essays in the Theory of International Politics* 201–5 (1966).
Huisken, Ron, *The Road to War on Iraq* (Strategic Defence Studies Centre, 2003).
Hull, Cordell, *The Memoirs of Cordell Hull*, 2 vols. (Macmillan Co., 1948).
Hume, David, *A Treatise upon Human Nature* (Prometheus Books (1992) [1739].
Huth, Paul K., *Standing Your Ground: Territorial Disputes and International Conflict* (University of Michigan Press, 1996).
Huth, Paul and Bruce Russett, 'What Makes Deterrence Work? Cases from 1900 to 1980', 36 World P. 496–526 (1984).
'Deterrence Failure and Crisis Escalation', 32 Int. Stud. Q. 29–45 (1988).

Institute for the Study of Conflict, *Annual of Power and Conflict 1980–1981* (The Institute, 1981).
Ioannou, Krateros, 'Propaganda', 3 Enc. Pub. IL 1135–8 (1997).
Ipsen, Knut, 'Das "Tokyo Trial" im Lichte des Seinerzeit Geltenden Völkerrechts', in Rolf Dietrich Herzberg (ed.), *Festschrift für Dietrich Oehler zum 70. Geburtstag* 505–15 (Carl Heymanns, 1985).
Völkerrecht (5th edn, C. H. Beck, 2004).
Jackson, Robert H., *Report of Robert H. Jackson, United States Representative to the International Conference on Military Trials, London, 1945*, Dept State Pub. 3080 (1949).
Jennings, Sir Robert Y., 'The Caroline and McLeod Cases', 32 Am. JIL 82–99 (1938).
'What is International Law and How Do We Tell It When We See It?', 37 Schw. Jb. IR 59–88 (1981).
Jentleson, Bruce W., 'The Reagan Administration and Coercive Diplomacy: Restraining More than Remaking Governments', 106 PSQ 57–82 (1991).
Jervis, Robert, *Perception and Misperception in International Politics* (Princeton University Press, 1976).
'Security Regimes', 36 Int. Org. 357–78 (1982).
Jian, Chen, *China's Road to the Korean War: The Making of the Sino-American Confrontation* (Columbia University Press, 1994).
Jie, Chen, 'China's Spratly Policy: With Special Reference to the Philippines and Malaysia', 34 Asian Surv. 893–903 (1994).
Jiménez de Aréchaga, Eduardo, 'International Law in the Past Third of a Century', 159 Rec. des Cours, vol. I, 1–344 (1978).
Johann, Heribert, *Begriff und Bedeutung des Ultimatums im Völkerrecht* (Dunker & Humblot, 1967).
Jones, Daniel M., Stuart A. Bremer and J. David Singer, 'Militarized Interstate Disputes, 1816–1992: Rationale, Coding Rules, and Empirical Patterns', 15 Conf. Mgmt & PS 163–213 (1996).
Jones, J. Mervyn, 'The Corfu Channel Case: Merits', 26 Brit. YBIL 447–53 (1949).
Kagan, Donald, *On the Origins of War and the Preservation of Peace* (Anchor Books, 1995).
Kahn, Hermann, *On Escalation: Metaphors and Scenarios* (Penguin Books, 1965).
Kant, Immanuel, *Zum Ewigen Frieden: Ein Philosophischer Entwurf* (Reclam, 1984) [1975].
Karsten, Peter, Peter D. Howell and Artes Frances Allen, *Military Threats: A Systematic Historical Analysis of the Determinants of Success* (Greenwood Press, 1984).
Kaul, B. M., *The Untold Story* 290–307 (Allied Publishers, 1967).
Kegley Jr, Charles W. and Gregory A. Raymond, 'Normative Restraints on the Use of Force Short of War', 23 J. Peace Res. 213–27 (1986).
Kelly, Patrick J., 'The Twilight of Customary International Law', 40 Va JIL 449–543 (2000).

Kelson, Hans, 'Collective Security and Collective Self-Defense Under the Charter of the United Nations', 42 Am. JIL 783–96 (1948).
Kennedy, Robert F., *Thirteen Days: A Memoir of the Cuban Missile Crisis* (W. W. Norton, 1969).
Keohane, Robert O., *After Hegemony: Cooperation and Discord in the World Political Economy* (Princeton University Press, 1989).
Keylor, William R., *The Twentieth Century World: An International History* (4th edn, Oxford University Press, 2001).
A World of Nations (Oxford University Press, 2003).
Khadiagala, Gilbert M., 'Uganda's Domestic and Regional Security in the 1970s', 31 J Mod. Afr. Stud. 231–55 (1993).
King, Gary, Robert O. Keohane and Sydney Verba, *Designing Social Inquiry: Scientific Inference in Qualitative Research* (Princeton University Press, 1994).
Kirgis, Frederic L., *Prior Consultation in International Law: A Study of State Practice* (University of Virginia Press, 1983).
'North Korea's Withdrawal from the Nonproliferation Treaty', *ASIL Insights* (Jan. 2003), http://www.asil.org/insights/insigh96.htm.
'North Korea's Missile Firings', *ASIL Insights* (Jul. 2006), http://www.asil.org/insights/2006/07/insights060724.html.
Klabbers, Jan, 'International Organizations in the Formation of Customary Law', in Enzo Cannizzaro and Paolo Palchetti (eds.), *Customary International Law on the Use of Force: A Methodological Approach* 179–95 (Martinus Nijhoff, 2005).
Knight, Jonathan, 'American Statecraft and the 1946 Black Sea Straits Controversy', 90 PSQ 451–75 (1975).
Koh, Harold Hongju, 'Why Do Nations Obey International Law?', 106 Yale LJ 2599–659 (1997).
Kohen, Marcelo G., 'The Notion of "State Survival" in International Law', in Laurence Boisson de Chazournes and Philippe Sands (eds.), *International Law, the International Court of Justice and Nuclear Weapons* 293–314 (Cambridge University Press, 1999).
Kolb, Robert, *Ius Contra Bellum: Le Droit International Relatif au Maintien de la Paix* (Helbling & Lichtenhahn, 2003).
Kontou, Nany, *The Termination and Revision of Treaties in the Light of New Customary Law* (Oxford University Press, 1994).
Korbel, Josef, 'The Kashmir Dispute After Six Years', 7 Int. Org. 498–510 (1953).
Koskenniemi, Martti, *From Apology to Utopia* (Cambridge University Press, 1989).
Kritsiotis, Dino, 'The Legality of the 1993 US Missile Strikes on Iraq and the Right of Self-Defence in International Law', 45 Int. & Comp. LQ 162–77 (1996).
Kunz, Josef L., 'Legality of the Security Council Resolutions of June 25 and 27, 1950', 45 Am. JIL 137–42 (1951).
Lai, B., 'The Effects of Different Types of Military Mobilization on the Outcome of International Crises', 48 J. Conf. Resol. 211–29 (2004).

Larson, Arthur, 'The Present Status of Propaganda in International Law', 31 L. & Cont. Prob. 439–51 (1966).

Lauren, Paul Gordon, 'Coercive Diplomacy and Ultimata: Theory in Practice and History', in Alexander L. George and William E. Simons, *The Limits of Coercive Diplomacy* 23–40 (2nd edn, Westview Press, 1994).

Lauterpacht, Elihu, 'River Boundaries: Legal Aspects of the Shatt-al-Arab Frontier', 9 Int. & Comp. LQ 208–36 (1960).

Lauterpacht, Hersch, *The Function of Law in the International Community* (Archon Books, 1933).

'"Resort to War" and the Interpretation of the Covenant During the Manchurian Dispute', 28 Am. JIL 43–60 (1934).

'Restrictive Interpretation and the Principle of Effectiveness in the Interpretation of Treaties', 26 Brit. YBIL 48–85 (1949).

Lebow, Richard Ned and Janice Gross Stein, *We All Lost the Cold War* (Princeton University Press, 1994).

'Deterrence and the Cold War', 110 PSQ 157–81 (1995).

Lee, Todd L. and Paul K. Huth, 'Legitimizing Dispute Settlement: International Legal Rulings as Domestic Political Cover', 100 Am. PSR 219–34 (2006).

Leng, Russell J. and J. David Singer, 'Militarized Interstate Crises: The BCOW Typology and its Applications', 32 Int. Stud. Q. 155–73 (1987).

Leng, Russell J. and Hugh G. Wheeler, 'Influence Strategies, Success, and War', 23 J. Conf. Resol. 655–84 (1979).

Liévano, Enrique Gaviria (ed.), *Nuestro Archipiélago de San Andrés y el Tratado con Nicaragua* (Plaza & Janes, 2001).

Lobel, Jules and Michael Ratner, 'Bypassing the Security Council: Ambiguous Authorizations to Use Force, Cease-Fires and the Iraqi Inspection Regime', 93 Am. JIL 124–55 (1999).

McCoubrey, Hilaire and Nigel D. White, *International Law and Armed Conflict* (Dartmouth, 1992).

McDougal, Myers S. and Florentino P. Feliciano, *Law and Minimum World Order: The Legal Regulation of International Coercion* (Yale University Press, 1961).

MacGibbon, I. C., 'Some Observations on the Part of Protest in International Law', 30 Brit. YBIL 293–319 (1954).

MacMillan, Margaret, *Peacemakers: The Paris Peace Conference and Its Attempt to End War* (John Murray, 2003).

Malawer, Stuart S., 'Imposed Treaties and International Law', Cal. WILJ 115, 156–8 (1977).

Mandel, Robert, 'The Effectiveness of Gunboat Diplomacy', 30 Int. Stud. Q. 59–76 (1986).

Mandelstam, M. André, *L'Interprétation du Pacte Briand-Kellog par les Gouvernements et les Parlaments des Etats Signataires* (Pedone, 1934).

Mayers, David, 'Containment and the Primacy of Diplomacy: George Kennan's Views, 1947–1948', 11 Int. Sec. 124–62 (1986).

Meisler, Stanley, *United Nations: The First Fifty Years* (Atlantic Monthly Press, 1995).
Mercer, Jonathan, *Reputation and International Politics* (Cornell University Press, 1996).
Milivojevic, Marko, 'The Spratly and Paracel Island Conflict', 31 *Survival* 70–7 (1991).
Moore, John B., *A Digest of International Law as Embodied in Diplomatic Discussions, Treaties and Other International Agreements*, 6 vols. (Government Printing Office, 1906).
Morrow, James D., *Game Theory for Political Scientists* (Princeton University Press, 1994).
Mueller, John, *Retreat from Doomsday: The Obsolescence of Major Wars* (Basic Books, 1989).
'Changing Attitudes Towards War: The Impact of the First World War', 21 Brit. JPS 1–28 (1991).
Murphy, Sean D., 'Contemporary Practice of the United States Relating to International Law', 93 Am. JIL 470–501, 628–67, 879–912 (1999).
'Efforts to Address Iraqi Compliance', 96 Am. JIL 956–62 (1999).
'Terrorism and the Concept of Armed Attack in Article 51 of the UN Charter', 43 Harv. ILJ 41–51 (2002).
'Use of Military Force to Disarm Iraq', 97 Am. JIL 419–32 (2003).
Myers, Matthew A., 'Deterrence and the Threat of Force Ban: Does the UN Charter Prohibit Some Military Exercises?', 162 Mil. LR 132–79 (1999).
Nanda, Ved P., and David Krieger, *Nuclear Weapons and the World Court* (Transnational, 1998).
Nathan, James A., *Soldiers, Statecraft, and History: Coercive Diplomacy and the International Order* (Praeger, 2002).
National Secretariate for Information, *The Invasion and Occupation of Goa in the World Press* (The Secretariate, 1962).
Neff, Stephen C., *War and the Law of Nations: A General History* (Cambridge University Press, 2005).
Neuhold, Hanspeter, *Internationale Konflikte: Verbotene und Erlaubte Mittel ihrer Austragung* (Springer Verlag, 1977).
Nolte, George, *Eingreifen auf Einladung: Zur Völkerrechtlichen Zulässigkeit des Einsatzes Fremder Truppen im Internen Konflikt auf Einladung der Regierung* (Springer Verlag, 1999).
Notter, Harley A. (ed.), *Postwar Foreign Policy Preparations 1939–1945* (Department of State Publications, 1949).
Occelli, Maria Benvenuta, '"Sinking" the Caroline: Why the Caroline Doctrine's Restrictions on Self-Defense Should Not be Regarded as Customary International Law', 4 San Diego ILJ 467–90 (2003).
Onuf, Nicholas G., 'Law and Lawyers in International Crises', 29 Int. Org. 1035–53 (1975).
Oppenheim, Lassa, *International Law: A Treatise*, 2 vols. (1st edn, Longman, 1906).
International Law: A Treatise, 2 vols. (7th edn, Longman, 1952).

OSCE, *Kosovo/Kosova, As Seen, as Told: An Analysis of the Human Rights Findings of the OSCE Kosovo Verification Mission* (Oct. 1998–Jun. 1999), http://www.osce.org/kosovo/.

Ostrom, Elinor, *Governing the Commons: The Evolution of Institutions for Collective Action* (Cambridge University Press, 1990).

Otte, Thomas G., 'Of Congress and Gunboats: Military Intervention in the Nineteenth Century', in Andrew M. Dorman and Thomas G. Otte (eds.), *Military Intervention: From Gunboat Diplomacy to Humanitarian Intervention* 19–52 (Dartmouth, 1995).

Owen, Art B., *Empirical Likelihood* (CRC Press, 2001).

Oxman, Bernard H., 'International Law and Naval and Air Operations at Sea', in Horace B. Robertson, Jr (ed.), *The Law of Naval Operations*, 64 US Nav. War CIL Stud. 18–37 (1991).

Paulus, Andreas L. and Jörn Müller, 'Security Council Resolution 1718 on North Korea's Nuclear Test', *ASIL Insights* (Nov. 2006), http://www.asil.org/insights/2006/11/insights061103.html.

Perry, William J., 'Desert Storm and Deterrence', 70 F. Aff. 66–82 (1991).

Peterson, Walter J., 'Deterrence and Compellence: A Critical Assessment of Conventional Wisdom', 30 Int. Stud. Q. 269–94 (1986).

Phillips, Warren and Richard Rimkunas, 'The Concept of Crisis in International Politics', 15 J. Conf. Resol. 259–72 (1978).

Politi, Mauro and Giuseppe Nesi (eds.), *The International Criminal Court and the Crime of Aggression* (Ashgate, 2004).

Polybius, *The Histories*, book 24 (Harvard University Press, 1927) [ca. 150 BC].

Popper, Karl R., *Logik der Forschung* (7th edn, Mohr, 1982) [1934].

Porret, Michel, (ed.) *Guerres et paix: Mélanges offerts à Jena-Claude Favez* (Georg, 2000).

Poundstone, William, *Prisoner's Dilemma: John von Neumann, Game Theory, and the Puzzle of the Bomb* (Oxford University Press, 1992).

Pritchard, John R. and Sonia M. Zaide (eds.), *The Tokyo War Crimes Trial: The Complete Transcripts of the Proceedings of the International Military Tribunal for the Far East* vol. XX, 49582–4 (1981).

Purdum, Todd S., *A Time of Our Choosing: America's War in Iraq* (Times Books/Henry Holt, 2003).

Raab, Dominic, '"Armed Attack" After the Oil Platforms Case', 17 Leid. JIL 719–35 (2004).

Ragazzi, Maurizio, *The Concept of International Obligations* Erga Omnes (Oxford University Press, 1997).

Ramazani, Rouhollah K., *The Persian Gulf: Iran's Role* (University Press of Virginia, 1972).

Randelzhofer, Albrecht, 'Art. 2(4)', in Bruno Simma (ed.), *The Charter of the United Nations: A Commentary*, vol. I, 112–36 (2nd edn, Oxford University Press, 2002).

'Article 51', in Bruno Simma (ed.), *The Charter of the United Nations: A Commentary*, vol. I, 788–806 (2nd edn, Oxford University Press, 2002).

Ratner, Steven R., '*Jus ad Bellum* and *Jus in Bello* after September 11', 96 Am. JIL 905–21 (2002).
'The Gulf of Sidra Incident of 1981: A Study of the Lawfulness of Peacetime Aerial Engagements', 10 Yale JIL 59–77 (1984).
Reisman, W. Michael and Andrew R. Willard (eds.), *International Incidents: The Law That Counts in World Politics* (Princeton University Press, 1988).
Ress, Georg, 'Interpretation', in Bruno Simma (ed.), *The Charter of the United Nations: A Commentary*, vol. I, 13–32 (2nd edn, Oxford University Press, 2002).
Richardson, James L., *Crisis Diplomacy: The Great Powers Since the Mid-Nineteenth Century* (Cambridge University Press, 1994).
Rifaat, Ahmed M., *International Aggression: A Study of the Legal Concept: Its Development and Definition in International Law* (Almqvist & Wiksell International, 1979).
Robel, Richard T., 'The Aegean Sea Continental Shelf Case', 18 Harv. JIL 649–75 (1977).
Roberts, Adam and Benedict Kingsbury (eds.), *United Nations, Divided World: The UN's Roles in International Relations* (Clarendon Press, 1988).
Robertson Jr, Horace B. (ed.), 'The Law of Naval Operations', 64 US Nav. War. CIL Stud. (1991).
Rojahn, Ondolf, 'Naval Demonstration', 3 Enc. Pub. IL 526–7 (1997).
'Ultimatum', 4 Enc. Pub. IL 1006–8 (2000).
Rose, S., 'Naval Activity in the Exclusive Economic Zone: Troubled Waters Ahead', 21 Ocean Dev. & IL 71–103 (1990).
Ross, Robert S., 'The 1995–96 Taiwan Strait Confrontation: Coercion, Credibility, and the Use of Force', 25 Int. Sec. 87–123 (2000).
Rubinoff, Arthur G., *India's Use of Force in Goa* (Popular Prakashan, 1971).
Russell, Bertrand, *Common Sense and Nuclear Warfare* (Simon & Schuster, 1959).
Russell, Ruth B. and Jeannette E. Muther, *A History of The United Nations Charter: The Role of the United States 1940–1945* (Brookings Institution, 1958).
Sadurska, Romana, 'Threats of Force', 82 Am. JIL 239–68 (1988).
St John, Ronald Bruce, *Libya and the United States: Two Centuries of Strife* (University of Pennsylvania Press, 2002).
Sample, Susan G., 'Military Buildups, War, and Realpolitik: A Multivariate Model', 42 J. Conf. Resol. 156–75 (1998).
Sapiro, Miriam, 'Iraq: The Shifting Sands of Preemptive Self-Defence', 97 Am. JIL 599–607 (2003).
Sartori, Anne, 'The Might of the Pen: A Reputational Theory of Communication in International Disputes', 56 Int. Org. 121–49 (2002).
Saxer, Urs, *Kosovo und das Völkerrecht: Ein Konfliktmanagement im Spannungsfeld von Menschenrechten, kollektiver Sicherheit und Unilateralismus* (Basler Schriften zur europäischen Integration, 1999).
Schachter, Oscar, 'The Quasi-Judicial Role of the Security Council and the General Assembly', 58 Am. JIL 960–5 (1964).

'The Twilight Existence of Nonbinding International Agreements', 71 Am. JIL 296–304 (1977).
'The Invisible College of International Lawyers', 72 Nw. ULR 217–26 (1977–8).
'The Right of States to Use Armed Force', 82 Mich. LR 1620–46 (1984).
'Entangled Treaty and Custom', in Yoram Dinstein (ed.), *International Law at a Time of Perplexity* 717–38 (M. Nijhoff, 1989).
'Self-Defense and the Rule of Law', 83 Am. JIL 259–77 (1989).
International Law in Theory and Practice (M. Nijhoff, 1991).
'United Nations Law', 88 Am. JIL 1–23 (1994).
Schelling, Thomas C., *The Strategy of Conflict* (Harvard University Press, 1960).
Arms and Influence (Yale University Press, 1966).
Schlochauer, Hans-Jürgen (ed.), *Wörterbuch des Völkerrechts* (2nd edn, De Gruyter, 1962).
Setear, John K., 'An Iterative Perspective on Treaties: A Synthesis of International Relations Theory and International Law', 37 Harv. ILJ 139–229 (1996).
Seydi, Süleyman, *The Turkish Straits and the Great Powers: From the Montreux Conventions to the Early Cold War 1936–1947* (Isis Press, 2003).
Shaw, Malcolm, *International Law* (5th edn, Cambridge University Press, 2003).
Shawcross, William, *Allies: The U.S., Britain, Europe and the War in Iraq* (Atlantic Books, 2003).
Shen, Jianming, 'Sovereignty, Statehood, Self-determination, and the Issue of Taiwan', 15 Am. UILR 1101 (2000).
Shultz, George P., *Turmoil and Triumph: My Years as Secretary of State* (Maxwell Macmillan, 1993).
Simma, Bruno, 'NATO, the UN and the Use of Force: Legal Aspects', 10 Eur. JIL 1–22 (1999).
(ed.), *The Charter of the United Nations: A Commentary*, 2 vols. (2nd edn, Oxford University Press, 2002).
Sinclair, Ian, *The Vienna Convention on the Law of Treaties* (2nd edn, Manchester University Press, 1984).
Sirriyeh, Hussein, 'Development of the Iraq-Iranian Dispute, 1847–1975', 20 J. Cont. Hist. 483–92 (1985).
Slantchev, Branislav L., 'Military Coercion in Interstate Crises', 99 Am. PSR. 533–47 (2005).
Slaughter, Anne-Marie, 'Chance to Reshape the U.N.', Wash. Post (13 Apr. 2003).
Sofaer, Abraham D., 'International Law and the Use of Force', 4 The Nat. Interest 53–64 (Fall 1988).
'On the Necessity of Pre-emption', 14 Eur. JIL 209–26 (2003).
Southall, Aidan, 'Social Disorganization in Uganda: Before, during, and after Amin', 18 J. Mod. Afr. Stud. 627–56 (1980).
Stanik, Joseph T., *El Dorado Canyon: Reagan's Undeclared War With Qaddafi* (Naval Institute Press, 2003).

Stein, Janice Gross, 'Reassurance in International Conflict Management', 106 PSQ 431–51 (1991).
Stern, Paul C. (ed.), *International Conflict Resolution after the Cold War* (National Academy Press, 2000).
Stevenson, David, 'Militarization and Diplomacy in Europe before 1914', 22 Int. Sec. 125–61 (1997).
Subedi, Surya P., *Land and Maritime Zones of Peace in International Law* (Clarendon Press, 1996).
Szasz, Paul C., 'The Security Council Starts Legislating', 96 Am. JIL 901–5 (2002).
Tams, Christian J., *Enforcing Obligations Erga Omnes in International Law* (Cambridge University Press, 2005).
Taylor, Alan J. P., *The Struggle for Mastery in Europe* (2nd edn, Clarendon Press, 1974).
Tschentscher, Axel, *The Basic Law (Grundgesetz): The Constitution of the Federal Republic of Germany (May 23rd, 1949)* (Jurisprudentia, 2002).
Tuchman, Barbara W., *The Guns of August* (Macmillan, 1962).
Tuck, Richard, *The Rights of War and Peace: Political Thought and the International Order from Grotius to Kant* (Oxford University Press, 1999).
Tulliu, Steve and Thomas Schmalberger, *Coming to Terms with Security: A Lexicon for Arms Control, Disarmament and Confidence-Building* (United Nations Publication, 2004).
Ullmann-Margalit, Edna, *The Emergence of Norms* (Oxford University Press, 1977).
Vagts, Alfred and Detlev Vagts, 'The Balance of Power in International Law: A History of an Idea', 73 Am. JIL 555–80 (1979).
Van Evera, Stephen, 'The Cult of the Offensive and the Origins of the First World War', 9 Int. Sec. 58–107 (1984).
Vasquez, John A., *The War Puzzle* (Cambridge University Press, 1993).
Vattel, Emer de, *Le Droit des Gens ou Principes de la Loi Naturelle, Appliqueé à la Conduite et aux Affaires des Nations et des Souverains* (Londres, 1958) [1758].
Vegetius Renatus, Flavius, *Epitoma Rei Militari* (Clarendon Press, 2004) [390].
Vertzberger, Yaacov Y. I., 'Foreign Policy Decisionmakers As Practical-Intuitive Historians: Applied History and Its Shortcomings', 30 Int. Stud. Q. 223–47 (1986).
Villiger, Mark E., *Customary International Law and Treaties: A Manual on the Theory and Practice of the Interrelation of Sources* (2nd edn, Kluwer Law International, 1997).
Vitzthum, Wolfgang Graf (ed.), *Völkerrecht* (3rd edn, Walter de Gruyter, 2004).
Voeten, Erik, 'Outside Options and the Logic of Security Council Action', 95 Am. PSR. 845–58 (2001).
'The Political Origins of the UN Security Council's Ability to Legitimize the Use of Force', 59 Int. Org. 527–57 (2005).
Walters, F. P., *A History of the League of Nations* (Oxford University Press, 1952).
Waltz, Kenneth, 'The Spread of Nuclear Weapons: More May Be Better', 117 *Adelphi Papers* (1981).

Wedgwood, Ruth, 'The Enforcement of Security Council Resolution 687: The Threat of Force Against Iraq's Weapons of Mass Destruction', 92 Am. JIL 724–8 (1998).

Weisburd, A. Mark, *Use of Force: The Practice of States Since World War II* (Pennsylvania State University Press, 1997).

Weller, Marc, 'The Rambouillet Conference on Kosovo', 75 Int. Aff. 211–51 (1999).

White, Nigel D. and Robert Cryer, 'Unilateral Enforcement of Resolution 687: A Threat Too Far?', 29 Cal. WJIL 243–83 (1999).

Whitton, John B., 'The United Nations Conference on Freedom of Information and the Movement Against International Propaganda', 43 Am. JIL 73–87 (1949).

'Hostile International Propaganda and International Law', 398 Ann. Am. Acad. P&SS 14–25 (1971).

Widmer, Hans, *Der Zwang im Völkerrecht* (Robert Noske, 1935).

Wiletts, Peter, *The Non-Aligned Movement: The Origins of a Third World Alliance* (Nichols Pub. Co., 1978).

Williams, John Fischer, 'Recent Interpretations of the Briand-Kellog Pact', 14 Int. Aff. 346–68 (1935).

Wilson, Andrew, 'The Aegean Dispute', 155 *Adelphi Papers* (1979).

Winfield, P. H., 'The History of Intervention in International Law', 3 Brit. YBIL 130–49 (1922–3).

Wolfke, Karol, *Custom in Present International Law* (2nd edn, Martinus Nyhoff Publishers, 1993).

Wolfram, Karl, *Vertrag und Spätere Praxis im Völkerrecht* (Springer, 1983).

Woodward, Bob, *Plan of Attack* (Simon & Schuster, 2004).

Wright, Claudia, 'Libya And The West: Headlong Into Confrontation?', 58 Int. Aff. 13–41 (1981–2).

Wright, Quincy, 'Opinion of Commission of Jurists on Janina-Corfu Affair', 18 Am. JIL 536–44 (1924).

'The Outlawry of War', 19 Am. JIL 76–103 (1925).

'The Stimson Note of January 7, 1932', 26 Am. JIL 342–8 (1932).

'The Meaning of the Pact of Paris', 27 Am. JIL 39–61 (1933).

'The Munich Settlement and International Law', 33 Am. JIL 12–32 (1939).

'The Crime of War Mongering', 42 Am. JIL 128–36 (1948).

The Role of International Law in the Elimination of War (Manchester University Press, 1961).

'The Goa Incident', 56 Am. JIL 617–32 (1962).

'The Cuban Quarantine', 57 Am. JIL 546–65 (1963).

A Study of War (updated and abridged edn, University of Chicago Press, 1964).

Yoo, John, 'International Law and the War on Iraq', 97 Am. JIL 563–76 (2003).

Young, Oran R., *The Politics of Force: Bargaining During International Crises* (Princeton University Press, 1968).

Zacher, Mark M., 'The Territorial Integrity Norm: International Boundaries and the Use of Force', 55 Int. Org. 215–50 (2001).

Zagare, Franck C. and D. Marc Kilgour, 'Deterrence Theory and the Spiral Model Revisited', 10 J. Theo. P. 59–87 (1998), at 63.
Zambelli, Mirko, *La Constatation des Situations de l'Article 39 de la Charte des Nations Unies par la Conseil de Sécurité: Le Champ d'Application des Pouvoirs prévus au Chapitre VII de la Charte des Nations Unies* (Helbing & Lichtenhahn, 2002).
Zhao, Suisheng (ed.), *Across the Taiwan Strait: Mainland China, Taiwan, and the 1995–1996 Crisis* (Routledge, 1999).
Zimmerman, Tim, 'Coercive Diplomacy and Libya', in Alexander L. George and William E. Simons (eds.), *The Limits of Coercive Diplomacy* 201–28 (Westview Press, 1994).

Index